Flutter
Apprentice

Second Edition

By Mike Katz, Kevin D Moore,

Vincent Ngo & Vincenzo Guzzi

Flutter Apprentice

By Michael Katz, Kevin David Moore, Vincent Ngo & Vincenzo Guzzi

Copyright ©2021 Razeware LLC.

ISBN: 978-1-950325-48-1

Table of Contents

Book License 11

Before You Begin 13

What You Need 15

Book Source Code & Forums 17
    About the Authors 20
    About the Editors 21

Acknowledgements 23
    Content Development 23

Introduction 25
    How to read this book 26

Section I: Build Your First Flutter App 29

Chapter 1: Getting Started 31
    What is Flutter? 32
    Flutter's history 37
    The Flutter architecture 38
    What's ahead 40
    Getting started 40
    Getting the Flutter SDK 41
    Trying it out 45
    Key points 49
    Where to go from here? 50

Chapter 2: Hello, Flutter 51
    Creating a new app 52
    Making the app yours 54
    Clearing the app 58
    Building a recipe list 59

Adding a recipe detail page 70
Key points.. 83
Where to go from here?.. 83

Section II: Everything's a Widget..................... 85

Chapter 3: Basic Widgets 87
Getting started 88
Styling your app... 90
Setting a theme 91
App structure and navigation... 97
Creating custom recipe cards 104
Key points 132
Where to go from here? 132

Chapter 4: Understanding Widgets 133
What is a widget?.. 134
Unboxing Card2 134
Rendering widgets 137
Getting started 140
Types of widgets... 150
Key points 159
Where to go from here? 159

Chapter 5: Scrollable Widgets............................. 161
Getting started 163
Introducing ListView 167
Setting up the Explore screen 168
Creating a FutureBuilder... 170
Building Recipes of the Day 172
Nested ListViews... 177
Creating the ListView for friends' posts............................. 181
Adding final touches to the Explore screen 185
Getting to know GridView 187

Building the Recipes screen 190
Other scrollable widgets 197
Challenges.. 199
Key points 201
Where to go from here? 201

Chapter 6: Interactive Widgets 203

Getting started 206
Creating the grocery item model.................................. 207
Creating the Grocery screen 209
Creating the empty Grocery screen............................... 212
Switching tabs 217
Managing tab state 221
Managing the grocery items....................................... 225
Adding new packages 228
Creating the screen to add grocery items......................... 229
Creating a grocery tile... 252
Building GroceryTile 255
Finishing GroceryTile 257
Saving the user's work.. 261
Creating GroceryListScreen 262
Adding gestures 264
Dismissing items with a swipe..................................... 267
Key points 272
Where to go from here? 272

Section III: Navigating Between Screens 273

Chapter 7: Routes & Navigation.......................... 275

Introducing Navigator... 276
Navigator 1.0 overview.. 277
Navigator 1.0's disadvantages 279
Navigator 2.0 overview.. 281

Navigation and unidirectional data flow 282
Is Navigator 2.0 always better than Navigator 1.0? 284
Getting started 284
Changes to the project files 285
Looking over the UI flow 288
Managing your app state 294
Creating the router 298
Using your app router 302
Adding screens 304
Showing the Splash screen 305
Displaying the Login screen 307
Transitioning from Login to Onboarding screen 309
Transitioning from Onboarding to Home 311
Handling tab selection 314
Showing the Grocery Item screen 315
Navigating to the Profile screen 320
Navigating to raywenderlich.com 323
Logging out 325
Handling the Android system's Back button 327
Key points 329
Where to go from here? 329

Chapter 8: Deep Links & Web URLs 331
Understanding deep links 333
Getting started 334
Overview of Fooderlich's paths 338
Recapping Navigator 2.0 341
Deep links under the hood 342
Creating a navigation state object 343
Creating a route information parser 347
Connecting the parser to the app router 348
Converting a URL to an app state 350

Converting the app state to a URL 352
Testing deep links.. 354
Running the web app 365
Key points 368
Where to go from here? 368

Section IV: Networking, Persistence and State ... 369

Chapter 9: Shared Preferences............................. 371
Getting started 374
Saving data 375
The shared_preferences plugin..................................... 376
Key points 388
Where to go from here? 388

Chapter 10: Serialization With JSON 389
What is JSON?... 390
Automating JSON serialization 391
Creating model classes 393
Key points 403
Where to go from here? 403

Chapter 11: Networking in Flutter 405
Signing up with the recipe API..................................... 406
Using the HTTP package 411
Connecting to the recipe service 411
Building the user interface 414
Key points 422
Where to go from here? 422

Chapter 12: Using the Chopper Library 423
Why Chopper?... 424
Preparing to use Chopper 424
Preparing the recipe service 426

Converting request and response 427
Encoding and decoding JSON 429
Using interceptors. 431
Generating the Chopper file. 433
Logging requests & responses. 435
Using the Chopper client 436
Key points 438
Where to go from here? 438

Chapter 13: State Management 439
Architecture. 440
Why you need state management. 441
Widget state. 442
Application state 443
Managing state in your app. 443
Using Provider. 448
UI Models. 448
Creating the recipe class 449
Convert data into models to display. 451
Creating a repository. 451
Creating a memory repository 454
Using a mock service 468
Other state management libraries 473
Key points 476
Where to go from here? 476

Chapter 14: Streams 477
Types of streams. 478
Adding streams to Recipe Finder. 481
Sending recipes over the stream 485
Exercise. 486
Switching between services. 487
Adding streams to Bookmarks 490

Adding streams to Groceries 492
Key points 495
Where to go from here? 495

Chapter 15: Saving Data With SQLite 497
Databases 498
Adding a database to the project 501
Adding an SQLite repository 516
Running the app 522
Using Moor 525
Key points 544
Where to go from here? 544

Section V: Deployment 545

Chapter 16: Platform Specific App Assets 547
Setting the app icon 548
Setting the app's name 556
Adding a launch screen 557
Key points 567
Where to go from here? 567

Chapter 17: Build & Release an Android App 569
Set up for release 570
Build an app bundle 575
Uploading to the Google Play Store 576
Uploading a build 589
Distribution 592
Key points 596
Where to go from here? 596

Chapter 18: Build & Release an iOS App 597
Creating the signing 598
Setting up the App Store 603

Uploading to the App Store 607

Sharing builds through TestFlight 614

Key points 621

Where to go from here? 621

Section VI: Working With Firebase Cloud Firestore 623

Chapter 19: Firebase Cloud Firestore 625

Getting started 626

What is a Cloud Firestore? 627

Setting up a Google project and Database 628

Creating Google Services files 633

Adding Flutter dependencies 641

Understanding Collections 641

Provider 644

Creating new messages 645

Reactively displaying messages 647

Authentication 650

Login screen 659

Key points 668

Where to go from here? 668

Conclusion 669

Appendices 671

Appendix A: Chapter 5 Solution 1 673

Appendix B: Chapter 5 Solution 2 677

Book License

By purchasing *Flutter Apprentice*, you have the following license:

- You are allowed to use and/or modify the source code in *Flutter Apprentice* in as many apps as you want, with no attribution required.

- You are allowed to use and/or modify all art, images and designs that are included in *Flutter Apprentice* in as many apps as you want, but must include this attribution line somewhere inside your app: "Artwork/images/designs: from *Flutter Apprentice*, available at www.raywenderlich.com".

- The source code included in *Flutter Apprentice* is for your personal use only. You are NOT allowed to distribute or sell the source code in *Flutter Apprentice* without prior authorization.

- This book is for your personal use only. You are NOT allowed to sell this book without prior authorization, or distribute it to friends, coworkers or students; they would need to purchase their own copies.

Before You Begin

This section tells you a few things you need to know before you get started, such as what you'll need for hardware and software, where to find the project files for this book, and more.

What You Need

To follow along with this book, you'll need the following:

- **Xcode 12.5.1 or later**. Xcode is iOS's main development tool, so you need it to build your Flutter app for iOS. You can download the latest version of Xcode from Apple's developer site here: apple.co/2asi58y or from the Mac App Store. Xcode 12.5.1 requires a Mac running **macOS Big Sur (11) or later**.

> **Note:** You also have the option of using Linux or Windows, but you won't be able to install Xcode or build apps for iOS on those platforms.

- **Cocoapods 1.10.2 or later**. Cocoapods is a dependency manager Flutter uses to run code on iOS.

- **Flutter SDK 2.5.1 or later**. You can download the Flutter SDK from the official Flutter site at https://flutter.dev/docs/get-started/install/macos. Installing the Flutter SDK will also install the **Dart SDK,** which you need to compile the Dart code in your Flutter apps.

- **Android Studio 2020.3.1 or later**, available at
  https://developer.android.com/studio. This is the IDE in which you'll develop the
  sample code in this book. It also includes the Android SDK and the build system
  for running Flutter apps on Android.

- **Flutter Plugin for Android Studio 60.1.2 or later**, installed by going to Android
  Studio **Preferences** on macOS (or **Settings** on Windows/Linux) and choosing
  Plugins, then searching for "Flutter".

You have the option of using **Visual Studio Code** for your Flutter development
environment instead of Android Studio. You'll still need to install Android Studio to
have access to the Android SDK and an Android emulator. If you choose to use Visual
Studio Code, follow the instructions on the official Flutter site at
https://flutter.dev/docs/get-started/editor?tab=vscode to get set up.

Chapter 1, "Getting Started" explains more about Flutter history and architecture.
You'll learn how to start using the Flutter SDK, then you'll see how to use Android
Studio and Xcode to build and run Flutter apps.

Book Source Code & Forums

Book source code

The materials for this book are all available in the GitHub repository here:

- https://github.com/raywenderlich/flta-materials

You can download the entire set of materials for the book from that page.

Forum

We've also set up an official forum for the book at https://forums.raywenderlich.com/c/books/flutter-apprentice/. This is a great place to ask questions about the book or to submit any errors you may find.

"To my children for providing encouragement and giving me just enough time to write."

— *Michael Katz*

"To my wife and family for putting up with me for always being on the computer and letting me create and learn."

— *Kevin David Moore*

"To my loving parents and sister. Thank you for always being there for me, especially during the hard times. To Ray and the entire RW team who started me on this journey, I am beyond grateful to be part of this family. To the Flutter community, without whom I would have nothing to create and share here."

— *Vincent Ngo*

"To my wife, Leanna. Thank you for introducing me to the wonderful world of literature, and for proof reading everything I've ever written."

— *Vincenzo Guzzi*

About the Authors

Michael Katz is champion baker. He's also a developer, architect, speaker, writer and avid homebrewer. He has contributed to several books on iOS development and is a long-time member of the https://raywenderlich.com/ tutorial team. He shares his home state of New York with his family, the world's best bagels, and the Yankees. When not at his computer, he's out on the trails, in his shop, or reading a good book (like this one!).

Kevin David Moore is an author of this book. Kevin has been developing Android apps for over 10 years and at many companies. He's written several articles at https://raywenderlich.com/ and created the "Programming in Kotlin" video series. He enjoys creating apps for fun and teaching others how to write Android apps. In addition to programming, he loves playing volleyball and running the sound system at church.

Vincent Ngo is an author of this book. A software developer by day at a growing startup, and an iOS/Flutter enthusiast by night, he believes that sharing knowledge is the best way to learn and grow as a techie. Vincent starts every morning with a Cà phê sữa đá (Vietnamese coffee) to fuel his day. He enjoys playing golf, meditating, and watching animated movies. You can find him on Twitter: https://twitter.com/vincentngo2.

Vincenzo Guzzi is an author of this book. He lives in Sweden with his wife and cat where he enjoys hiking, snowboarding, reading books, and growing tomatoes. When he's not writing Android code as a Senior Engineer for Spotify, he's staying up late creating Flutter applications and writing tutorials for raywenderlich.com. You can find him on Twitter at https://twitter.com/vguzzi_dev, or follow him on Instagram at https://www.instagram.com/vguzzidev/ to see some of his tomatoes!

About the Editors

Stephanie Patterson is the tech editor for this book. Stef is passionate about helping others learn, which includes mentoring, writing and editing documentation, data wrangling and coding by example. Throughout most of her career, she has worked as a senior SQL developer and analyst. In 2013, she started creating iOS apps using raywenderlich.com books and articles. Now, thanks to Flutter, Stef is creating natively compiled cross-platform apps. Stef loves movies, trivia nights, Sci-Fi and spending time with her husband, daughter and their Chiweenie, Gracie. You can find her on Twitter at https://twitter.com/geekmespeakstef.

Sandra Grauschopf is the editor of this book. She is a freelance writer, editor, and content strategist as well as the Editing Team Lead at https://raywenderlich.com/. She loves to untangle tortured sentences and to travel the world with a trusty book in her hand.

Cesare Rocchi is the final pass editor for this book. Cesare runs https://studiomagnolia.com, an interactive studio that creates compelling web and mobile applications. He blogs at https://www.upbeat.it. You can find him on Twitter at https://twitter.com/_funkyboy.

Content Development

We would like to thank **Tim Sneath** and **Chris Sells** from Google. Both provided key insights and constant encouragement during the gestation and development of this book.

We would also like to thank **Joe Howard** for his work as an FPE for the book in its early stages. Joe's path to software development began in the fields of computational physics and systems engineering. He started as a web developer and also has been a native mobile developer on iOS and Android since 2009. Joe has a passion for system and enterprise architecture including building robust, testable, maintainable, and scalable systems. He currently focuses on the full stack using web frameworks like React and Angular, Node.js microservices, GraphQL, and devops tools like Docker, Kubernetes, and Terraform. He lives in Boston and is a Senior Architect at CVS Health.

Introduction

Welcome to *Flutter Apprentice*!

Flutter is an incredible user interface (UI) toolkit that lets you build apps for iOS and Android — and even the web and desktop platforms like macOS, Windows and Linux — all from a single codebase.

Flutter has all the benefits of other cross-platform tools, especially because you're targeting multiple platforms from one codebase. Furthermore, it improves upon most cross-platform tools thanks to a super-fast rendering engine that makes your Flutter apps perform as native apps.

In addition, Flutter features are generally independent of native features, since you use Flutter's own type of UI elements, called widgets, to create your UI. And Flutter has the ability to work with native code, so you can integrate your Flutter app with native features when you need to.

If you're coming from a platform like iOS or Android, you'll find the Flutter development experience refreshing! Thanks to a feature called "hot reload", you rarely need to rebuild your apps as you develop them. A running app in a simulator or emulator will refresh with code changes automatically as you save your source files!

In this book, you'll see how to build full-featured Flutter apps, gain experience with a wide range of Flutter widgets and learn how to deploy your apps to mobile app stores.

How to read this book

In the first section of the book, you'll learn how to set up a Flutter development environment. Once that's done, you'll start building your first Flutter app.

The next two sections focus on UI development with Flutter widgets. You'll see just how impressive Flutter user interfaces can be.

The fourth section switches to building a new app. You'll use it to learn about using networking and databases with Flutter, as well as the all-important topic of state management.

The book's final section shows you how to incorporate platform-specific assets into your app, then demonstrate how to deploy your apps to the mobile app stores.

Here's a breakdown of these five main sections of the book:

Section I: Build Your First Flutter App

The chapters in this section introduce you to Flutter, get you up and running with a Flutter development environment and walk you through building your first Flutter app.

You'll learn about where Flutter came from and why it exists, understand the structure of Flutter projects and see how to create the UI of a Flutter app.

You'll also get your first introduction to the key component found in Flutter user interfaces: widgets!

Section II: Everything's a Widget

In this section, you'll start to build a full-featured recipe app named **Fooderlich**. You'll gain an understanding the wide range of widgets available in Flutter and put them to use. Then you'll learn the theory of how widgets work behind the scenes.

Finally, you'll dive deeper into layout widgets, scrollable widgets and interactive widgets.

Section III: Navigating Between Screens

You'll continue working on the Fooderlich app in this section, learning about navigating between screens and working with deep links.

Topics you'll learn include Navigator 2.0 and Flutter Web.

Section IV: Networking, Persistence & State

Most apps interact with the network to retrieve data and then persist that data locally in some form of cache, such as a database. In this section, you'll build a new app that lets you search the Internet for recipes, bookmark recipes and save their ingredients into a shopping list.

You'll learn about making network requests, parsing the network JSON response and saving data in a SQLite database. You'll also get an introduction to using Dart streams.

Finally, this section will dive deeper into the important topic of app state, which determines where and how to refresh data in the UI as a user interacts with your app.

Section V: Deployment

Building an app for you own devices is great; sharing your app with the world is even better!

In this section, you'll go over the steps and processes to release your apps to the iOS App Store and Google Play Store. You'll also see how to use platform-specific assets in your apps.

Section I: Build Your First Flutter App

The chapters in this section will introduce you to Flutter, get you up and running with a Flutter development environment and walk you through building your first Flutter app.

You'll learn about where Flutter came from and why it exists, understand the structure of Flutter projects, and see how to create the user interface of a Flutter app.

You'll also get your first introduction to the key component found in Flutter user interfaces: Widgets!

Chapter 1: Getting Started

By Michael Katz

Congratulations. By opening "The Flutter Apprentice", you've taken your first step toward becoming a Flutter master. This book will be your guide to learning the **Flutter UI Toolkit**, Google's platform for building apps for mobile, desktop and web from a single codebase.

The five sections of this book will progressively teach you how to create an app using Flutter. You'll learn all about **widgets**, which are components that you compose to build your apps. You'll also learn about navigation and transitions, handling state and network management. Finally, you'll learn how to deploy the app to testers and users.

This book assumes you're familiar with development for a native mobile platform, such as iOS with Swift or Android with Kotlin… but you don't need to be an expert by any means. These chapters will show you how to build a Flutter app from scratch, so if you're completely new, you'll catch up just fine.

What is Flutter?

In the simplest terms, Flutter is a software development toolkit from Google for building cross-platform apps. Flutter apps consist of a series of packages, plugins and widgets — but that's not all. Flutter is a process, a philosophy and a community as well.

It's also the easiest way to get an app up and running on any one platform, let alone multiple. You can be more productive than you thought possible thanks to Flutter's declarative, widget-based UI structure, first-class support for reactive programming, cross platform abstractions and its virtual machine that allows for hot reloading of code changes.

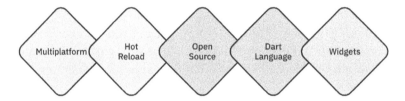

One thing Flutter is *not* is a language. Flutter uses **Dart** as its programming language. If you know Kotlin, Swift, Java or Typescript, you'll find Dart familiar, since it's an object-oriented C-style language.

You can compile Dart to native code, which makes it fast. It also uses a virtual machine (VM) with a special feature: **hot reload**. This lets you update your code and see the changes live without redeploying it.

For years, programmers have been promised the ability to **write once and run anywhere**; Flutter may well be the best attempt yet at achieving that goal.

Seriously?

Yes, Flutter is that awesome. You *can* build a high-quality app that's performant and looks great, very quickly. This book will show you how.

In the first few chapters, you'll get your feet under you with the basic UI. By the end of the book, you'll be able to build apps that look great and perform well.

And it truly does work well with both desktop and web.

Other cross-platform toolkits have tried to abstract the underlying OS by adding a layer on top of the native UI layer. This leaves the developer with the lowest common set of features available — not to mention, degraded performance.

In contrast, Flutter's widgets exist parallel to native widgets due to its custom user interface rendering engine, **Skia**. That means that the toolkit controls how the UI looks and behaves, which allows for consistent behavior between platforms. From a performance perspective, there's no penalty from additional layers of abstraction.

Who's Flutter for?

Flutter is for both the new or experienced developer who wants to start a mobile app with minimal overhead. Flutter is for someone looking to make an app that runs on multiple devices, either right away or in the future. It's for someone who prefers to build declarative UIs with the support of a large, open-source community.

Additionally, Flutter is for developers with experience on one platform who want to develop an app that works across many. This is doubly true if you're a web developer with deep Javascript or Typescript knowledge, but haven't gotten started on mobile yet. You can learn both major mobile platforms at once!

If you don't have an existing app, Flutter is a great way to develop something quickly to validate an idea or to build a full, multi-platform production app.

On the other hand, if you already have a great app on one platform with the native toolkits, then you should evaluate your ongoing maintenance costs to see if it makes sense to build out for the other platforms by using Flutter or the native toolkits.

Great things about Flutter

Here's just a sample of some of the great things about using Flutter:

- Flutter is **open-source**. That means you can watch its evolution and know what's coming — and even try out new features in development. You can also create your own patches and packages or contribute code. And you can be involved in the community to help others or contribute to its future direction.

- Flutter uses the **Dart** programming language. Dart (https://dart.dev) is a modern, UI-focused language that's compiled to native ARM or x86 code or cross-compiled to Javascript. It supports all the great language features people have come to like and expect, such as async/await for concurrency management and **type inference** for clean, type-safe code.

- One of the best features of Flutter is **hot reload**. Hot reload allows you to make updates to the code and the UI that rebuild the widget tree, then deliver them live to emulators and devices — without having to reload state or recompile your app.

- Sometimes, you make changes that affect too much of the widget tree or app state to hot reload easily. In those cases, you can use **hot restart**. Hot restart takes a little longer than hot reload because it loads the changes, restarts the app and resets the state, but it's still faster than a **full restart**, which recompiles and redeploys. You need to use a full restart when you make certain significant changes to the code, including anything changing state management.

- These restart features leverage Dart's VM to inject the updated code, so they're only available in debug mode and not in a production app.

- Other cross-platform toolkits produce apps with a stock look and feel — boring! Flutter is purposely attractive, using Google's **Material Design** out of the box. It's also easy to apply Cupertino widgets to get an iOS-like appearance. The UI is fully customizable, allowing you to make an app that looks right for your brand.

- Flutter comes with great animations and transitions, and you can build custom widgets as well. Because widgets are **composable**, you can be creative and flexible with the UI. For example, you can put videos behind a scroll view or put a toolbar on top of a canvas.

- The sheer number of widgets and the declarative syntax for building UIs lets you be extremely productive, building a rich app quickly with minimal overhead and boilerplate. Stateful widgets are bound to data and automatically update as the data model changes.

- If you've used SwiftUI or Jetpack Compose recently, you're already familiar with many of Flutter's concepts. But Flutter is even better — it has fewer limitations on the tools and you can build for multiple platforms at once.

- Flutter was designed with **accessibility** in mind, with out-of-the-box support for dynamic font sizes and screen readers and a ton of best practices around language, contrast and interaction methods.

- Platform integration is important for accessing libraries written in other languages or using platform-specific features that don't have a Flutter support package yet. Flutter supports C and C++ interoperability as well as **platform channels** for connecting to Kotlin and Java on Android and Swift or Objective-C on iOS.

Are you convinced yet?

If you're not yet convinced that there's a place for Flutter, check out the showcase: https://flutter.dev/showcase.

There, you see the top companies using Flutter and how diverse the apps you can make with it are. These aren't limited to "JSON-in-a-table" apps, but also include media-rich dynamic and interactive apps.

These apps help you be more productive, better informed, communicate more easily and have more fun. Flutter's native performance and system integrations make it a better choice than a web or hybrid app for most mobile applications.

Popular apps from some of the world's biggest companies are built with Flutter. These include:

- Very Good Ventures

- Tencent

- Realtor.com

- Google Assistant

- New York Times

- Policygenius

- Google Stadia

Take a look at some recent examples:

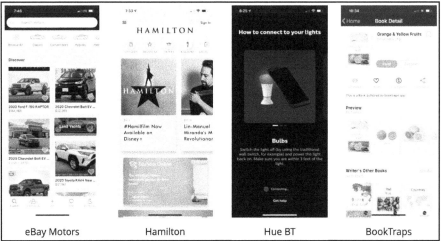

| eBay Motors | Hamilton | Hue BT | BookTraps |

When not to use Flutter

Flutter isn't the best tool for every application. Here are some areas where Flutter is an evolving platform.

Games and audio

While you can create simple 2D games using Flutter, for complex 2D and 3D games, you'd probably prefer to base your app on a cross-platform game engine technology like Unity or Unreal. They have more domain-specific features like physics, sprite and asset management, game state management, multiplayer support and so on.

Flutter doesn't have a sophisticated audio engine yet, so audio editing or mixing apps are at a disadvantage over those that are purpose-built for a specific platform.

Apps with specific native SDK needs

Flutter supports many, but not all, native features. Fortunately, you can usually create bridges to platform-specific code. However, if the app is highly integrated with a device's features and platform SDKs, it might be worth writing the app using the platform-specific tools. Flutter also produces app binaries that are bigger in size than those built with platform frameworks.

Flutter might not be a practical choice if you are only interested in a single platform app and you have deep knowledge of that platform's tools and languages. For example, if you're working with a highly-customized iOS app based on CloudKit that uses all the native hardware, MLKit, StoreKit, extensions and so on, maintaining and taking advantage of those features will be easier using SwiftUI. Of course, the same goes for a heavily-biased Android app using Jetpack Compose.

Certain platforms

Flutter doesn't run everywhere. It doesn't support Apple **Bitcode** yet, which means that it doesn't support watchOS, tvOS or certain iOS app extensions. Its support for the web is still in its early days, which means that Flutter has many features and performance improvements ahead of it — but they're coming.

Since Flutter doesn't run on watches or TVs yet, you'll have to build those components natively and attach them to a Flutter-based mobile app. Depending on how sophisticated those other apps are, it might not be worth the hassle to write both native and Flutter code.

Flutter's history

Flutter comes from a tradition of trying to improve web performance. It's built on top of several open-source technologies developed at Google to bring native performance and modern programming to the web through Chrome.

The Flutter team chose the Dart language, which Google also developed, for its productivity enhancements. Its object-oriented type system and support for reactive and asynchronous programming give it clear advantages over Javascript. Most importantly, Google built the Dart VM into the Chrome browser, allowing web apps written in Dart to run at native speeds.

Another piece of the puzzle is the inclusion of Skia as the graphics rendering layer. Skia is another Google-based open source project that powers the graphics on Android, Chrome browsers, Chrome OS and Firefox. It runs directly on the GPU using Vulcan on Android and Metal on iOS, making the graphics layer fast on mobile devices. Its API allows Flutter widgets to render quickly and consistently, regardless of the host platform.

The Flutter architecture

Flutter has a modular, layered architecture. This allows you to write your application logic once and have consistent behavior across platforms, even though the underlying engine code differs depending on the platform. The layered architecture also exposes different points for customization and overriding, as necessary.

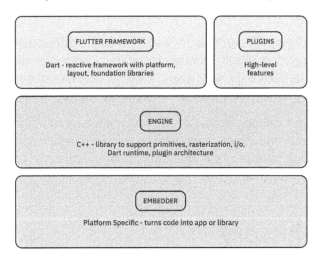

The Flutter architecture consists of three main layers:

1. The **Framework** layer is written in Dart and contains the high-level libraries that you'll use directly to build apps. This includes the UI theme, widgets, layout and animations, gestures and foundational building blocks. Alongside the main Flutter framework are **plugins**: high-level features like JSON serialization, geolocation, camera access, in-app payments and so on. This plugin-based architecture lets you include only the features your app needs.

2. The **Engine** layer contains the core C++ libraries that make up the primitives that support Flutter apps. The engine implements the low-level primitives of the Flutter API, such as I/O, graphics, text layout, accessibility, the plugin architecture and the Dart runtime. The engine is also responsible for rasterizing Flutter scenes for fast rendering onscreen.

3. The **Embedder** is different for each target platform and handles packaging the code as a stand-alone app or embedded module.

Each of the architecture layers is made up of other sublayers and modules, making them almost fractal. Of particular import to general app development is the makeup of the framework layer:

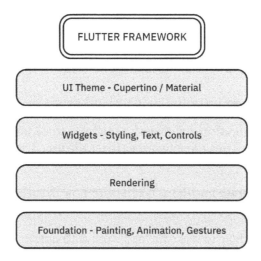

The Flutter framework consists of several sublayers:

- At the top is the **UI theme**, which uses either the Material (Android) or Cupertino (iOS) design language. This affects how the controls appear, allowing you to make your app look just like a native one.

- The **widget layer** is where you'll spend the bulk of your UI programming time. This is where you compose design and interactive elements to make up the app.

- Beneath the widgets layer is the **rendering layer**, which is the abstraction for building a layout.

- The **foundation layer** provides basic building blocks, like animations and gestures, that build up the higher layers.

What's ahead

This book is divided into five sections:

- Section 1 is the **introduction**. You're here! In this section, you'll get an overview of Flutter, learn how to get started and make sure you have everything set up to develop great apps. You'll build a simple app to get a taste of the Dart language and Flutter SDKs.

- Section 2 is all about **widgets**, the building blocks you use to make your app.

- Section 3 covers **navigation** and **deep links**. If you think about widgets as making up screens, navigation ties them together to let the user accomplish various tasks within the app.

- Section 4 goes over **state** and **data**. You'll learn how to save data and work with local persistence and networking.

- Section 5 shows you how to make the app work with **native platforms** as well as how to **deploy** your app.

By the end of the book, you'll be able to take an idea, turn it into a great-looking multi-platform app and submit it for publication.

Getting started

Now that you've decided Flutter is right for you, your next step is to get the tools necessary to build Flutter apps: the Flutter SDK and Dart compiler. You'll also need an IDE with a Flutter plugin along with the tools to build and deploy for the various platforms. The latter means Xcode for iOS and Android Studio for Android.

To start, visit https://flutter.dev/. This portal is the source of truth for any installation instructions or API changes that occur between this book's publication and the time you read it. If there are any contradictions, the information at **flutter.dev** supersedes.

What you need

- A computer. You can develop Flutter apps on Windows, macOS, Linux or ChromeOS. However, Xcode only runs on macOS, making a Mac necessary to build and deploy apps for iOS.

> **Note**: Because of the Xcode limitation for macOS, this book uses the Flutter toolchain on Mac. You can follow along on any platform of your choice — just skip any iOS- or Mac-specific steps.

- The Flutter SDK.

- An editor, such as Android Studio or Visual Studio Code.

- At least one device. You can run in an iOS Simulator or Android emulator, but running Flutter apps on a physical device will give you the true user experience.

- Developer accounts (optional). To deploy to the Apple App Store or Google Play Store, you'll need a valid account on each.

Getting the Flutter SDK

The first step is to download the SDK. You can follow the steps on **flutter.dev** or jump right in here:https://flutter.dev/docs/development/tools/sdk/releases.

One thing to note is that Flutter organizes its SDK around **channels**, which are different development branches. New features or platform support will be available first on a **beta channel** for developers to try out. This is a great way to get early access to certain features like new platforms or native SDK support.

For this book and development in general, use the **stable channel**. That branch has been vetted and tested and has little chance of breaking.

Follow the instructions to download the SDK from
https://flutter.dev/docs/get-started/install/macos#get-sdk.
Installation is as simple as unarchiving and putting the **bin** folder in your path.

Once you do that, you'll have access to the Flutter command-line app, which is your starting point. To check you've set it up correctly, run the following command in a terminal:

```
flutter help
```

In response, you should see the main help instructions:

```
Manage your Flutter app development.

Common commands:

  flutter create <output directory>
    Create a new Flutter project in the specified directory.

  flutter run [options]
    Run your Flutter application on an attached device or in an
emulator.

Usage: flutter <command> [arguments]
...
```

These `flutter` subcommands are a gateway to all the tools that come with Flutter. You'll see project management tools, package management tools and tools to run and test your apps. You'll dive into many of these in this and future chapters.

Getting everything else

In addition to the Flutter SDKs, you'll need Java, the Android SDK, the iOS SDKs and an IDE with Flutter extensions. To make this process easier, Flutter includes the **Flutter Doctor**, which guides you through installing all the missing tools.

Just run:

```
flutter doctor
```

That checks for all the necessary components and provides the links or instructions to download ones you're missing.

Here's an example:

```
Doctor summary (to see all details, run flutter doctor -v):
[✓] Flutter (Channel stable, 2.5.1, on macOS 11.5 20G71 darwin-
x64, locale en-US)
[✗] Android toolchain - develop for Android devices
    ✗ Flutter requires Android SDK 30 and the Android BuildTools
30.0.2
```

```
        To update using sdkmanager, run:
          "/Users/michael/Library/Android/sdk/tools/bin/
sdkmanager"
            "platforms;android-30" "build-tools;30.0.2"
        or visit https://flutter.dev/docs/get-started/install/
macos
        for detailed instructions.
[!] Xcode - develop for iOS and macOS (Xcode 12.5.1)
    ✗ CocoaPods not installed.
        CocoaPods is used to retrieve the iOS platform side's
plugin
        code that responds to your plugin usage on the Dart
side.
        Without CocoaPods, plugins will not work on iOS or
macOS.
        For more info, see https://flutter.dev/platform-plugins
      To install:
        sudo gem install cocoapods
[✗] Chrome - develop for the web (Cannot find Chrome executable
at
    /Applications/Google Chrome.app/Contents/MacOS/Google
Chrome)
    ! Cannot find Chrome. Try setting CHROME_EXECUTABLE to a
Chrome executable.
[!] Android Studio (not installed)

[⬚] Connected device (the doctor check crashed)
    ✗ Due to an error, the doctor check did not complete. If the
error message below is not helpful, please let us know
        about this issue at https://github.com/flutter/flutter/
issues.
    ✗ Exception: Unable to run "adb", check your Android SDK
installation and ANDROID_HOME environment variable:
        /Users/michael/Library/Android/sdk/platform-tools/adb

! Doctor found issues in 4 categories.
```

In this example output, Flutter Doctor has identified a series of issues: mainly, no Java, an outdated Android toolchain and that CocoaPods, Android Studio and Google Chrome are missing.

The tool has helpfully suggested commands and links to get the missing dependencies. The tool also terminated before completing, which is common if it doesn't find major dependencies.

For your specific setup, follow the suggestions to install whatever you're missing. Then keep running flutter doctor until you get all green checkmarks. You'll likely have to run it more than a couple of times to clear all the issues.

> **Note**: If Flutter Doctor's suggestions don't work, you may have to manually install missing tools, like Java or Android Studio, by following the instructions on their respective websites. Just take it one step at a time. Setting up the development environment is the hardest part of working with Flutter.

Setting up an IDE

The Flutter team officially supports three editors: Android Studio, Visual Studio Code and Emacs. However, there are many other editors that support the Dart language, work with the Flutter command line or have third-party Flutter plugins.

This book's examples use Android Studio, but the code and examples will all work in your editor of choice. Flutter Doctor will have you install this IDE anyway, to get all the Android tools, so using Android Studio keeps you from having to install additional editors. Additionally, Flutter Doctor will tell you to install the Android Studio **Flutter plugin**, which also triggers an install of the **Dart plugin** for Android Studio.

Once you go through all of the `flutter doctor` steps, you'll have everything you need to create Flutter apps in Android studio. If you see **Create New Flutter project** in the Android Studio welcome window, you're good to go.

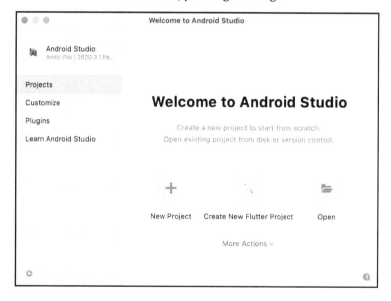

Trying it out

Downloading all the components is the hardest part of getting a Flutter app up and running. Next, you'll try actually building an app.

There are two recommended ways to create a new project: with the IDE or through the `flutter` command-line tool in a terminal. In this chapter, you'll use the IDE shortcut and in the next chapter, you'll use the command line.

In Android Studio, click the **Create New Flutter Project** option. Leave the default app selected and click the **Next** button to continue to the next screen.

For this example, you can keep the default values or change them to something more convenient. Click the **Next** button to continue.

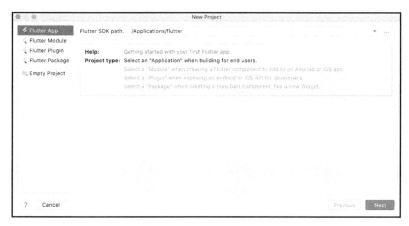

The options here let you include platform support or change the package name. You'll learn more about these options later. For now, click the **Finish** button.

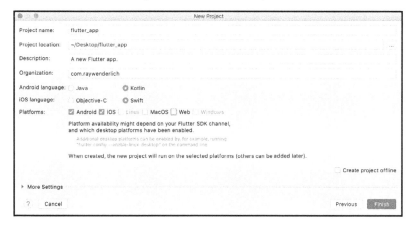

If you use Visual Studio Code, the process is similar. To create a new project, use **View ‣ Command Palette… ‣ Flutter: New Project**. After that, click through the project form that comes up.

With either editor, you might see pop-ups or messages to download or update various tools and components. Follow the directions until you resolve the messages.

For example, this Android Studio banner shows: **'Pub get' has not been run**. Clicking **Get dependencies** resolves this.

The template project

The default new project is the same in either editor. It's a simple Flutter demo. The demo app counts the number of times you tap a button.

To give it a try, select a connected device, an iOS simulator or an Android emulator.

Launch the app by clicking the **Run** icon:

It might take a while to compile and launch the first time. When you're done, you'll
see the following:

Congratulations, you've made your first Flutter app! Click the button and see the
increment response update the label.

All the code for this app is in **lib\main.dart** in the default project. Feel free to take a look at it.

Throughout the rest of this book, you'll dive into Flutter apps, widgets, state, themes and many other concepts that will help you build beautiful apps.

Bonus: Try hot reload

You'll learn a lot more about hot reload in future chapters, but it's just too cool of a feature to not indulge in a little taste at this point. Before starting, adjust your IDE window so you can see both it and the simulator or emulator with your app running in it.

In **main.dart**, find the following Text widget:

```
Text(
  'You have pushed the button this many times:',
),
```

Next, change the string to: **'Thou hast pushed the button this many times:'** to give it a faux-medieval flair.

Here's the not-so-tricky part: Just save the file. Now, look at the running app and observe the change.

Et voila! Your changes reload without stopping the app and redeploying.

Sometimes, saving the file does not automatically trigger the hot reload. In that case, just press the **Hot Reload** icon, which looks like a lightning bolt, in the toolbar.

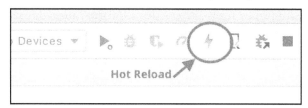

Key points

- Flutter is a **software development toolkit** from Google for building cross-platform apps using the Dart programming language.

- With Flutter, you can build a **high-quality app** that's performant and looks great, very quickly.

- Flutter is for both **new** and **experienced developers** who want to start a mobile app with minimal overhead.

- Install the **Flutter SDK** and associated tools using instructions found at https://flutter.dev.

- The `flutter doctor` command helps you install and update your Flutter tools.

- This book will mostly use **Android Studio** as the IDE for Flutter development.

Where to go from here?

Your home for all things Flutter is **flutter.dev** (and **dart.dev** for the Dart language). If you get stuck at any of the installation steps, go there for updated instructions.

flutter.dev contains the official documentation and reference pages, which you can find at https://flutter.dev/docs. These will be your source for complete and up-to-date information about the SDKs.

Also, there's https://flutter.dev/community, which has links to all the official Flutter communities on multiple social media platforms. In particular, check out the Google Developers' Flutter YouTube channel: https://www.youtube.com/c/flutterdev/.

Finally, available on raywenderlich.com is *The Dart Apprentice*, a companion book to learn more about Dart. For a quick start, check out this free **Dart Basics** article https://www.raywenderlich.com/4482551-dart-basics or the video course **Programming in Dart: Fundamentals**, available at https://www.raywenderlich.com/4921688-programming-in-dart-fundamentals.

Chapter 2: Hello, Flutter

By Michael Katz

Now that you've had a short introduction, you're ready to start your Flutter apprenticeship. Your first task is to build a basic app from scratch, giving you the chance to get the hang of the tools and the basic Flutter app structure. You'll customize the app and find out how to use a few popular widgets like `ListView` and `Slider` to update its UI in response to changes.

Creating a simple app will let you see just how quick and easy it is to build cross-platform apps with Flutter — and it will give you a quick win.

By the end of the chapter, you'll have built a lightweight recipe app. Since you're just starting to learn Flutter, your app will offer a hard-coded list of recipes and let you use a `Slider` to recalculate quantities based on the number of servings.

Here's what your finished app will look like:

All you need to start this chapter is to have Flutter set up. If the `flutter doctor` results show no errors, you're ready to get started. Otherwise, go back to Chapter 1, "Getting Started", to set up your environment.

Creating a new app

There are two simple ways to start a new Flutter app. In the last chapter, you created a new app project through the IDE. Alternatively, you can create an app with the `flutter` command. You'll use the second option here.

Open a terminal window, then navigate to the location where you want to create a new folder for the project. For example, you can use this book's materials and go to **flta-materials/02-hello-flutter/projects/starter/**.

Creating a new project is straightforward. In the terminal, run:

```
flutter create recipes
```

This command creates a new app in a new folder, both named **recipes**. It has the demo app code, as you saw in the previous chapter, with support for running on iOS and Android.

Using your IDE, open the **recipes** folder as an existing project.

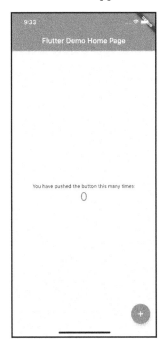

Build and run and you'll see the same demo app as in Chapter 1, "Getting Started".

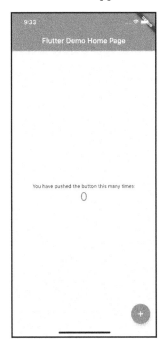

Tapping the + button increments the counter.

Making the app yours

The ready-made app is a good place to start because the `flutter create` command puts all the boilerplate together for you to get up and running. But this is not *your* app. It's literally **MyApp**, as you can see near the top of **main.dart**:

```
class MyApp extends StatelessWidget {
```

This defines a new Dart `class` named `MyApp` which **extends** — or inherits from — `StatelessWidget`. In Flutter, almost everything that makes up the user interface is a **Widget**. A `StatelessWidget` doesn't change after you build it. You'll learn a lot more about widgets and state in the next section. For now, just think of `MyApp` as the container for the app.

Since you're building a recipe app, you don't want your main `class` to be named `MyApp` — you want it to be `RecipeApp`.

While you could change it manually in multiple places, you'll reduce the chance of a copy-and-paste error or typo by using the IDE's **rename** action instead. This lets you rename a symbol at its definition and all its callers at the same time.

In Android Studio, you'll find this either under the **Refactor ▸ Rename** menu item or by right-clicking on `MyApp` in `class MyApp...` and navigating to **Refactor ▸ Rename**. Rename **MyApp** to be **RecipeApp**. The result will look like this:

```
void main() {
  runApp(RecipeApp());
}
class RecipeApp extends StatelessWidget {
```

`main()` is the entry point for the code when the app launches. `runApp()` tells Flutter which is the top-level widget for the app.

A hot reload won't include the code changes you just made. To run the new code you need to perform a hot restart. In this specific case you won'd notice any change in the UI.

Note: As mentioned in Chapter 1, "Getting Started", when you save your changes, hot reload automatically runs and updates the UI. If this doesn't happen, check your IDE settings for Flutter to make sure it's enabled. If you don't want it to trigger it when you save changes you can run it manually. The shortcut for Android Studio is **Command-**.

With hot reload you can quickly see the effect of code changes and the app state is preserved. For example, if the user was in a "logged in" state before the code changed, a hot reload will preserve such a state and you won't need to log in again to test your changes.

If you've made significant changes, like adding a new property to a state or changed `main()` like in the case above, then you need to hot restart, so that the new change is detected and included in the new build.

For even bigger changes, like adding dependencies or assets, you need to a full build and run.

Styling your app

To continue making this into a new app, you'll customize the appearance of your widgets next. Replace RecipeApp's build() with:

```
// 1
@override
Widget build(BuildContext context) {
  // 2
  final ThemeData theme = ThemeData();
  // 3
  return MaterialApp(
    // 4
    title: 'Recipe Calculator',
    // 5
    theme: theme.copyWith(
        colorScheme: theme.colorScheme.copyWith(
            primary: Colors.grey,
            secondary: Colors.black,
        ),
    ),
    // 6
    home: const MyHomePage(title: 'Recipe Calculator'),
  );
}
```

This code changes the appearance of the app:

1. A widget's build() method is the entry point for composing together other widgets to make a new widget.

2. A theme determines visual aspects like color. The default ThemeData will show the standard Material defaults.

3. MaterialApp uses Material Design and is the widget that will be included in RecipeApp.

4. The title of the app is a description that the device uses to identify the app. The UI won't display this.

5. By copying the theme and replacing the color scheme with an updated copy lets you change the app's colors. Here, the primary color is Colors.grey and the secondary color is Colors.black.

6. This still uses the same MyHomePage widget as before, but now, you've updated the title and displayed it on the device.

When you relaunch the app now, you'll see the same widgets, but they have a more sophisticated style.

You've taken the first step towards making the app your own by customizing the MaterialApp body. You'll finish cleaning up the app in the next section.

Clearing the app

You've themed the app, but it's still displaying the counter demo. Clearing the screen is your next step. To start, replace the _MyHomePageState class with:

```
class _MyHomePageState extends State<MyHomePage> {
  @override
  Widget build(BuildContext context) {
    // 1
    return Scaffold(
      // 2
      appBar: AppBar(
        title: Text(widget.title),
      ),
      // 3
      body: SafeArea(
        // TODO: Replace child: Container()
        // 4
        child: Container(),
      ),
    );
  }

  // TODO: Add buildRecipeCard() here
}
```

A quick look at what this shows:

1. A Scaffold provides the high-level structure for a screen. In this case, you're using two properties.

2. AppBar gets a title property by using a Text widget that has a title passed in from home: MyHomePage(title: 'Recipe Calculator') in the previous step.

3. body has SafeArea, which keeps the app from getting too close to the operating system interfaces such as the notch or interactive areas like the Home Indicator at the bottom of some iOS screens.

4. SafeArea has a child widget, which is an empty Container widget.

One hot reload later, and you're left with a clean app:

Building a recipe list

An empty recipe app isn't very useful. The app should have a nice list of recipes for the user to scroll through. Before you can display these, however, you need the data to fill out the UI.

Adding a data model

You'll use `Recipe` as the main data structure for recipes in this app.

Create a new **Dart file** in the **lib** folder, named **recipe.dart**.

Add the following class to the file:

```
class Recipe {
  String label;
  String imageUrl;
  // TODO: Add servings and ingredients here

  Recipe(
    this.label,
    this.imageUrl,
  );
  // TODO; Add List<Recipe> here
}

// TODO: Add Ingredient() here
```

This is the start of a `Recipe` model with a label and an image.

You'll also need to supply some data for the app to display. In a full-featured app, you'd load this data either from a local database or a JSON-based API. For the sake of simplicity as you get started with Flutter, however, you'll use hard-coded data in this chapter.

Add the following method to `Recipe` by replacing `// TODO: Add List<Recipe>` `here` with:

```
static List<Recipe> samples = [
  Recipe(
    'Spaghetti and Meatballs',
    'assets/2126711929_ef763de2b3_w.jpg',
  ),
  Recipe(
    'Tomato Soup',
    'assets/27729023535_a57606c1be.jpg',
  ),
  Recipe(
    'Grilled Cheese',
    'assets/3187380632_5056654a19_b.jpg',
  ),
  Recipe(
    'Chocolate Chip Cookies',
    'assets/15992102771_b92f4cc00a_b.jpg',
  ),
```

```
  Recipe(
    'Taco Salad',
    'assets/8533381643_a31a99e8a6_c.jpg',
  ),
  Recipe(
    'Hawaiian Pizza',
    'assets/15452035777_294cefced5_c.jpg',
  ),
];
```

This is a hard-coded list of recipes. You'll add more detail later, but right now, it's just a list of names and images.

> **Note:** A `List` is an ordered collection of items; in some programming languages, it's called an array. `List` indexes start with 0.

You've created a `List` with images, but you don't have any images in your project yet. To add them, go to **Finder** and copy the **assets** folder from the top level of **02-hello-flutter** in the book materials of your project's folder structure. When you're done, it should live at the same level as the **lib** folder. That way, the app will be able to find the images when you run it.

You'll notice that by copy-pasting in Finder, the folder and images automatically display in the Android Studio project list.

But just adding assets to the project doesn't display them in the app. To tell the app to include those assets, open **pubspec.yaml** in the **recipes** project root folder.

Under `# To add assets to your application...` add the following lines:

```
assets:
  - assets/
```

These lines specify that **assets/** is an assets folder and must be included with the app. Make sure that the first line here is aligned with the `uses-material-design: true` line above it.

Displaying the list

With the data ready to go, your next step is to create a place for the data to go *to*.

Back in **main.dart**, you need to import the data file so the code in **main.dart** can find it. Add the following to the top of the file, under the other import lines:

```
import 'recipe.dart';
```

Next, in _MyHomePageState SafeArea's child, find and replace // TODO: Replace child: Container() and the two lines beneath it with:

```
// 4
child: ListView.builder(
  // 5
  itemCount: Recipe.samples.length,
  // 6
  itemBuilder: (BuildContext context, int index) {
    // 7
    // TODO: Update to return Recipe card
    return Text(Recipe.samples[index].label);
  },
),
```

This code does the following:

4. Builds a list using ListView.

5. itemCount determines the number of rows the list has. In this case, length is the number of objects in the Recipe.samples list.

6. itemBuilder builds the widget tree for each row.

7. A Text widget displays the name of the recipe.

Perform a hot reload now and you'll see the following list:

Putting the list into a card

It's great that you're displaying real data now, but this is barely an app. To spice things up a notch, you need to add images to go along with the titles.

To do this, you'll use a Card. In Material Design, Cards define an area of the UI where you've laid out related information about a specific entity. For example, a Card in a music app might have labels for an album's title, artist and release date along with an image for the album cover and maybe a control for rating it with stars.

Your recipe Card will show the recipe's label and image. Its widget tree will have the following structure:

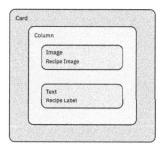

In **main.dart**, at the bottom of _MyHomePageState create a **custom widget** by replacing // TODO: Add buildRecipeCard() here with:

```
Widget buildRecipeCard(Recipe recipe) {
  // 1
  return Card(
    // 2
    child: Column(
      // 3
      children: <Widget>[
        // 4
        Image(image: AssetImage(recipe.imageUrl)),
        // 5
        Text(recipe.label),
      ],
    ),
  );
}
```

Here's how you define your new custom Card widget:

1. You return a Card from buildRecipeCard().

2. The Card's child property is a Column. A Column is a widget that defines a vertical layout.

3. The `Column` has two `children`.

4. The first child is an `Image` widget. `AssetImage` states that the image is fetched from the local **asset** bundle defined in **pubspec.yaml**.

5. A `Text` widget is the second child. It will contain the `recipe.label` value.

To use the card, go to `_MyHomePageState` and replace `// TODO: Update to return Recipe card` and the `return` line below it with this:

```
// TODO: Add GestureDetector
return buildRecipeCard(Recipe.samples[index]);
```

That instructs the `itemBuilder` to use the custom `Card` widget for each recipe in the `samples` list.

Hot restart the app to see the image and text cards.

Notice that `Card` doesn't default to a flat square at the bottom of the widget. Material Design provides a standard corner radius and drop shadow.

Looking at the widget tree

Now's a good time to think about the widget tree of the overall app. Do you remember that it started with `RecipeApp` from `main()`?

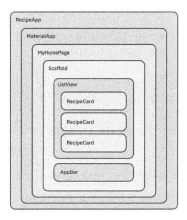

`RecipeApp` built a `MaterialApp`, which in turn used `MyHomePage` as its home. That builds a `Scaffold` with an `AppBar` and a `ListView`. You then updated the `ListView` builder to make a `Card` for each item.

Thinking about the widget tree helps explain the app as the layout gets more complicated and as you add interactivity. Fortunately, you don't have to hand-draw a diagram each time.

In Android Studio, open the **Flutter Inspector** from the **View ▸ Tool Windows ▸ Flutter Inspector** menu while your app is running. This opens a powerful UI debugging tool.

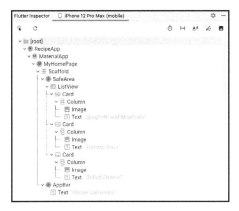

This view shows you all the widgets onscreen and how they are composed. As you scroll, you can refresh the tree. You might notice the number of cards change. That's because the List doesn't keep every item in memory at once to improve performance. You'll cover more about how that works in a later chapter.

Making it look nice

The default cards look okay, but they're not as nice as they could be. With a few added extras, you can spiffy the card up. These include wrapping widgets in layout widgets like Padding or specifying additional styling parameters.

Get started by replacing buildRecipeCard() with:

```
Widget buildRecipeCard(Recipe recipe) {
  return Card(
    // 1
    elevation: 2.0,
    // 2
    shape: RoundedRectangleBorder(
      borderRadius: BorderRadius.circular(10.0)),
    // 3
    child: Padding(
      padding: const EdgeInsets.all(16.0),
      // 4
      child: Column(
        children: <Widget>[
          Image(image: AssetImage(recipe.imageUrl)),
          // 5
          const SizedBox(
            height: 14.0,
          ),
          // 6
          Text(
            recipe.label,
            style: const TextStyle(
              fontSize: 20.0,
              fontWeight: FontWeight.w700,
              fontFamily: 'Palatino',
            ),
          )
        ],
      ),
    ),
  );
}
```

This has a few updates to look at:

1. A card's `elevation` determines *how high off the screen* the card is, affecting its shadow.

2. `shape` handles the shape of the card. This code defines a rounded rectangle with a `10.0` corner radius.

3. `Padding` insets its child's contents by the specified `padding` value.

4. The padding child is still the same vertical `Column` with the image and text.

5. Between the image and text is a `SizedBox`. This is a blank view with a fixed size.

6. You can customize `Text` widgets with a `style` object. In this case, you've specified a `Palatino` font with a size of `20.0` and a bold weight of `w700`.

Hot reload and you'll see a more styled list.

You can play around with these values to get the list to look "just right" for you. With hot reload, it's easy to make changes and instantly see their effect on the running app.

Using the Widget inspector, you'll see the added Padding and SizedBox widgets. When you select a widget, such as the SizedBox, it shows you all its real-time properties in a separate pane, which includes the ones you set explicitly and those that were inherited or set by default.

Selecting a widget also highlights where it was defined in the source.

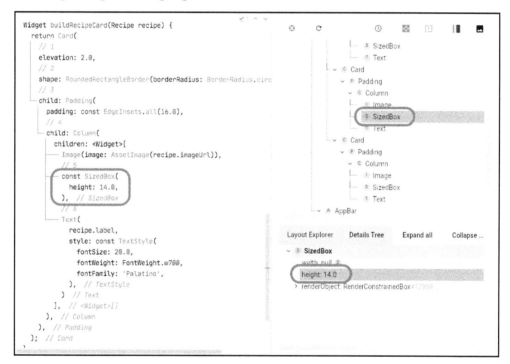

Note: You may need to click the **Refresh Tree** button to reload the widget structure in the inspector. See Chapter 4, "Understanding Widgets" for more details.

Adding a recipe detail page

You now have a pretty list, but the app isn't interactive yet. What would make it great is to show the user details about a recipe when they tap the card. You'll start implementing this by making the card react to a tap.

Making a tap response

Inside `_MyHomePageState`, locate `// TODO: Add GestureDetector` and replace the `return` statement beneath it with the following:

```
// 7
return GestureDetector(
  // 8
  onTap: () {
    // 9
    Navigator.push(
      context,
      MaterialPageRoute(
        builder: (context) {
          // 10
          // TODO: Replace return with return RecipeDetail()
          return Text('Detail page');
        },
      ),
    );
  },
  // 11
  child: buildRecipeCard(Recipe.samples[index]),
);
```

This introduces a few new widgets and concepts. Looking at the lines one at a time:

7. Introduces a `GestureDetector` widget, which, as the name implies, detects gestures.

8. Implements an `onTap` function, which is the callback called when the widget is tapped.

9. The `Navigator` widget manages a stack of pages. Calling `push()` with a `MaterialPageRoute` will push a new Material page onto the stack. Section III, "Navigating Between Screens", will cover navigation in a lot more detail.

10. `builder` creates the destination page widget.

11. `GestureDetector`'s child widget defines the area where the gesture is active.

Hot reload the app and now each card is tappable. **Tap** a recipe and you'll see a black **Detail page**:

Creating an actual target page

The resulting page is obviously just a placeholder. Not only is it ugly, but because it doesn't have all the normal page trappings, the user is now stuck here, at least on iOS devices without a back button. But don't worry, you can fix that!

In **lib**, create a new **Dart file** named **recipe_detail.dart**.

Now, add this code to the file, ignore the red squiggles:

```
import 'package:flutter/material.dart';
import 'recipe.dart';

class RecipeDetail extends StatefulWidget {
  final Recipe recipe;

  const RecipeDetail({
    Key? key,
```

```
    required this.recipe,
  }) : super(key: key);

  @override
  _RecipeDetailState createState() {
    return _RecipeDetailState();
  }
}

// TODO: Add _RecipeDetailState here
```

This creates a new StatefulWidget which has an initializer that takes the Recipe details to display. This is a StatefulWidget because you'll add some interactive state to this page later.

You need _RecipeDetailState to build the widget, replace // TODO: Add _RecipeDetailState here with:

```
class _RecipeDetailState extends State<RecipeDetail> {
  // TODO: Add _sliderVal here

  @override
  Widget build(BuildContext context) {
    // 1
    return Scaffold(
      appBar: AppBar(
        title: Text(widget.recipe.label),
      ),
      // 2
      body: SafeArea(
        // 3
        child: Column(
          children: <Widget>[
            // 4
            SizedBox(
              height: 300,
              width: double.infinity,
              child: Image(
                image: AssetImage(widget.recipe.imageUrl),
              ),
            ),
            // 5
            const SizedBox(
              height: 4,
            ),
            // 6
            Text(
              widget.recipe.label,
              style: const TextStyle(fontSize: 18),
            ),
            // TODO: Add Expanded
```

```
            // TODO: Add Slider() here
          ],
        ),
      ),
    );
  }
}
```

The body of the widget is the same as you've already seen. Here are a few things to notice:

1. `Scaffold` defines the page's general structure.

2. In the body, there's a `SafeArea`, a `Column` with a `Container`, a `SizedBox` and `Text` children.

3. `SafeArea` keeps the app from getting too close to the operating system interfaces, such as the notch or the interactive area of most iPhones.

4. One new thing is the `SizedBox` around the `Image`, which defines resizable bounds for the image. Here, the `height` is fixed at 300 but the `width` will adjust to fit the aspect ratio. The unit of measurement in Flutter is **logical pixels**.

5. There is a spacer `SizedBox`.

6. The `Text` for the `label` has a `style` that's a little different than the main `Card`, to show you how much customizability is available.

Next, go back to **main.dart** and add the following line to the top of the file:

```
import 'recipe_detail.dart';
```

Then find `// TODO: Replace return with return RecipeDetail()` replace it and the existing `return` statement with:

```
return RecipeDetail(recipe: Recipe.samples[index]);
```

Perform a hot restart by choosing **Run ▸ Flutter Hot Restart** from the menu to set the app state back to the original list. Tapping a recipe card will now show the RecipeDetail page.

> **Note**: You need to use hot restart here because hot reload won't update the UI after you update the state.

Because you now have a Scaffold with an appBar, Flutter will automatically include a back button to return the user to the main list.

Adding ingredients

To complete the detail page, you'll need to add additional details to the Recipe class. Before you can do that, you have to add an ingredient list to the recipes.

Open **recipe.dart** and replace // TODO: Add Ingredient() here with the following class:

```
class Ingredient {
  double quantity;
  String measure;
  String name;

  Ingredient(
    this.quantity,
    this.measure,
    this.name,
  );
}
```

This is a simple data container for an ingredient. It has a name, a unit of measure — like "cup" or "tablespoon" — and a quantity.

At the top of the Recipe class, replace // TODO: Add servings and ingredients here with the following:

```
int servings;
List<Ingredient> ingredients;
```

This adds properties to specify that serving is how many people the specified quantity feeds and ingredients is a simple list.

To use these new properties, go to your samples list inside the Recipe class and change the Recipe constructor from:

```
Recipe(
  this.label,
  this.imageUrl,
);
```

to:

```
Recipe(
  this.label,
  this.imageUrl,
  this.servings,
  this.ingredients,
);
```

You'll see red squiggles under part of your code because the values for `servings` and `ingredients` have not been set. You'll fix that next.

```
Recipe(
   this.label,
   this.imageUrl,
   this.servings,
   this.ingredients,
);

static List<Recipe> samples = [
   Recipe(
      'Spaghetti and Meatballs',
      'assets/2126711929_ef763de2b3_w.jpg',
   ),
   Recipe(
      'Tomato Soup',
      'assets/27729023535_a57606c1be.jpg',
   ),
```

To include the new `servings` and `ingredients` properties, replace the existing `samples` definition with the following:

```
static List<Recipe> samples = [
  Recipe(
    'Spaghetti and Meatballs',
    'assets/2126711929_ef763de2b3_w.jpg',
    4,
    [
      Ingredient(1, 'box', 'Spaghetti',),
      Ingredient(4, '', 'Frozen Meatballs',),
      Ingredient(0.5, 'jar', 'sauce',),
    ],
  ),
  Recipe(
    'Tomato Soup',
    'assets/27729023535_a57606c1be.jpg',
    2,
    [
      Ingredient(1, 'can', 'Tomato Soup',),
    ],
  ),
  Recipe(
    'Grilled Cheese',
    'assets/3187380632_5056654a19_b.jpg',
    1,
    [
      Ingredient(2, 'slices', 'Cheese',),
      Ingredient(2, 'slices', 'Bread',),
    ],
  ),
```

```
    Recipe(
      'Chocolate Chip Cookies',
      'assets/15992102771_b92f4cc00a_b.jpg',
      24,
      [
        Ingredient(4, 'cups', 'flour',),
        Ingredient(2, 'cups', 'sugar',),
        Ingredient(0.5, 'cups', 'chocolate chips',),
      ],
    ),
    Recipe(
      'Taco Salad',
      'assets/8533381643_a31a99e8a6_c.jpg',
      1,
      [
        Ingredient(4, 'oz', 'nachos',),
        Ingredient(3, 'oz', 'taco meat',),
        Ingredient(0.5, 'cup', 'cheese',),
        Ingredient(0.25, 'cup', 'chopped tomatoes',),
      ],
    ),
    Recipe(
      'Hawaiian Pizza',
      'assets/15452035777_294cefced5_c.jpg',
      4,
      [
        Ingredient(1, 'item', 'pizza',),
        Ingredient(1, 'cup', 'pineapple',),
        Ingredient(8, 'oz', 'ham',),
      ],
    ),
  ];
```

That fills out an ingredient list for these items. Please don't cook these at home, these are just examples. :]

Hot reload the app now. No changes will be visible, but it should build successfully.

Showing the ingredients

A recipe doesn't do much good without the ingredients. Now, you're ready to add a widget to display them.

In **recipe_detail.dart**, replace // TODO: Add Expanded with:

```
// 7
Expanded(
  // 8
  child: ListView.builder(
    padding: const EdgeInsets.all(7.0),
    itemCount: widget.recipe.ingredients.length,
    itemBuilder: (BuildContext context, int index) {
      final ingredient = widget.recipe.ingredients[index];
      // 9
      // TODO: Add ingredient.quantity
      return Text(
        '${ingredient.quantity} ${ingredient.measure} $
```

```
{ingredient.name}');
    },
  ),
),
```

This code adds:

7. An Expanded widget, which expands to fill the space in a Column. This way, the ingredient list will take up the space not filled by the other widgets.

8. A ListView, with one row per ingredient.

9. A Text that uses **string interpolation** to populate a string with runtime values. You use the ${expression} syntax inside the string literal to denote these.

Hot restart by choosing **Run ▸ Flutter Hot Restart** and navigate to a detail page to see the ingredients.

Nice job, the screen now shows the recipe name and the ingredients. Next, you'll add a feature to make it interactive.

Adding a serving slider

You're currently showing the ingredients for a suggested serving. Wouldn't it be great if you could change the desired quantity and have the amount of ingredients update automatically?

You'll do this by adding a **Slider** widget to allow the user to adjust the number of servings.

First, create an instance variable to store the slider value at the top of _RecipeDetailState by replacing // TODO: Add _sliderVal here:

```
int _sliderVal = 1;
```

Now find // TODO: Add Slider() here replace it with the following:

```
Slider(
  // 10
  min: 1,
  max: 10,
  divisions: 10,
  // 11
  label: '${_sliderVal * widget.recipe.servings} servings',
  // 12
  value: _sliderVal.toDouble(),
  // 13
  onChanged: (newValue) {
    setState(() {
      _sliderVal = newValue.round();
    });
  },
  // 14
  activeColor: Colors.green,
  inactiveColor: Colors.black,
),
```

Slider presents a round thumb that can be dragged along a track to change a value. Here's how it works:

10. You use min, max and divisions to define how the slider moves. In this case, it moves between the values of 1 and 10, with 10 discreet stops. That is, it can only have values of 1, 2, 3, 4, 5, 6, 7, 8, 9 or 10.

11. label updates as the _sliderVal changes and displays a scaled number of servings.

12. The slider works in double values, so this converts the int variable.

13. Conversely, when the slider changes, this uses `round()` to convert the `double` slider value to an `int`, then saves it in `_sliderVal`.

14. This sets the slider's colors to something more "on brand". The `activeColor` is the section between the minimum value and the thumb, and the `inactiveColor` represents the rest.

Hot reload the app, adjust the slider and see the value reflected in the indicator.

Updating the recipe

It's great to see the changed value reflected in the slider, but right now, it doesn't affect the recipe itself.

To do that, you just have to change the `Expanded` ingredients `itemBuilder` return statement to include the current value of `_sliderVal` as a factor for each ingredient.

Replace `// TODO: Add ingredient.quantity` and the whole `return` statement beneath it with:

```
return Text('${ingredient.quantity * _sliderVal} '
            '${ingredient.measure} '
            '${ingredient.name}');
```

After a hot reload, you'll see that the recipe's ingredients change when you move the slider.

That's it! You've now built a cool, interactive Flutter app that works just the same on iOS and Android.

In the next few sections, you'll continue to explore how widgets and state work. You'll also learn about important functionality like networking.

Key points

- Build a new app with `flutter create`.

- Use widgets to compose a screen with controls and layout.

- Use widget parameters for styling.

- A `MaterialApp` widget specifies the app, and `Scaffold` specifies the high-level structure of a given screen.

- State allows for interactive widgets.

- When state changes, you usually need to hot restart the app instead of hot reload. In some case, you may also need to rebuild and restart the app entirely.

Where to go from here?

Congratulations, you've written your first app!

To get a sense of all the widget options available, the documentation at https://api.flutter.dev/ should be your starting point. In particular, the Material library https://api.flutter.dev/flutter/material/material-library.html and Widgets library https://api.flutter.dev/flutter/widgets/widgets-library.html will cover most of what you can put onscreen. Those pages list all the parameters, and often have in-browser interactive sections where you can experiment.

Chapter 3, "Basic Widgets", is all about using widgets and Chapter 4, "Understanding Widgets", goes into more detail on the theory behind widgets. Future chapters will go into more depth about other concepts briefly introduced in this chapter.

Section II: Everything's a Widget

In this section you'll start to build a full-featured recipe app named **Fooderlich**. You'll gain an understanding of and use a wide range of widgets available in Flutter, and learn about the theory of how widgets work behind the scenes.

You'll then dive deeper into layout widgets, scrollable widgets and interactive widgets.

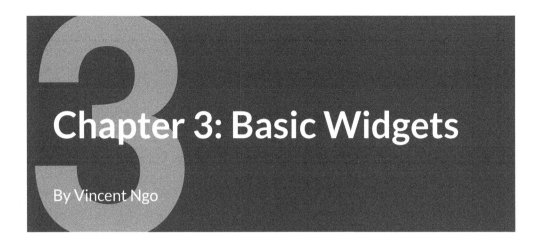

Chapter 3: Basic Widgets

By Vincent Ngo

As you know, everything in Flutter is a widget. But how do you know which widget to use when? In this chapter, you'll explore three categories of basic widgets, which you can use for:

- Structure and navigation

- Displaying information

- Positioning widgets

By the end of this chapter, you'll use those different types of widgets to build the foundation of an app called **Fooderlich**, a social recipe app. You'll build out the app's structure and learn how to create three different recipe cards: the main recipe card, an author card and an explore card.

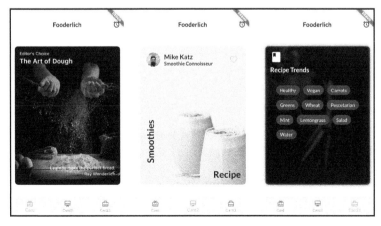

Ready? Dive in by taking a look at the starter project.

Getting started

Start by downloading this chapter's project from the book materials repo https://github.com/raywenderlich/flta-materials.

Locate the **projects** folder and open **starter**. If your IDE has a banner that reads **'Pub get' has not been run**, click **Get dependencies** to resolve the issue.

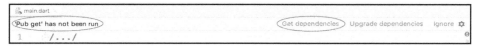

Run the app from Android Studio and you'll see an app bar and some simple text:

main.dart is the starting point for any Flutter app. Open it and you'll see the following:

```dart
import 'package:flutter/material.dart';

void main() {
  // 1
  runApp(const Fooderlich());
}

class Fooderlich extends StatelessWidget {
  // 2
  const Fooderlich({Key? key}) : super(key: key);
  @override
  Widget build(BuildContext context) {
    // TODO: Create theme
    // TODO: Apply Home widget
    // 3
    return MaterialApp(
      // TODO: Add theme
      title: 'Fooderlich',
      // 4
      home: Scaffold(
        // TODO: Style the title
        appBar: AppBar(title: const Text('Fooderlich')),
        // TODO: Style the body text
        body: const Center(child: Text('Let\'s get cooking
🦉')),
      ),
    );
  }
}
```

Take a moment to explore what the code does:

1. Everything in Flutter starts with a widget. `runApp()` takes in the root widget `Fooderlich`.

2. Every stateless widget must override the `build()` method.

3. The `Fooderlich` widget starts by composing a `MaterialApp` widget to give it a **Material Design** system look and feel. See https://material.io for more details about it.

4. The `MaterialApp` widget contains a `Scaffold` widget, which defines the layout and structure of the app. The scaffold has two properties: an `appBar` and a body. An `Appbar`'s `title` contains a `Text` widget. The body has a `Center` widget, whose `child` property is a `Text` widget.

Styling your app

Since Flutter is cross-platform, it's only natural for Google's UI Toolkit to support the visual design systems of both Android and iOS.

Android uses the **Material Design** system, which you'd import like this:

```
import 'package:flutter/material.dart';
```

iOS uses the **Cupertino** system. Here's how you'd import it:

```
import 'package:flutter/cupertino.dart';
```

To keep things simple, a rule of thumb is to pick only one design system for your UI. Imagine having to create **if-else** statements just to manage the two designs, let alone support different transitions and OS version compatibility.

Throughout this book, you'll learn to use the **Material Design** system. You'll find the look and feel of Material Design is quite customizable!

> **Note**: Switching between Material and Cupertino is beyond the scope of this book. For more information about what these packages offer in terms of UI components, check out:
>
> • Material UI Components:
>
> https://flutter.dev/docs/development/ui/widgets/material
>
> • Cupertino UI Components:
>
> https://flutter.dev/docs/development/ui/widgets/cupertino

Now that you have settled on a design, you'll set a theme for your app in the next section.

Setting a theme

You might notice the current app looks a little boring with the default blue, so you'll spice it up with a custom theme! Your first step is to select the font for your app to use.

Using Google fonts

The `google_fonts` package supports over 900 fonts to help you style your text. It's already included **pubspec.yaml** and you have already added it to the app when clicking **Pub Get** before. You'll use this package to apply a custom font to your theme class.

Defining a theme class

To share colors and font styles throughout your app, you'll provide a `ThemeData` object to `MaterialApp`. In the **lib** directory, open **fooderlich_theme.dart**, which contains a predefined theme for your app.

Take a look at the code:

```
import 'package:flutter/material.dart';
import 'package:google_fonts/google_fonts.dart';

class FooderlichTheme {
  // 1
  static TextTheme lightTextTheme = TextTheme(
    bodyText1: GoogleFonts.openSans(
      fontSize: 14.0,
      fontWeight: FontWeight.w700,
      color: Colors.black,
    ),
    headline1: GoogleFonts.openSans(
      fontSize: 32.0,
      fontWeight: FontWeight.bold,
      color: Colors.black,
    ),
    headline2: GoogleFonts.openSans(
      fontSize: 21.0,
      fontWeight: FontWeight.w700,
      color: Colors.black,
    ),
    headline3: GoogleFonts.openSans(
      fontSize: 16.0,
      fontWeight: FontWeight.w600,
      color: Colors.black,
```

```
    ),
    headline6: GoogleFonts.openSans(
      fontSize: 20.0,
      fontWeight: FontWeight.w600,
      color: Colors.black,
    ),
  );

  // 2
  static TextTheme darkTextTheme = TextTheme(
    bodyText1: GoogleFonts.openSans(
      fontSize: 14.0,
      fontWeight: FontWeight.w700,
      color: Colors.white,
    ),
    headline1: GoogleFonts.openSans(
      fontSize: 32.0,
      fontWeight: FontWeight.bold,
      color: Colors.white,
    ),
    headline2: GoogleFonts.openSans(
      fontSize: 21.0,
      fontWeight: FontWeight.w700,
      color: Colors.white,
    ),
    headline3: GoogleFonts.openSans(
      fontSize: 16.0,
      fontWeight: FontWeight.w600,
      color: Colors.white,
    ),
    headline6: GoogleFonts.openSans(
      fontSize: 20.0,
      fontWeight: FontWeight.w600,
      color: Colors.white,
    ),
  );

  // 3
  static ThemeData light() {
    return ThemeData(
      brightness: Brightness.light,
      checkboxTheme: CheckboxThemeData(
        fillColor: MaterialStateColor.resolveWith(
          (states) {
            return Colors.black;
          },
        ),
      ),
      appBarTheme: const AppBarTheme(
        foregroundColor: Colors.black,
        backgroundColor: Colors.white,
      ),
      floatingActionButtonTheme: const
```

```
FloatingActionButtonThemeData(
        foregroundColor: Colors.white,
        backgroundColor: Colors.black,
      ),
      bottomNavigationBarTheme: const
BottomNavigationBarThemeData(
        selectedItemColor: Colors.green,
      ),
      textTheme: lightTextTheme,
    );
  }

  // 4
  static ThemeData dark() {
    return ThemeData(
      brightness: Brightness.dark,
      appBarTheme: AppBarTheme(
        foregroundColor: Colors.white,
        backgroundColor: Colors.grey[900],
      ),
      floatingActionButtonTheme: const
FloatingActionButtonThemeData(
        foregroundColor: Colors.white,
        backgroundColor: Colors.green,
      ),
      bottomNavigationBarTheme: const
BottomNavigationBarThemeData(
        selectedItemColor: Colors.green,
      ),
      textTheme: darkTextTheme,
    );
  }
}
```

This code does the following:

1. Declares a TextTheme called lightTextTheme, which uses the Google font **Open Sans** and has a predefined font size and weight. Most importantly, the color of the text is black.

2. Then it defines darkTextTheme. In this case, the text is white.

3. Next, it defines a static method, light, which returns the color tones for a light theme using the lightTextTheme you created in step 1.

4. Finally, it declares a static method, dark, which returns the color tones for a dark theme using the darkTextTheme you created in step 2.

Your next step is to utilize the theme.

Using the theme

In **main.dart**, import your theme by adding the following beneath the existing import statement:

```
import 'fooderlich_theme.dart';
```

Then replace the comment //TODO: Create theme with the following:

```
final theme = FooderlichTheme.dark();
```

To apply the new theme replace the comment // TODO: Add theme with the following:

```
theme: theme,
```

Next replace the comment // TODO: Style the title and the line below it with the following:

```
appBar: AppBar(
        title: Text(
          'Fooderlich',
          style: theme.textTheme.headline6,
        ),
      ),
```

Finally, locate the comment // TODO: Style the body text and replace it and the code below it with the following:

```
body: Center(
    child: Text('Let\'s get cooking 🍳',
        style: theme.textTheme.headline1),
  ),
```

After all your updates, your code should look like this:

```
// 1
import 'fooderlich_theme.dart';

void main() {
  runApp(const Fooderlich());
}

class Fooderlich extends StatelessWidget {
  const Fooderlich({Key? key}) : super(key: key);
  @override
```

```
Widget build(BuildContext context) {
  // 2
  final theme = FooderlichTheme.dark();
  // TODO: Apply Home widget
  return MaterialApp(
    // 3
    theme: theme,
    title: 'Fooderlich',
    home: Scaffold(
      appBar: AppBar(
        title: Text('Fooderlich',
                // 4
                style: theme.textTheme.headline6,
              ),
      ),
      body: Center(
        child: Text('Let\'s get cooking 🍳',
                // 5
                style: theme.textTheme.headline1,
              ),
      ),
    ),
  );
}
```

To recap, your updates:

1. Imported the `FooderlichTheme`.

2. Defined a variable that holds the theme.

3. Added the `MaterialApp` widget's `theme` property.

4. Added `AppBar` text styling.

5. Finally, added body text styling.

Save your changes. Thanks to hot reload, you'll see the updated theme nearly immediately.

To see the difference between light and dark mode, change the theme between `FooderlichTheme.dark()` and `FooderlichTheme.light()`. The two themes look like this:

> **Note**: It's generally a good idea to establish a common theme object for your app — especially when you work with designers. That gives you a **single source of truth** to access your theme across all your widgets.

Next, you'll learn about an important aspect of building an app — understanding which app structure to use.

App structure and navigation

Establishing your app's structure from the beginning is important for the user experience. Applying the right navigation structure makes it easy for your users to navigate the information in your app.

Fooderlich uses the `Scaffold` widget for its starting app structure. `Scaffold` is one of the most commonly-used Material widgets in Flutter. Next, you'll learn how to implement it in your app.

Using Scaffold

The `Scaffold` widget implements all your basic visual layout structure needs. It's composed of the following parts:

- AppBar
- BottomSheet
- BottomNavigationBar
- Drawer
- FloatingActionButton
- SnackBar

`Scaffold` has a lot of functionality out of the box!

The following diagram represents some of the aforementioned items as well as showing left and right nav options:

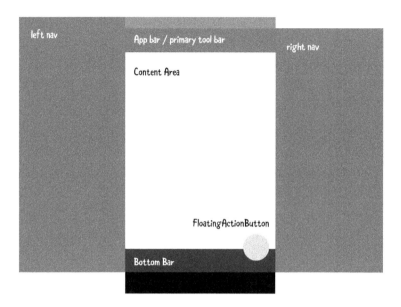

For more information, check out Flutter's documentation on **Material Components widgets**, including app structure and navigation:
https://flutter.dev/docs/development/ui/widgets/material

Now, it's time to add more functionality.

Setting up the Home widget

As you build large-scale apps, you'll start to compose a staircase of widgets. Widgets composed of other widgets can get really long and messy. It's a good idea to break your widgets into separate files for readability.

To avoid making your code overly complicated, you'll create the first of these separate files now.

Scaffold needs to handle some state changes, via a **StatefulWidget**. Your next step is to move code out of **main.dart** into a new StatefulWidget named Home.

In the **lib** directory, create a new file called **home.dart** and add the following:

```dart
import 'package:flutter/material.dart';

// 1
class Home extends StatefulWidget {
  const Home({Key? key}) : super(key: key);

  @override
  _HomeState createState() => _HomeState();
}

class _HomeState extends State<Home> {
  // TODO: Add state variables and functions

  @override
  Widget build(BuildContext context) {
    return Scaffold(
      appBar: AppBar(
        title: Text(
          'Fooderlich',
          // 2
          style: Theme.of(context).textTheme.headline6,
        ),
      ),
      // TODO: Show selected tab
      body: Center(
          child: Text('Let\'s get cooking 😋 ',
              // 3
              style: Theme.of(context).textTheme.headline1)),
      // TODO: Add bottom navigation bar
    );
  }
}
```

Most of the `Scaffold` code looks like what you have in **main.dart**, but there are a few changes:

1. Your new class extends `StatefulWidget`.

2. The `AppBar` style now reads: `Theme.of(context).textTheme.headline6` instead of: `theme.textTheme.headline6`. `Theme.of(context)` returns the nearest Theme in the widget tree. If the widget has a defined Theme, it returns that. Otherwise, it returns the app's theme.

3. As with the `AppBar`, you've also updated the `Text` style to use the `Theme.of(context)`.

Go back to **main.dart**, which you need to update so it can use the new Home widget. At the top, add the following import statement:

```
import 'home.dart';
```

Next replace `// TODO: Apply Home widget` and all the `return MaterialApp()` code below it with the following:

```
return MaterialApp(
  theme: theme,
  title: 'Fooderlich',
  home: const Home(),
);
```

With that done, you'll move on to addressing `Scaffold`'s bottom navigation.

Adding a BottomNavigationBar

Your next step is to add a bottom navigation bar to the scaffold. This will let your users navigate between tabs.

Return to **home.dart**, locate `// TODO: Add bottom navigation bar` and replace it with the following code:

```
// 4
bottomNavigationBar: BottomNavigationBar(
  // 5
  selectedItemColor:
    Theme.of(context).textSelectionTheme.selectionColor,
  // TODO: Set selected tab bar
  // 6
  items: <BottomNavigationBarItem>[
    const BottomNavigationBarItem(
      icon: Icon(Icons.card_giftcard),
      label: 'Card',
    ),
    const BottomNavigationBarItem(
      icon: Icon(Icons.card_giftcard),
      label: 'Card2',
    ),
    const BottomNavigationBarItem(
      icon: Icon(Icons.card_giftcard),
      label: 'Card3',
    ),
  ],
),
```

Take a moment to review the code. Here, you:

4. Defined a `BottomNavigationBar`.

5. Set the selection color of an item when tapped.

6. Defined three bottom navigation tab bar items.

With that done, your app looks like this:

Now that you've set up the bottom navigation bar, you need to implement the navigation between tab bar items.

Navigating between items

Before you can let the user switch between tab bar items, you need to know which index they selected.

Locate `// TODO: Add state variables and functions` and replace it with the following:

```
// 7
int _selectedIndex = 0;

// 8
static List<Widget> pages = <Widget>[
```

```
    // TODO: Replace with Card1
    Container(color: Colors.red),
    // TODO: Replace with Card2
    Container(color: Colors.green),
    // TODO: Replace with Card3
    Container(color: Colors.blue)
  ];

  // 9
  void _onItemTapped(int index) {
    setState(() {
      _selectedIndex = index;
    });
  }
```

Here's what you've added with this code:

7. _selectedIndex keeps track of which tab is currently selected. The underscore in _selectedIndex signifies it's private. The selected index is the **state** being tracked by _HomeState.

8. Here, you define the widgets that will display on each tab. For now, when you tap between the different tab bar items, it shows container widgets of different colors. Soon, you'll replace each of these with card widgets.

9. This function handles tapped tab bar items. Here, you set the index of the item that the user pressed. setState() notifies the framework that the state of this object has changed, then rebuilds this widget internally.

> **Note**: In the next chapter, you'll learn more about how widgets work under the hood. Stay tuned.

Next, locate // TODO: Show selected tab and replace it and the body in the Scaffold with:

```
  body: pages[_selectedIndex],
```

As the framework rebuilds the widgets, it displays the container widget for the selected tab bar item.

Indicating the selected tab bar item

Now, you want to indicate to the user which tab bar item they currently have selected. Locate `// TODO: Set selected tab bar` and add the following code:

```
// 10
currentIndex: _selectedIndex,
// 11
onTap: _onItemTapped,
```

Here's what's going on with this code:

10. `currentIndex` will tell the bottom navigation bar which tab bar item to highlight.

11. When the user taps on a tab bar item, it calls the `_onItemTapped` handler, which updates the state with the correct `index`. In this case, it changes the color.

Because you've made changes to the state, you have two options to see the changes. You can either stop your app and restart it, which takes a bit of time, or you can use hot restart, which rebuilds your app in a matter of seconds.

Press the **Hot Restart** button on the **Run** window to see how fast it is:

After restarting, your app will look different for each tab bar item, like this:

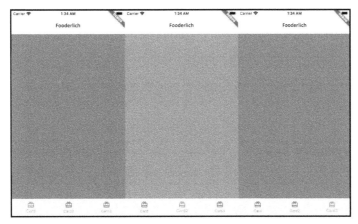

Now that you've set up your tab navigation, it's time to create beautiful recipe cards!

Creating custom recipe cards

In this section, you'll compose three recipe cards by combining a mixture of display and layout widgets.

Display widgets handle what the user sees onscreen. Examples of display widgets include:

- Text
- Image
- Button

Layout widgets help with the arrangement of widgets. Examples of layout widgets include:

- Container
- Padding
- Stack
- Column
- SizedBox
- Row

> **Note**: Flutter has a plethora of layout widgets to choose from, but this chapter only covers the most common.
>
> For more examples, check out
>
> https://flutter.dev/docs/development/ui/widgets/layout.

Composing Card1: the main recipe card

The first card you'll compose looks like this:

Card1 is composed of the following widgets:

- **Container**: Groups all the other widgets together. It applies **Padding** and uses a **BoxDecoration** to describe how to apply shadows and rounded corners.

- **Stack**: Layers widgets on top of each other.

- **Text**: Displays the recipe content, like title, subtitle and author.

- **Image**: Shows the recipe's art.

In the **lib** directory, create a new file called **card1.dart** and add the following code to it:

```dart
import 'package:flutter/material.dart';

class Card1 extends StatelessWidget {
  const Card1({Key? key}) : super(key: key);
  // 1
  final String category = 'Editor\'s Choice';
  final String title = 'The Art of Dough';
  final String description = 'Learn to make the perfect bread.';
  final String chef = 'Ray Wenderlich';

  // 2
  @override
  Widget build(BuildContext context) {
    // 3
    return Center(
      // TODO: Card1 Decorate Container
      child: Container(),
    );
  }
}
```

Take a moment to go over the code:

1. Define string variables to display on the card. This is just sample data to help build the card.

2. Every stateless widget comes with a `build()` method that you override.

3. Start with a `Container` laid out in the center.

Next, open **home.dart** and add the following import:

```dart
import 'card1.dart';
```

Locate `// TODO: Replace with Card1` and replace the first container with the following:

```dart
const Card1(),
```

You've now set up `Card1`. Hot restart, and the app currently looks like this:

It's a little bland, isn't it? For your next step, you'll spice it up with an image.

Adding the image

Switch to **card1.dart**. Locate `// TODO: Card1 Decorate Container` and replace the empty `Container()` below it with the following:

```
Container(
  // TODO: Add a stack of text
  // 1
  padding: const EdgeInsets.all(16),
  // 2
  constraints: const BoxConstraints.expand(
    width: 350,
    height: 450,
  ),
  // 3
  decoration: const BoxDecoration(
    // 4
    image: DecorationImage(
      // 5
      image: AssetImage('assets/mag1.png'),
      // 6
      fit: BoxFit.cover,
    ),
```

```
    // 7
    borderRadius: BorderRadius.all(Radius.circular(10.0)),
  ),
),
```

Here are the arguments you added to `Container`:

1. Apply a padding of 16 on all sides of the box. Flutter units are specified in **logical pixels**, which are like **dp** on Android.

2. Constrain the container's size to a width of 350 and a height of 450.

3. Apply `BoxDecoration`. This describes how to draw a box.

4. In `BoxDecoration`, set up `DecorationImage`, which tells the box to paint an image.

5. Set which image to paint in the box using an `AssetImage`, an image found in the starter project assets.

6. Cover the entire box with that image.

7. Apply a corner radius of 10 to all sides of the container.

Save your changes to hot reload. Your app now looks like this:

Much better! But you still need to tell the user what they're looking at.

Adding the text

You're going to add three lines of text describing what the card does. Start by adding the following import statement to the top of the **card1.dart** file so that you can use your Theme:

```
import 'fooderlich_theme.dart';
```

Next locate `// TODO: Add a stack of text` and replace it with the following:

```
child: Stack(
  children: [
    Text(
      category,
      style: FooderlichTheme.darkTextTheme.bodyText1,
    ),
    Text(
      title,
      style: FooderlichTheme.darkTextTheme.headline5,
    ),
    Text(
      description,
      style: FooderlichTheme.darkTextTheme.bodyText1,
    ),
    Text(
      chef,
      style: FooderlichTheme.darkTextTheme.bodyText1,
    ),
  ],
),
```

Stack places these new widgets on top of each other. Here's how it looks:

Well, that's not quite right. Next, you'll position the text so it's readable.

Positioning the text

Replace the Stack() you just added with the following:

```
Stack(
  children: [
    // 8
    Text(
      category,
      style: FooderlichTheme.darkTextTheme.bodyText1,
    ),
    // 9
    Positioned(
      child: Text(
        title,
        style: FooderlichTheme.darkTextTheme.headline2,
      ),
      top: 20,
    ),
    // 10
    Positioned(
      child: Text(
        description,
        style: FooderlichTheme.darkTextTheme.bodyText1,
```

```
      ),
      bottom: 30,
      right: 0,
    ),
    // 11
    Positioned(
      child: Text(
        chef,
        style: FooderlichTheme.darkTextTheme.bodyText1,
      ),
      bottom: 10,
      right: 0,
    )
  ],
),
```

For the relevant Text, you apply a Positioned widget. That widget controls where you position the Text in the Stack. Here are the positions you're using:

8. The category, **Editor's Choice**, stays where it is. Remember, Container already applies a padding of 16 on all sides.

9. You place the title 20 pixels from the top.

10. Here, you position the description 30 pixels from the bottom and 0 to the right.

11. Finally, you position the chef's name 10 pixels from the bottom-right.

After these updates, the app looks like this:

Great, the first card is finished now. It's time to move on to the next!

Composing Card2: the author card

It's time to start composing the next card, the author card. Here's how it will look by the time you're done:

Despite the differences in appearance, `Card2` is similar to `Card1`. It's composed of the following widgets:

- A `Container` with a `BoxDecoration` displaying an image with rounded corners.

- A custom author widget that displays the author's profile picture, name and job title.

- Text widgets — but this time, notice **Smoothies** has a vertical rotation.

- `IconButton` with a heart on the top-right.

In the **lib** directory, create a new file called **card2.dart**. Add the following code:

```
import 'package:flutter/material.dart';

class Card2 extends StatelessWidget {
  const Card2({Key? key}) : super(key: key);
  @override
  Widget build(BuildContext context) {
    return Center(
      // 1
      child: Container(
        constraints: const BoxConstraints.expand(
          width: 350,
          height: 450,
        ),
        decoration: const BoxDecoration(
          image: DecorationImage(
            image: AssetImage('assets/mag5.png'),
            fit: BoxFit.cover,
          ),
          borderRadius: BorderRadius.all(
            Radius.circular(10.0),
          ),
        ),
        // 2
        child: Column(
          children: [
            // TODO 1: add author information
            // TODO 4: add Positioned text
          ],
        ),
      ),
    );
  }
}
```

Taking a quick look at the code, you'll notice the following:

1. The Center widget has a Container child widget which has three properties, the first two being constraints and decoration.

2. The third property is child and it has a Column widget, which displays its children vertically.

> **Note**: If you ever want to look at all your TODO entries, open the **TODO** tab in Android Studio and you'll see something similar:

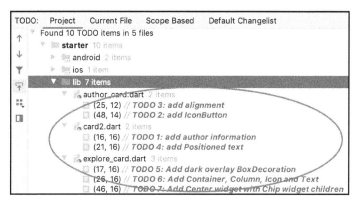

Card2's initial setup is similar to Card1. In **home.dart**, import Card2 as follows:

```
import 'card2.dart';
```

Next, locate // TODO: Replace with Card2 and replace it and the second Container() with:

```
const Card2(),
```

Then, perform a hot restart.

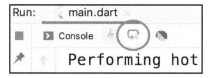

Tap the **Card2** tab bar item. Your app should look like this:

Here's how Card2's layout will look after you've added the Column's children widgets:

The column will display the following two widgets vertically:

- The author's card

- The recipe's titles

Your next step is to build these widgets.

Composing the author card

The following widgets make up the `AuthorCard`:

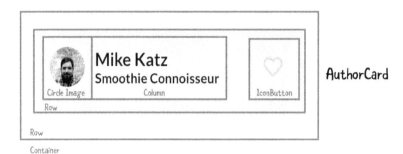

- **Container**: Groups all the widgets together.

- **Row**: Lays out the widgets horizontally and in the following order: `CircleImage`, `Column` and `IconButton`.

- **Column**: Lays out the two `Text` widgets vertically, with the name of the author above the author's title.

- **CircleImage**: A custom widget you'll create next to show the author avatar.

- **IconButton**: A button that shows an icon.

Creating a circular avatar widget

Your first step is to create the author's circular avatar.

In the **lib** directory, create a new file called **circle_image.dart**. Add the following code:

```dart
import 'package:flutter/material.dart';

class CircleImage extends StatelessWidget {
  // 1
  const CircleImage({
    Key? key,
    this.imageProvider,
    this.imageRadius = 20,
  }) : super(key: key);

  // 2
  final double imageRadius;
  final ImageProvider? imageProvider;

  @override
  Widget build(BuildContext context) {
    // 3
    return CircleAvatar(
      backgroundColor: Colors.white,
      radius: imageRadius,
      // 4
      child: CircleAvatar(
        radius: imageRadius - 5,
        backgroundImage: imageProvider,
      ),
    );
  }
}
```

Here's how you created this new custom widget:

1. `CircleImage` has two parameters: `imageProvider` and `imageRadius`.

2. The `imageRadius` and `imageProvider` property declarations.

3. `CircleAvatar` is a widget provided by the Material library. It's defined as a white circle with a radius of `imageRadius`.

4. Within the outer circle is another `CircleAvatar`, which is a smaller circle that includes the user's profile image. Making the inner circle smaller gives you the white border effect.

Setting up the AuthorCard widget

In the **lib** directory, create a new file called **author_card.dart**. Add the following code:

```
import 'package:flutter/material.dart';
import 'fooderlich_theme.dart';
import 'circle_image.dart';

class AuthorCard extends StatelessWidget {
  // 1
  final String authorName;
  final String title;
  final ImageProvider? imageProvider;

  const AuthorCard({
    Key? key,
    required this.authorName,
    required this.title,
    this.imageProvider,
  }) : super(key: key);

  // 2
  @override
  Widget build(BuildContext context) {
    // TODO: Replace return Container(...);
    return Container(
      padding: const EdgeInsets.all(16),
      child: Row(
        children: [],
      ),
    );
  }
}
```

Here's how this code works:

1. `AuthorCard` has three properties: `authorName`, the author's job `title` and the profile image, which `imageProvider` handles.

2. `AuthorCard` is grouped in a container and uses a `Row` widget to lay out the other widgets horizontally.

You'll come back to this widget later. For now, you'll set things up so that hot reload will refresh the UI while you complete this widget.

Adding the AuthorCard widget to Card2

Open **card2.dart** and add the following imports:

```
import 'author_card.dart';
```

Then, locate `// TODO 1: add author information` and replace it with the
following:

```
const AuthorCard(
  authorName: 'Mike Katz',
  title: 'Smoothie Connoisseur',
  imageProvider: AssetImage('assets/author_katz.jpeg'),
),
```

Now that you've added the `AuthorCard`, it's time to go back to composing the author
card widget itself.

Composing the AuthorCard widget

Open **author_card.dart**. Find `// TODO: Replace return Container(...);` and
replace it and `return Container(...);` with the following:

```
return Container(
  padding: const EdgeInsets.all(16),
  child: Row(
    // TODO 3: add alignment
    children: [
      // 1
      Row(
        children: [
          CircleImage(
            imageProvider: imageProvider,
            imageRadius: 28,
          ),
          // 2
          const SizedBox(width: 8),
          // 3
          Column(
            crossAxisAlignment: CrossAxisAlignment.start,
            children: [
              Text(
                authorName,
                style: FooderlichTheme.lightTextTheme.headline2,
              ),
              Text(
                title,
                style: FooderlichTheme.lightTextTheme.headline3,
              )
```

```
        ],
      ),
    ],
  ),
),
// TODO 2: add IconButton
  ],
),
);
```

Notice that the container has two Row widgets nested within each other. Here's what the code does:

1. The inner Row groups the CircleImage and the author's Text information.

2. Applies 8 pixels of padding between the image and the text.

3. Lays out the author's name and job title vertically using a Column.

Hot reload and tap **Card2**'s tab bar button. Your app will now look like this:

Looking good, but there are a few important elements you still need to add.

Adding the IconButton widget

Next, you need to add the heart-shaped `IconButton` widget after the inner `Row` widget. The user will click this icon when they want to favorite a recipe.

Start by locating `// TODO 2: add IconButton` and replacing it with the code below:

```
IconButton(
  // 4
  icon: const Icon(Icons.favorite_border),
  iconSize: 30,
  color: Colors.grey[400],
  // 5
  onPressed: () {
    const snackBar = SnackBar(content: Text('Favorite
Pressed'));
    ScaffoldMessenger.of(context).showSnackBar(snackBar);
  }),
```

Here's a quick breakdown:

4. Set the icon, size and color of the icon.

5. When the user presses the icon, display a `snackbar`.

> **Note**: A snackbar is useful to briefly display information to users when an action has taken place. For example, when you delete an email, you can provide a user with an action to undo. In this case, the snackbar will tell the user that they have liked a recipe.

When you press the **heart** icon, your app will look like this:

Next, still in **author_card.dart**, locate `// TODO 3: add alignment` and replace it with the following:

```
mainAxisAlignment: MainAxisAlignment.spaceBetween,
```

The outer Row widget applies a `spaceBetween` alignment. This adds extra space evenly between the outer row's children, placing the `IconButton` at the far right of the screen.

Just one important element left to add: the text.

Composing the text

Return to **card2.dart**, and add the theme import:

```
import 'fooderlich_theme.dart';
```

Then locate `// TODO 4: add Positioned` text and replace it with the following:

```
// 1
Expanded(
  // 2
  child: Stack(
    children: [
      // 3
      Positioned(
        bottom: 16,
        right: 16,
        child: Text(
          'Recipe',
          style: FooderlichTheme.lightTextTheme.headline1,
        ),
      ),
      // 4
      Positioned(
        bottom: 70,
        left: 16,
        child: RotatedBox(
          quarterTurns: 3,
          child: Text(
            'Smoothies',
            style: FooderlichTheme.lightTextTheme.headline1,
          ),
        ),
      ),
    ],
  ),
),
```

Notice how convenient it is to use `FooderlichTheme` to apply text styles.

Now, take a look at the code:

1. With `Expanded`, you fill in the remaining available space.

2. Apply a `Stack` widget to position the texts on top of each other.

3. Position the first text 16 pixels from the bottom and 16 pixels from the right.

4. Finally, position the second text 70 pixels from the bottom and 16 pixels from the left. Also apply a `RotatedBox` widget, which rotates the text clockwise three `quarterTurns`. This makes it appear vertical.

After saving and hot reloading, `Card2` will look like this:

And that's all you need to do for the second card. Next, you'll move on to the final card.

Composing Card3: the explore card

`Card3` is the last card you'll create for this chapter. This card lets the user explore trends to find the recipes they want to try.

The following widgets compose `Card3`:

- `Container` and `BoxDecoration` display image and rounded corners, similar to the cards above.

- You use a second `Container` to make the image darker and translucent so the white text is easier to read.

- Show an icon and the title.

- Show a collection of `Chip` widgets, which display recipe attributes like **Healthy** or **Vegan**.

In the **lib** directory, create a new file called **card3.dart**. Add the following code:

```dart
import 'package:flutter/material.dart';
import 'fooderlich_theme.dart';

class Card3 extends StatelessWidget {
  const Card3({Key? key}) : super(key: key);
  @override
  Widget build(BuildContext context) {
    return Center(
      child: Container(
        constraints: const BoxConstraints.expand(
          width: 350,
          height: 450,
        ),
        decoration: const BoxDecoration(
          image: DecorationImage(
            image: AssetImage('assets/mag2.png'),
            fit: BoxFit.cover,
          ),
          borderRadius: BorderRadius.all(Radius.circular(10.0)),
        ),
        child: Stack(
          children: [
            // TODO 5: add dark overlay BoxDecoration
            // TODO 6: Add Container, Column, Icon and Text
            // TODO 7: Add Center widget with Chip widget
children
          ],
        ),
      ),
    );
  }
}
```

Similar to the previous cards, this sets up the basic container and box decorations for your card.

The initial setup of Card3 is just like Card1 and Card2. In **home.dart** add the needed import at the top of the file:

```
import 'card3.dart';
```

Next, locate // TODO: Replace with Card3 and replace it and the container with the following:

```
const Card3(),
```

Perform a hot restart by clicking the button in the **Run** panel.

Tap the **Card3** tab bar item. Your app will look like this:

So far, the card just has the typical card theme and the image. You'll add the other elements next.

Composing the dark overlay

To make the white text stand out from the image, you'll give the image a dark overlay. Just as you've done before, you'll use Stack to overlay other widgets on top of the image.

In **card3.dart**, locate `// TODO 5: add dark overlay BoxDecoration` add replace it with the following code in the `Stack`:

```
Container(
  decoration: BoxDecoration(
    // 1
    color: Colors.black.withOpacity(0.6),
    // 2
    borderRadius: const BorderRadius.all(Radius.circular(10.0)),
  ),
),
```

Adding this code does the following:

1. You add a container with a color overlay with a 60% semi-transparent background to make the image appear darker.

2. This gives the appearance of rounded image corners.

Your app now looks like this:

Great! Now for some text.

Composing the header

The next thing you want to do is to add the **Recipe Trends** text and icon. To do this, replace // TODO 6: Add Container, Column, Icon and Text with:

```
Container(
  // 3
  padding: const EdgeInsets.all(16),
  // 4
  child: Column(
    // 5
    crossAxisAlignment: CrossAxisAlignment.start,
    children: [
      // 6
      const Icon(
        Icons.book,
        color: Colors.white,
        size: 40,
      ),
      // 7
      const SizedBox(height: 8),
      // 8
      Text(
        'Recipe Trends',
        style: FooderlichTheme.darkTextTheme.headline2,
      ),
      // 9
      const SizedBox(height: 30),
    ],
  ),
),
```

Here's what you do with this code:

3. Apply padding of 16 pixels on all sides.

4. Set up a child Column to lay out the widgets vertically.

5. Position all the widgets to the **left** of the column.

6. Add a book icon.

7. Apply an 8-pixel space vertically.

8. Add the text widget.

9. Apply a 30-pixel space vertically.

Save the file, and your card now looks like this:

Great, next you'll add the chips with the recipe categories.

Composing the chips

Locate `// TODO 7: Add Center widget with Chip widget children` and replace it with the following:

```
Center(
  // 11
  child: Wrap(
    // 12
    alignment: WrapAlignment.start,
    // 13
    spacing: 12,
    // 14
    children: [
      Chip(
        label: Text('Healthy',
            style: FooderlichTheme.darkTextTheme.bodyText1),
        backgroundColor: Colors.black.withOpacity(0.7),
        onDeleted: () {
          print('delete');
        },
      ),
      Chip(
        label: Text('Vegan',
            style: FooderlichTheme.darkTextTheme.bodyText1),
```

```
      backgroundColor: Colors.black.withOpacity(0.7),
      onDeleted: () {
        print('delete');
      },
    ),
    Chip(
      label: Text('Carrots',
          style: FooderlichTheme.darkTextTheme.bodyText1),
      backgroundColor: Colors.black.withOpacity(0.7),
    ),
  ],
 ),
),
```

Here's a breakdown of this code:

10. You add a `Center` widget.

11. `Wrap` is a layout widget that attempts to lay out each of its children adjacent to the previous children. If there's not enough space, it wraps to the next line.

12. Place the children as close to the left, i.e. the `start`, as possible.

13. Apply a 12-pixel space between each child.

14. Add the list of `Chip` widgets.

> **Note**: A `Chip` widget is a display element that displays text and image avatars, and also performs user actions such as tap and delete. For more about chip widgets, check out this awesome tutorial by Pinkesh Darji:
>
> https://medium.com/aubergine-solutions/1c46217dca9b

Save your changes and hot restart. Now, your card looks like this:

Add more `Chip` widgets by duplicating the `Chip()` code above. This gives you the chance to see the `Wrap` layout widget in action, as shown below:

You did it! You've finished this chapter. Along the way, you've applied three different categories of widgets. You learned how to use structural widgets to organize different screens, and you created three custom recipe cards and applied different widget layouts to each of them.

Well done!

Key points

- Three main categories of widgets are: structure and navigation; displaying information; and, positioning widgets.

- There are two main visual design systems available in Flutter, **Material** and **Cupertino**. They help you build apps that look native on Android and iOS, respectively.

- Using the **Material** theme, you can build quite varied user interface elements to give your app a custom look and feel.

- It's generally a good idea to establish a common theme object for your app, giving you a single source of truth for your app's style.

- The **Scaffold** widget implements all your basic visual layout structure needs.

- The **Container** widget can be used to group other widgets together.

- The **Stack** widget layers child widgets on top of each other.

Where to go from here?

There's a wealth of Material Design widgets to play with, not to mention other types of widgets — too many to cover in a single chapter.

Fortunately, the Flutter team created a Widget UI component library that shows how each widget works! Check it out here: https://gallery.flutter.dev/

In this chapter, you got started right off with using widgets to build a nice user interface. In the next chapter, you'll dive into the theory of widgets to help you better understand how to use them.

Chapter 4: Understanding Widgets

By Vincent Ngo

You may have heard that everything in Flutter is a widget. While that might not be absolutely true, most of the time when you're building apps, you only see the top layer: **widgets**. In this chapter, you'll dive into widget theory. You'll explore:

- Widgets

- Widget rendering

- Flutter Inspector

- Types of widgets

- Widget lifecycle

It's time to jump in!

> **Note:** This chapter is mostly theoretical. You'll make just a few code changes to the project near the end of the chapter.

What is a widget?

A **widget** is a building block for your user interface. Using widgets is like combining Legos. Like Legos, you can mix and match widgets to create something amazing.

Flutter's declarative nature makes it super easy to build a UI with widgets. A widget is a blueprint for displaying your app **state**.

$$UI = f(state)$$
Screen   Build

You can think of widgets as a function of UI. Given a state, the `build()` method of a widget constructs the widget UI.

Unboxing Card2

In the previous chapter, you created three recipe cards. Now, you'll look in more detail at the widgets that compose **Card2**:

Do you remember which widgets you needed to build this card?

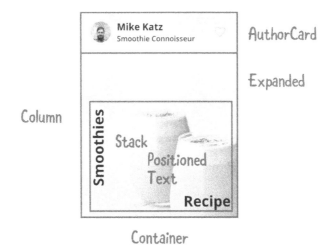

Recall that the card consists of the following:

- **Container widget**: Styles, decorates and positions widgets.

- **Column widget**: Displays other widgets vertically.

- **AuthorCard custom widget**: Displays the author's information.

- **Expanded widget**: Uses a widget to fill the remaining space.

- **Stack widget**: Places widgets on top of each other.

- **Positioned widget**: Controls a widget's position in the stack.

Widget trees

Every widget contains a build() method. In this method, you create a UI composition by nesting widgets within other widgets. This forms a **tree-like data structure**. Each widget can contain other widgets, commonly called **children**. Below is a visualization of **Card2**'s widget tree:

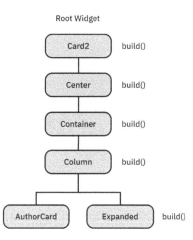

You can also break down AuthorCard and Expanded:

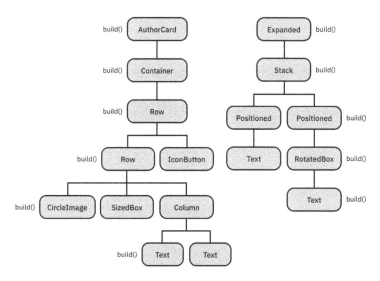

The widget tree provides a blueprint that describes how you want to lay out your UI. The framework traverses the nodes in the tree and calls each build() method to compose your entire UI.

Rendering widgets

In Chapter 1, "Getting Started", you learned that Flutter's architecture contains three layers:

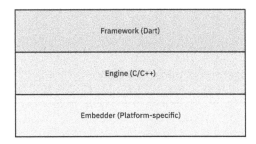

In this chapter, you'll focus on the **framework layer**. You can break this layer into four parts:

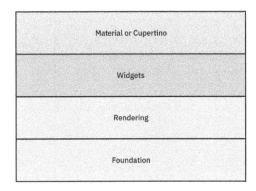

- **Material** and **Cupertino** are UI control libraries built on top of the widget layer. They make your UI look and feel like Android and iOS apps, respectively.

- The **Widgets** layer is a composition abstraction on widgets. It contains all the primitive classes needed to create UI controls. Check out the official documentation here: https://api.flutter.dev/flutter/widgets/widgets-library.html.

- The **Rendering** layer is a layout abstraction that draws and handles the widget's layout. Imagine having to recompute every widget's coordinates and frames manually. Yuck!

- **Foundation**, also known as the **dart:ui** layer, contains core libraries that handle animation, painting and gestures.

Three trees

Flutter's framework actually manages not one, but three trees in parallel:

- Widget Tree
- Element Tree
- RenderObject Tree

Here's how a single widget works under the hood:

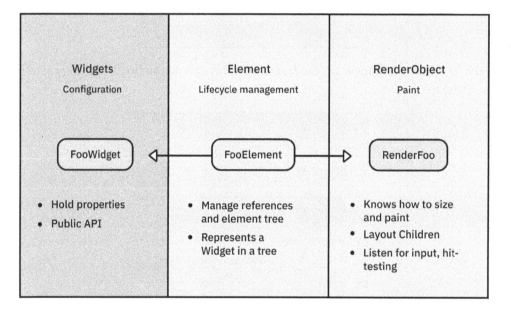

1. **Widget**: The public API or blueprint for the framework. Developers usually just deal with composing widgets.

2. **Element**: Manages a widget and a widget's render object. For every widget instance in the tree, there is a corresponding element.

3. **RenderObject**: Responsible for drawing and laying out a specific widget instance. Also handles user interactions, like hit-testing and gestures.

Types of elements

There are two types of elements:

1. **ComponentElement**: A type of element that's composed of other elements. This corresponds to composing widgets inside other widgets.

2. **RenderObjectElement**: A type of element that holds a render object.

You can think of **ComponentElement** as a group of elements, and **RenderObjectElement** as a single element. Remember that each element contains a render object to perform widget painting, layout and hit testing.

Example trees for Card2

The image below shows an example of the three trees for the **Card2** UI:

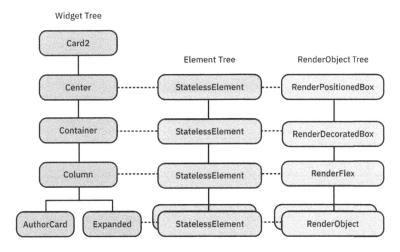

As you saw in previous chapters, Flutter starts to build your app by calling `runApp()`. Every widget's `build()` method then composes a subtree of widgets. For each widget in the widget tree, Flutter creates a corresponding **element**.

The element tree manages each widget instance and associates a render object to tell the framework how to render a particular widget.

> **Note**: For more details on Flutter widget rendering, check out the Flutter team's talk they gave in China on how to render widgets:
>
> https://youtu.be/996ZgFRENMs.

Getting started

Open the **starter** project in Android Studio, run `flutter pub get` if necessary, then run the app. You'll see the **Fooderlich** app from the previous chapter:

Next, open **DevTools** by tapping the **blue Dart** icon, as shown below:

DevTools will open in your browser. Select a widget on the left to see its layout on the right.

> **Note:** It works best with the Google Chrome web browser. Click the ⚙ icon to switch between dark and light mode!

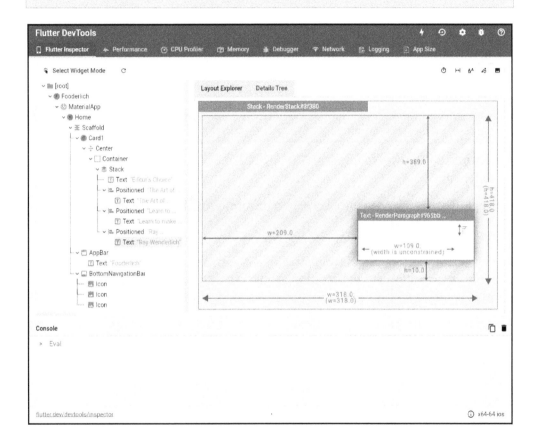

DevTools overview

DevTools provides all kinds of awesome tools to help you debug your Flutter app. These include:

- **Flutter Inspector**: Used to explore and debug the widget tree.

- **Performance**: Allows you to analyze Flutter frame charts, timeline events and CPU profiler.

- **CPU Profiler**: Allows you to record and profile your Flutter app session.

- **Memory**: Shows how objects in Dart are allocated, which helps find memory leaks.

- **Debugger**: Supports breakpoints and variable inspection on the call stack. Also allows you to step through code right within DevTools.

- **Network**: Allows you to inspect HTTP, HTTPS and web socket traffic within your Flutter app.

- **Logging**: Displays events fired on the Dart runtime and app-level log events.

- **App Size**: Helps you analyze your total app size.

There are many different tools to play with, but in this chapter, you'll only look at the **Flutter Inspector**. For information about how the other tools work, check out:https://flutter.dev/docs/development/tools/devtools/overview.

Flutter Inspector

The Flutter Inspector has four key benefits. It helps you:

- Visualize your widget tree.

- Inspect the properties of a specific widget in the tree.

- Experiment with different layout configurations using the **Layout Explorer**.

- Enable slow animation to show how your transitions look.

Flutter Inspector tools

Here are some of the important tools to use with the Flutter Inspector.

- **Select Widget Mode**: When enabled, this allows you to tap a particular widget on a device or simulator to inspect its properties.

Clicking any element in the widget tree also highlights the widget on the device and jumps to the exact line of code. How cool is that!

- **Refresh Tree**: Simply reloads the current widget's info.

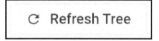

- **Slow Animation**: Slows down the animation so you can visually inspect the UI transitions.

- **Show Guidelines**: Shows visual debugging hints. That allows you to check the borders, paddings and alignment of your widgets.

Here's a screenshot of how it looks on a device:

- **Show Baselines**: When enabled, this tells RenderBox to paint a line under each text's baseline.

Here, you can see the green line under the baseline of each Text widget:

- **Highlight Repaints**: Adds a random border to a widget every time Flutter repaints it. This is useful if you want to find unnecessary repaints.

If you feel bored, you can spice things up by enabling disco mode, as shown below:

- **Highlight Oversized Images**: Tells you which images in your app are oversized.

If an image is oversized it will invert the image's colors and flip it upside down. As shown below:

Inspecting the widget tree

In the emulator, select the first tab, then click **Refresh Tree** in the DevTools. Finally, select Card1 and click **Details Tree** tab, as shown below:

Note that:

- In the left panel, there's a portion of the Flutter widget tree under investigation, starting from the root.

- When you tap a specific widget in the tree, you can inspect its sub-tree, as shown in the **Details Tree** tab on the right panel.

- The Details Tree represents the element tree and displays all the important properties that make up the widget. Notice that it references **renderObject**.

The Details Tree is a great way for you to inspect and experiment with how a specific widget property works.

Click a Text widget and you'll see all the properties you can configure:

How useful is this? You can examine all the properties, and if something doesn't make sense, you can pull up the Flutter widget documentation to read more about that property!

Inspecting like a pro

Besides checking the properties in **Details Tree**, you can evaluate your widgets in two other ways:

1. Hover over any widget and it will show a pop-up with all the properties.

2. Click on a widget to print the widget's object, properties and state in the console.

As shown below:

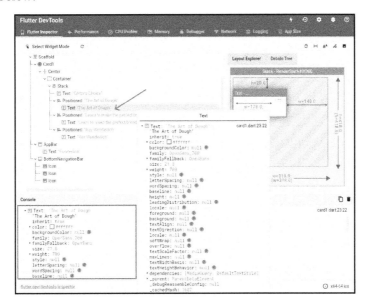

Layout Explorer

Next, click the **Layout Explorer** tab, as shown below:

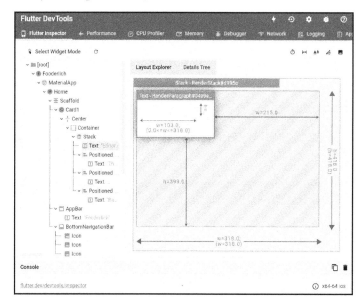

You can use the Layout Explorer to visualize how your Text widget is laid out within the Stack.

Next, follow these instructions:

1. Make sure your device is running and DevTools is open in your browser.

2. Click **Card3** in the bottom navigation bar.

3. Click the **Refresh Tree** button.

4. Select the **Column** element in the tree.

5. Click **Layout Explorer**.

You'll see the following:

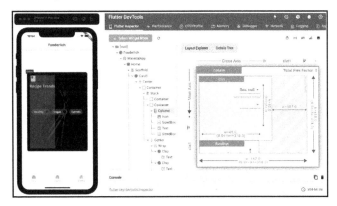

The Layout Explorer is handy for modifying flex widget layouts in real time.

The explorer supports modifying:

- `mainAxisAlignment`
- `crossAxisAlignment`
- `flex`

Click **start** within the **Main Axis** and change the value to **end**. Notice that the **Recipe Trends** text is now at the bottom of the card:

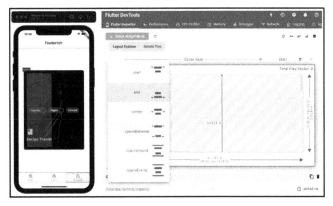

This is useful when you need to inspect and tweak layouts at runtime.Feel free to experiment and play around with the Layout Explorer. You can create simple column or row widgets to mess around with the layout axis.

You now have all the tools you need to debug widgets! In the next section, you'll learn about the types of widgets and when to use them.

Types of widgets

There are three major types of widgets: **Stateless**, **Stateful** and **Inherited**. All widgets are immutable but some have state attached to them using their element. You'll learn more about the differences between these next.

Stateless widgets

You can't alter the state or properties of Stateless widget once it's built. When your properties don't need to change over time, it's generally a good idea to start with a stateless widget.

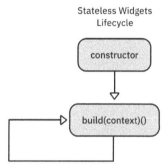

The lifecycle of a stateless widget starts with a constructor, which you can pass parameters to, and a `build()` method, which you override. The visual description of the widget is determined by the `build()` method.

The following events trigger this kind of widget to update:

1. The widget is inserted into the widget tree for the first time.

2. The state of a dependency or inherited widget — ancestor nodes — changes.

Stateful widgets

Stateful widgets preserve state, which is useful when parts of your UI need to change dynamically.

For example, one good time to use a stateful widget is when a user taps a **Favorite** button to toggle a simple Boolean value on and off.

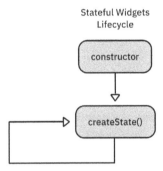

Stateful widgets store their mutable state in a separate `State` class. That's why every stateful widget must override and implement `createState()`.

Next, take a look at the stateful widget's lifecycle.

State object lifecycle

Every widget's build() method takes a BuildContext as an argument. The build context tells you where you are in the tree of widgets. You can access the **element** for any widget through the BuildContext. Later, you'll see why the build context is important, especially for accessing state information from parent widgets.

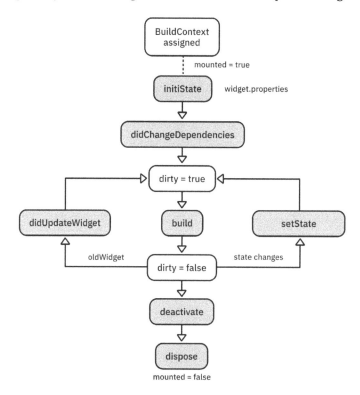

Now, take a closer look at the lifecycle:

1. When you assign the build context to the widget, an internal flag, mounted, is set to true. This lets the framework know that this widget is currently on the widget tree.

2. initState() is the first method called after a widget is created. This is similar to onCreate() in Android or viewDidLoad() in iOS.

3. The first time the framework builds a widget, it calls didChangeDependencies() after initState(). It might call didChangeDependencies() again if your state object depends on an **inherited widget** that has changed. There is more on inherited widgets below.

4. Finally, the framework calls `build()` after `didChangeDependencies()`. This function is the most important for developers because it's called every time a widget needs rendering. Every widget in the tree triggers a `build()` method recursively, so this operation has to be very fast.

> **Note**: You should always perform heavy computational functions asynchronously and store their results as part of the state for later use with the `build()` function. `build()` should never do anything that's computationally demanding. This is similar to how you think of the iOS or Android main thread. For example, you should never make a network call that stalls the UI rendering.

5. The framework calls `didUpdateWidget(_)` when a parent widget makes a change or needs to redraw the UI. When that happens, you'll get the `oldWidget` instance as a parameter so you can compare it with your current widget and do any additional logic.

6. Whenever you want to modify the state in your widget, you call `setState()`. The framework then marks the widget as `dirty` and triggers a `build()` again.

> **Note**: Asynchronous code should always check if the `mounted` property is true before calling `setstate()`, because the widget may no longer be part of the widget tree.

7. When you remove the object from the tree, the framework calls `deactivate()`. The framework can, in some cases, reinsert the state object into another part of the tree.

8. The framework calls `dispose()` when you permanently remove the object and its state from the tree. This method is very important because you'll need it to handle memory cleanup, such as unsubscribing streams and disposing of animations or controllers.

The rule of thumb for `dispose()` is to check any properties you define in your state and make sure you've disposed of them properly.

Adding stateful widgets

Card2 is currently a StatelessWidget. Notice that the **Heart** button on the top-right currently only displays a SnackBar(), but nothing else like turning a solid color like a typical **Favorite** button. This isn't because you haven't hooked up any actions. It's because the widget, as it is, can't manage state dynamically. To fix this, you'll change this card into a StatefulWidget.

AuthorCard is nested within Card2. Open **author_card.dart** and right-click on AuthorCard. Then click **Show Context Actions** from the menu that pops up:

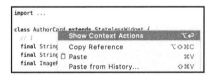

Select **Convert to StatefulWidget**. Instead of converting manually, you can just use this menu shortcut to do it automatically:

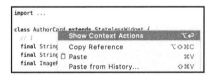

There are now two classes:

```
class AuthorCard extends StatefulWidget {
  ...

  @override
  _AuthorCardState createState() => _AuthorCardState();
}
```

```
class _AuthorCardState extends State<AuthorCard> {
  @override
  Widget build(BuildContext context) {
    ...
  }
}
```

A couple of things to notice in the code above:

- The refactor converted `AuthorCard` from a `StatelessWidget` into a `StatefulWidget`. It added a `createState()` implementation.

- The refactor also created the `_AuthorCardState` state class. It stores mutable data that can change over the lifetime of the widget.

Implementing favorites

In `_AuthorCardState`, add the following property right after the class declaration:

```
bool _isFavorited = false;
```

Now that you've created a new state, you need to manage it. Replace the current `IconButton` in `_AuthorCardState` with the following:

```
IconButton(
  // 1
  icon: Icon(_isFavorited ? Icons.favorite :
Icons.favorite_border),
  iconSize: 30,
  // 2
  color: Colors.red[400],
  onPressed: () {
    // 3
    setState(() {
      _isFavorited = !_isFavorited;
    });
  },
)
```

Here's how the new state works:

1. First, it checks if the user has favorited this recipe card. If t rue, it shows a filled heart. If false, it shows an outlined heart.

2. It changes the color to red to give the app more life.

3. When the user presses the `IconButton`, it toggles the `_isFavorited` state via a call to `setState()`.

Save the change to trigger a hot reload and see the heart button toggle on and off when you tap it, as shown below:

Examining the widget tree

Now that you've turned `AuthorCard` into a stateful widget, your next step is to look at how the element tree manages state changes.

Recall that the framework will construct the widget tree and, for every widget instance, create an element object. The element, in this case, is a `StatefulElement` and it manages the state object, as shown below:

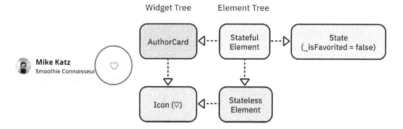

When the user taps the heart button, `setState()` runs and toggles `_isFavorited` to true. Internally, the state object marks this element as **dirty**. That triggers a call to `build()`.

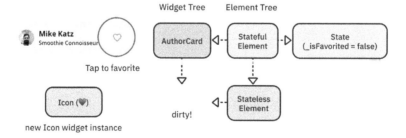

This is where the element object shows its strength. It removes the old widget and replaces it with a new instance of Icon that contains the filled heart icon.

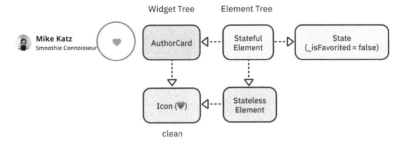

Rather than reconstructing the whole tree, the framework only updates the widgets that need to be changed. It walks down the tree hierarchy and checks for what's changed. It reuses everything else.

Now, what happens when you need to access data from some other widget, located elsewhere in the hierarchy? You use inherited widgets.

Inherited widgets

Inherited widgets let you access state information from the parent elements in the tree hierarchy.

Imagine you have a piece of data way up in the widget tree that you want to access. One solution is to pass the data down as a parameter on each nested widget — but that quickly becomes annoying and cumbersome.

Wouldn't it be great if there was a centralized way to access such data?

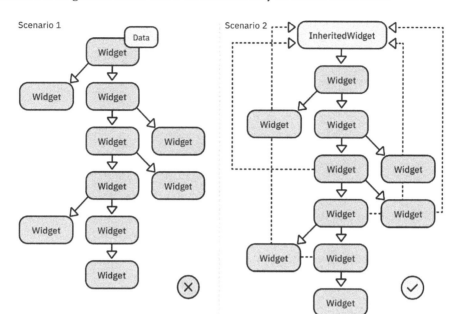

That's where inherited widgets come in! By adding an inherited widget in your tree, you can reference the data from any of its descendants. This is known as **lifting state up**.

For example, you use an inherited widget when:

- Accessing a Theme object to change the UI's appearance.

- Calling an API service object to fetch data from the web.

- Subscribing to streams to update the UI according to the data received.

Inherited widgets are an advanced topic. You'll learn more about them in Section 4, "Networking, Persistence and State", which covers state management and the **Provider** package—a wrapper around an inherited widget.

Key points

- Flutter maintains three trees in parallel: the `Widget`, `Element` and `RenderObject` trees.

- A Flutter app is performant because it maintains its structure and only updates the widgets that need redrawing.

- The **Flutter Inspector** is a useful tool to debug, experiment with and inspect a widget tree.

- You should always start by creating `StatelessWidgets` and only use `StatefulWidgets` when you need to manage and maintain the state of your widget.

- Inherited widgets are a good solution to access state from the top of the tree.

Where to go from here?

If you want to learn more theory about how widgets work, check out the following links:

- Detailed architectural overview of Flutter and widgets: https://flutter.dev/docs/resources/architectural-overview.

- The Flutter team created a YouTube series explaining widgets under the hood: https://www.youtube.com/playlist?list=PLjxrf2q8roU2HdJQDjJzOeO6J3FoFLWr2.

- The Flutter team gave a talk in China on how to render widgets: https://youtu.be/996ZgFRENMs.

In the next chapter, you'll get back to more practical concerns and see how to create scrollable widgets.

Chapter 5: Scrollable Widgets

By Vincent Ngo

Building scrollable content is an essential part of UI development. There's only so much information a user can process at a time, let alone fit on an entire screen in the palm of your hand!

In this chapter, you'll learn everything you need to know about scrollable widgets. In particular, you'll learn:

- How to use `ListView`.

- How to nest scroll views.

- How to leverage the power of `GridView`.

You'll continue to build your recipe app, **Fooderlich**, by adding two new screens: **Explore** and **Recipes**. The first shows popular recipes for the day along with what your friends are cooking.

The second displays a library of recipes, handy if you're still on the fence about what to cook today. :]

By the end of this chapter, you'll be a scrollable widget wizard!

Getting started

Open the starter project in Android Studio, then run `flutter pub get` if necessary and run the app.

You'll see colored screens as shown below:

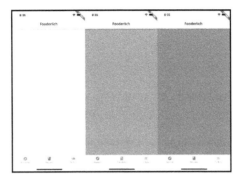

Project files

There are new files in this starter project to help you out. Before you learn how to create scrollable widgets, take a look at them.

Assets folder

The **assets** directory contains all JSON files and images that you'll use to build your app.

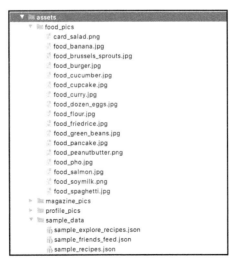

Sample images

- **food_pics**: Contains the food pictures you'll display throughout the app.

- **magazine_pics**: All the food magazine background images you'll display on card widgets.

- **profile_pics**: Contains raywenderlich.com team member pictures.

JSON Data

The **sample_data** directory contains three JSON files:

- **sample_explore_recipes.json**: A list of recipes to display on the home screen. Sometimes, users might want recommendations for what to cook today!

- **sample_friends_feed.json**: This list contains samples of your friends' posts, in case you're curious about what your friends are cooking up!

- **sample_recipes.json**: A list of recipes including details about the duration and cooking difficulty of each.

New classes

In the **lib** directory, you'll also notice three new folders, as shown below:

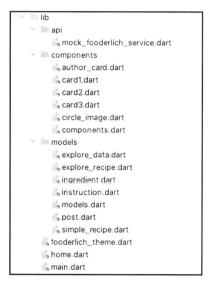

API folder

The **api** folder contains a mock service class.

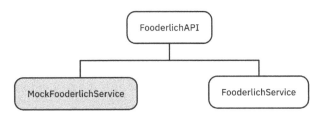

`MockFooderlichService` is a service class that mocks a server response. It has `async` functions that wait to load data from a sample JSON and decode it to recipe model objects.

In this chapter, you'll use two API calls:

- **getExploreData()**: Returns `ExploreData`. Internally, it makes a batch request and returns two lists: recipes to explore and friend posts.

- **getRecipes()**: Returns the list of recipes.

> **Note**: Unfamiliar with how `async` works in Dart? Check out Chapter 10, "Asynchronous Programming" in **Dart Apprentice** (https://bit.ly/2Yoo0VO) or read this article to learn more:https://dart.dev/codelabs/async-await.

> **Pro tip**: Sometimes your back-end service is not ready to consume. Creating a mock service object is a flexible way to build your UI. Instead of creating many recipe mock objects, all you have to do is change a JSON file.

Models folder

You'll use these six model objects to build your app's UI:

- **ExploreRecipe**: All of the details about a recipe. It contains ingredients, instructions, duration and a whole lot more.

- **Ingredient**: A single ingredient. This is part of `ExploreRecipe`.

- **Instruction**: A single instruction to cook the recipe. It's part of `ExploreRecipe`.

- **Post**: Describes a friend's post. A post is similar to a tweet and represents what your social network is cooking.

- **ExploreData**: Groups two datasets. It contains a list of `ExploreRecipes` and a list of `Posts`.

- **SimpleRecipe**: How difficult a recipe is to cook.

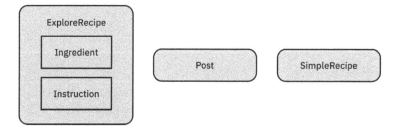

Feel free to explore the different properties each model object contains!

> **Note**: **models.dart** is a **barrel** file. It exports all your model objects and makes it convenient to import them later on. Think of this as grouping many imports into a single file.

Components folder

lib/components contains all your custom widgets.

> **Note**: **components.dart** is another **barrel** file that groups all imports in a single file.

Notice that every single `Card` now requires an `ExploreRecipe` instance.

That's it for getting up to speed on the new starter project files!

Now that you have a mock service and model objects, you can focus on scrollable widgets!

Introducing ListView

ListView is a very popular Flutter component. It's a linear scrollable widget that arranges its children linearly and supports horizontal and vertical scrolling.

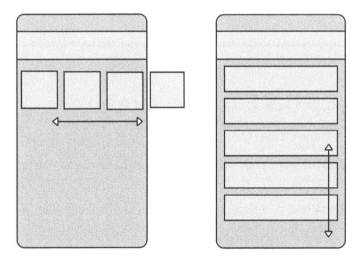

> **Fun fact**: `Column` and `Row` widgets are like `ListView` but without the scroll view.

Introducing Constructors

A `ListView` has four constructors:

- The default constructor takes an explicit list of widgets called `children`. That will construct every single child in the list, even the ones that aren't visible. You should use this if you have a small number of children.

- `ListView.builder()` takes in an `IndexedWidgetBuilder` and builds the list on demand. It will only construct the children that are visible onscreen. You should use this if you need to display a large or infinite number of items.

- `ListView.separated()` takes **two** `IndexedWidgetBuilders`: `itemBuilder` and `seperatorBuilder`. This is useful if you want to place a separator widget between your items.

- `ListView.custom()` gives you more fine-grain control over your child items.

> **Note**: For more details about ListView constructors, check out the official documentation:https://api.flutter.dev/flutter/widgets/ListView-class.html

Next, you'll learn how to use the first three constructors!

Setting up the Explore screen

The first screen you'll create is the `ExploreScreen`. It contains two sections:

- **TodayRecipeListView**: A horizontal scroll view that lets you pan through different cards.

- **FriendPostListView**: A vertical scroll view that shows what your friends are cooking.

In the **lib** folder, create a new directory called **screens**.

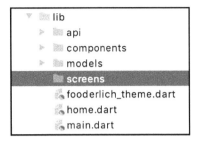

Within the new directory, create a new file called **explore_screen.dart** and add the following code:

```
import 'package:flutter/material.dart';

import '../components/components.dart';
import '../models/models.dart';
import '../api/mock_fooderlich_service.dart';

class ExploreScreen extends StatelessWidget {
  // 1
  final mockService = MockFooderlichService();

  ExploreScreen({Key? key}) : super(key: key);

  @override
  Widget build(BuildContext context) {
    // 2
    // TODO 1: Add TodayRecipeListView FutureBuilder
    return const Center(
      child: Text('Explore Screen'),
    );
  }
}
```

Here's how the code works:

1. Create a `MockFooderlichService`, to mock server responses.

2. Display a placeholder text. You'll replace this later.

Updating the navigation pages

In **home.dart**, locate `// TODO: Replace with ExploreScreen` and replace the line below with the following:

```
ExploreScreen(),
```

This will display the newly created `ExploreScreen` in the first tab.

Make sure the new `ExploreScreen` has been imported. If your IDE didn't add it automatically, add this import:

```
import 'screens/explore_screen.dart';
```

Hot restart the app. It will look like this:

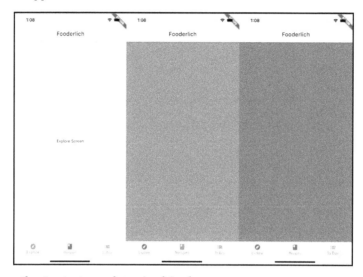

You'll replace the `Containers` later in this chapter.

Creating a FutureBuilder

How do you display your UI with an asynchronous task?

`MockFooderlichService` contains asynchronous functions that return a `Future` object. `FutureBuilder` comes in handy here, as it helps you determine the state of a future. For example, it tells you whether data is still loading or the fetch has finished.

In **explore_screen.dart**, replace the whole `return` statement below `// TODO 1: Add TodayRecipeListView FutureBuilder` with the following code:

```
// 1
return FutureBuilder(
  // 2
  future: mockService.getExploreData(),
  // 3
  builder: (context, AsyncSnapshot<ExploreData> snapshot) {
```

```
    // TODO: Add Nested List Views
    // 4
    if (snapshot.connectionState == ConnectionState.done) {
      // 5
      final recipes = snapshot.data?.todayRecipes ?? [];
      // TODO: Replace this with TodayRecipeListView
      return Center(
          child: Container(
              child: const Text('Show TodayRecipeListView'),
          ),
      );
    } else {
      // 6
      return const Center(
          child: CircularProgressIndicator(),
      );
    }
  },
);
```

Here's what the code does:

1. Within the widget's `build()`, you create a `FutureBuilder`.

2. The `FutureBuilder` takes in a `Future` as a parameter. `getExploreData()` creates a future that will, in turn, return an `ExploreData` instance. That instance will contain two lists, `todayRecipes` and `friendPosts`.

3. Within `builder`, you use `snapshot` to check the current state of the `Future`.

4. Now, the `Future` is complete and you can extract the data to pass to your widget.

5. `snapshot.data` returns `ExploreData`, from which you extract `todayRecipes` to pass to the list view. Right now, you show a simple text as a placeholder. You'll build a `TodayRecipeListView` soon.

6. The future is still loading, so you show a spinner to let the user know something is happening.

> **Note**: For more information, check out Flutter's `FutureBuilder` documentation:
>
> https://api.flutter.dev/flutter/widgets/FutureBuilder-class.html.

Perform a hot reload. You'll see the loading spinner first. After the future completes, it shows the placeholder text.

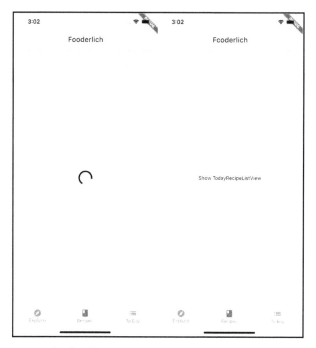

Now that you've set up the loading UI, it's time to build the actual list view!

Building Recipes of the Day

The first scrollable component you'll build is `TodayRecipeListView`. This is the top section of the `ExploreScreen`. It will be a horizontal list view.

In **lib/components**, create a new file called **today_recipe_list_view.dart**. Add the following code:

```
import 'package:flutter/material.dart';

// 1
import '../components/components.dart';
import '../models/models.dart';

class TodayRecipeListView extends StatelessWidget {
  // 2
  final List<ExploreRecipe> recipes;

  const TodayRecipeListView({
```

```
    Key? key,
    required this.recipes,
  }) : super(key: key);

  @override
  Widget build(BuildContext context) {
    // 3
    return Padding(
      padding: const EdgeInsets.only(
        left: 16,
        right: 16,
        top: 16,
      ),
      // 4
      child: Column(
        crossAxisAlignment: CrossAxisAlignment.start,
        children: [
          // 5
          Text(
            'Recipes of the Day 🔍',
            style: Theme.of(context).textTheme.headline1),
          // 6
          const SizedBox(height: 16),
          // 7
          Container(
            height: 400,
            // TODO: Add ListView Here
            color: Colors.grey,
          ),
        ],
      ),
    );
  }

  // TODO: Add buildCard() widget here

}
```

Here's how the code works:

1. Import the barrel files, **component.dart** and **models.dart**, so you can use data models and UI components.

2. `TodayRecipeListView` needs a list of recipes to display.

3. Within `build()`, start by applying some padding.

4. Add a `Column` to place widgets in a vertical layout.

5. In the column, add a `Text`. This is the header for the Recipes of the Day.

6. Add a 16-point-tall `SizedBox`, to supply some padding.

7. Add a `Container`, 400 points tall, and set the background color to **grey**. This container will hold your horizontal list view.

Adding ListView for today's recipes

Open **components.dart** and add the following export:

```
export 'today_recipe_list_view.dart';
```

This means you don't have to call additional imports when you use the new component.

Next, open **explore_screen.dart** and replace the `return` statement below the comment `// TODO: Replace this with TodayRecipeListView` with the following:

```
return TodayRecipeListView(recipes: recipes);
```

If your app is still running, it will now look like this:

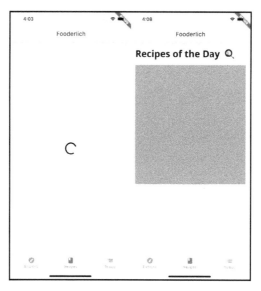

Now it's finally time to add the `ListView`.

In **today_recipe_list_view.dart**, replace the comment `// TODO: Add ListView Here` and the `color:` line below it with the following:

```
// 1
color: Colors.transparent,
// 2
child: ListView.separated(
  // 3
  scrollDirection: Axis.horizontal,
  // 4
  itemCount: recipes.length,
  // 5
  itemBuilder: (context, index) {
    // 6
    final recipe = recipes[index];
    return buildCard(recipe);
  },
  // 7
  separatorBuilder: (context, index) {
    // 8
    return const SizedBox(width: 16);
  },
),
```

Here's how the code works:

1. Change the color from grey to transparent.

2. Create `ListView.separated`. Remember, this widget creates two `IndexedWidgetBuilders`.

3. Set the scroll direction to the `horizontal` axis.

4. Set the number of items in the list view.

5. Create the `itemBuilder` callback, which will go through every item in the list.

6. Get the recipe for the current index and build the card.

7. Create the `separatorBuilder` callback, which will go through every item in the list.

8. For every item, you create a `SizedBox` to space every item 16 points apart.

Next, you need to actually build the card. Replace `// TODO: Add buildCard()`
`widget here` with the following:

```
Widget buildCard(ExploreRecipe recipe) {
  if (recipe.cardType == RecipeCardType.card1) {
    return Card1(recipe: recipe);
  } else if (recipe.cardType == RecipeCardType.card2) {
    return Card2(recipe: recipe);
  } else if (recipe.cardType == RecipeCardType.card3) {
    return Card3(recipe: recipe);
  } else {
    throw Exception('This card doesn\'t exist yet');
  }
}
```

This function builds the card for each item. Every `ExploreRecipe` has a `cardType`.
This helps you determine which `Card` to create for that recipe.

Save the change to trigger a hot restart, and Fooderlich will now look like this:

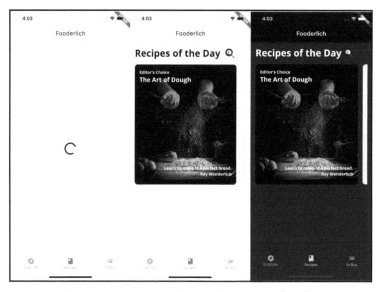

Finally, you can scroll through the list of beautiful recipes for the day. Don't forget,
you can switch the theme in **main.dart** to dark mode!

Next, you'll build the bottom section of `ExploreScreen`.

Nested ListViews

There are two approaches to building the bottom section: the Column approach and the Nested ListView approach. You'll take a look at each of them now.

Column approach

You could put the two list views in a `Column`. A `Column` arranges items in a vertical layout, so that makes sense right?

The diagram shows two **rectangular boundaries** that represent two scrollable areas.

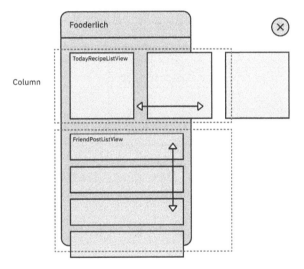

The pros and cons to this approach are:

- `TodayRecipeListView` is OK because the scroll is in the horizontal direction. All the cards also fit on the screen and look great!

- `FriendPostListView` scrolls in the vertical direction, but it only has a small scroll area. So as a user, you can't see very many of your friend's posts at once.

This approach has a bad user experience because the content area is too small! The `Cards` already take up most of the screen. How much room will there be for the vertical scroll area on small devices?

Nested ListView approach

In the second approach, you nest multiple list views in a parent list view.

The diagram shows one big **rectangular boundary**.

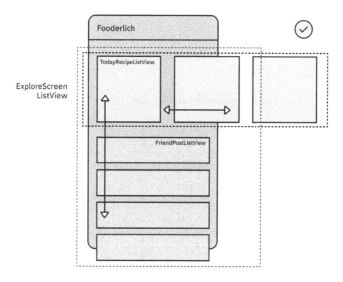

`ExploreScreen` holds the parent `ListView`. Since there are only two child `ListViews`, you can use the default constructor, which returns an explicit list of children.

The benefits of this approach are:

1. The scroll area is a lot bigger, using 70–80% of the screen.

2. You can view more of your friends' posts.

3. You can continue to scroll `TodayRecipeListView` in the horizontal direction.

4. When you scroll upward, Flutter listens to the scroll event of the parent `ListView`. So it will scroll both `TodayRecipeListView` and `FriendPostListView` upwards, giving you more room to view all the content!

Nested `ListView` sounds like a better approach, doesn't it?

Adding the nested ListView

First, open **explore_screen.dart** and replace build() with the following:

```
@override
Widget build(BuildContext context) {
  // 1
  return FutureBuilder(
    // 2
    future: mockService.getExploreData(),
    // 3
    builder: (context, AsyncSnapshot<ExploreData> snapshot) {
      // 4
      if (snapshot.connectionState == ConnectionState.done) {
        // 5
        return ListView(
          // 6
          scrollDirection: Axis.vertical,
          children: [
            // 7
            TodayRecipeListView(recipes:
snapshot.data?.todayRecipes ?? []),
            // 8
            const SizedBox(height: 16),
            // 9
            // TODO: Replace this with FriendPostListView
            Container(
              height: 400,
              color: Colors.green,
            ),
          ],
        );
      } else {
        // 10
        return const Center(child: CircularProgressIndicator());
      }
    },
  );
}
```

Here's how the code works:

1. This is the FutureBuilder from before. It runs an asynchronous task and lets you know the state of the future.

2. Use your mock service to call getExploreData(). This returns an ExploreData object future.

3. Check the state of the future within the builder callback.

4. Check if the future is complete.

5. When the future is complete, return the primary ListView. This holds an explicit list of children. In this scenario, the primary ListView will hold the other two ListViews as children.

6. Set the scroll direction to vertical, although that's the default value.

7. The first item in children is TodayRecipeListView. You pass in the list of todayRecipes from ExploreData.

8. Add a 16-point vertical space so the lists aren't too close to each other.

9. Add a green placeholder container. You'll create and add the FriendPostListView later.

10. If the future hasn't finished loading yet, show a circular progress indicator.

Your app now looks like this:

Notice that you can still scroll the Cards horizontally. When you scroll up and down, you'll notice the entire area scrolls!

Now that you have the desired scroll behavior, it's time to build FriendPostListView.

Creating the ListView for friends' posts

First, you'll create the items for the list view to display. When those are ready, you'll build a vertical list view to display them.

Here's how `FriendPostTile` will look:

 Cooking up some steak 🥩 today, state should be rare, medium or medium well?
50 mins ago

It's time to get started!

Building the tile for a friend's post

Within **lib/components**, create a new file called **friend_post_tile.dart**. Add the following code:

```dart
import 'package:flutter/material.dart';

import '../components/components.dart';
import '../models/models.dart';

class FriendPostTile extends StatelessWidget {
  final Post post;

  const FriendPostTile({
    Key? key,
    required this.post,
  }) : super(key: key);

  @override
  Widget build(BuildContext context) {
    // 1
    return Row(
      crossAxisAlignment: CrossAxisAlignment.start,
      mainAxisAlignment: MainAxisAlignment.start,
      children: [
        // 2
        CircleImage(
          imageProvider: AssetImage(post.profileImageUrl),
          imageRadius: 20,
        ),
        // 3
        const SizedBox(width: 16),
        // 4
        Expanded(
          // 5
```

```
        child: Column(
          crossAxisAlignment: CrossAxisAlignment.start,
          children: [
            // 6
            Text(post.comment),
            // 7
            Text(
              '${post.timestamp} mins ago',
              style: const TextStyle(fontWeight:
FontWeight.w700),
            ),
          ],
        ),
      ),
    ],
  );
  }
}
```

Here's how the code works:

1. Create a Row to arrange the widgets horizontally.

2. The first element is a circular avatar, which displays the image asset associated with the post.

3. Apply a 16-point padding.

4. Create Expanded, which makes the children fill the rest of the container.

5. Establish a Column to arrange the widgets vertically.

6. Create a Text to display your friend's comments.

7. Create another Text to display the timestamp of a post.

> **Note**: There's no height restriction on FriendPostTile. That means the text can expand to many lines as long as it's in a scroll view! This is like iOS's dynamic table views and autosizing TextViews in Android.

Open **components.dart** and add the following:

```
export 'friend_post_tile.dart';
```

Now, it's time to create your vertical ListView.

Creating FriendPostListView

In **lib/components**, create a new file called **friend_post_list_view.dart** and add the following code:

```
import 'package:flutter/material.dart';

import '../models/models.dart';
import 'components.dart';

class FriendPostListView extends StatelessWidget {
  // 1
  final List<Post> friendPosts;

  const FriendPostListView({
    Key? key,
    required this.friendPosts,
  }) : super(key: key);

  @override
  Widget build(BuildContext context) {
    // 2
    return Padding(
      padding: const EdgeInsets.only(
        left: 16,
        right: 16,
        top: 0,
      ),
      // 3
      child: Column(
        crossAxisAlignment: CrossAxisAlignment.start,
        children: [
          // 4
          Text('Social Chefs 👨‍🍳',
              style: Theme.of(context).textTheme.headline1),
          // 5
          const SizedBox(height: 16),
          // TODO: Add PostListView here
          // 6
          const SizedBox(height: 16),
        ],
      ),
    );
  }
}
```

Here's how the code works:

1. FriendPostListView requires a list of Posts.

2. Apply a left and right padding widget of 16 points.

3. Create a Column to position the Text followed by the posts in a vertical layout.

4. Create the Text widget header.

5. Apply a spacing of 16 points vertically.

6. Leave some padding at the end of the list.

Next, add the following code below // TODO: Add PostListView here:

```
// 1
ListView.separated(
  // 2
  primary: false,
  // 3
  physics: const NeverScrollableScrollPhysics(),
  // 4
  shrinkWrap: true,
  scrollDirection: Axis.vertical,
  itemCount: friendPosts.length,
  itemBuilder: (context, index) {
    // 5
    final post = friendPosts[index];
    return FriendPostTile(post: post);
  },
  separatorBuilder: (context, index) {
    // 6
    return const SizedBox(height: 16);
  },
),
```

Here's how you defined the new ListView:

1. Create ListView.separated with two IndexWidgetBuilder callbacks.

2. Since you're nesting two list views, it's a good idea to set primary to **false**. That lets Flutter know that this isn't the primary scroll view.

3. Set the scrolling physics to NeverScrollableScrollPhysics. Even though you set primary to false, it's also a good idea to disable the scrolling for this list view. That will propagate up to the parent list view.

4. Set shrinkWrap to true to create a **fixed-length** scrollable list of items. This gives it a fixed height. If this were **false**, you'd get an unbounded height error.

5. For every item in the list, create a `FriendPostTile`.

6. For every item, also create a `SizedBox` to space each item by 16 points.

> **Note**: There are several different types of scroll physics you can play with:
>
> • `AlwaysScrollableScrollPhysics`
>
> • `BouncingScrollPhysics`
>
> • `ClampingScrollPhysics`
>
> • `FixedExtentScrollPhysics`
>
> • `NeverScrollableScrollPhysics`
>
> • `PageScrollPhysicsRange`
>
> • `MaintainingScrollPhysics`
>
> Find more details at
>
> https://api.flutter.dev/flutter/widgets/ScrollPhysics-class.html.

Open **components.dart** and add the following export:

```
export 'friend_post_list_view.dart';
```

And that's it. Now, you'll finish up the **Explore** screen and your app will have a cool new feature!

Adding final touches to the Explore screen

Open **explore_screen.dart** and replace the `Container` code below the comment `// TODO: Replace this with FriendPostListView` with the following:

```
FriendPostListView(friendPosts: snapshot.data?.friendPosts ??
[]),
```

Here, you create a `FriendPostListView` and extract `friendPosts` from `ExploreData`.

Restart or hot reload the app. The final **Explore** screen should look like the following in light mode:

Here's what it looks like in dark mode:

Aren't nested scroll views a neat technique? :]

Now, it's time to play with grid views.

Getting to know GridView

GridView is a 2D array of scrollable widgets. It arranges the children in a grid and supports horizontal and vertical scrolling.

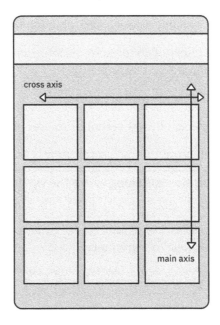

Getting used to GridView is easy. Like ListView, it inherits from ScrollView, so their constructors are very similar.

GridView has five types of constructors:

- The **default** takes an explicit list of widgets.
- GridView.builder()
- GridView.count()
- GridView.custom()
- GridView.extent()

The builder() and count() constructors are the most common. You'll have no problem getting used to these since ListView uses similar ones.

Key parameters

Here are some parameters you should pay attention to:

- **crossAxisSpacing**: The spacing between each child in the cross axis.

- **mainAxisSpacing**: The spacing between each child on the main axis.

- **crossAxisCount**: The number of children in the cross axis. You can also think of this as the number of columns you want in a grid.

- **shrinkWrap**. Controls the fixed scroll area size.

- **physics**: Controls how the scroll view responds to user input.

- **primary**: Helps Flutter determine which scroll view is the primary one.

- **scrollDirection**: Controls the axis along which the view will scroll.

> **Note**: GridView has a plethora of parameters to experiment and play with. Check out Greg Perry's article to learn more:
>
> https://medium.com/@greg.perry/decode-gridview-9b123553e604.

Understanding the cross and main axis?

What's the difference between the **main** and **cross** axis? Remember that Columns and Rows are like ListViews, but without a scroll view.

The main axis always corresponds to the scroll direction!

If your scroll direction is horizontal, you can think of this as a Row. The main axis represents the horizontal direction, as shown below:

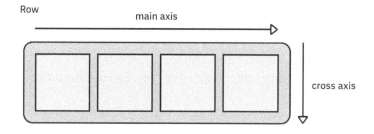

If your scroll direction is vertical, you can think of it as a `Column`. The main axis represents the vertical direction, as shown below:

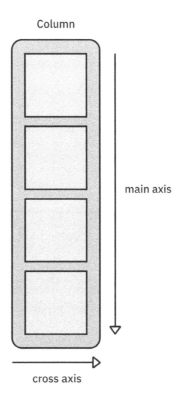

Grid delegates

Grid delegates help figure out the spacing and the number of columns to use to lay out the children in a `GridView`.

Aside from customizing your own grid delegates, Flutter provides two delegates you can use out of the box:

- `SliverGridDelegateWithFixedCrossAxisCount`
- `SliverGridDelegateWithMaxCrossAxisExtent`

The first creates a layout that has a fixed number of tiles along the cross axis. The second creates a layout with tiles that have a maximum cross axis extent.

Building the Recipes screen

You are now ready to build the Recipes screen! In the **screens** directory, create a new file called **recipes_screen.dart**. Add the following code:

```dart
import 'package:flutter/material.dart';

import '../models/models.dart';
import '../api/mock_fooderlich_service.dart';
import '../components/components.dart';

class RecipesScreen extends StatelessWidget {
  // 1
  final exploreService = MockFooderlichService();

  RecipesScreen({Key? key}) : super(key: key);

  @override
  Widget build(BuildContext context) {
    // 2
    return FutureBuilder(
        // 3
        future: exploreService.getRecipes(),
        builder: (context, AsyncSnapshot<List<SimpleRecipe>>
snapshot) {
          // 4
          if (snapshot.connectionState == ConnectionState.done)
{
            // TODO: Add RecipesGridView Here
            // 5
            return const Center(child: Text('Recipes Screen'));
          } else {
            // 6
            return const Center(child:
CircularProgressIndicator());
          }
        },
    );
  }
}
```

The code has a similar setup to `ExploreScreen`. To create it, you:

1. Create a mock service.

2. Create a `FutureBuilder`.

3. Use `getRecipes()` to return the list of recipes to display. This function returns a future list of `SimpleRecipes`.

4. Check if the future is complete.

5. Add a placeholder text until you build `RecipesGridView`.

6. Show a circular loading indicator if the future isn't complete yet.

In **home.dart**, add the following `import`:

```
import 'screens/recipes_screen.dart';
```

Next locate the comment `// TODO: Replace with RecipesScreen` and replace the `Container` beneath it with the following:

```
RecipesScreen(),
```

Perform a hot restart to see the first step of the new recipes screen:

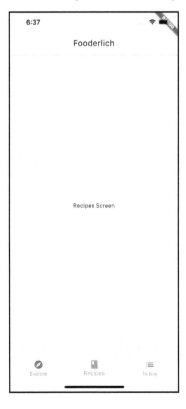

Creating the recipe thumbnail

Before you create the grid view, you need a widget to display in the grid. Here's the thumbnail widget you'll create:

It's a simple tile that displays the picture, the name and the duration of a recipe.

In **lib/components**, create a new file called **recipe_thumbnail.dart** and add the following code:

```
import 'package:flutter/material.dart';

import '../models/models.dart';

class RecipeThumbnail extends StatelessWidget {
  // 1
  final SimpleRecipe recipe;

  const RecipeThumbnail({
    Key? key,
    required this.recipe,
  }) : super(key: key);

  @override
  Widget build(BuildContext context) {
    // 2
    return Container(
      padding: const EdgeInsets.all(8),
      // 3
      child: Column(
        crossAxisAlignment: CrossAxisAlignment.start,
        children: [
          // 4
          Expanded(
            // 5
            child: ClipRRect(
              child: Image.asset(
                '${recipe.dishImage}',
                fit: BoxFit.cover,
```

```
          ),
          borderRadius: BorderRadius.circular(12),
        ),
      ),
      // 6
      const SizedBox(height: 10),
      // 7
      Text(
        recipe.title,
        maxLines: 1,
        style: Theme.of(context).textTheme.bodyText1,
      ),
      Text(
        recipe.duration,
        style: Theme.of(context).textTheme.bodyText1,
      )
    ],
  ),
 );
 }
}
```

Here's how the code works:

1. This class requires a `SimpleRecipe` as a parameter. That helps configure your widget.

2. Create a `Container` with 8-point padding all around.

3. Use a `Column` to apply a vertical layout.

4. The first element of the column is `Expanded`, which widget holds on to an `Image`. You want the image to fill the remaining space.

5. The `Image` is within the `ClipRRect`, which clips the image to make the borders rounded.

6. Add some room between the image and the other widgets.

7. Add the remaining `Text`s: one to display the recipe's title and another to display the duration.

Next, open **components.dart** and add the following export:

```
export 'recipe_thumbnail.dart';
```

Now, you're ready to create your grid view!

Creating the recipes GridView

In **lib/components**, create a new file called **recipes_grid_view.dart** and add the
following code:

```
import 'package:flutter/material.dart';

import '../components/components.dart';
import '../models/models.dart';

class RecipesGridView extends StatelessWidget {
  // 1
  final List<SimpleRecipe> recipes;

  const RecipesGridView({
    Key? key,
    required this.recipes,
  }) : super(key: key);

  @override
  Widget build(BuildContext context) {
    // 2
    return Padding(
      padding: const EdgeInsets.only(
        left: 16,
        right: 16,
        top: 16,
      ),
      // 3
      child: GridView.builder(
        // 4
        itemCount: recipes.length,
        // 5
        gridDelegate:
            const
SliverGridDelegateWithFixedCrossAxisCount(crossAxisCount: 2),
        itemBuilder: (context, index) {
          // 6
          final simpleRecipe = recipes[index];
          return RecipeThumbnail(recipe: simpleRecipe);
        },
      ),
    );
  }
}
```

A `GridView` is similar to a `ListView`. Here's how it works:

1. `RecipesGridView` requires a list of recipes to display in a grid.

2. Apply a 16 point padding on the left, right, and top.

3. Create a `GridView.builder`, which displays only the items visible onscreen.

4. Tell the grid view how many items will be in the grid.

5. Add `SliverGridDelegateWithFixedCrossAxisCount` and set the `crossAxisCount` to 2. That means that there will be only two columns.

6. For every index, fetch the recipe and create a corresponding `RecipeThumbnail`.

Open **components.dart** and add the following export:

```
export 'recipes_grid_view.dart';
```

Using the recipes GridView

Open **recipes_screen.dart** and replace the `return` statement below the comment `// TODO: Add RecipesGridView Here` with the following:

```
return RecipesGridView(recipes: snapshot.data ?? []);
```

When the list of recipes has been loaded this will display them in a grid layout.

Congratulations, you've now set up your RecipesScreen!

If you still have your app running, perform a hot reload. The new screen will look like this:

And that's it, you're done. Congratulations!

Fun fact: Did you know ListView and GridView widgets are implemented using Slivers? Think of slivers as an interface for scrollable widgets. ListView inherits from BoxScrollView and under the hood is a CustomScrollView with a single SliverList.

Check out the implementation for BoxScrollView here:

https://git.io/JabcO.

> **Note**: Slivers are just part of a scrollable area. A benefit of using slivers is to lazily load items in as it scrolls into view. This makes the list efficient, especially with a large number of children in your list.
>
> To explore more on slivers check out the following links:
>
> https://www.raywenderlich.com/19539821-slivers-in-flutter-getting-started
>
> https://www.youtube.com/watch?v=mSc7qFzxHDw

Other scrollable widgets

There are many more scrollable widgets for various use cases. Here are some not covered in this chapter:

- **CustomScrollView**: A widget that creates custom scroll effects using slivers. Ever wonder how to collapse your navigation header on scroll? Use `CustomScrollView` for more fine-grain control over your scrollable area!

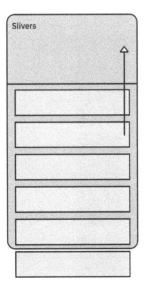 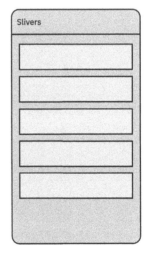

- **PageView**: A scrollable widget that scrolls page by page, making it perfect for an onboarding flow. It also supports a vertical scroll direction.

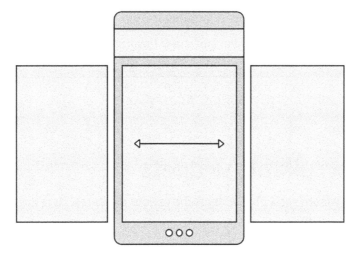

- **StaggeredGridView**: A grid view package that supports columns and rows of varying sizes. If you need to support dynamic height and custom layouts, this is the most popular package.

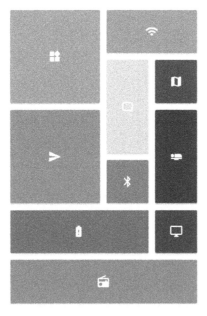

Now it's time for some challenges.

Challenges

Challenge 1: Add a scroll listener

So far, you've built some scrollable widgets, but how do you listen to scroll events?

For this challenge, try adding a scroll controller to `ExploreScreen`. Print two statements to the console:

1. `print('i am at the bottom!')` if the user scrolls to the bottom.

2. `print('i am at the top!')` if the user scrolls to the top.

You can view the scroll controller API documentation here:
https://api.flutter.dev/flutter/widgets/ScrollController-class.html.

Here's a step-by-step hint:

1.) Make `ExploreScreen` a stateful widget.

2.) Create an instance of `ScrollController` in the `initState()`.

3.) Create `scrollListener()` to listen to the scroll position.

4.) Add a scroll listener to the scroll controller.

5.) Add the scroll controller to the `ListView`.

6.) Dispose your scroll `scrollListener()`.

Solution

See Appendix A.

Challenge 2: Add a new GridView layout

Try using `SliverGridDelegateWithMaxCrossAxisExtent` to create the grid layout below, which displays recipes in only one column:

Solution

See Appendix B.

Key points

- **ListView** and **GridView** support both horizontal and vertical scroll directions.
- The **primary** property lets Flutter know which scroll view is the primary scroll view.
- **physics** in a scroll view lets you change the user scroll interaction.
- Especially in a **nested list view**, remember to set `shrinkWrap` to **true** so you can give the scroll view a fixed height for all the items in the list.
- Use a **FutureBuilder** to wait for an asynchronous task to complete.
- You can nest scrollable widgets. For example, you can place a grid view within a list view. Unleash your wildest imagination!
- Use **ScrollController** and **ScrollNotification** to control or listen to scroll behavior.
- **Barrel** files are handy to group imports together. They also let you import many widgets using a single file.

Where to go from here?

At this point, you've learned how to create `ListViews` and `GridViews`. They are much easier to use than iOS's `UITableView` and Android's `RecyclerView`, right? Building scrollable widgets is an important skill you should master!

Flutter makes it easy to build and use such scrollable widgets. It offers the flexibility to scroll in any direction and the power to nest scrollable widgets. With the skills you've learned, you can build cool scroll interactions.

You're ready to look like a pro in front of your friends :]

For more examples check out the Flutter Gallery at https://gallery.flutter.dev/#/, which showcases some great examples to test out.

In the next chapter, you'll take a look at some more interactive widgets.

Chapter 6: Interactive Widgets

By Vincent Ngo

In the previous chapter, you learned how to capture lots of data with scrollable widgets. But how do you make an app more engaging? How do you collect input and feedback from your users?

In this chapter, you'll explore interactive widgets. In particular, you'll learn to create:

- Gesture-based widgets

- Time and date picker widgets

- Input and selection widgets

- Dismissable widgets

You'll continue to work on **Fooderlich**, building the final tab: **To Buy**. This tab allows the user to create a grocery list of items to buy, make modifications to them, and check them off their TODO list when they're done. They'll be able to **add**, **remove** and **update** the items in the list.

You'll also get a quick introduction to **Provider**, a package that helps you manage state and notify components that there's updated data to display.

You'll start by building an empty screen. If there are no grocery items available, the user has two options:

1. Click **Browse Recipes** to view other recipes.

2. Click the + button to add a new grocery item.

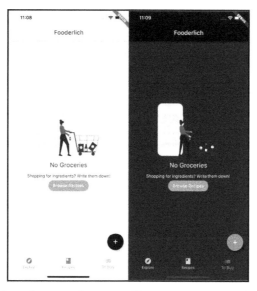

When the user taps the + button, the app will present a screen for the user to create an item:

The screen consists of the following data attributes:

- The name of the item.

- A tag that shows the item's importance level.

- The date and time when you want to buy this item.

- The color you want to label this item.

- The quantity of the item.

Also, when you create the item, the app will show a preview of the item itself! How cool is that?

When you create your first item, the grocery list replaces the empty screen:

The user will be able to take four actions on this new screen:

1. Tap a grocery item to update some information.

2. Tap the checkbox to mark an item as complete.

3. Swipe away the item to delete it.

4. Create and add another item to the list.

By the end of this chapter, you'll have built a functional TODO list for users to manage their grocery items. You'll even add light and dark mode support!

It's time to get started.

Getting started

Open the starter project in Android Studio and run `flutter pub get`, if necessary. Then, run the app.

You'll see the **Fooderlich** app from the previous chapter. When you tap the **To Buy** tab, you'll see a blue screen. Don't worry, soon you'll add an image so your users won't think there's a problem.

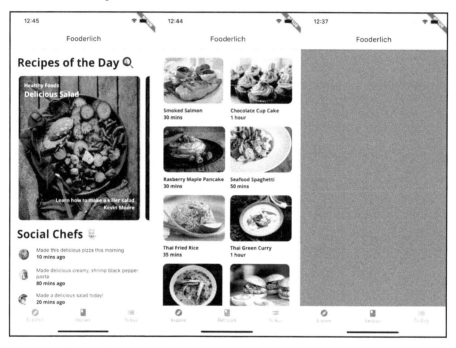

Inside **assets/fooderlich_assets**, you'll find a new image.

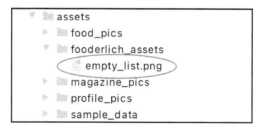

You'll display **empty_list.png** when there aren't any items in the list.

Now, it's time to add some code!

Creating the grocery item model

First, you'll set up the model for the information you want to save about the items. In the **models** directory, create a new file called **grocery_item.dart**, then add the following code:

```dart
import 'package:flutter/painting.dart';

// 1
enum Importance {
  low,
  medium,
  high,
}

class GroceryItem {
  // 2
  final String id;
  // 3
  final String name;
  final Importance importance;
  final Color color;
  final int quantity;
  final DateTime date;
  final bool isComplete;

  GroceryItem({
    required this.id,
    required this.name,
```

```
      required this.importance,
      required this.color,
      required this.quantity,
      required this.date,
      this.isComplete = false,
  });

  // 4
  GroceryItem copyWith({
    String? id,
    String? name,
    Importance? importance,
    Color? color,
    int? quantity,
    DateTime? date,
    bool? isComplete,
  }) {
    return GroceryItem(
        id: id ?? this.id,
        name: name ?? this.name,
        importance: importance ?? this.importance,
        color: color ?? this.color,
        quantity: quantity ?? this.quantity,
        date: date ?? this.date,
        isComplete: isComplete ?? this.isComplete);
  }
}
```

Take a moment to explore what **grocery_item.dart** contains:

1. Importance is an enum that you'll use to tag the importance of an item: low, medium or high.

2. Each GroceryItem must have a unique id to differentiate the items from one other.

3. A user can set the name, level of importance, color label, quantity and date, as well as marking completed items.

4. copyWith copies and creates a completely new instance of GroceryItem. This will be useful later, when you manage the state of the items.

Next, you need to add this new code to the barrel file.

Open the **models/models.dart** barrel file and add the following:

```
export 'grocery_item.dart';
```

> **Note**: Remember that the purpose of a barrel file is to group common Dart files together. This allows you to group classes that are commonly used together so you only have to import a single file — in this case, **models.dart**.

Creating the Grocery screen

Now that you've set up your model, it's time to create the Grocery screen. This screen will display one of two views:

`EmptyGroceryScreen` will display when there are no items. After the user adds at least one item, you'll display `GroceryListScreen` instead.

Building GroceryScreen

The first thing you need to do is create `GroceryScreen`, which determines whether to display the empty or list screen.

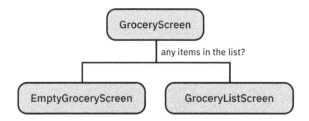

Within the **screens** directory, create a new Dart file called **grocery_screen.dart**. Then, add the following code:

```
import 'package:flutter/material.dart';

class GroceryScreen extends StatelessWidget {
  const GroceryScreen({Key? key}) : super(key: key);

  @override
  Widget build(BuildContext context) {
    // TODO 2: Replace with EmptyGroceryScreen
    return Container(color: Colors.green);
  }
  // TODO: Add buildGroceryScreen
}
```

For now, this will just show a green screen. You'll replace this with something more informative later.

Displaying the Grocery screen

Your next task is to give your users a way to see the new page — when it's ready, that is. When you click on the **To Buy** tab, it needs to show `GroceryScreen`, not the solid color.

Do this by opening **home.dart** and adding the following import:

```
import 'screens/grocery_screen.dart';
```

Then, locate `// TODO 1: Replace with grocery screen` and replace `Container` with the following:

```
const GroceryScreen(),
```

This substitutes the existing empty container with the new screen.

With the app running, perform a hot restart, then tap the **To Buy** tab. You'll now see a green screen instead of a blue one.

Great! That's progress, right? Well, it'll get better after you create the screens. You'll start doing that now, with the Grocery screen that will display when the list is empty.

Creating the empty Grocery screen

Within the **screens** directory, create a new Dart file called
empty_grocery_screen.dart and add the following:

```
import 'package:flutter/material.dart';

class EmptyGroceryScreen extends StatelessWidget {
  const EmptyGroceryScreen({Key? key}) : super(key: key);

  @override
  Widget build(BuildContext context) {
    // TODO 3: Replace and add layout widgets
    return Container(color: Colors.purple);
  }
}
```

This is the first simple implementation of `EmptyGroceryScreen`. You'll replace the
placeholder `Container` with other widgets soon.

Adding the empty screen

Before you continue building `EmptyGroceryScreen`, you need to set up the widget
for hot reload so you can see your updates live.

Open **grocery_screen.dart** and add the following import:

```
import 'empty_grocery_screen.dart';
```

Locate `// TODO 2: Replace with EmptyGroceryScreen` and replace the whole
`return` statement beneath it with:

```
// TODO 4: Add a scaffold widget
return const EmptyGroceryScreen();
```

Now, you'll see the following purple screen:

Great! Now, you'll be able to see your changes live after you code them.

Adding layout widgets

Next, you'll lay the foundation for the final look of the page by adding widgets that handle the layout of the empty Grocery screen.

Open **empty_grocery_screen.dart** and locate `// TODO 3: Replace and add layout widgets`. Replace the line below it with the following:

```
// 1
return Padding(
  padding: const EdgeInsets.all(30.0),
  // 2
  child: Center(
      // 3
      child: Column(
        mainAxisAlignment: MainAxisAlignment.center,
        children: [
```

```
        // TODO 4: Add empty image
        // TODO 5: Add empty screen title
        // TODO 6: Add empty screen subtitle
        // TODO 7: Add browse recipes button
      ],
    ),
  ),
);
```

Here's what you've added:

1. **Padding**: Adds 30 pixels on all sides.

2. **Center**: Places all the other widgets in the center.

3. **Column**: Handles the vertical layouts of the other widgets.

The app will now look like this:

Now, it's time to make your screen more interesting!

Adding the visual pieces

Finally, it's time to go beyond a colorful screen and add some text and images.

Still in **empty_grocery_screen.dart**, locate `// TODO 4: Add empty image` and replace it with the following:

```
// 1
Flexible(
  // 2
  child: AspectRatio(
    aspectRatio: 1 / 1,
    child: Image.asset('assets/fooderlich_assets/
empty_list.png'),
  ),
),
```

Here's how the code works:

1. **Flexible** gives a child the ability to fill the available space in the main axis.

2. **AspectRatio** sizes its child to the specified `aspectRatio`. Although `aspectRatio` is a double, the Flutter documentation recommends writing it as `width / height` instead of the calculated result. In this case, you want a square aspect ratio of `1 / 1` and not `1.0`.

> **Note**: Dart does the calculation for you to provide the double. What if you'd wanted a 16:9 ratio? You'd put `16 / 9` and not `1.5`.

Next, replace `// TODO 5: Add empty screen title` with the following:

```
const Text(
  'No Groceries',
  style: TextStyle(fontSize: 21.0),
),
```

Here, you added a title using `Text`, placed below the image.

Next, locate `// TODO 6: Add empty screen subtitle` and replace it with the following:

```
const SizedBox(height: 16.0),
const Text(
  'Shopping for ingredients?\n'
  'Tap the + button to write them down!',
```

```
    textAlign: TextAlign.center,
  ),
```

As you just did with the title, you've added a subtitle with a 16-pixel box between it and the title above.

Finally, replace `// TODO 7: Add browse recipes` button with the following:

```
MaterialButton(
  textColor: Colors.white,
  child: const Text('Browse Recipes'),
  shape: RoundedRectangleBorder(
      borderRadius: BorderRadius.circular(30.0),
  ),
  color: Colors.green,
  onPressed: () {
    // TODO 8: Go to Recipes Tab
  },
),
```

Now, you've added a rounded green `MaterialButton`.

> **Note**: There are many other styles of buttons you can choose from! See https://flutter.dev/docs/development/ui/widgets/material#Buttons for more options.

Now, check out your app. It will look like this:

Great! Now, users will know that their grocery list is empty. Next, you'll add a handler so that tapping the **Browse Recipes** button brings you to the **Recipes** tab.

Switching tabs

You have two options to implement switching to the **Recipes** tab:

1. **Standard callback**: Pass a callback from the parent widget all the way down the widget tree to a descendant widget. When ready, it fires the callback at each level up the tree and calls setState() to rebuild the Home widget's subtree.

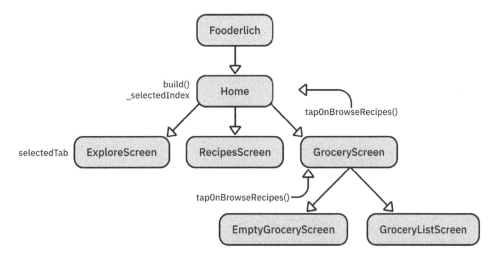

This approach is OK for small projects, but as your project gets larger, it becomes annoying and complicated. Imagine having to pass a callback at every level of the widget tree. It's hard to maintain and excessively couples your widgets to one another.

2. **Provider**: Wraps around inherited widgets. This package allows you to provide data and state information to descendant widgets.

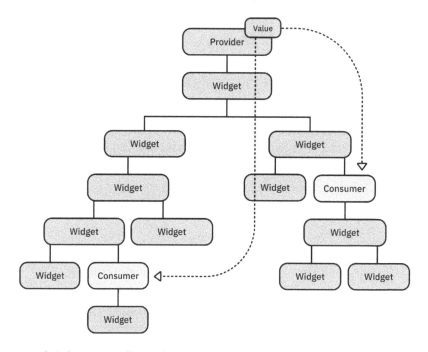

This approach is better. It allows descendant widgets in the subtree to access state information.

Instead of callbacks, you just wrap Consumers around your widgets. Every time a state changes, those Consumers rebuild the subtree below it.

It's **Provider** time!

Provider overview

Provider is a convenient way to pass state down the widget tree and rebuild your UI when changes occur. You'll add it to your project next.

Before you do that, however, you need to understand four concepts:

1. ChangeNotifier is extended by a class to provide change notifications to its listeners.

2. ChangeNotifierProvider listens for changes to a ChangeNotifier. Widgets below it can access the state object and listen to state changes.

3. `Consumer` wraps around part of a widget tree. It rebuilds part of a subtree when the state it listens to changes.

4. `Provider.of` allows descendant widgets to access the state object. If you only need access to the state object and don't need to listen for changes, use this!

> **Note**: This is a quick overview of how Provider works. You'll learn more about using Provider for state management in Chapter 13, "State Management".

Adding Provider

Open **pubspec.yaml** and add the following package under **dependencies** beneath `google_fonts`:

```
provider: ^6.0.0
```

Save the file and run `flutter pub get`.

Creating a tab manager

In the **models** directory, create a new file called **tab_manager.dart** and add the following code:

```dart
import 'package:flutter/material.dart';

// 1
class TabManager extends ChangeNotifier {
  // 2
  int selectedTab = 0;

  // 3
  void goToTab(index) {
    // 4
    selectedTab = index;
    // 5
    notifyListeners();
  }

  // 6
  void goToRecipes() {
    selectedTab = 1;
    // 7
    notifyListeners();
  }
}
```

TabManager manages the tab index that the user taps. This code does the following:

1. TabManager extends ChangeNotifier. This allows the object to provide change notifications to its listeners.

2. selectedTab keeps track of which tab the user tapped.

3. goToTab is a simple function that modifies the current tab index.

4. Stores the index of the new tab the user tapped.

5. Calls notifyListeners() to notify all widgets listening to this state.

6. goToRecipes() is a specific function that sets selectedTab to the **Recipes** tab, which is at index **1**.

7. Notifies all widgets listening to TabManager that **Recipes** is the selected tab.

Next, add TabManager to **models.dart**:

```
export 'tab_manager.dart';
```

Awesome! Now, you have a simple tab manager to manage the current tab index. It's time to provide this to your widgets.

Managing tab state

So how will you use Provider? Here's a blueprint:

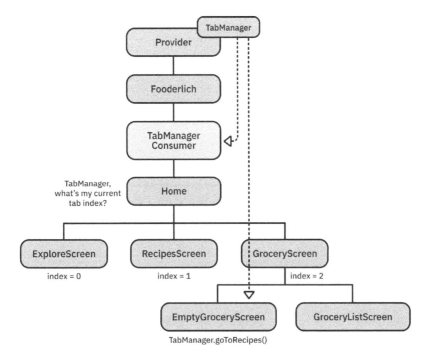

These are the steps you'll take:

- Provide the TabManager change notifier at the root level of Fooderlich. This allows descendant widgets to access the tab manager.

- Wrap a Consumer around Home. This ensures that Home displays the right screen anytime TabManager's tab index changes.

- Since Provider is a wrapper around inherited widgets, EmptyGroceryScreen can access the TabManager state object through its context.

- goToRecipes() changes the tab index, notifying Consumer, which then rebuilds Home with the correct tab to display.

Sounds easy, right? Well, then, it's time to jump in.

Providing TabManager

First, you need to provide `TabManager` at Fooderlich's top level to let descendant widgets access the state object.

Open **main.dart** and add the following imports:

```
import 'package:provider/provider.dart';
import 'models/models.dart';
```

Then, locate `// TODO 8: Replace Home with MultiProvider` and replace home with the following:

```
// 1
home: MultiProvider(
  providers: [
    // 2
    ChangeNotifierProvider(create: (context) => TabManager()),
    // TODO 10: Add GroceryManager Provider
  ],
  child: const Home(),
),
```

Here's how the code works:

1. You assign `MultiProvider` as a property of `Home`. This accepts a list of providers for `Home`'s descendant widgets to access.

2. `ChangeNotifierProvider` creates an instance of `TabManager`, which listens to tab index changes and notifies its listeners.

> **Note**: Use `MultiProvider` when you need to provide more than one `Provider` to a widget tree. Later, you'll also add a `GroceryManager` state object to manage the list of items.

Adding a TabManager consumer

Now, it's time to set up the consumer so the app can listen to changes broadcast by `TabManager`.

Open **home.dart** and add the following imports:

```
import 'package:provider/provider.dart';
import 'models/models.dart';
```

Next, locate `// TODO 9: Wrap inside a Consumer Widget` and replace the whole body of `build()` with the following:

```
// 1
return Consumer<TabManager>(builder: (context, tabManager,
child) {
  return Scaffold(
      appBar: AppBar(
          title: Text(
            'Fooderlich',
            style: Theme.of(context).textTheme.headline6,
          ),
      ),
      // 2
      // TODO: Replace body
      body: pages[tabManager.selectedTab],
      bottomNavigationBar: BottomNavigationBar(
          selectedItemColor: Theme.of(context)
            .textSelectionTheme.selectionColor,
          // 3
          currentIndex: tabManager.selectedTab,
          onTap: (index) {
            // 4
            tabManager.goToTab(index);
          },
          items: <BottomNavigationBarItem>[
            const BottomNavigationBarItem(
                icon: Icon(Icons.explore),
                label: 'Explore',
            ),
            const BottomNavigationBarItem(
                icon: Icon(Icons.book),
                label: 'Recipes',
            ),
            const BottomNavigationBarItem(
                icon: Icon(Icons.list),
                label: 'To Buy',
            ),
          ],
      ),
  );
  },
);
```

Here's how the code works:

1. Wraps all the widgets inside `Consumer`. When `TabManager` changes, the widgets below it will rebuild.

2. Displays the correct page widget, based on the current tab index.

3. Sets the current index of `BottomNavigationBar`.

4. Calls `manager.goToTab()` when the user taps a different tab, to notify other widgets that the index changed.

Now, since you've added `Consumer<TabManager>`, you no longer need `_onItemTapped()`. Locate the method and delete it, as well as the `int _selectedIndex = 0;` declaration.

Switching to the Recipes tab

There's one last step to implement the ability to switch between tabs.

Open **empty_grocery_screen.dart** and add the following imports:

```
import 'package:provider/provider.dart';
import '../models/models.dart';
```

Then, locate `// TODO 8: Go to Recipes Tab` and replace it with the following:

```
Provider.of<TabManager>(context, listen: false).goToRecipes();
```

Here, you use `Provider.of()` to access the model object, `TabManager`. `goToRecipes()` sets the index to the **Recipes** tab. This notifies `Consumer` to rebuild `Home` with the right tab index.

On the **To Buy** tab, tap the **Browse Recipes** button. It will now navigate to the recipes screen.

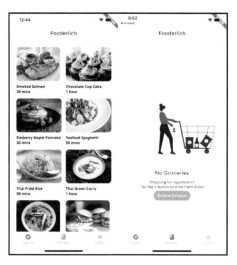

Great! Now it's time to create some grocery items.

Managing the grocery items

Before you display or create grocery items, you need a way to manage them.

In the **models** directory, create a new file called **grocery_manager.dart**. Add the following:

```
import 'package:flutter/material.dart';
import 'grocery_item.dart';

class GroceryManager extends ChangeNotifier {
  // 1
  final _groceryItems = <GroceryItem>[];

  // 2
  List<GroceryItem> get groceryItems =>
List.unmodifiable(_groceryItems);

  // 3
  void deleteItem(int index) {
    _groceryItems.removeAt(index);
    notifyListeners();
  }

  // 4
  void addItem(GroceryItem item) {
    _groceryItems.add(item);
    notifyListeners();
  }

  // 5
  void updateItem(GroceryItem item, int index) {
    _groceryItems[index] = item;
    notifyListeners();
  }

  // 6
  void completeItem(int index, bool change) {
    final item = _groceryItems[index];
    _groceryItems[index] = item.copyWith(isComplete: change);
    notifyListeners();
  }
}
```

GroceryManager extends ChangeNotifier to notify its listener about state changes. Here's how GroceryManager works:

1. This manager holds a private array of _groceryItems. Only the manager can change and update grocery items.

2. Provides a public getter method for groceryItems, which is unmodifiable. External entities can only read the list of grocery items.

3. deleteItem() deletes an item at a particular index.

4. addItem() adds a new grocery item at the end of the list.

5. updateItem() replaces the old item at a given index with a new item.

6. completeItem() toggles the isComplete flag on and off.

Each of these methods calls notifyListeners(). This notifies widgets of changes to GroceryManager that require a rebuild.

Next, open the barrel file, **models.dart**, and add the following:

```
export 'grocery_manager.dart';
```

This lets other classes use the new manager.

Adding GroceryManager as a provider

Much like you did with TabManager you'll now add GroceryManager as a provider.

Open **main.dart** and locate // TODO 10: Add GroceryManager Provider. Replace it with:

```
ChangeNotifierProvider(create: (context) => GroceryManager()),
```

All descendant widgets of Fooderlich can now listen to or access GroceryManager!

Consuming the changes

How does the **To Buy** screen react to changes in the grocery list? So far, it doesn't, but you're now ready to hook up the new manager with the view that displays grocery items. :]

Open **grocery_screen.dart** and add the following imports:

```
import 'package:provider/provider.dart';
import '../models/models.dart';
```

Find `// TODO: Add buildGroceryScreen` and replace it with the following code:

```
Widget buildGroceryScreen() {
  // 1
  return Consumer<GroceryManager>(
    // 2
    builder: (context, manager, child) {
      // 3
      if (manager.groceryItems.isNotEmpty) {
        // TODO 25: Add GroceryListScreen
        return Container();
      } else {
        // 4
        return const EmptyGroceryScreen();
      }
    },
  );
}
```

`buildGroceryScreen()` is a helper function that decides which widget tree to construct. Here's how it works:

1. You wrap your widgets inside a `Consumer`, which listens for `GroceryManager` state changes.

2. `Consumer` rebuilds the widgets below itself when the grocery manager items changes.

3. If there are grocery items in the list, show the `GroceryListScreen`. You will create this screen soon.

4. If there are no grocery items, show the `EmptyGroceryScreen`.

> **Tip:** You should only wrap a `Consumer` around widgets that need it. For example, wrapping a consumer widget at the top level would force it to rebuild the entire tree!

Next, locate `// TODO 4: add a scaffold` widget and replace the line below it with the following:

```
// 5
return Scaffold(
  // 6
  floatingActionButton: FloatingActionButton(
    child: const Icon(Icons.add),
    onPressed: () {
      // TODO 11: Present GroceryItemScreen
    },
  ),
  // 7
  body: buildGroceryScreen(),
);
```

Here's how the code works:

5. The main layout structure for `GroceryScreen` is a scaffold.

6. Adds a floating action button with a + icon. Tapping the button presents the screen to create or add an item. You'll build this screen later.

7. Builds the rest of the Grocery screen's subtree. That's coming up next!

`GroceryScreen` is all set up to switch between the empty and list screens. Now, it's time to create grocery items!

Adding new packages

Before going any further, you need to add three new packages. Open **pubspec.yaml** and add the following under `dependencies`:

```
flutter_colorpicker: ^0.6.0
intl: ^0.17.0
uuid: ^3.0.4
```

Here's what each of them does:

*   **flutter_colorpicker**: Provides a material color picker for your app.

*   **intl**: Provides internationalization and localization utilities. You'll use this to format dates.

*   **uuid**: Generates unique keys for each grocery item. This helps you know which item to add, update or remove.

Don't forget to run `flutter pub get` after updating **pubspec.yaml** entries.

The next screen you'll create is `GroceryItemScreen`, which gives users a way to edit or create new grocery items.

Creating the screen to add grocery items

In the **screens** directory, create a new file called **grocery_item_screen.dart** and add the following:

```
import 'package:flutter/material.dart';
import 'package:google_fonts/google_fonts.dart';
import 'package:flutter_colorpicker/flutter_colorpicker.dart';
import 'package:intl/intl.dart';
import 'package:uuid/uuid.dart';
import '../models/models.dart';

class GroceryItemScreen extends StatefulWidget {
  // 1
  final Function(GroceryItem) onCreate;
  // 2
  final Function(GroceryItem) onUpdate;
  // 3
  final GroceryItem? originalItem;
  // 4
  final bool isUpdating;

  const GroceryItemScreen({
    Key? key,
    required this.onCreate,
    required this.onUpdate,
    this.originalItem,
  })  : isUpdating = (originalItem != null),
        super(key: key);

  @override
  _GroceryItemScreenState createState() =>
  _GroceryItemScreenState();
}

class _GroceryItemScreenState extends State<GroceryItemScreen> {
  // TODO: Add grocery item screen state properties

  @override
  Widget build(BuildContext context) {
    // TODO 12: Add GroceryItemScreen Scaffold
    return Container(color: Colors.orange);
  }
}
```

```
// TODO: Add buildNameField()

// TODO: Add buildImportanceField()

// TODO: ADD buildDateField()

// TODO: Add buildTimeField()

// TODO: Add buildColorPicker()

// TODO: Add buildQuantityField()

}
```

Take a moment to understand the properties you added:

1. `onCreate` is a callback that lets you know when a new item is created.

2. `onUpdate` is a callback that returns the updated grocery item.

3. The grocery item that the user clicked.

4. `isUpdating` determines whether the user is creating or editing an item.

Before you continue building `GroceryItemScreen`, you need to present this widget.

Presenting GroceryItemScreen

Open **grocery_screen.dart** and add the following import:

```
import 'grocery_item_screen.dart';
```

Then, locate `//TODO 11: Present GroceryItemScreen` and replace it with the following code:

```
// 1
final manager = Provider.of<GroceryManager>(
  context,
  listen: false);
// 2
Navigator.push(
  context,
  // 3
  MaterialPageRoute(
    // 4
    builder: (context) => GroceryItemScreen(
      // 5
      onCreate: (item) {
        // 6
```

```
      manager.addItem(item);
      // 7
      Navigator.pop(context);
    },
    // 8
    onUpdate: (item) {},
  ),
 ),
);
```

Here's how the code works:

1. Returns the `GroceryManager` available in the tree.

2. `Navigator.push()` adds a new route to the stack of routes.

3. `MaterialPageRoute` replaces the entire screen with a platform-specific transition. In Android, for example, it slides upwards and fades in. In iOS, it slides in from the right.

4. Creates a new `GroceryItemScreen` within the route's builder callback.

5. `onCreate` defines what to do with the created item.

6. `addItem()` adds this new item to the list of items.

7. Once the item is added to the list, pop removes the top navigation route item, `GroceryItemScreen`, to show the list of grocery items.

8. `onUpdate` will never get called since you are creating a new item.

> **Note**: For now, you just need to know that `Navigator.push()` presents a new screen and `Navigator.pop` removes it again. You'll dive deeper into `Navigator` in the next chapter.

Tap the + button on your running app and you'll see the following:

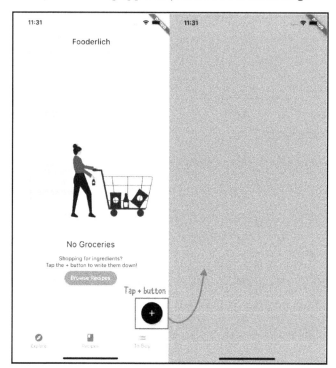

Onwards!

Adding GroceryItemScreen's state properties

Now, it's time to give the grocery items some properties to make them more useful.

Start by opening **grocery_item_screen.dart** and locating `// TODO: Add grocery item screen state properties`. Replace it with the following:

```
final _nameController = TextEditingController();
String _name = '';
Importance _importance = Importance.low,
DateTime _dueDate = DateTime.now();
TimeOfDay _timeOfDay = TimeOfDay.now();
Color _currentColor = Colors.green;
int _currentSliderValue = 0;

// TODO: Add initState()

// TODO: Add dispose()
```

Ignore any tan squiggles — these will go away as you add more code.

_GroceryItemScreenState manages six different values:

1. _nameController is a TextEditingController. This controller listens for text changes. It controls the value displayed in a text field.

2. _name stores the name of the item.

3. _importance stores the importance level.

4. _dueDate stores the current date and time.

5. _timeOfDay stores the current time.

6. _currentColor stores the color label.

7. _currentSliderValue stores the quantity of an item.

These properties will create the final GroceryItem.

Next, within _GroceryItemScreenState, find // TODO: Add initState() and replace it with:

```
@override
void initState() {
  // 1
  final originalItem = widget.originalItem;
  if (originalItem != null) {
    _nameController.text = originalItem.name;
    _name = originalItem.name;
    _currentSliderValue = originalItem.quantity;
    _importance = originalItem.importance;
    _currentColor = originalItem.color;
    final date = originalItem.date;
    _timeOfDay = TimeOfDay(hour: date.hour, minute:
date.minute);
    _dueDate = date;
  }

  // 2
  _nameController.addListener(() {
    setState(() {
      _name = _nameController.text;
    });
  });

  super.initState();
}
```

Before a widget builds, `initState()` initializes its properties before use.

1. When the `originalItem` is not null, the user is editing an existing item. In this case, you must configure the widget to show the item's values.

2. Adds a listener to listen for text field changes. When the text changes, you set the `_name`.

This newly added code made those tan squiggles disappear. :]

Soon, you'll add some layout widgets to align the items properly on the screen. However, before you do, you have a bit more code to add to clean everything up.

Finally, replace `// TODO: Add dispose()` with the following:

```
@override
void dispose() {
  _nameController.dispose();
  super.dispose();
}
```

This will `dispose` your `TextEditingController` when you no longer need it.

Now that you've completed your configuration and cleaned it up, it's time to add some layout widgets!

Adding GroceryItemScreen's layout widgets

Still in **grocery_item_screen.dart**, locate `// TODO 12: Add GroceryItemScreen Scaffold` and replace the line below it with the following:

```
// 1
return Scaffold(
  // 2
  appBar: AppBar(
    actions: [
      IconButton(
          icon: const Icon(Icons.check),
          onPressed: () {
            // TODO 24: Add callback handler
          },)
    ],
    // 3
    elevation: 0.0,
    // 4
    title: Text(
      'Grocery Item',
      style: GoogleFonts.lato(fontWeight: FontWeight.w600),
```

```
                ),
    ),
    // 5
    body: Container(
      padding: const EdgeInsets.all(16.0),
      child: ListView(
        children: [
          // TODO 13: Add name TextField
          // TODO 14: Add Importance selection
          // TODO 15: Add date picker
          // TODO 16: Add time picker
          // TODO 17: Add color picker
          // TODO 18: Add slider
          // TODO: 19: Add Grocery Tile
        ],
      ),
    ),
  );
```

Here's how the code works:

1. `Scaffold` defines the main layout and structure of the entire screen.

2. Includes an app bar with one action button. The user will tap this button when they've finished creating an item.

3. Sets elevation to `0.0`, removing the shadow under the app bar.

4. Sets the title of the app bar.

5. Shows a `ListView`, padded by 16 pixels on every side, within the body of the scaffold. You'll fill this list view with a bunch of interactive widgets soon.

Your screen now looks like this:

It's a bit bare, but not for long. Now that you have the main layout structure, it's time to add interactive widgets!

Adding the text field to enter a grocery name

The first input widget you'll create is a `TextField`, which is a helpful widget when you need the user to enter some text. In this case, it will capture the name of the grocery item.

There are two ways to listen for text changes. You can either:

1. Implement an `onChanged` callback handler.

2. Supply `TextEditingController` to `TextField` and add a listener for text changes. This approach allows more fine-grained control over your text field, such as changing the text field's value based on a certain logic.

You'll use the second approach. `TextEditingController` allows you to set the initial value.

> **Note**: You can find more information about text fields here:
>
> https://flutter.dev/docs/cookbook/forms/text-field-changes

Still in **grocery_item_screen.dart**, find and replace `// TODO: Add buildNameField()` with the following code:

```
Widget buildNameField() {
  // 1
  return Column(
    // 2
    crossAxisAlignment: CrossAxisAlignment.start,
    children: [
      // 3
      Text(
        'Item Name',
        style: GoogleFonts.lato(fontSize: 28.0),
      ),
      // 4
      TextField(
        // 5
        controller: _nameController,
        // 6
        cursorColor: _currentColor,
        // 7
        decoration: InputDecoration(
          // 8
          hintText: 'E.g. Apples, Banana, 1 Bag of salt',
          // 9
          enabledBorder: const UnderlineInputBorder(
            borderSide: BorderSide(color: Colors.white),
          ),
          focusedBorder: UnderlineInputBorder(
            borderSide: BorderSide(color: _currentColor),
          ),
          border: UnderlineInputBorder(
            borderSide: BorderSide(color: _currentColor),
          ),
        ),
      ),
    ],
  );
}
```

Here's what's happening above:

1. Creates a `Column` to lay elements out vertically.

2. Aligns all widgets in the column to the left.

3. Adds a `Text` that's styled using `GoogleFonts`.

4. Adds a `TextField` to enter the name of the item.

5. Sets the `TextField`'s `TextEditingController`.

6. Sets the cursor color.

7. Styles the text field using `InputDecoration`.

8. Includes a hint to give users an example of what to write.

9. Customizes the text field's border color.

Next, locate `// TODO 13: Add name TextField` and replace it with:

```
buildNameField(),
```

Run the app and it will look like this:

On to the next input widget!

Building the importance widget

Your next step is to let the users choose how important a grocery item is. You'll do this using a `Chip`. This widget represents information about an entity. You can present a collection of chips for the user to select.

Understanding chips

There are four different types of chip widgets:

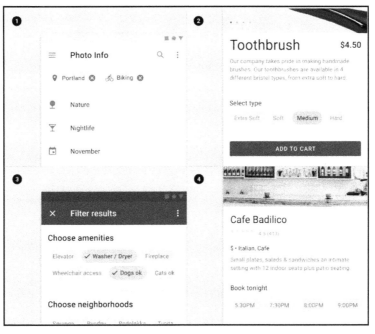

Image from: https://material.io/components/chips/flutter#types

1. **InputChip**: Converts input into chips. An example would be user preference UI flows, such as asking the types of new media they like.

2. **ChoiceChip**: Allows the user to make a single selection given a set of options.

3. **FilterChip**: Allows the user to select multiple answers given a set of options.

4. **ActionChip**: A button that's styled like a chip.

> **Note**: For more information about chips, check out:
>
> https://material.io/components/chips/flutter#types

Here, you'll use a ChoiceChip to let users choose the importance level of a grocery item.

Continuing in **grocery_item_screen.dart**, replace // TODO: buildImportanceField() with:

```
Widget buildImportanceField() {
  // 1
  return Column(
    crossAxisAlignment: CrossAxisAlignment.start,
    children: [
      // 2
      Text(
        'Importance',
        style: GoogleFonts.lato(fontSize: 28.0),
      ),
      // 3
      Wrap(
        spacing: 10.0,
        children: [
          // 4
          ChoiceChip(
            // 5
            selectedColor: Colors.black,
            // 6
            selected: _importance == Importance.low,
            label: const Text(
              'low',
              style: TextStyle(color: Colors.white),
            ),
            // 7
            onSelected: (selected) {
              setState(() => _importance = Importance.low);
            },
          ),
          ChoiceChip(
            selectedColor: Colors.black,
            selected: _importance == Importance.medium,
            label: const Text(
              'medium',
              style: TextStyle(color: Colors.white),
            ),
            onSelected: (selected) {
              setState(() => _importance = Importance.medium);
            },
          ),
```

```
            ChoiceChip(
              selectedColor: Colors.black,
              selected: _importance == Importance.high,
              label: const Text(
                'high',
                style: TextStyle(color: Colors.white),
              ),
              onSelected: (selected) {
                setState(() => _importance = Importance.high);
              },
            ),
          ],
        )
      ],
    );
  }
```

In the code above, you:

1. Use a `Column` to lay out the widgets vertically.

2. Add `Text`.

3. Add `Wrap` and space each child widget 10 pixels apart. `Wrap` lays out children horizontally. When there's no more room, it wraps to the next line.

4. Create a `ChoiceChip` for the user to select the **low** priority.

5. Set the selected chip's background color to black.

6. Check whether the user selected this `ChoiceChip`.

7. Update `_importance`, if the user selected this choice.

You then repeat steps four through seven two more times for the medium and high priority `ChoiceChips`.

> **Note**: For more information, check out this animated video of how `Wrap` works! https://youtu.be/z5iw2SeFx2M

Next, locate `// TODO 14: Add Importance selection` and replace it with:

```
buildImportanceField(),
```

Run the app. It will currently look like this:

Now, it's time to add the date by which the user needs to get this item!

Building the date widget

DatePicker is a useful widget when you need the user to enter a date. You'll use it here to let the user set a deadline to buy their grocery item.

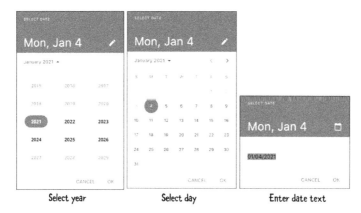

Select year   Select day   Enter date text

To use it, replace `// TODO: ADD buildDateField()` with the following:

```
Widget buildDateField(BuildContext context) {
  // 1
  return Column(
    crossAxisAlignment: CrossAxisAlignment.start,
    children: [
      // 2
      Row(
        // 3
        mainAxisAlignment: MainAxisAlignment.spaceBetween,
        children: [
          // 4
          Text(
            'Date',
            style: GoogleFonts.lato(fontSize: 28.0),
          ),
          // 5
          TextButton(
            child: const Text('Select'),
            // 6
            onPressed: () async {
              final currentDate = DateTime.now();
              // 7
              final selectedDate = await showDatePicker(
                context: context,
                initialDate: currentDate,
                firstDate: currentDate,
                lastDate: DateTime(currentDate.year + 5),
              );
              // 8
              setState(() {
                if (selectedDate != null) {
                  _dueDate = selectedDate;
                }
              });
            },
          ),
        ],
      ),
      // 9
      Text('${DateFormat('yyyy-MM-dd').format(_dueDate)}'),
    ],
  );
}
```

Here's how the code works:

1. Adds a `Column` to lay out elements vertically.

2. Adds a `Row` to lay out elements horizontally.

3. Adds a space between elements in the row.

4. Adds the date `Text`.

5. Adds a `TextButton` to confirm the selected value.

6. Gets the current date when the user presses the button.

7. Presents the date picker. You restrict the date picker and only allow the user to pick a date from today until five years in the future.

8. Sets `_dueDate` after the user selects a date.

9. Format the current date and display it with a `Text`.

Next, locate `// TODO 15: Add date picker` and replace it with:

```
buildDateField(context),
```

Run the app. It will now look like this:

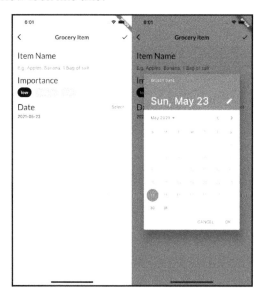

Up next — the time picker!

Building the time widget

Now that the user can set the date when they want to buy an item, you'll also let them set the time. To do this, you'll use `TimePicker` — a widget that's useful when you need the user to enter the time.

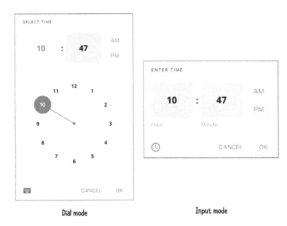

Dial mode   Input mode

To do this, replace `// TODO: Add buildTimeField()` with the following code:

```
Widget buildTimeField(BuildContext context) {
  return Column(
    crossAxisAlignment: CrossAxisAlignment.start,
    children: [
      Row(
        mainAxisAlignment: MainAxisAlignment.spaceBetween,
        children: [
          Text(
            'Time of Day',
            style: GoogleFonts.lato(fontSize: 28.0),
          ),
          TextButton(
            child: const Text('Select'),
            onPressed: () async {
              // 1
              final timeOfDay = await showTimePicker(
                // 2
                initialTime: TimeOfDay.now(),
                context: context,
              );

              // 3
              setState(() {
                if (timeOfDay != null) {
                  _timeOfDay = timeOfDay;
                }
```

```
            });
          },
        ),
      ],
    ),
    Text('${_timeOfDay.format(context)}'),
  ],
  );
}
```

This has the same setup as `buildDateField()`. Here's how the code for the time picker works:

1. Shows the time picker when the user taps the **Select** button.

2. Sets the initial time displayed in the time picker to the current time.

3. Once the user selects the time widget, it updates `_timeOfDay`.

Next, locate `// TODO 16: Add time picker` and replace it with:

```
buildTimeField(context),
```

Run the app to see the following:

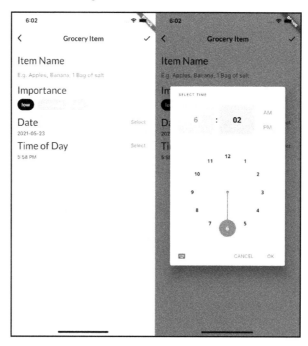

Building the color picker widget

Now, you're ready to let the user pick a color to tag the grocery items. For this, you'll use a third-party widget, ColorPicker, which presents the user with a color palette.

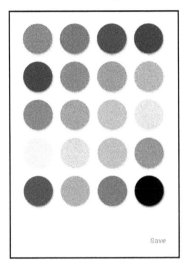

First, find and replace // TODO: Add buildColorPicker() with:

```
Widget buildColorPicker(BuildContext context) {
  // 1
  return Row(
    mainAxisAlignment: MainAxisAlignment.spaceBetween,
    children: [
      // 2
      Row(
        children: [
          Container(
            height: 50.0,
            width: 10.0,
            color: _currentColor,
          ),
          const SizedBox(width: 8.0),
          Text(
            'Color',
            style: GoogleFonts.lato(fontSize: 28.0),
          ),
        ],
      ),
      // 3
      TextButton(
        child: const Text('Select'),
        onPressed: () {
          // 4
```

```
          showDialog(
            context: context,
            builder: (context) {
              // 5
              return AlertDialog(
                content: BlockPicker(
                  pickerColor: Colors.white,
                  // 6
                  onColorChanged: (color) {
                    setState(() => _currentColor = color);
                  },
                ),
                actions: [
                  // 7
                  TextButton(
                    child: const Text('Save'),
                    onPressed: () {
                      Navigator.of(context).pop();
                    },
                  ),
                ],
              );
            },
          );
        },
      ),
    ],
  );
}
```

Here's how it works:

1. Adds a Row widget to layout the color picker section in the horizontal direction.

2. Creates a child Row and groups the following widgets:

• A Container to display the selected color.

• An 8-pixel-wide SizedBox.

• A Text to display the color picker's title.

3. Adds a TextButton.

4. Shows a pop-up dialog when the user taps the button.

5. Wraps BlockPicker inside AlertDialog.

6. Updates `_currentColor` when the user selects a color.

7. Adds an action button in the dialog. When the user taps **Save**, it dismisses the dialog.

> **Note**: For more information about `AlertDialog`, check out:
>
> https://api.flutter.dev/flutter/material/AlertDialog-class.html.

Next, add the color picker to the app. Locate `// TODO 17: Add color picker` and replace it with:

```
const SizedBox(height: 10.0),
buildColorPicker(context),
```

After running the app, it will look like this:

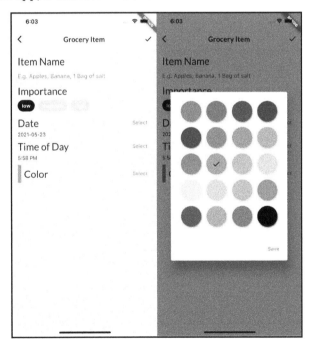

Great! Now the user can tag their grocery list items with colors to make them easier to identify.

Building a quantity widget

For your next step, you'll let the user indicate how much of any given item they need. For this, you'll use a widget that's useful for capturing a quantity or amount: `Slider`.

Below `buildColorPicker()`, replace `// TODO: Add buildQuantityField()` with:

```
Widget buildQuantityField() {
  // 1
  return Column(
    crossAxisAlignment: CrossAxisAlignment.start,
    children: [
      // 2
      Row(
        crossAxisAlignment: CrossAxisAlignment.baseline,
        textBaseline: TextBaseline.alphabetic,
        children: [
          Text(
            'Quantity',
            style: GoogleFonts.lato(fontSize: 28.0),
          ),
          const SizedBox(width: 16.0),
          Text(
            _currentSliderValue.toInt().toString(),
            style: GoogleFonts.lato(fontSize: 18.0),
          ),
        ],
      ),
      // 3
      Slider(
        // 4
        inactiveColor: _currentColor.withOpacity(0.5),
        activeColor: _currentColor,
        // 5
        value: _currentSliderValue.toDouble(),
        // 6
        min: 0.0,
        max: 100.0,
        // 7
        divisions: 100,
        // 8
        label: _currentSliderValue.toInt().toString(),
        // 9
        onChanged: (double value) {
          setState(
```

```
        () {
          _currentSliderValue = value.toInt();
        },
      );
    },
  ),
  ],
  );
}
```

In the code above, you:

1. Lay out your widgets vertically, using a `Column`.

2. Add a title and the quantity labels to the quantity section by creating a `Row` that contains two `Text`s. You use a `SizedBox` to separate the `Text`s.

3. Add a `Slider`.

4. Set the active and inactive colors.

5. Set the current slider value.

6. Set the slider's minimum and maximum value.

7. Set how you want the slider to increment.

8. Set the label above the slider. Here, you want to show the current value above the slider.

9. Update `_currentSliderValue` when the value changes.

Now, you're ready to use the slider. Locate `// TODO 18: Add slider` and replace it with:

```
const SizedBox(height: 10.0),
buildQuantityField(),
```

Run the app to see:

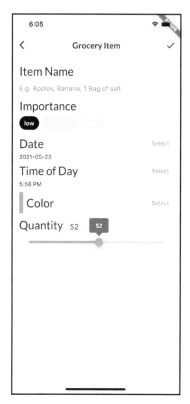

Now, all the input widgets are complete. Awesome! But keep **grocery_item_screen.dart** open, you'll make some more updates soon.

Wouldn't it be great if you could preview what the grocery item looks like while you are creating it? That's your next task.

Creating a grocery tile

Start by creating `GroceryTile`. Here's what it looks like:

In **lib/components**, create a new file called **grocery_tile.dart**. Then add the following code:

```dart
import 'package:flutter/material.dart';
import 'package:google_fonts/google_fonts.dart';
import 'package:intl/intl.dart';
import '../models/grocery_item.dart';

class GroceryTile extends StatelessWidget {
  // 1
  final GroceryItem item;
  // 2
  final Function(bool?)? onComplete;
  // 3
  final TextDecoration textDecoration;

  // 4
  GroceryTile({
    Key? key,
    required this.item,
    this.onComplete,
  }) : textDecoration =
    item.isComplete ? TextDecoration.lineThrough :
TextDecoration.none,
    super(key: key);

  @override
  Widget build(BuildContext context) {
    // TODO 21: Change this Widget
    return Container(
      height: 100.0,
      // TODO 20: Replace this color
      color: Colors.red,
    );
  }

  // TODO: Add BuildImportance()

  // TODO: Add buildDate()

  // TODO: Add buildCheckbox()
}
```

Here's how GroceryTile is set up:

1. You include a GroceryItem to configure the tile.

2. onComplete is a callback handler that lets you know whether the user toggled the checkbox on or off.

3. textDecoration helps style all the Texts.

4. When you initialize a `GroceryTile`, you check the item to see if the user marked it as complete. If so, you show a **strike** through the text. Otherwise, you display the text as normal.

Now that you've completed `GroceryTile`'s initial setup, it's time to add more functionality to the screen. Since you'll work on it again soon, keep **grocery_tile.dart** open.

Using GroceryTile

Switch back to **grocery_item_screen.dart** and add the following import:

```
import '../components/grocery_tile.dart';
```

Then locate `// TODO: 19: Add Grocery Tile` and replace it with the following:

```
GroceryTile(
  item: GroceryItem(
    id: 'previewMode',
    name: _name,
    importance: _importance,
    color: _currentColor,
    quantity: _currentSliderValue,
    date: DateTime(
      _dueDate.year,
      _dueDate.month,
      _dueDate.day,
      _timeOfDay.hour,
      _timeOfDay.minute,
    ),
  ),
),
```

This code uses all the state properties of the widget to create a `GroceryItem`, then passes it to `GroceryTile` to configure itself.

Your app should look similar to this:

Now, it's time to turn that red box into a grocery item!

Building GroceryTile

Now that you've set up the live update, it's time to add more details to your grocery tile.

Displaying the importance label

So far, you've let the user pick the importance level for each grocery item, but you're not displaying that information. To fix this, switch back to **grocery_tile.dart**, locate `// TODO: Add BuildImportance()` and replace it with:

```
Widget buildImportance() {
  if (item.importance == Importance.low) {
    return Text(
```

```
        'Low',
        style: GoogleFonts.lato(decoration: textDecoration));
    } else if (item.importance == Importance.medium) {
      return Text(
        'Medium',
        style: GoogleFonts.lato(
          fontWeight: FontWeight.w800,
          decoration: textDecoration));
    } else if (item.importance == Importance.high) {
      return Text(
        'High',
        style: GoogleFonts.lato(
          color: Colors.red,
          fontWeight: FontWeight.w900,
          decoration: textDecoration,
        ),
      );
    } else {
      throw Exception('This importance type does not exist');
    }
  }
```

Here, you've created a helper method to construct the importance label. You check the item's `importance` and display the correct `Text`.

Displaying the selected date

Now, you need to fix the same problem with the date to buy the groceries. To do this, add the following code below `buildImportance()`:

```
Widget buildDate() {
  final dateFormatter = DateFormat('MMMM dd h:mm a');
  final dateString = dateFormatter.format(item.date);
  return Text(
    dateString,
    style: TextStyle(decoration: textDecoration),
  );
}
```

Here, you created a helper method to format and convert `DateTime` into a `dateString` format.

Displaying the checkbox

Similarly, you've added the functionality to let the user mark an item as complete, but haven't shown the checkbox anywhere.

Fix this by replacing `TODO: Add buildCheckbox()` with:

```
Widget buildCheckbox() {
  return Checkbox(
    // 1
    value: item.isComplete,
    // 2
    onChanged: onComplete,
  );
}
```

Here, you create `Checkbox`, which:

1. Toggles the checkbox on or off based on `item.isComplete`.

2. Triggers the `onComplete` callback when the user taps the checkbox.

Now that you've set up all your helper widgets, it's time to put all the pieces together!

Finishing GroceryTile

At this point, you're ready to put all the elements in place to finish building the **GroceryTile** widget.

Locate `// TODO 20: Replace this color` and replace the TODO message and the `color: Colors.red,` line with:

```
child: Row(
  mainAxisAlignment: MainAxisAlignment.spaceBetween,
  children: [
    // TODO 22: Add Row to group (name, date, importance)
    // TODO 23: Add Row to group (quantity, checkbox)
  ],
),
```

Here, you're preparing the Row to host all the elements of the item.

Now, locate `// TODO 21: Change this Widget` and notice that `Container` has a squiggle under it. In the **Dart Analysis** tab, there's also an information warning message: **SizedBox for whitespace**. That's due to the lint rules. `Container()` requires more processing than `SizedBox()`.

Since you only need to define the height of the box, you don't need a container; you only need something to give you some space.

To fix this, change the word `Container` to `SizedBox`. You'll notice the squiggle and the related message in the Dart Analysis tab are now gone. :]

Since it no longer applies, delete `// TODO 21: Change this Widget` as well.

Next, you'll group elements into two separate rows to create the following effect:

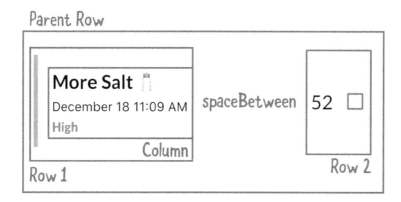

- **Row 1**: Groups the color label and a column containing the name, date and importance.

- **Row 2**: Groups the quantity and the checkbox.

Adding the first row

Locate `// TODO 22: Add Row to group (name, date, importance)` and replace it with the following:

```
// 2
Container(width: 5.0, color: item.color),
// 3
const SizedBox(width: 16.0),
// 4
Column(
  mainAxisAlignment: MainAxisAlignment.center,
  crossAxisAlignment: CrossAxisAlignment.start,
  children: [
    // 5
    Text(
      item.name,
      style: GoogleFonts.lato(
        decoration: textDecoration,
        fontSize: 21.0,
        fontWeight: FontWeight.bold),
    ),
```

```
      const SizedBox(height: 4.0),
      buildDate(),
      const SizedBox(height: 4.0),
      buildImportance(),
    ],
  ),
),
```

In this code, you:

1. Add a Row to lay out elements in the horizontal direction.

2. Add a container widget with the item's color. This helps to color-code items.

3. Space the elements 16 pixels apart.

4. Add a Column to lay out elements in the vertical direction.

5. Lay out elements spaced 4 pixels apart in the following order: item name, date and importance.

> **Note**: If you're not seeing your app update when you add these new features, you might need to hot restart, navigate to the **To Buy** screen and add a new grocery item.

As you make changes to the screen options and add more code, you'll see those updates in a newly added tile. Here's an example:

Showing the checkbox

Next, locate // TODO 23: Add Row to group (quantity, checkbox) and replace it with the following:

```
// 6
Row(
  children: [
    // 7
    Text(item.quantity.toString(),
        style:
            GoogleFonts.lato(
              decoration: textDecoration,
              fontSize: 21.0),
        ),
    // 8
    buildCheckbox(),
  ],
),
```

Here's how the code works:

6. Add a Row to lay out elements in the horizontal direction.

7. Then add a Text to display the item's quantity.

8. Finally, add the checkbox.

Your app should look similar to this:

Change some of your choices, such as the name or quantity, and see the tile update automatically. A user can now preview grocery items while they create them!

Saving the user's work

For the finishing touch, the user needs to be able to save the item.

Switch back to **grocery_item_screen.dart**, locate `// TODO 24: Add callback handler` and replace it with the following:

```
// 1
final groceryItem = GroceryItem(
    id: widget.originalItem?.id ?? const Uuid().v1(),
    name: _nameController.text,
    importance: _importance,
    color: _currentColor,
    quantity: _currentSliderValue,
    date: DateTime(
      _dueDate.year,
      _dueDate.month,
      _dueDate.day,
      _timeOfDay.hour,
      _timeOfDay.minute,
    ),
);

if (widget.isUpdating) {
  // 2
  widget.onUpdate(groceryItem);
} else {
  // 3
  widget.onCreate(groceryItem);
}
```

Here's what's going on above:

1. When the user taps **Save**, you take all the state properties and create a `GroceryItem`.

2. If the user is updating an existing item, call `onUpdate`.

3. If the user is creating a new item, call `onCreate`.

This is pretty much all you need to create an item! Finally, it's time to display the list of items.

Creating GroceryListScreen

In **screens**, create a new file called **grocery_list_screen.dart**.

Add the following code:

```
import 'package:flutter/material.dart';
import '../components/grocery_tile.dart';
import '../models/models.dart';
import 'grocery_item_screen.dart';

class GroceryListScreen extends StatelessWidget {
  final GroceryManager manager;

  const GroceryListScreen({
    Key? key,
    required this.manager,
  }) : super(key: key);

  @override
  Widget build(BuildContext context) {
    // TODO 26: Replace with ListView
    return Container();
  }
}
```

This is the initial setup for `GroceryListScreen`. It requires a `GroceryManager` so it can get the list of grocery items to display in the list.

Adding items to the Grocery screen

Open **grocery_screen.dart** and add the following imports:

```
import 'grocery_list_screen.dart';
```

Then locate `// TODO 25: Add GroceryListScreen` and replace the line below it with:

```
return GroceryListScreen(manager: manager);
```

The grocery list will display if the user has items in the list. Now, it's time to create that list!

Creating a GroceryList view

Open **grocery_list_screen.dart**, then locate `// TODO 26: Replace with ListView` and replace the existing `return` line below it with the following:

```
// 1
final groceryItems = manager.groceryItems;
// 2
return Padding(
  padding: const EdgeInsets.all(16.0),
  // 3
  child: ListView.separated(
      // 4
      itemCount: groceryItems.length,
      itemBuilder: (context, index) {
        final item = groceryItems[index];
        // TODO 28: Wrap in a Dismissable
        // TODO 27: Wrap in an InkWell
        // 5
        return GroceryTile(
          key: Key(item.id),
          item: item,
          // 6
          onComplete: (change) {
            // 7
            if (change != null) {
              manager.completeItem(index, change);
            }
          },);
      },
      // 8
      separatorBuilder: (context, index) {
        return const SizedBox(height: 16.0);
      },
    ),
  );
```

In the code above, you:

1. Get the list of grocery items from the manager.

2. Apply padding of 16 pixels all around this screen.

3. Add `ListView`.

4. Set the number of items in the list.

5. For each item in the list, get the current item and construct a `GroceryTile`.

6. Return `onComplete` when the user taps the checkbox.

7. Check if there is a change and update the item's `isComplete` status.

8. Space each grocery item 16 pixels apart.

Hot restart, add an item in the tile and tap the checkmark in the top-right corner. That will bring you to this screen:

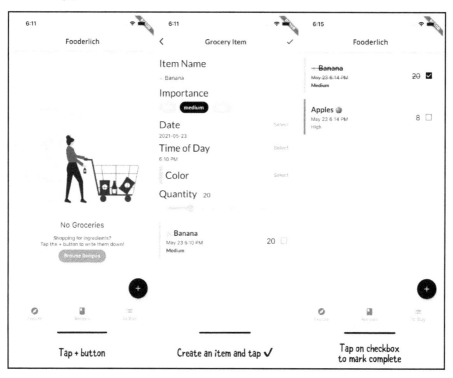

Great, now you can view the list of grocery items and mark an item complete! But how do you tap an existing item to update it? Guess what, that's your next step. :]

Adding gestures

Before you add gestures, here is a quick overview!

Gesture-based widgets detect different user touch behaviors. You wrap gesture widgets around other widgets that need touch behavior.

Gesture widgets try to recognize what type of gesture the user performed — for example, if they tapped, double-tapped, long-pressed or panned.

The two most common gesture widgets are:

1. **GestureDetector**: Provides other controls, like dragging.

2. **InkWell**: Provides animated ripple feedback. For example, when the user taps a UI element you use it to display a splash animation, as shown below:

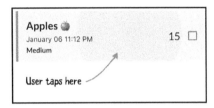

Gestures behavior

Another thing to be aware of with gesture widgets is HitTestBehavior, which controls how the gesture behaves during a hit test.

There are three types of behavior:

- **deferToChild**: Passes the touch event down the widget tree. This is the default behavior for GestureDetector.

- **opaque**: Prevents widgets in the background from receiving touch events.

- **translucent**: Allows widgets in the background to receive touch events.

These gesture widgets support tap, double-tap, long-press, panning and many other gestures. For more information, check out: https://flutter.dev/docs/development/ui/advanced/gestures.

Now, it's time to add a gesture!

Adding an InkWell

Open **grocery_list_screen.dart**, locate // TODO 27: Wrap in an InkWell and replace the existing return GroceryTile() code with the following:

```
// 1
return InkWell(
  child: GroceryTile(
    key: Key(item.id),
    item: item,
    onComplete: (change) {
      if (change != null) {
        manager.completeItem(index, change);
      }
    }),
  // 2
  onTap: () {
    Navigator.push(
        context,
        MaterialPageRoute(
            builder: (context) => GroceryItemScreen(
              originalItem: item,
              // 3
              onUpdate: (item) {
                // 4
                manager.updateItem(item, index);
                // 5
                Navigator.pop(context);
              },
              // 6
              onCreate: (item) {},
            ),
        ),
    );
  },
);
```

Here's how the code works:

1. You wrap GroceryTile inside an InkWell.

2. When the gesture recognizes a tap, it presents GroceryItemScreen, letting the user edit the current item.

3. GroceryItemScreen calls onUpdate when the user updates an item.

4. `GroceryManager` updates the item at the particular index.

5. Dismisses `GroceryItemScreen`.

6. `onCreate` will not be called since you are updating an existing item.

With the app running, you can now tap a grocery item and make an update.

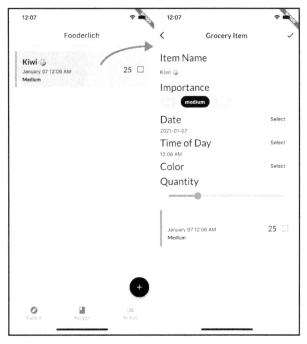

Great job! You can create and update an item. But what about deleting items you no longer need?

Dismissing items with a swipe

Next, you'll learn how to dismiss or delete items from the list. You'll use `Dismissible`, a widget that clears items from the list when the user swipes left or right. It even supports swiping in the vertical direction.

Within **grocery_list_screen.dart**, locate `// TODO 28: Wrap in a Dismissable.` Wrapping a widget with another widget sounds complicated, but it's not. You could do it manually, but why not use a built-in feature of the IDE? Especially since the feature also includes the closing `)`; so you don't have to add it manually.

Put your cursor on the widget you wish to wrap — in this case, `Inkwell` — and a light bulb will appear.

```
// TODO 28: Wrap in a Dismissable
// 1
return InkWell(
      ld: GroceryTile(
        key: Key(item.id),
        item: item,
        onComplete: (change) {
          manager.completeItem(index, change);
        }), // GroceryTile
      // 2
      onTap: () {
```

When you click the light bulb, a list appears. The image below was made with Android Studio, but VSCode also has a list, though it may be in a different order.

```
// TODO 28: Wrap in a Dismissable
// 1
         return InkWell(
Wrap with widget...      ►  GroceryTile(
Wrap with Center
Wrap with Column          /: Key(item.id),
Wrap with Container       em: item,
Wrap with Padding         Complete: (change) {
Wrap with Row             manager.completeItem(index, change);
Wrap with SizedBox        , // GroceryTile
Wrap with StreamBuilder
Remove this widget
Press ⌥Space to open preview
                          onTap: () {
```

Clicking **Wrap with widget...** wraps a new widget around your existing widget, including adding the closing `)`;.

```
// TODO 28: Wrap in a Dismissable
// 1
return widget(
  child: InkWell(
    child: GroceryTile(
        key: Key(item.id),
        item: item,
        onComplete: (change) {
          manager.completeItem(index, change);
        }), // GroceryTile
      // 2
      onTap: () {
        Navigator.push(
```

In normal circumstances, you'd type the widget you want. In this case, just highlight the widget(child:

```
// TODO 28: Wrap in a Dismissable
// 1
return widget(
  child: InkWell(
    child: GroceryTile(
      key: Key(item.id),
      item: item,
      onComplete: (change) {
        manager.completeItem(index, change);
      }), // GroceryTile
    // 2
    onTap: () {
      Navigator.push(
```

and replace the highlighted code with this:

```
Dismissible(
  // 6
  key: Key(item.id),
  // 7
  direction: DismissDirection.endToStart,
  // 8
  background: Container(
    color: Colors.red,
    alignment: Alignment.centerRight,
    child: const Icon(Icons.delete_forever,
      color: Colors.white, size: 50.0)),
  // 9
  onDismissed: (direction) {
    // 10
    manager.deleteItem(index);
    // 11
    ScaffoldMessenger.of(context).showSnackBar(
      SnackBar(content: Text('${item.name} dismissed')));
  },
  child:
```

You've now wrapped InkWell inside a Dismissible. Here's how it works:

6. The dismissible widget includes a Key. Flutter needs this to find and remove the right element in the tree.

7. Sets the direction the user can swipe to dismiss.

8. Selects the background widget to display behind the widget you're swiping. In this case, the background widget is red with a white trash can Icon aligned in the center and to the right of the Container.

9. `onDismissed` lets you know when the user swiped away a `GroceryTile`.

10. Lets the grocery manager handle deleting the item, given an index.

11. Shows a snack bar widget to let the user know which item they deleted.

All done! Try dismissing an item by swiping from right to left. Awesome, right? :]

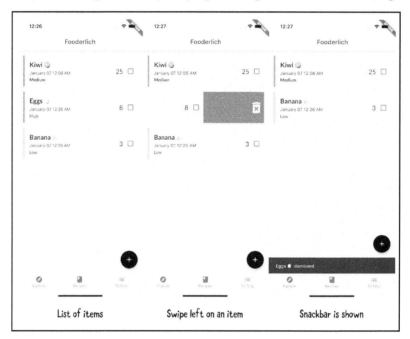

List of items   Swipe left on an item   Snackbar is shown

Caching your page selection

You're almost done, but there's one final thing to tweak! Did you notice any problems when you switched tabs?

There are two issues to fix:

- A spinner shows up every time you switch tabs. This indicates that data reloads every time.

- The app doesn't preserve the scroll position when you switch to another tab.

It's time to fix these problems!

Open **home.dart** and, within `build()`, find `// TODO: Replace body` replace it and the body line with the following:

```
body: IndexedStack(index: tabManager.selectedTab, children:
pages),
```

`IndexedStack` allows you to easily switch widgets in your app. It only shows one child widget at a time, but it preserves the state of all the children. Yes, there *is* a widget for that!

Now, scroll and switch to different tabs. You'll notice that the app now preserves all the states across all the children. Nice work!

Key points

- You can pass data around with **callbacks** or **provider packages**.

- If you need to pass data one level up, use **callbacks**.

- If you need to pass data deep in the widget tree, use **providers**.

- **Provider** is a state management helper that acts as a wrapper around inherited widgets.

- **Provider** helps expose state model objects to widgets below it.

- `Consumer` listens for changes to values and rebuilds the widgets below itself.

- Split your widgets by screen to keep code modular and organized.

- Create `manager` objects to manage functions and state changes in one place.

- Gesture widgets recognize and determine the type of touch event. They provide callbacks to react to events like `onTap` or `onDrag`.

- You can use dismissible widgets to swipe away items in a list.

Where to go from here?

There are many ways to engage and collect data from your users. You've learned to pass data around using callbacks and providers. You learned to create different input widgets. You also learned to apply touch events to navigate to parts of your app.

That's a lot, but you've only scratched the surface! There's a plethora of widgets out there. You can explore other packages at https://pub.dev/, a place where you can find the most popular widgets created by the Flutter community!

In the next section, you'll dive into navigation.

Section III: Navigating Between Screens

You'll continue working on the Fooderlich app in this section, learning about navigating between screens and working with deep links.

Topics you'll learn include Navigator 2.0 and Flutter Web.

Chapter 7: Routes & Navigation

By Vincent Ngo

Navigation, or how users switch between different screens, is an important concept to master. Good navigation keeps your app organized and helps users find their way around your app without getting frustrated.

In the previous chapter, you got a small taste of navigation when you created a grocery list for users to manage what to buy. When the user taps an item, it shows the item details:

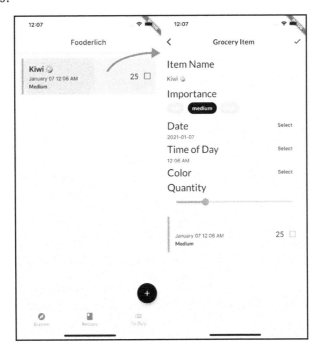

But this uses the imperative style of navigation, known as **Navigator 1.0**. In this chapter, you'll learn to navigate between screens the declarative way.

You'll cover the following topics:

- Quick overview of `Navigator` 1.0.

- Overview of `Navigator` 2.0 and how to use it.

- How to drive navigation through state by using the **provider** package.

- How to handle the Android system's back button.

By the end of this chapter, you will know everything you need to navigate to different screens!

> **Note**: If you'd like to skip straight to the code, jump ahead to the **Getting Started** section. If you'd like to learn the theory first, read on!

Introducing Navigator

If you come from an iOS background, you might be familiar with **UINavigationController**. This controller defines a stack-based scheme to manage and navigate between view controllers.

In Android, you use **Jetpack Navigation** to manage various fragments.

In Flutter, you use a **Navigator** widget to manage your screens or pages. You can think of **screens** or **pages** as **routes**.

> **Note**: This chapter uses these terms interchangeably because they all mean the same thing.

A **stack** is a data structure that manages pages. You insert the elements last-in, first-out (LIFO), and only the element at the top of the stack is visible to the user.

For example, when a user views a list of grocery items, tapping an item **pushes** `GroceryItemScreen` to the top of the stack. Once the user finishes making changes, you **pop** it off the stack.

Here's a top-level and a side-level view of the navigation stack:

Now, it's time for a quick overview of Navigator 1.0.

Navigator 1.0 overview

Before the release of Flutter 1.22, you could only shift between screens by issuing direct commands like "show this now" or "remove the current screen and go back to the previous one". Navigator 1.0 provides a simple set of APIs for you to navigate between screens. The most common ones include:

- push(): Adds a new route on the stack.

- pop(): Removes a route from the stack.

So how do you add a navigator to your app?

Most Flutter apps start with WidgetsApp as the root widget.

> **Note**: So far you have used `MaterialApp`, which extends `WidgetsApp`.

`WidgetsApp` wraps many other common widgets that your app requires. Among these wrapped widgets are a top-level `Navigator` to manage the pages you push and pop.

Pushing and popping routes

To show another screen to the user, you need to push a `Route` onto the `Navigator` stack. Here's an example of that code:

```
bool result = await Navigator.push<bool>(
  context,
  MaterialPageRoute<bool>(
    builder: (BuildContext context) => OnboardingScreen()
  ),
);
```

Here, `MaterialPageRoute` returns an instance of your new screen widget. `Navigator` returns the result of the push whenever the screen pops off the stack.

Here's how you pop a route off the stack:

```
Navigator.pop(context);
```

This seems easy enough. So why not just use Navigator 1.0? Well, it has a few disadvantages.

Navigator 1.0's disadvantages

The imperative API may seem natural and easy to use but, in practice, it's hard to manage and scale.

The first is that there's no good way to manage your pages without keeping a mental map of where you push and pop a screen.

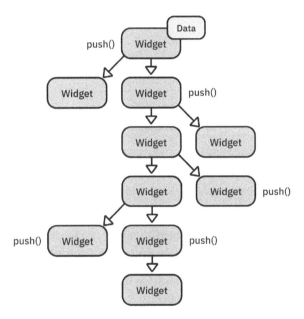

Imagine a new developer has just joined your team. Where would they even start? They'd surely be confused.

Moreover, Navigator 1.0 doesn't expose the route stack to developers. This makes it difficult to handle complicated cases, like adding and removing a screen between pages.

For example, in Fooderlich, you want to show the Onboarding screen only if the user hasn't completed the onboarding yet. Handling that with Navigator 1.0 is complicated.

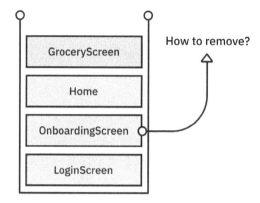

Another disadvantage is that Navigator 1.0 does not update the web URL path. Any time you go to a new page, you only see the base URL, like so: **www.localhost:8000/ #/**. Additionally, the web browser's forward and backward buttons may not work as expected.

Finally, on Android devices, the **Back** button might not work with Navigator 1.0 when you have nested navigators or when you add Flutter to your host Android app.

Wouldn't it be great if there was a declarative API that solves most of these pain points? That's why **Navigator 2.0** was born!

Navigator 2.0 overview

Flutter 1.22 introduced Navigator 2.0, a new declarative API that allows you to take full control of your navigation stack. It aims to feel more Flutter-like while solving the pain points of Navigator 1.0. Its main goals include:

- **Exposing the navigator's page stack**: You can now manage your pages. More power, more control!

- **Backward-compatible with imperative API**: You can use both imperative and declarative styles in the same app.

- **Handle operating system events**: Works better with events like the Android system's Back button.

- **Manage nested navigators**: Gives you control over which navigator has priority.

- **Manage navigation state**: Lets you parse routes and handles web URLs and deep linking.

Here are the new abstractions that make up Navigator 2.0's declarative API:

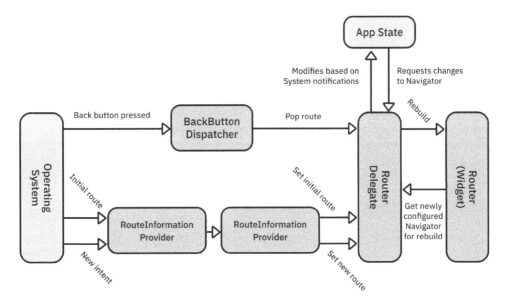

It includes the following key components:

- **Page**: An abstract class that describes the configuration for a route.

- **Router**: Handles configuring the list of pages the Navigator displays.

- **RouterDelegate**: defines how the router listens for changes to the app state to rebuild the navigator's configuration.

- **RouteInformationProvider**: Provides `RouteInformation` to the router.

- **RouteInformationParser**: Parses route information into a user-defined data type.

- **BackButtonDispatcher**: Reports presses on the platform system's Back button to the router.

- **TransitionDelegate**: Decides how pages transition into and out of the screen.

> **Note**: This chapter will mainly focus on the use of Navigator and RouterDelegate. In the next chapter, you'll dive deeper into the other components.

Navigation and unidirectional data flow

The imperative API is very basic, forcing you to place `push()` and `pop()` functions all over your widget hierarchy — which couples all your widgets! To present another screen, you also have to place callbacks up the widget hierarchy.

With the new declarative API, you can now manage your navigation state unidirectionally. The widgets are state-driven, as shown here:

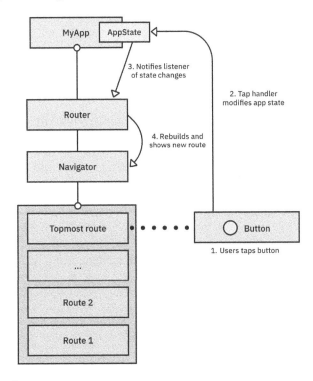

Here's how it works:

1. A user taps on a button.

2. The button handler tells the app state to update.

3. The router is a listener of the state, so it receives a notification when the state changes.

4. Based on the new state changes, the router reconfigures the list of pages for the navigator.

5. Navigator detects if there's a new page in the list and handles the transitions to show the page.

That's it! Instead of having to build a mental mind map of how every screen presents and dismisses, the state drives which pages appear.

Is Navigator 2.0 always better than Navigator 1.0?

If you have an existing project, you don't have to migrate or convert your existing code to use the new API.

Here are some tips to help you decide which is more useful for you:

- **For medium to large apps**: Consider using a declarative API and a router widget. You may have to manage a lot of your navigation state.

- **For small apps**: For rapid prototyping or creating a small app for demos, the imperative API is suitable. Sometimes push and pop are all you need!

Next, you'll get some hands-on experience with Navigator 2.0.

> **Note**: This chapter will focus on implementing Navigator 2.0. To learn more about Navigator 1.0, check:
>
> • **Flutter's Dev Cookbook Tutorials**:
>
> https://flutter.dev/docs/cookbook/navigation.
>
> • **Flutter Navigation: Getting Started by Filip Babić**:
>
> https://www.raywenderlich.com/4562634-flutter-navigation-getting-started.

Getting started

Open the starter project in Android Studio, run `flutter pub get`, then run the app.

> **Note**: It's better to start with the starter project rather than continuing with the project from the last chapter because the starter project contains some changes specific to this chapter.

You'll see that the **Fooderlich** app only shows a Splash screen.

Don't worry, you'll connect all the screens soon. You'll build a simple flow that features a login screen and an onboarding widget before showing the existing tab-based app you've built so far. But first, you'll take a look at the changes to the project files.

Changes to the project files

Before you dive into navigation, there are new files in this starter project to help you out.

In **main.dart**, Fooderlich is now a StatefulWidget. It'll listen to state changes and rebuild corresponding widgets accordingly.

Fooderlich now supports the user setting for dark mode.

What's new in the screens folder

There are eight new changes in **lib/screens/**:

- **splash_screen.dart**: Configures the initial Splash screen.

- **login_screen.dart**: Allows the user to log in.

- **onboarding_screen.dart**: Guides the user through a series of steps to learn more about the app.

- **profile_screen.dart**: Allows users to check their profile, update settings and log out.

- **home.dart**: Now includes a **Profile** button on the top-right for the user to view their profile.

- **screens.dart**: A barrel file that groups all the screens into a single import.

Later, you'll use these to construct your authentication UI flow.

Changes to the models folder

There are a few changes to files in **lib/models/**.

tab_manager.dart has been removed. Instead, you'll manage the user's tab selection in **app_state_manager.dart**, which you'll build soon.

In addition, there are three new model objects:

- **fooderlich_pages.dart**: Describes a list of unique keys for each page.

- **user.dart**: Describes a single user. Includes information like the user's role, profile picture, full name and app settings.

- **profile_manager.dart**: Manages the user's profile state by, for example, getting the user's info, checking if the user is viewing their profile and setting dark mode.

Additional assets

assets/ contains new images, which you'll use to build the new onboarding guide.

New packages

There are two new packages in **pubspec.yaml**:

```
smooth_page_indicator: ^1.0.0+2
webview_flutter: ^2.0.13
```

Here's what they do:

- **smooth_page_indicator**: Shows a page indicator when you scroll through pages.

- **webview_flutter**: Provides a `WebView` widget to show web content on the iOS or Android platform.

Android SDK version

If you open **android/app/build.gradle** you will notice that the `minSdkVersion` is now 19, as shown below:

```
android {
    defaultConfig {
        ...
        minSdkVersion 19
        ...
    }
}
```

This is because webview_flutter depends on Android SDK 19 or higher to enable hybrid composition.

Note: For more information check out the webview_flutter documentation https://pub.dev/packages/webview_flutter

Now that you know what's changed, you'll get a quick overview of the UI flow you'll build in this chapter.

Looking over the UI flow

Here are the first three screens you show the user:

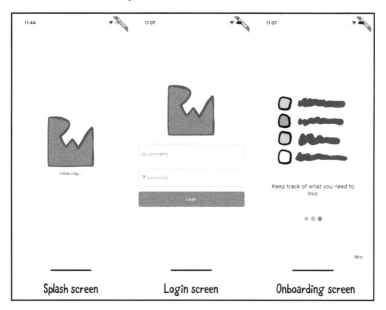

Splash screen   Login screen   Onboarding screen

1. When the user launches the app, the first screen they'll see is the **Splash screen**. This gives the developer the chance to initialize and configure the app.

2. Once initialized, the user navigates to the **Login screen**. The user must now enter their **username** and **password**, then tap **Login**.

3. Once the user logs in, an **Onboarding screen** shows them how to use the app. The user has two choices: swipe through a guide to learn more about the app or skip.

From the Onboarding screen, the user goes to the app's **Home**. They can now start using the app.

The app presents the user with three tabs with these options:

1. **Explore**: View recipes for the day and see what their friends are cooking up.

2. **Recipes**: Browse a collection of recipes they want to cook.

3. **To Buy**: Add ingredients or items to their grocery list.

Next, the user can either tap the **Add** button or, if the grocery list isn't empty, they can tap an existing item. This will present the **Grocery Item** screen, as shown below:

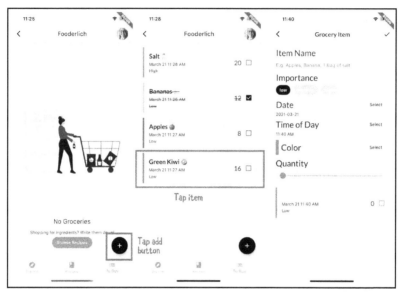

Now, how does the user view their profile or log out? They start by tapping the profile avatar, as shown below:

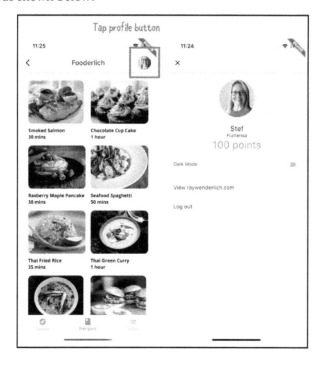

On the **Profile** screen, they can do the following:

- View their profile and see how many points they've earned.

- Change the app theme to dark mode.

- Visit the raywenderlich.com website.

- Log out of the app.

Below is an example of a user toggling dark mode on and then opening raywenderlich.com.

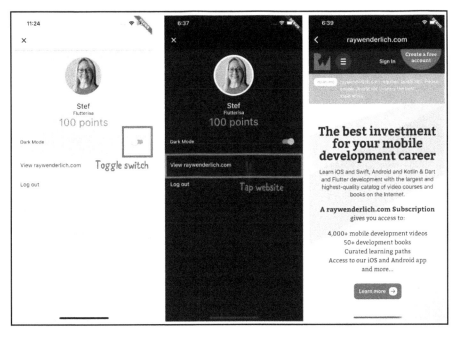

When you tap **Log out**, it reinitializes the app and goes to the Login screen, as shown below:

Here's a bird's eye view of the entire navigation hierarchy:

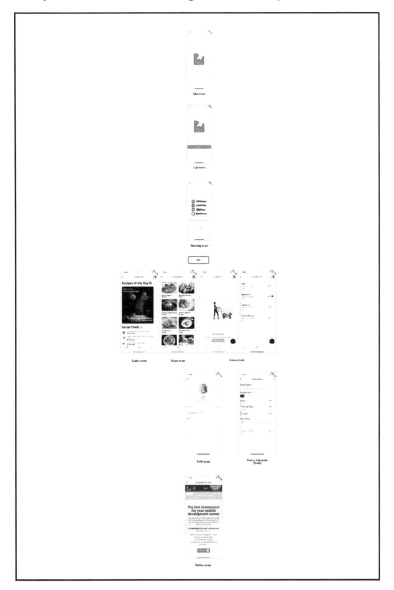

> **Note**: There's a large-scale version of the image in the **assets** folder of this chapter's materials.

Your app is going to be awesome when it's finished. Now, it's time to add some code!

Managing your app state

The first step is to define your app state, how it can change and which components it notifies when a change occurs.

In the **models** directory, create a new file called **app_state_manager.dart** and add the following:

```
import 'dart:async';
import 'package:flutter/material.dart';

// 1
class FooderlichTab {
  static const int explore = 0;
  static const int recipes = 1;
  static const int toBuy = 2;
}

class AppStateManager extends ChangeNotifier {
  // 2
  bool _initialized = false;
  // 3
  bool _loggedIn = false;
  // 4
  bool _onboardingComplete = false;
  // 5
  int _selectedTab = FooderlichTab.explore;

  // 6
  bool get isInitialized => _initialized;
  bool get isLoggedIn => _loggedIn;
  bool get isOnboardingComplete => _onboardingComplete;
  int get getSelectedTab => _selectedTab;

  // TODO: Add initializeApp
  // TODO: Add login
  // TODO: Add completeOnboarding
  // TODO: Add goToTab
  // TODO: Add goToRecipes
  // TODO: Add logout
}
```

AppStateManager manages the app's navigation state. Take a moment to understand the properties you added:

1. Creates constants for each tab the user taps.

2. _initialized checks if the app is initialized.

3. _loggedIn lets you check if the user has logged in.

4. _onboardingComplete checks if the user completed the onboarding flow.

5. _selectedTab keeps track of which tab the user is on.

6. These are getter methods for each property. You cannot change these properties outside AppStateManager. This is important for the unidirectional flow architecture, where you don't change state directly but only via function calls or dispatched events.

Now, it's time to learn how to modify the app state. You'll create functions to change each of the properties declared above.

Initializing the app

Within the same file, locate // TODO: Add initializeApp and replace it with the following:

```
void initializeApp() {
  // 7
  Timer(const Duration(milliseconds: 2000), () {
    // 8
    _initialized = true;
    // 9
    notifyListeners();
  },
  );
}
```

Here's how the code works:

7. Sets a delayed timer for 2,000 milliseconds before executing the closure. This sets how long the app screen will display after the user starts the app.

8. Sets initialized to **true**.

9. Notifies all listeners.

Logging in

Next, locate // TODO: Add login and replace it with the following:

```
void login(String username, String password) {
  // 10
  _loggedIn = true;
  // 11
  notifyListeners();
}
```

This function takes in a username and a password. Here's what it does:

10. Sets `loggedIn` to **true**.

11. Notifies all listeners.

> **Note**: In a real scenario, you'd make an API request to log in. In this case, however, you're just using a mock.

Completing the onboarding

Next, locate `// TODO: Add completeOnboarding` and replace it with the following:

```
void completeOnboarding() {
  _onboardingComplete = true;
  notifyListeners();
}
```

Calling `completeOnboarding()` will notify all listeners that the user has completed the onboarding guide.

Setting the selected tab

Locate `// TODO: Add goToTab` and replace it with the following:

```
void goToTab(index) {
  _selectedTab = index;
  notifyListeners();
}
```

`goToTab` sets the index of `_selectedTab` and notifies all listeners.

Navigating to the Recipes tab

Locate `// TODO: Add goToRecipes` and replace it with the following:

```
void goToRecipes() {
  _selectedTab = FooderlichTab.recipes;
  notifyListeners();
}
```

This is a helper function that goes straight to the recipes tab.

Adding the log out capability

Locate `// TODO: Add logout` and replace it with the following:

```
void logout() {
  // 12
  _loggedIn = false;
  _onboardingComplete = false;
  _initialized = false;
  _selectedTab = 0;

  // 13
  initializeApp();
  // 14
  notifyListeners();
}
```

When the user logs out, the code above:

12. Resets all app state properties.

13. Reinitializes the app.

14. Notifies all listeners of state change.

Notice that all these functions follow the same pattern: they set some values that aren't publicly exposed and then notify listeners. This is the essence of the unidirectional data flow architecture you're implementing.

Finally, open **lib/models/models.dart** and add the following:

```
export 'app_state_manager.dart';
```

This way, you add the newly created `AppStateManager` to the barrel file. You now have a well-defined model of the app state and a mechanism that notifies listeners of state changes. This is great progress. Now, you'll use it in the app!

Using the new AppStateManager

Open **lib/main.dart**, locate `// TODO: Create AppStateManager` and replace it with the following:

```
final _appStateManager = AppStateManager();
```

Here, you initialize the `AppStateManager`.

Next, locate `// TODO: Add AppStateManager ChangeNotifierProvider` and replace it with the following:

```
ChangeNotifierProvider(create: (context) => _appStateManager,),
```

This creates a change provider for `AppStateManager`, so widget descendants can access or listen to the app state.

That's all! Notice how you defined your app's state first? Any developer looking at this file can tell how the user interacts with the Fooderlich app.

Don't close **main.dart**, you're going to update it again soon. Next, you'll add a router.

Creating the router

`Router` configures the list of pages the Navigator displays. It listens to state managers and, based on the state changes, configures the list of page routes.

Under **lib/**, create a new directory called **navigation**. Within that folder, create a new file called **app_router.dart**. Add the following code:

```
import 'package:flutter/material.dart';

import '../models/models.dart';
import '../screens/screens.dart';

// 1
class AppRouter extends RouterDelegate
    with ChangeNotifier, PopNavigatorRouterDelegateMixin {
  // 2
  @override
  final GlobalKey<NavigatorState> navigatorKey;

  // 3
  final AppStateManager appStateManager;
  // 4
  final GroceryManager groceryManager;
  // 5
  final ProfileManager profileManager;

  AppRouter({
    required this.appStateManager,
    required this.groceryManager,
    required this.profileManager,
  })
      : navigatorKey = GlobalKey<NavigatorState>() {
```

```
    // TODO: Add Listeners
  }

  // TODO: Dispose listeners

  // 6
  @override
  Widget build(BuildContext context) {
    // 7
    return Navigator(
      // 8
      key: navigatorKey,
      // TODO: Add onPopPage
      // 9
      pages: [
        // TODO: Add SplashScreen
        // TODO: Add LoginScreen
        // TODO: Add OnboardingScreen
        // TODO: Add Home
        // TODO: Create new item
        // TODO: Select GroceryItemScreen
        // TODO: Add Profile Screen
        // TODO: Add WebView Screen
      ],
    );
  }

  // TODO: Add _handlePopPage

  // 10
  @override
  Future<void> setNewRoutePath(configuration) async => null;
}
```

Here's how the router widget works:

1. It extends RouterDelegate. The system will tell the router to build and configure a navigator widget.

2. Declares GlobalKey, a unique key across the entire app.

3. Declares AppStateManager. The router will listen to app state changes to configure the navigator's list of pages.

4. Declares GroceryManager to listen to the user's state when you create or edit an item.

5. Declares ProfileManager to listen to the user profile state.

6. RouterDelegate requires you to add a build(). This configures your navigator and pages.

7. Configures a `Navigator`.

8. Uses the `navigatorKey`, which is required to retrieve the current navigator.

9. Declares pages, the stack of pages that describes your navigation stack.

10. Sets `setNewRoutePath` to `null` since you aren't supporting Flutter web apps yet. Don't worry about that for now, you'll learn more about that topic in the next chapter.

> **Note**: How is this declarative? Instead of telling the navigator what to do with `push()` and `pop()`, you tell it: when the state is **x**, render **y** pages.

Now that you've defined your router, you'll let it handle routing requests.

Handling pop events

Locate `// TOOD: Add _handlePopPage` and replace it with the following:

```
bool _handlePopPage(
  // 1
  Route<dynamic> route,
  // 2
  result) {
  // 3
  if (!route.didPop(result)) {
    // 4
    return false;
  }

  // 5
  // TODO: Handle Onboarding and splash
  // TODO: Handle state when user closes grocery item screen
  // TODO: Handle state when user closes profile screen
  // TODO: Handle state when user closes WebView screen
    // 6
  return true;
}
```

When the user taps the **Back** button or triggers a system back button event, it fires a helper method, `onPopPage`.

Here's how it works:

1. This is the current `Route`, which contains information like `RouteSettings` to retrieve the route's name and arguments.

2. `result` is the value that returns when the route completes — a value that a dialog returns, for example.

3. Checks if the current route's pop succeeded.

4. If it failed, return `false`.

5. If the route pop succeeds, this checks the different routes and triggers the appropriate state changes.

Now, to use this callback helper, locate `// TODO: Add onPopPage` and replace it with the following:

```
onPopPage: _handlePopPage,
```

This way, it's called every time a page pops from the stack.

Adding state listeners

Now, you need to connect the state managers. When the state changes, the router will reconfigure the navigator with a new set of pages.

Locate `// TODO: Add Listeners` and replace it with the following:

```
appStateManager.addListener(notifyListeners);
groceryManager.addListener(notifyListeners);
profileManager.addListener(notifyListeners);
```

Here's what the state managers do:

*   **appStateManager**: Determines the state of the app. It manages whether the app initialized login and if the user completed the onboarding.

*   **groceryManager**: Manages the list of grocery items and the item selection state.

*   **profileManager**: Manages the user's profile and settings.

When you dispose the router, you must remove all listeners. Forgetting to do this will throw an exception.

Locate `// TODO: Dispose listeners` and replace it with the following:

```
@override
void dispose() {
    appStateManager.removeListener(notifyListeners);
  groceryManager.removeListener(notifyListeners);
    profileManager.removeListener(notifyListeners);
    super.dispose();
}
```

Congratulations, you just set up your router widget. Now, it's time to use it! Keep **app_router.dart** open, you'll use it again soon.

Using your app router

The newly created router needs to know who the managers are, so you'll now connect it to the state, grocery and profile managers.

Open **main.dart** and locate `// TODO: Import app_router`. Replace it with the following:

```
import 'navigation/app_router.dart';
```

Next, locate `// TODO: Define AppRouter` and replace it with the following:

```
late AppRouter _appRouter;
```

Now, locate `// TODO: Initialize app router` and replace it with the following:

```
@override
void initState() {
  _appRouter = AppRouter(
    appStateManager: _appStateManager,
    groceryManager: _groceryManager,
    profileManager: _profileManager,
  );
  super.initState();
}
```

You've now initialized your app router in `initState()` before you use it. Keep **main.dart** open.

For your next step, locate `// TODO: Replace with Router` widget. Replace it and the existing `home: const SplashScreen(),` line with the following code:

```
home: Router(
    routerDelegate: _appRouter,
  // TODO: Add backButtonDispatcher
),
```

You don't need the Splash screen import anymore. Go ahead and **remove** the following code:

```
import 'screens/splash_screen.dart';
```

Your router is all set now! It's time to let it play with screens.

Adding screens

With all the infrastructure in place, it's now time to define which screen to display according to the route. But first, check out the current situation.Build and run on iOS. You'll notice an exception in the **Run** tab:

```
======== Exception caught by widgets library ==============================
Navigator.onGenerateRoute was null, but the route named "/" was referenced.
The relevant error-causing widget was:
    Router<dynamic> file:///Users/
```

Even worse, the simulator might display the red screen of death:

That's because `Navigator` pages can't be empty. The app threw an exception because it can't generate a route. You'll fix that by adding screens next.

Showing the Splash screen

You'll start from the beginning, displaying the Splash screen.

Open **lib/screens/splash_screen.dart** and add the following imports:

```
import 'package:provider/provider.dart';
import '../models/models.dart';
```

Next, locate `// TODO: SplashScreen MaterialPage Helper` and replace it with the following:

```
static MaterialPage page() {
  return MaterialPage(
    name: FooderlichPages.splashPath,
      key: ValueKey(FooderlichPages.splashPath),
      child: const SplashScreen(),
  );
}
```

Here, you define a static method to create a `MaterialPage` that sets the appropriate unique identifier and creates `SplashScreen`.

Next locate `// TODO: Initialize App` and replace it with the following:

```
Provider.of<AppStateManager>(context, listen:
false).initializeApp();
```

Here, you use the current context to retrieve the `AppStateManager` to initialize the app.

Now, you want to add the Splash screen that displays while the app is starting.

Go back to **app_router.dart**, locate `// TODO: Add SplashScreen` and replace it with the following:

```
if (!appStateManager.isInitialized) SplashScreen.page(),
```

Here, you check if the app is initialized. If it's not, you show the Splash screen.

Perform a hot restart and you'll see the following screen flash by:

You'll still see an error but don't worry, it will go away shortly.

Congratulations, you just set up your first route! Now, it'll be much easier to prepare the other routes. Leave **app_router.dart** open.

The next set of code updates will follow a similar pattern:

- Update the screen code to trigger state changes via managers.

- Update the router code to handle new state changes, according to the route set as current.

Displaying the Login screen

You'll now implement the first step of the routing logic: displaying the Login screen after the Splash screen if the user isn't logged in.

Open **lib/screens/login_screen.dart** and add the following import:

```
import 'package:provider/provider.dart';
import '../models/models.dart';
```

Next, locate `// TODO: LoginScreen MaterialPage Helper` and replace it with the following:

```
static MaterialPage page() {
  return MaterialPage(
      name: FooderlichPages.loginPath,
      key: ValueKey(FooderlichPages.loginPath),
      child: const LoginScreen(),
  );
}
```

Here, you define a static method that creates a `MaterialPage`, sets a unique key and creates `LoginScreen`. Keep **login_screen.dart** open.

Switch back to **app_router.dart**, locate `// TODO: Add LoginScreen` and replace it with the following:

```
if (appStateManager.isInitialized && !
appStateManager.isLoggedIn)
LoginScreen.page(),
```

This code says that if the app initialized and the user hasn't logged in, it should show the login page.

Trigger a hot restart. You'll see the Splash screen for a few seconds, followed by the Login screen:

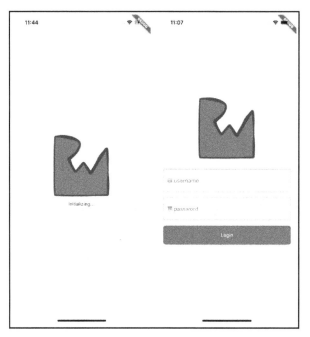

Congratulations, the error has disappeared and you have successfully implemented routes. The final step is to handle changes to the login state.

Back in **login_screen.dart**, locate `// TODO: Login -> Navigate to home` and replace it with the following:

```
Provider.of<AppStateManager>(context, listen: false)
  .login('mockUsername', 'mockPassword');
```

This uses `AppStateManager` to call a function that updates the user's login status. What happens when the login state changes? Glad you asked, that's the next step. :]

Transitioning from Login to Onboarding screen

When the user is logged in, you want to show the Onboarding screen.

Open **lib/screens/onboarding_screen.dart** and add the following imports:

```
import 'package:provider/provider.dart';
import '../models/models.dart';
```

Next, locate `// TODO: Add OnboardingScreen MaterialPage Helper` and replace it with the following:

```
static MaterialPage page() {
  return MaterialPage(
      name: FooderlichPages.onboardingPath,
      key: ValueKey(FooderlichPages.onboardingPath),
      child: const OnboardingScreen(),
  );
}
```

Here, you configure a `MaterialPage`, set the onboarding page's unique key and create the Onboarding screen widget.

Return to **app_router.dart**, locate `// TODO: Add OnboardingScreen` and replace it with the following:

```
if (appStateManager.isLoggedIn &&
    !appStateManager.isOnboardingComplete)
  OnboardingScreen.page(),
```

Here, you're showing the Onboarding screen if the user is logged in but hasn't completed the Onboarding Guide yet.

Perform another hot restart then tap the **Login** button. You'll see the Onboarding screen appear.

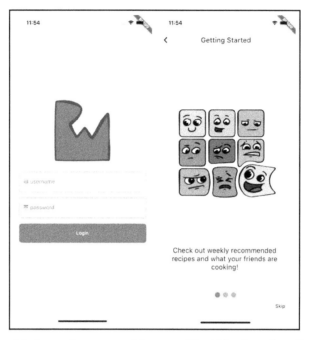

Congratulations, this is good progress. Now, you'll add logic to handle changes triggered within the Onboarding screen.

Handling the Skip and Back buttons in Onboarding

When the user taps the **Skip** button rather than going through the Onboarding guide, you want to show the usual home screen.

In **onboarding_screen.dart**, locate `// TODO: Onboarding -> Navigate to home` and replace it with the following:

```
Provider.of<AppStateManager>(context, listen: false)
    .completeOnboarding();
```

Here, tapping **Skip** triggers `completeOnboarding()`, which updates the state and indicates that the user completed onboarding. It's not working yet, so don't panic if you see an error.

Next, you want to deal with what happens when the user taps **Back** on the Onboarding screen.

Go back to **app_router.dart**, locate `TODO: Handle Onboarding and Splash` and replace it with the following:

```
if (route.settings.name == FooderlichPages.onboardingPath) {
  appStateManager.logout();
}
```

If the user taps the **Back** button from the Onboarding screen, it calls `logout()`. This resets the entire app state and the user has to log in again.

The app will return to the Splash screen to reinitialize, as shown below:

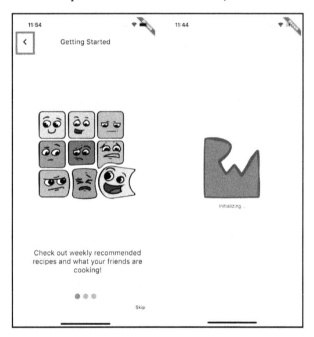

Transitioning from Onboarding to Home

When the user taps **Skip**, the app will show the Home screen. Open **lib/screens/home.dart** and add the following imports:

```
import 'package:provider/provider.dart';
import '../models/models.dart';
```

Next, locate `// TODO: Home MaterialPage Helper` and replace it with the following:

```
static MaterialPage page(int currentTab) {
  return MaterialPage(
      name: FooderlichPages.home,
      key: ValueKey(FooderlichPages.home),
      child: Home(
        currentTab: currentTab,
      ),
  );
}
```

Here, you've created a static `MaterialPage` helper with the current tab to display on the Home screen. Keep **home.dart** open.

Return to **app_router.dart**, locate `// TODO: Add Home` and replace it with the following:

```
if (appStateManager.isOnboardingComplete)
Home.page(appStateManager.getSelectedTab),
```

This tells your app to show the home page only when the user completes onboarding.

Finally, you can see the onboarding in action!

Hot restart, navigate to the Onboarding screen by tapping the **Login** button and then tap the **Skip** button. You'll now see the Home screen. Congratulations!

You'll notice that you can't switch to different tabs. That's because you haven't set up the state handling yet. You'll do that next.

Handling tab selection

Open **home.dart**, locate `// TODO: Wrap Consumer for AppStateManager` and replace it with the following:

```
return Consumer<AppStateManager>(
  builder: (context, appStateManager, child) {
```

Ignore any red squiggles for now.

Next, scroll down to the end of the widget and replace `// TODO: Add closing },);` with the following:

```
},);
```

Make sure you have auto-format turned on and save the file to reformat.

You've just wrapped your entire widget inside a `Consumer`. `Consumer` will listen for app state changes and rebuild its inner widget accordingly.

Next, locate `// TODO: Update user's selected tab` and replace it with the following:

```
Provider.of<AppStateManager>(context, listen: false)
    .goToTab(index);
```

Here, you specify that tapping a tab calls `goToTab()`.

Handling the Browse Recipes button

Now, you want to add that tapping the **Browse Recipes** button brings the user to the **Recipes** tab.

Open **empty_grocery_screen.dart** add the following imports:

```
import 'package:provider/provider.dart';
import '../models/models.dart';
```

Next, locate `// TODO: Update user's selected tab` and replace it with the following:

```
Provider.of<AppStateManager>(context, listen: false)
    .goToRecipes();
```

Here, you specify that tapping **Browse Recipes** calls `goToRecipes()`. This is similar to what you did for tabs.

To test it, tap the **To Buy** tab in the bottom navigation bar, then tap the **Browse Recipes** button. Notice that the app goes to the **Recipes** tab, as shown below:

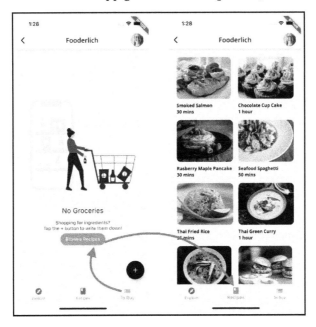

Showing the Grocery Item screen

Next, you'll connect the Grocery Item screen. Open **lib/screens/grocery_item_screen.dart**. Locate `// TODO: GroceryItemScreen MaterialPage Helper` and replace it with the following:

```
static MaterialPage page(
    {GroceryItem? item,
    int index = -1,
    required Function(GroceryItem) onCreate,
    required Function(GroceryItem, int) onUpdate,
    }) {
```

```
    return MaterialPage(
        name: FooderlichPages.groceryItemDetails,
        key: ValueKey(FooderlichPages.groceryItemDetails),
        child: GroceryItemScreen(
          originalItem: item,
          index: index,
          onCreate: onCreate,
          onUpdate: onUpdate,
        ),
    );
  }
```

Here, you create a static page helper that wraps `GroceryItemScreen` in a `MaterialPage`. The Grocery Item screen requires:

1. The original grocery item, if any. Otherwise, it assumes the user is creating a new grocery item.

2. The selected grocery item's index.

3. `onCreate` when the user finishes creating the new item.

4. `onUpdate` when the user finishes updating an item.

Next, you'll implement the Grocery Item screen. There are two ways to show it:

1. The user taps the + button to create a new grocery item.

2. The user taps an existing grocery item to edit it.

You'll enable these features next.

Creating a new grocery item

Open **lib/screens/grocery_screen.dart** and locate `// TODO: Create New Item`. Replace it with the following:

```
  Provider.of<GroceryManager>(context, listen:
  false).createNewItem();
```

Here, you trigger a call to `createNewItem()` when the user taps the + button.

Next, go back to **app_router.dart**, locate `// TODO: Create new item` and replace it with the following:

```
  // 1
  if (groceryManager.isCreatingNewItem)
  // 2
```

```
GroceryItemScreen.page(
  onCreate: (item) {
    // 3
    groceryManager.addItem(item);
  }, onUpdate: (item, index) {
    // 4 No update
  },
),
```

Here's how this lets you navigate to a new grocery item:

1. Checks if the user is creating a new grocery item.

2. If so, shows the Grocery Item screen.

3. Once the user saves the item, updates the grocery list.

4. onUpdate only gets called when the user updates an existing item.

With your app running, perform a hot restart. You'll now be able to create a new grocery item, as shown below:

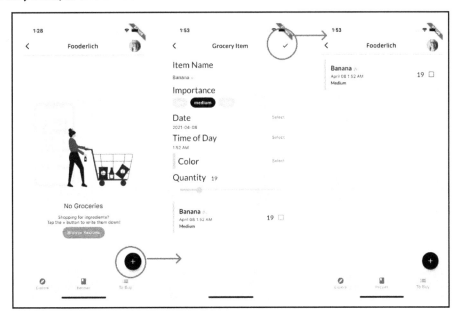

Editing an existing grocery item

Open **grocery_list_screen.dart**, locate `// TODO: Tap on grocery item` and replace it with the following:

```
manager.groceryItemTapped(index);
```

This fires `groceryItemTapped()` to let listeners know that the user selected a grocery item.

Now, return to **app_router.dart**, locate `// TODO: Select GroceryItemScreen` and replace with the following:

```
// 1
if (groceryManager.selectedIndex != -1)
  // 2
  GroceryItemScreen.page(
    item: groceryManager.selectedGroceryItem,
    index: groceryManager.selectedIndex,
    onUpdate: (item, index) {
      // 3
      groceryManager.updateItem(item, index);
    },
    onCreate: (_) {
      // 4 No create
    }
  ),
```

Here's how the code works:

1. Checks to see if a grocery item is selected.

2. If so, creates the Grocery Item screen page.

3. When the user changes and saves an item, it updates the item at the current index.

4. `onCreate` only gets called when the user adds a new item.

Now, you're able to tap on a grocery item, edit it and save it!

Dismissing the Grocery Item screen

Sometimes, a user starts to add a grocery item, then changes their mind. To cover this case, open **app_router.dart**, locate `// TODO: Handle state when user closes grocery item screen` and replace it with the following:

```
if (route.settings.name == FooderlichPages.groceryItemDetails) {
    groceryManager.groceryItemTapped(-1);
}
```

This ensures that the appropriate state is reset when the user taps the back button from the Grocery Item screen.

Hot restart and then test the sequence again:

1. Tap the + button to create a new grocery item.

2. From the To Buy screen tap on the new item to edit it.

3. Tap the < button to go back.

Notice that the app now works as expected.

Navigating to the Profile screen

The user can't navigate to the Profile screen yet. Before you can fix that, you need to handle the state changes.

Open **home.dart**, locate `// TODO: home -> profile` and replace it with the following:

```
Provider.of<ProfileManager>(context, listen: false)
  .tapOnProfile(true);
```

This triggers `tapOnProfile()` whenever the user taps the Profile button.

Now that the user can get to the Profile screen, they need to be able to close it again.

Open **lib/screens/profile_screen.dart**, locate `// TODO: Close Profile Screen` and replace it with the following:

```
Provider.of<ProfileManager>(context, listen: false)
  .tapOnProfile(false);
```

This handles the action that occurs when the user taps the **X** (close) button. It updates the profile state so the navigator removes the Profile screen.

Now, locate `// TODO: ProfileScreen MaterialPage Helper` and replace it with the following:

```
static MaterialPage page(User user) {
  return MaterialPage(
      name: FooderlichPages.profilePath,
      key: ValueKey(FooderlichPages.profilePath),
      child: ProfileScreen(user: user),
  );
}
```

Here, you create a helper `MaterialPage` for the Profile screen. It requires a user object.

Next, open **app_router.dart**, locate `// TODO: Add Profile Screen` and replace it with the following:

```
if (profileManager.didSelectUser)
  ProfileScreen.page(profileManager.getUser),
```

This checks the profile manager to see if the user selected their profile. If so, it shows the Profile screen.

Perform a hot reload and tap the user's avatar. It will now present the Profile screen:

Open **app_router.dart**, locate `// TODO: Handle state when user closes profile screen` and replace it with the following:

```
if (route.settings.name == FooderlichPages.profilePath) {
  profileManager.tapOnProfile(false);
}
```

This checks to see if the route you are popping is indeed the `profilePath`, then tells the `profileManager` that the Profile screen is not visible anymore.

Now tap the **X** button and the Profile screen will disappear.

Navigating to raywenderlich.com

Within the Profile screen, you can do three things:

1. Change the dark mode setting.

2. Visit raywenderlich.com.

3. Log out.

Next, you'll handle the WebView screen.

Transitioning from Profile to WebView

Return to **profile_screen.dart**, locate `// TODO: Open raywenderlich.com WebView` and replace it with the following:

```
Provider.of<ProfileManager>(context, listen: false)
  .tapOnRaywenderlich(true);
```

Here, you are saying to call `tapOnRaywenderlich()` when the user taps the corresponding button. This triggers a rebuild on your router widget and adds the WebView screen.

Now, open **webview_screen.dart** and import the following:

```
import '../models/models.dart';
```

Next, locate `// TODO: WebViewScreen MaterialPage Helper` and replace it with the following:

```
static MaterialPage page() {
  return MaterialPage(
      name: FooderlichPages.raywenderlich,
      key: ValueKey(FooderlichPages.raywenderlich),
      child: const WebViewScreen(),
  );
}
```

Here, you create a static `MaterialPage` that wraps a WebView screen widget.

Next, go back to **app_router.dart**. Locate `// TODO: Add WebView Screen` and replace it with the following:

```
if (profileManager.didTapOnRaywenderlich)
WebViewScreen.page(),
```

This checks if the user tapped the option to go to the raywenderlich.com website. If so, it presents the WebView screen.

Hot reload and go to the Profile screen. Now, tap **View raywenderlich.com** and you'll see it present in a web view, as shown below:

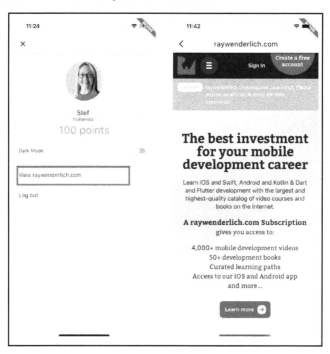

What about closing the view?

Still in **app_router.dart**, locate `// TODO: Handle state when user closes WebView screen` and replace it with the following:

```
if (route.settings.name == FooderlichPages.raywenderlich) {
  profileManager.tapOnRaywenderlich(false);
}
```

Here, you check if the name of the route setting is **raywenderlich**, then call the appropriate method on `profileManager`.

Next, you'll work on the log out functionality.

Logging out

To handle logging out the user, go to **profile_screen.dart** and locate `// TODO: Logout user`. Replace it with the following:

```
// 1
Provider.of<ProfileManager>(context, listen: false)
    .tapOnProfile(false);
// 2
Provider.of<AppStateManager>(context, listen: false).logout();
```

Here's what happens when the log out action triggers:

1. Sets the user profile tap state to **false**.

2. Calls `logout()`, which resets the entire app state.

Save your changes. Now, tap **Log out** from the Profile screen and you'll notice it goes
back to the Splash screen, as shown below:

Next, you'll address the Android system **Back** button.

Handling the Android system's Back button

If you have been running the project on iOS, stop the app on your existing device or simulator.Now, build and run your app on an **Android** device or emulator. Do the following tasks:

1. Navigate through the app to the **To Buy** tab.

2. Tap the + button.

3. Tap the Android system **Back** button, not the app's **Back** button.

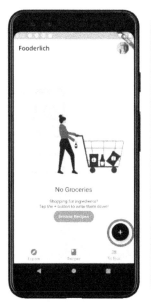 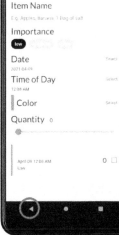 

Tap on + button   Tap on Android back button   Expect the previous screen but exit app

You expect it to go back to the previous page. Instead, it exits the entire app!

To fix this, open **main.dart**, locate `// TODO: Add backButtonDispatcher` and replace it with the following:

```
backButtonDispatcher: RootBackButtonDispatcher(),
```

Here, you set the router widget's `BackButtonDispatcher`, which listens to the platform pop route notifications. When the user taps the Android system **Back** button, it triggers the router delegate's `onPopPage` callback.

Hot restart your app and try the same steps again.

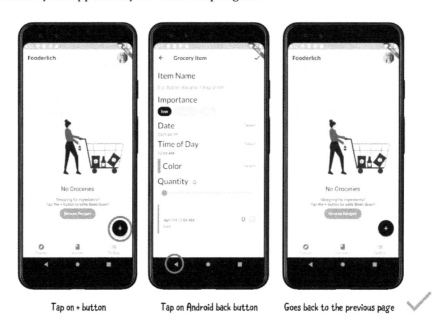

Tap on + button   Tap on Android back button   Goes back to the previous page

Woo-hoo, it behaves as expected! Congratulations, you've now completed the entire UI navigation flow.

Key points

- You can wrap another router in a **containing widget**.

- **Navigator 1.0** is useful for quick and simple prototypes, presenting alerts and dialogs.

- **Navigator 2.0** is useful when you need more control and organization when managing the navigation stack.

- In Navigator 2.0, the navigator widget holds a list of `MaterialPage` objects.

- Use a **router widget** to listen to navigation state changes and configure your navigator's list of pages.

- Setting the router's **Back** button dispatcher lets you listen to platform system events.

Where to go from here?

You've now learned how to navigate between screens the declarative way. Instead of calling `push()` and `pop()` in different widgets, you use multiple state managers to manage your state.

You also learned to create a router widget, which encapsulates and configures all the page routes for a navigator. Now, you can easily manage your navigation flow in a single router object!

To learn about this topic here are some recommendations for high-level theory and walk-throughs:

- To understand the motivation behind Navigator 2.0, check out the design document: https://bit.ly/3BcjjMU.

- Watch this Navigator 2.0 presentation by Chun-Heng Tai, who contributed to the declarative API: https://youtu.be/xFFQKvcad3s?t=3158.

- In this video, Simon Lightfoot walks you through a Navigator 2.0 example: https://www.youtube.com/watch?v=Y6kh5UonEZ0.

- Flutter Navigation 2.0 by Dominik Roszkowski goes through the differences between Navigator 1.0 and 2.0, including a video example: https://youtu.be/JmfYeF4gUu0?t=9728.

- For in-depth knowledge about Navigator, check out Flutter's documentation: https://api.flutter.dev/flutter/widgets/Navigator-class.html.

Other libraries to check out

Navigator 2.0 can be a little hard to understand and manage on its own. The packages below wrap around the Navigator 2.0 API to make routing and navigation easier:

- https://pub.dev/packages/beamer

- https://pub.dev/packages/flow_builder

- https://pub.dev/packages/fluro

- https://pub.dev/packages/vrouter

- https://pub.dev/packages/auto_route

There are so many more things you can do with Navigator 2.0. In the next chapter, you'll look at supporting web URLs and deep linking!

Chapter 8: Deep Links & Web URLs

By Vincent Ngo

Sometimes, opening your app and working through the navigation to get to a screen is just too much trouble for the user. Redirecting to a specific part of your app is a powerful marketing tool for user engagement. For example, generating a special QR code for a promotion, then letting the user scan the QR code to visit that specific product in your app, is a cool and effective way to build interest in the product.

In the last chapter, you learned how to use Navigator 2.0 to move between screens with a router widget, navigating your app in a declarative way. Now, you'll learn to use more features of Navigator 2.0. Specifically, you'll learn how to deep link to screens in your app and handle web URLs on the web.

For example, here's how **Fooderlich** will look in the Chrome web browser:

By the end of this chapter, you'll know how to:

- Parse URL strings and query parameters.

- Convert a URL to and from your app state.

- Support deep linking on iOS and Android.

- Support URL-driven navigation in the browser for Flutter web apps.

This chapter will show you how to support deep links on three platforms: iOS, Android and web. You'll be able to direct users to any screen of your choice.

> **Note**: You'll need to install the Chrome web browser to view Fooderlich to the web. If you don't have Chrome already, you can get it from https://www.google.com/chrome/. The Flutter web project can run on other browsers, but this chapter only covers testing and development on Chrome.

Understanding deep links

A **deep link** is a URL that navigates to a specific destination in your mobile app. You can think of deep links like a URL address you enter into a web browser to go to a specific page of a website rather than the home page.

Deep links help with user engagement and business marketing. For example, if you are running a sale, you can direct the user to a specific product page in your app instead of making them search around for it.

Imagine that Fooderlich has its own website. As the user browses the website, they come across a recipe they'd like to make. By using deep linking, you could let users click on the recipe to open the app directly on the **Grocery Item** screen and immediately start adding ingredients to their shopping list. This saves them time and makes the app more enjoyable.

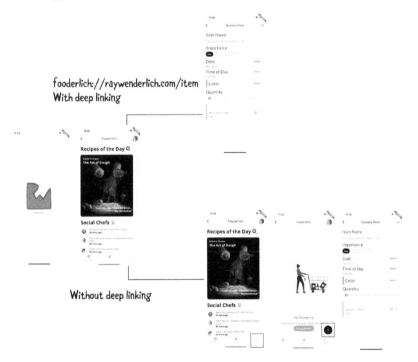

- With deep linking, Fooderlich is more automated. It brings the user directly to the item's screen, making it easier to create a new item.

- Without deep linking, it's more manual. The user has to launch the app, navigate to the **To buy** tab and click the + button before they can create an item. That takes three steps instead of one, and likely some head-scratching too!

Types of deep links

There are three types of deep links:

- **URI schemes**: An app's own URI scheme. **fooderlich://raywenderlich.com/home** is an example of Fooderlich's URI scheme. This form of deep link only works if the user has installed your app.

- **iOS Universal Links**: In the root of your web domain, you place a file that points to a specific app ID to know whether to open your app or to direct the user to the App Store. You must register that specific app ID with Apple to handle links from that domain.

- **Android App Links**: These are like iOS Universal Links, but for the Android platform. Android App Links take users to a link's specific content directly in your app. They leverage HTTP URLs and are associated with a website. For users that don't have your app installed, these links will go directly to the content of your website.

In this chapter, you'll only look at **URI Schemes**. For more information on how to set up iOS Universal Links and Android App Links, check out the following:

- **iOS Universal Links**:
  https://www.raywenderlich.com/6080-universal-links-make-the-connection.

- **Android App Links**:
  https://www.raywenderlich.com/18330247-deep-links-in-android-getting-started.

Getting started

> **Note**: We recommend that you use the starter project for this chapter rather than continuing with the project from the last chapter.

Open the starter project in Android Studio and run `flutter pub get`. Then, run the app on iOS or Android.

You'll see that the **Fooderlich** app shows the Login screen.

Soon, you'll be able to redirect the user to different parts of the app. But first, take a moment to review what's changed in the starter project since the last chapter.

Project files

Before you dive into parsing URLs, check out the new files in this starter project.

Screens folder

There's one change in **lib/screens/**:

- **profile_screen.dart**: Handles two different cases when the user opens raywenderlich.com.

- If the user is on mobile, it opens the website in a web view.

- If the user is on a web browser, it opens the website in a different tab.

Models folder

There's two new additions in **lib/models/**:

- **app_cache.dart**: Helps to cache user info, such as the user login and onboarding statuses. It checks the cache to see if the user needs to log in or complete the onboarding process.

- **app_state_manager.dart**: Depends on AppCache to check the user login and onboarding status. When the app calls initializeApp(), it checks the app cache to update the appropriate state.

New packages

There are two new packages in **pubspec.yaml**:

```
url_launcher: ^6.0.10
shared_preferences: ^2.0.7
```

Here's what each of them does:

- **url_launcher**: A cross-platform library to help launch a URL.

- **shared_preferences**: Wraps platform-specific persistent storage for simple data. AppCache uses this package to store the user login and onboarding state.

New Flutter web project

The starter project includes a pre-built Flutter web project.

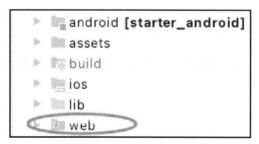

> **Note**: To speed things up, the web project is pre-built in your starter project. To learn how to create a Flutter web app, check out: https://bit.ly/3iBa5m9.

Setting up deep links

To enable deep linking on iOS and Android, you have to add some metadata tags in the respective platforms.

Setting up deep links on iOS

Open **ios/Runner/Info.plist**. You'll see some new key-value pairs, which enable deep linking for iOS:

```
<key>FlutterDeepLinkingEnabled</key>
<true/>
<key>CFBundleURLTypes</key>
<array>
  <dict>
  <key>CFBundleTypeRole</key>
  <string>Editor</string>
  <key>CFBundleURLName</key>
  <string>raywenderlich.com</string>
  <key>CFBundleURLSchemes</key>
  <array>
  <string>fooderlich</string>
  </array>
  </dict>
</array>
```

CFBundleURLName is a unique URL that distinguishes your app from others that use the same scheme. fooderlich is the name of the URL scheme you'll use later.

Setting up deep links on Android

Open **android/app/src/main/AndroidManifest.xml**. Here you'll also find two new definitions in the <data> tag:

```
<!-- Deep linking -->
<meta-data android:name="flutter_deeplinking_enabled"
android:value="true" />
<intent-filter>
<action android:name="android.intent.action.VIEW" />
<category android:name="android.intent.category.DEFAULT" />
<category android:name="android.intent.category.BROWSABLE" />
<data
  android:scheme="fooderlich"
  android:host="raywenderlich.com" />
</intent-filter>
```

Like iOS, you set the same values for scheme and host.

When you create a deep link for Fooderlich, the custom URL scheme looks like this:

```
fooderlich://raywenderlich.com/<path>
```

Now, for a quick overview of the URL paths you'll create.

Overview of Fooderlich's paths

You have many options when it comes to which of Fooderlich's various screens you can deep link to. Here are all the possible paths you can redirect your users to:

Path: /

The app initializes and checks the app cache to see if the user is logged in and has completed the onboarding guide.

- **/login**: Redirect to the Login screen if the user isn't logged in yet.

- **/onboarding**: Redirects to the Onboarding screen if the user hasn't completed the onboarding.

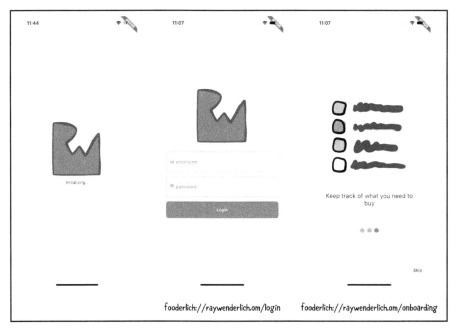

Path: /home?tab=[index]

The /home path redirects to the Home screen only if the user has logged in and completed onboarding. It contains one query parameter, tab, which directs to a tab index. As shown in the screenshots below, the tab index is 0, 1 or 2 respectively.

Path: /profile

If the user has logged in and completed onboarding, /profile will redirect to the Profile screen.

Path: /item?id=[uuid]

/item redirects to the Grocery Item screen. It contains one query parameter, id. There are two scenarios:

1. If query parameter id has a value, it will redirect to a specific item in the list.

2. If there is no query parameter, it shows an empty item screen for the user to create a new item.

You can see the result in the middle screenshot below.

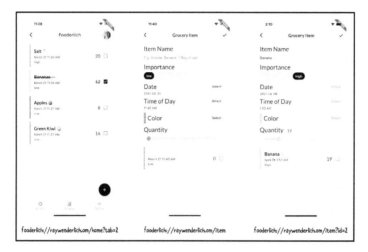

> **Note**: Keep in mind that these URL paths will work the same for both mobile and web apps.
>
> When you deep link on mobile, you'll use the following URI scheme:
>
> fooderlich://raywenderlich.com/
>
> On the web, the URI scheme is like any web browser URL:
>
> http://localhost:60738/#/

Before you start implementing deep links, take a moment for a quick Navigator 2.0 recap.

Recapping Navigator 2.0

In the last chapter, you learned how to set up four components: **RouterDelegate**, **Router**, **Navigator** and **BackButtonDispatcher**.

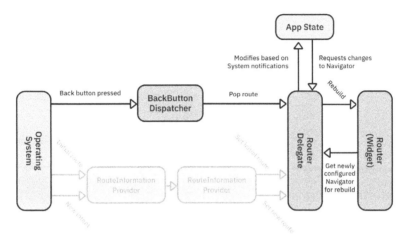

- **Router** is a widget that extends `RouterDelegate`. The router ensures that the messages are passed to `RouterDelegate`.

- **Navigator** defines a stack of `MaterialPages` in a declarative way. It also handles any `onPopPage` events.

- **BackButtonDispatcher** handles platform-specific system back button presses. It listens to requests by the OS and notifies the router delegate to pop a route.

The next two components you'll look at are **RouteInformationProvider** and **RouteInformationParser**.

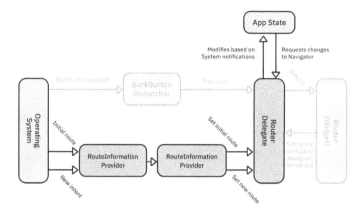

- **RouteInformationProvider**: Provides the route information to the router. It informs the router about the initial route and notifies the router of new intents. You don't have to create this class, the default implementation is usually all you need.

- **RouteInformationParser**: Gets the route string from `RouteInformationProvider`, then parses the URL string to a generic user-defined data type. This data type is a navigation configuration.

Deep links under the hood

For deep links to work, you need to do two key things: convert a URL to an app state and convert an app state to a URL. Next, you'll see both in detail.

Converting a URL to an app state

The first part of supporting deep links is to figure out which state of the app corresponds to a specific URL. Here's how the conversion happens:

1. The user enters a new URL triggered by a deep link or by changing the URL in the web browser's address bar.

2. Within `RouteInformationParser`, `parseRouteInformation()` converts the URL string into a user-defined data type. This is called the **navigation state**. This data type includes the path and the query parameters. You'll build this soon.

3. The router then calls `setNewRoutePath()`, which converts your navigation state into an app state. It will then use the current app state to configure the navigator stack.

Converting the app state to a URL string

When the user taps a button or the app state changes, you need to change the current URL. Here's what happens when you set up your app to handle URLs:

1. The router calls `routerDelegate`'s `notifyListeners()` to let Flutter know that it needs to update the current URL.

2. It uses `currentConfiguration()` to convert your app state back to a navigation state.

3. `restoreRouteInformation()` then converts your navigation state into a URL string. On a Flutter web app, this updates the URL bar's address.

> **Note**: As you recall, navigation state is just a user-defined data type. It converts a URL string into a proper data type. This object holds information about your navigation, including:
>
> • The URL path or location.
>
> • The query parameters.

In the next section, `AppLink` is the data type that encapsulates the URL string.

Enough theory, it's time to get started!

Creating a navigation state object

`AppLink` is the intermediary object between a URL string and your app state. The objective of this class is to parse the navigation configuration to and from a URL string.

In **lib/navigation**, create a new file called **app_link.dart** and add the following:

```
class AppLink {
  // 1
  static const String kHomePath = '/home';
  static const String kOnboardingPath = '/onboarding';
```

```
    static const String kLoginPath = '/login';
    static const String kProfilePath = '/profile';
    static const String kItemPath = '/item';
    // 2
    static const String kTabParam = 'tab';
    static const String kIdParam = 'id';
    // 3
    String? location;
    // 4
    int? currentTab;
    // 5
    String? itemId;
    // 6
    AppLink({
      this.location,
      this.currentTab,
      this.itemId,
    });

  // TODO: Add fromLocation

  // TODO: Add toLocation

  }
```

AppLink is your navigation state object. Take a moment to understand the properties you added. In the code above, you:

1. Create constants for each URL path.

2. Create constants for each of the query parameters you'll support.

3. Store the path of the URL using location.

4. Use currentTab to store the tab you want to redirect the user to.

5. Store the ID of the item you want to view in itemId.

6. Initialize the app link with the location and the two query parameters.

Converting a URL string to an AppLink

AppLink is an object that helps store the route information. It helps to parse the URL string to a route and vice versa, converting the route information back to a URL string. It essentially encapsulates all the logic that transforms a simple string into a state and back.

Next locate // TODO: Add fromLocation and add the following:

```
static AppLink fromLocation(String? location) {
    // 1
    location = Uri.decodeFull(location ?? '');
    // 2
    final uri = Uri.parse(location);
    final params = uri.queryParameters;

    // 3
    final currentTab = int.tryParse(params[AppLink.kTabParam] ??
'');
    // 4
    final itemId = params[AppLink.kIdParam];
    // 5
    final link = AppLink(
      location: uri.path,
      currentTab: currentTab,
      itemId: itemId,
    );
    // 6
    return link;
}
```

fromLocation() converts a URL string to an AppLink:

1. First, you need to decode the URL. URLs often include special characters in their paths, so you need to **percent-encode** the URL path. For example, you'd encode hello!world to hello%21world.

2. Parse the URI for query parameter keys and key-value pairs.

3. Extract the currentTab from the URL path if it exists.

4. Extract the itemId from the URL path if it exists.

5. Create the AppLink by passing in the query parameters you extract from the URL string.

6. Return the instance of AppLink.

Converting an AppLink to a URL string

The app will also need the converse transformation, from AppLink to simple string.

Locate `// TODO: Add toLocation` and add the following:

```
String toLocation() {
  // 1
  String addKeyValPair({
    required String key,
    String? value,
  }) =>
      value == null ? '' : '${key}=$value&';
  // 2
  switch (location) {
    // 3
    case kLoginPath:
      return kLoginPath;
    // 4
    case kOnboardingPath:
      return kOnboardingPath;
    // 5
    case kProfilePath:
      return kProfilePath;
    // 6
    case kItemPath:
      var loc = '$kItemPath?';
      loc += addKeyValPair(
        key: kIdParam,
        value: itemId,
      );
      return Uri.encodeFull(loc);
    // 7
    default:
      var loc = '$kHomePath?';
      loc += addKeyValPair(
        key: kTabParam,
        value: currentTab.toString(),
      );
      return Uri.encodeFull(loc);
  }
}
```

This converts `AppLink` back to a URI string. Here's how it works. You:

1. Create an internal function that formats the query parameter key-value pair into a string format.

2. Go through each defined path.

3. If the path is `kLoginPath`, return the right string path: `/login`.

4. If the path is `kOnboardingPath`, return the right string path: `/onboarding`.

5. If the path is `kProfilePath`, return the right string path: `/profile`.

6. If the path is `kItemPath`, return the right string path: `/item`, and if there are any parameters, append `?id=${id}`.

7. If the path is invalid, default to the path `/home`. If the user selected a tab, append `?tab=${tabIndex}`.

Next, you'll use `RouteInformationParser` to parse route information into `AppLink`.

Creating a route information parser

In the **navigation** directory, create a new file called **app_route_parser.dart** and add the following:

```
import 'package:flutter/material.dart';

import 'app_link.dart';

// 1
class AppRouteParser extends RouteInformationParser<AppLink> {
  // 2
  @override
  Future<AppLink> parseRouteInformation(
      RouteInformation routeInformation) async {
    // 3
    final link =
AppLink.fromLocation(routeInformation.location);
    return link;
  }

  // 4
  @override
  RouteInformation restoreRouteInformation(AppLink appLink) {
    // 5
    final location = appLink.toLocation();
    // 6
```

```
        return RouteInformation(location: location);
    }
}
```

Here's how the code works:

1. `AppRouteParser` extends `RouteInformationParser`. Notice it takes a generic type. In this case, your type is `AppLink`, which holds all the route and navigation information.

2. The first method you need to override is `parseRouteInformation()`. The route information contains the URL string.

3. Take the route information and build an instance of `AppLink` from it.

4. The second method you need to override is `restoreRouteInformation()`.

5. This function passes in an `AppLink` object. You ask `AppLink` to give you back the URL string.

6. You wrap it in `RouteInformation` to pass it along.

Connecting the parser to the app router

Now that you've set up your `RouteInformationParser`, it's time to connect it to your router delegate.

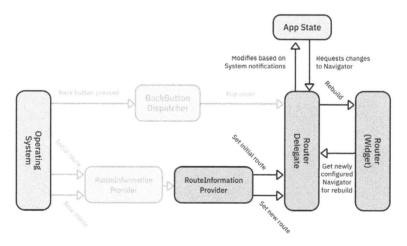

Open **lib/main.dart**, locate `// TODO: Initialize RouteInformationParser` and replace it with the following:

```
final routeParser = AppRouteParser();
```

Here, you initialize your app route parser. If it didn't auto-import, be sure to add the following to the top:

```
import 'navigation/app_route_parser.dart';
```

Next, locate `// TODO: Replace with Material.router` and replace the whole `return` statement below it with the following:

```
return MaterialApp.router(
  theme: theme,
  title: 'Fooderlich',
  backButtonDispatcher: RootBackButtonDispatcher(),
  // 1
  routeInformationParser: routeParser,
  // 2
  routerDelegate: _appRouter,
);
```

You've created a `MaterialApp` that initializes an internal router. Here's what it does:

1. Set `routeParser`. Remember that the route information parser's job is to convert the app state to and from a URL string.

2. `routerDelegate` helps construct the stack of pages that represents your app state.

At this point, you might see some red squiggles or errors in the simulator. You'll fix them soon.

Converting a URL to an app state

When the user enters a new URL on the web or triggers a deep link on mobile, RouteInformationProvider notifies RouteInformationParser that there's a new route, as shown below:

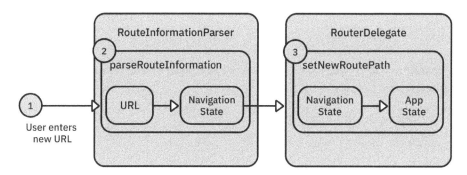

Here is the process that goes from a URL to an app state:

1. The user enters a new URL in the web browser's address bar.

2. RouteInformationParser parses the new route into your navigation state, an instance of AppLink.

3. Based on the navigation state, RouterDelegate updates the app state to reflect the new changes.

Configuring navigation

Quick theory test: Where's the logic that maps a specific URL path to a specific screen? It's in setNewRoutePath()!

Open **lib/navigation/app_router.dart**, locate // TODO: Add <AppLink> and replace it and the space just before it with the following:

```
<AppLink>
```

Remember that AppLink encapsulates all the route information. The code above sets the RouterDelegate's user-defined data type to AppLink.

If the imports aren't already added at the top, add the following:

```
import 'app_link.dart';
```

Next, locate `// TODO: Replace` `setNewRoutePath` and replace the comment and
the code below with the following:

```
// 1
@override
Future<void> setNewRoutePath(AppLink newLink) async {
  // 2
  switch (newLink.location) {
    // 3
    case AppLink.kProfilePath:
      profileManager.tapOnProfile(true);
      break;
    // 4
    case AppLink.kItemPath:
      // 5
      final itemId = newLink.itemId;
      if (itemId != null) {
        groceryManager.setSelectedGroceryItem(itemId);
      } else {
        // 6
        groceryManager.createNewItem();
      }
      // 7
      profileManager.tapOnProfile(false);
      break;
    // 8
    case AppLink.kHomePath:
      // 9
      appStateManager.goToTab(newLink.currentTab ?? 0);
      // 10
      profileManager.tapOnProfile(false);
      groceryManager.groceryItemTapped(-1);
      break;
    // 11
    default:
      break;
  }
}
```

Here's how you convert your app link to an app state:

1. You call `setNewRoutePath()` when a new route is pushed. It passes along an
   `AppLink`. This is your navigation configuration.

2. Use a `switch` to check every location.

3. If the new location is `/profile`, show the Profile screen.

4. Check if the new location starts with `/item`.

5. If `itemId` is not null, set the selected grocery item and show the Grocery Item screen.

6. If `itemId` is null, show an empty Grocery Item screen.

7. Hide the Profile screen.

8. If the new location is `/home`.

9. Set the currently selected tab.

10. Make sure the Profile screen and Grocery Item screen are hidden.

11. If the location does not exist, do nothing.

Converting the app state to a URL

At this point, you've converted a URL to an app state. Next, you need to do the opposite. When the user taps a button or navigates to another screen, you need to convert the app state back to a URL string. For the web app, this will synchronize the browser's address bar.

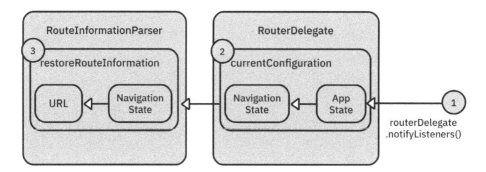

1. When the user presses a button or modifies a state, `notifyListeners()` fires.

2. `RouteInformationParser` asks for the current navigation configuration, so you must convert your app state to an `AppLink`.

3. `RouteInformationParser` then calls `restoreRouteInformation` and converts `AppLink` to a URL string.

Still in **lib/navigation/app_router.dart**, locate `// TODO: Convert app state to applink` and replace it with the following:

```
AppLink getCurrentPath() {
  // 1
  if (!appStateManager.isLoggedIn) {
    return AppLink(location: AppLink.kLoginPath);
  // 2
  } else if (!appStateManager.isOnboardingComplete) {
    return AppLink(location: AppLink.kOnboardingPath);
  // 3
  } else if (profileManager.didSelectUser) {
    return AppLink(location: AppLink.kProfilePath);
  // 4
  } else if (groceryManager.isCreatingNewItem) {
    return AppLink(location: AppLink.kItemPath);
  // 5
  } else if (groceryManager.selectedGroceryItem != null) {
    final id = groceryManager.selectedGroceryItem?.id;
    return AppLink(location: AppLink.kItemPath, itemId: id);
  // 6
  } else {
    return AppLink(
        location: AppLink.kHomePath,
        currentTab: appStateManager.getSelectedTab);
  }
}
```

This is a helper function that converts the app state to an `AppLink` object. Here's how it works:

1. If the user hasn't logged in, return the app link with the login path.

2. If the user hasn't completed onboarding, return the app link with the onboarding path.

3. If the user taps the profile, return the app link with the profile path.

4. If the user taps the + button to create a new grocery item, return the app link with the item path.

5. If the user selected an existing item, return an app link with the item path and the item's `id`.

6. If none of the conditions are met, default by returning to the home path with the selected tab.

Next, locate `// TODO: Apply configuration helper` and replace it with the following:

```
@override
AppLink get currentConfiguration => getCurrentPath();
```

Accessing `currentConfiguration` calls the helper, `getCurrentPath()`, which checks the app state and returns the right app link configuration.

Congratulations, you've now set everything up! Now, you get to see your work in action.

> **Note**: This may seem like a lot of boilerplate code to maintain the mapping between state and routes. There are other navigator 2.0 packages that try to address this problem. You may check out:
>
> • https://pub.dev/packages/auto_route
>
> • https://pub.dev/packages/fluro
>
> • https://pub.dev/packages/beamer

Testing deep links

For your next step, you'll test how deep linking works on iOS, Android and the web.

Testing deep links on iOS

In Android Studio, select an iOS device and press the **Run** button:

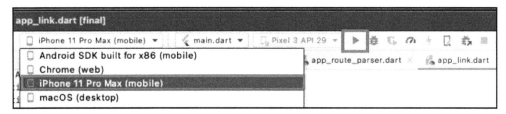

Once the simulator is running, log in and complete the onboarding, as shown below:

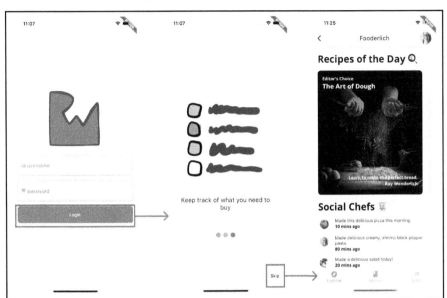

Deep linking to the Home screen

Enter the following in your terminal:

```
xcrun simctl openurl booted 'fooderlich://raywenderlich.com/
home?tab=1'
```

> **Note**: Entering it in Android Studio's terminal may cause a popup to appear on the simulator. If so, allow it to proceed.

In the simulator, this automatically switches to Fooderlich's second tab, as shown below:

Deep linking to the Profile screen

Next, run the following command:

```
xcrun simctl openurl booted 'fooderlich://raywenderlich.com/
profile'
```

This opens the Profile screen, as shown below:

Deep linking to create a new item

Next, run the following command:

```
xcrun simctl openurl booted 'fooderlich://raywenderlich.com/
item'
```

The Grocery Item screen will now show:

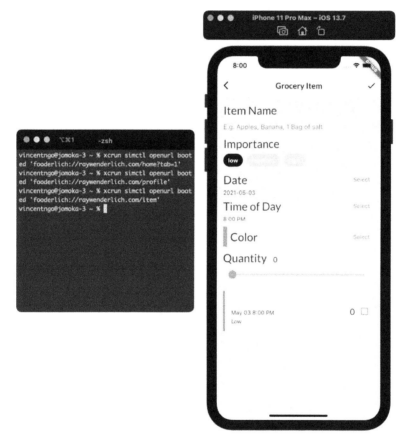

Following this pattern, you can build paths to any location in your app!

Resetting the cache in the iOS simulator

Recall that `AppStateManager` checks with `AppCache` to see whether the user is logged in or has onboarded. If you want to reset the cache to see the Login screen again, you have two options:

1. Go to the Profile view and tap **Log out**. This invalidates the app cache.

2. If you are running on an iOS simulator, you can select **Erase All Content and Settings...** to clear the cache.

> **Note**: This will delete any other apps that you have on the simulator.

Testing deep links on Android

Stop running on iOS. Open Android Studio, select an Android device and click the **Play** button:

Once the simulator or device is running, log in and complete the onboarding process, as shown below:

Deep linking to the Home screen

Enter the following in your terminal:

```
~/Library/Android/sdk/platform-tools/adb shell am start -a
android.intent.action.VIEW \
    -c android.intent.category.BROWSABLE \
    -d 'fooderlich://raywenderlich.com/home?tab=1'
```

> **Note**: If you receive a message in Terminal like: `Warning: Activity not started, intent has been delivered to currently running top-most instance`, just ignore it. It only means that the app is already running.
>
> The full path is listed to ensure that if you don't have adb in your $PATH, you can still execute this command. The \ at the end of each line is to nicely format the script across multiple lines.

This directs to the second tab of Fooderlich, as shown below:

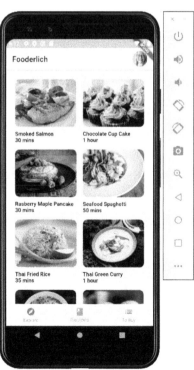

Deep linking to the Profile screen

Next, run the following command:

```
~/Library/Android/sdk/platform-tools/adb shell am start -a
android.intent.action.VIEW \
    -c android.intent.category.BROWSABLE \
    -d 'fooderlich://raywenderlich.com/profile'
```

This opens the Profile screen, as shown below:

Deep linking to Create New Item

Next, run the following command:

```
~/Library/Android/sdk/platform-tools/adb shell am start -a
android.intent.action.VIEW \
    -c android.intent.category.BROWSABLE \
    -d 'fooderlich://raywenderlich.com/item'
```

The Grocery Item screen will appear, as shown below:

Resetting the cache in Android

If you need to reset your user cache, here's what you do:

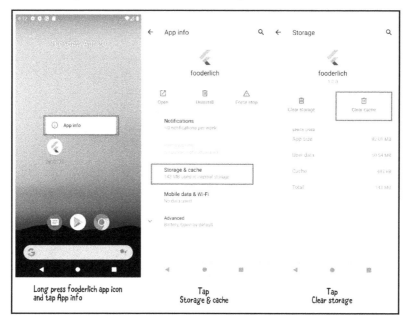

1. Long-press the Fooderlich app icon, then tap **App info**.

2. Next, tap **Storage & cache**.

3. Finally, tap **Clear cache**. This will wipe your cache.

Now, it's time to test how Fooderlich handles URLs on the web.

Running the web app

Note: As of **Flutter v2.5** when you run Flutter Web you may see a scroll controller exception. As shown below:

```
The provided ScrollController is currently attached to more than
one ScrollPosition.
```

This is a false exception and the web app will still work. If you want the exception to go away you can set a scroll controller on each scrollable widget. Track the issue here: https://github.com/flutter/flutter/issues/89864

Stop running on Android. In Android Studio, select **Chrome (web)** and click the **Run** button:

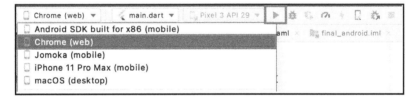

Note: Your data won't persist between app launches. That's because Flutter web runs the equivalent of incognito mode during development.

If you build and release your Flutter web app, it will work as expected. For more information on how to build for release, check:

https://flutter.dev/docs/deployment/web#building-the-app-for-release.

Go through the Fooderlich UI flow and you'll see that the web browser's address bar changes:

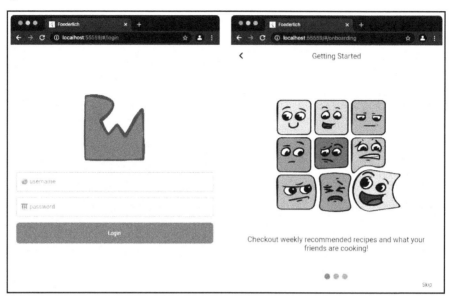

If you change the tab query parameter's value to **0**, **1** or **2**, the app will automatically switch to that tab.

Next, note that tapping the + button opens the grocery item.

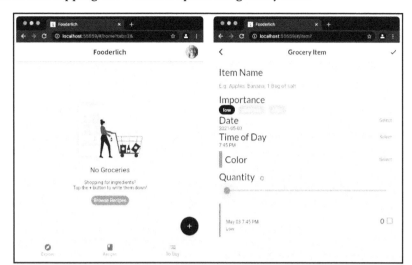

One cool thing to notice is that the app stores the entire browser history.

Tap the **Back** and **Forward** buttons and the app will restore that state! How cool is that? Another thing you can do is long-press the **Back** button to jump to a specific state in the browser history.

Congratulations on learning how to work with deep links in your Flutter app!

Key points

- The app notifies `RouteInformationProvider` when there's a new route.

- The provider passes the route information to `RouteInformationParser` to parse the URL string.

- The parser converts app state to and from a URL string.

- `AppLink` models the navigation state. It is a user-defined data type that encapsulates information about a URL string.

- In development mode, the Flutter web app does not persist data between app launches. The web app generated in release mode will work on the other browsers.

Where to go from here?

If you're curious about how to remove the # symbol from a URL in the web app, check out: https://flutter.dev/docs/development/ui/navigation/url-strategies.

Look at how gSkinner's **flutter-folio** app handles navigation. The idea of an app link came from this sample project. Check out their example here: https://github.com/gskinnerTeam/flutter-folio.

You can see examples of two different types of web renderers here: https://flutter.dev/docs/development/tools/web-renderers.

You learned how to extend Navigator 2.0 to support deep links and to synchronize a web browser's URL address bar. This helps bring users to specific destinations within your app, building better user engagement!

Being able to manage your navigation state for multiple platforms is truly amazing!

Section IV: Networking, Persistence and State

Most apps interact with the network to retrieve data and then persist that data locally in some form of cache, such as a database. In this section, you'll build a new app that lets you search the Internet for recipes, bookmark recipes, and save their ingredients into a shopping list.

You'll learn about making network requests, parsing the network JSON response, and saving data in a SQLite database. You'll also get an introduction to using Dart streams.

Finally, this section will also dive deeper into the important topic of app state, which determines where and how your user interface stores and refreshes data in the user interface as a user interacts with your app.

Chapter 9: Shared Preferences

By Kevin David Moore

Picture this: You're browsing recipes and find one you like. You're in a hurry and want to bookmark it to check it later. Can you build a Flutter app that does that? You sure can! Read on to find out how.

In this chapter, your goal is to learn how to use the **shared_preferences** plugin to save important pieces of information to your device.

You'll start with a new project that shows three tabs at the bottom of the screen for three different views: Recipes, Bookmarks and Groceries.

The first screen is where you'll search for recipes you want to prepare. Once you find a recipe you like, just bookmark it and the app will add the recipe to your **Bookmarks** page and also add all the ingredients you need to your shopping list. You'll use a web API to search for recipes and store the ones you bookmark in a local database.

The completed app will look something like:

This shows the **Recipes** tab with the results you get when searching for **Pasta**. It's as easy as typing in the search text field and pressing the **Search** icon. The app stores your search term history in the combo box to the right of the text field.

When you tap a card, you'll see something like:

To save a recipe, just tap the **Bookmark** button. When you navigate to the **Bookmarks** tab, you'll see that the recipe has been saved:

If you don't want the recipe anymore, swipe left or right and you'll see a delete button that allows you to remove it from the list of bookmarked recipes.

The **Groceries** tab shows the ingredients you need to make the recipes you've bookmarked.

You'll build this app over the next few chapters. In this chapter, you'll use shared preferences to save simple data like the selected tab and also to cache the searched items in the Recipes tab.

By the end of the chapter, you'll know:

- What shared preferences are.

- How to use the shared_preferences plugin to save and retrieve objects.

Now that you know what your goal is, it's time to jump in!

Getting started

Open the **starter** project for this chapter in Android Studio, run `flutter pub get`, then run the app.

Notice the three tabs at the bottom — each will show a different screen when you tap it. Only the Recipes screen currently shows any UI. It looks like this:

App libraries

The starter project includes the following libraries in **pubspec.yaml**:

```
dependencies:
  ...
  cached_network_image: ^3.1.0
  flutter_slidable: ^0.6.0
  flutter_svg: ^0.22.0
```

Here's what they help you do:

- **cached_network_image**: Download and cache the images you'll use in the app.

- **flutter_slidable**: Build a widget that lets the user slide a card left and right to perform different actions, like deleting a saved recipe.

- **flutter_svg**: Load SVG images without the need to use a program to convert them to vector files.

Now that you've had a look at the libraries, take a moment to think about how you save data before you begin coding your app.

Saving data

There are three primary ways to save data to your device:

1. Write formatted data, like JSON, to a file.

2. Use a library or plugin to write simple data to a shared location.

3. Use a SQLite database.

Writing data to a file is simple, but it requires you to handle reading and writing data in the correct format and order.

You can also use a library or plugin to write simple data to a shared location managed by the platform, like iOS and Android. This is what you'll do in this chapter.

For more complex data, you can save the information to a local database. You'll learn more about that in Chapter 15, "Saving Data With SQLite".

Why save small bits of data?

There are many reasons to save small bits of data. For example, you could save the user ID when the user has logged in — or if the user has logged in at all. You could also save the onboarding state or data that the user has bookmarked to consult later.

Note that this simple data saved to a shared location is lost when the user uninstalls the app.

The shared_preferences plugin

shared_preferences is a Flutter plugin that allows you to save data in a key-value format so you can easily retrieve it later. Behind the scenes, it uses the aptly named **SharedPreferences** on Android and the similar **UserDefaults** on iOS.

For this app, you'll learn to use the plugin by saving the search terms the user entered as well as the tab that's currently selected.

One of the great things about this plugin is that it doesn't require any setup or configuration. Just create an instance of the plugin and you're ready to fetch and save data.

> **Note**: The shared_preferences plugin gives you a quick way to persist and retrieve data, but it only supports saving simple properties like strings, numbers, and boolean values.
>
> In later chapters, you'll learn about alternatives that you can use when you want to save complex data.
>
> Be aware that shared_preferences is not a good fit to store sensitive data. To store passwords or access tokens, check out the Android Keystore for Android and Keychain Services for iOS, or consider using the **flutter_secure_storage** plugin.

To use shared_preferences, you need to first add it as a dependency. Open **pubspec.yaml** and, underneath the `flutter_svg` library, add:

```
shared_preferences: ^2.0.7
```

Make sure you indent it the same as the other libraries.

Now, click the **Pub Get** button to get the shared_preferences library.

You can also run pub get from the command line:

```
flutter pub get
```

You're now ready to store data. You'll start by saving the searches the user makes so they can easily select them again in the future.

Saving UI states

You'll use shared_preferences to save a list of saved searches in this section. Later, you'll also save the tab that the user has selected so the app always opens to that tab.

You'll start by preparing your search to store that information.

Adding an entry to the search list

First, you'll change the UI so that when the user presses the search icon, the app will add the search entry to the search list.

Open **ui/recipes/recipe_list.dart**, locate // TODO: Add imports and replace it with:

```
import 'package:shared_preferences/shared_preferences.dart';
import '../widgets/custom_dropdown.dart';
import '../colors.dart';
```

That imports the shared_preferences plugin, a custom widget to display a drop-down menu and a helper class to set colors.

Next, you'll give each search term a unique key. Find // TODO: Add key and replace it with:

```
static const String prefSearchKey = 'previousSearches';
```

All preferences need to use a unique key or they'll be overwritten. Here, you're simply defining a constant for the preference key.

Next, replace `// TODO: Add searches array` with

```
List<String> previousSearches = <String>[];
```

This clears the way for you to save the user's previous searches and keep track of the current search.

Running code in the background

To understand the code you'll add next, you need to know a bit about running code in the background.

Most modern UI toolkits have a main thread that runs the UI code. Any code that takes a long time needs to run on a different thread or process so it doesn't block the UI. Dart uses a technique similar to JavaScript to achieve this. The language includes these two keywords:

- `async`
- `await`

`async` marks a method or code section as **asynchronous**. You then use the `await` keyword inside that method to wait until an asynchronous process finishes in the background.

Dart also has a class named Future, which indicates that the method promises a future result. SharedPreferences.getInstance() returns Future<SharedPreferences>, which you use to retrieve an instance of the SharedPreferences class. You'll see that in action next.

Saving previous searches

Now that you've laid some groundwork, you're ready to implement saving the searches.

Still in **recipe_list.dart**, find // TODO: Add savePreviousSearches and replace it with:

```
void savePreviousSearches() async {
  // 1
  final prefs = await SharedPreferences.getInstance();
  // 2
  prefs.setStringList(prefSearchKey, previousSearches);
}
```

Here, you use the async keyword to indicate that this method will run asynchronously. It also:

1. Uses the await keyword to wait for an instance of SharedPreferences.

2. Saves the list of previous searches using the prefSearchKey key.

Next, add the following method:

```
void getPreviousSearches() async {
  // 1
  final prefs = await SharedPreferences.getInstance();
  // 2
  if (prefs.containsKey(prefSearchKey)) {
    // 3
    final searches = prefs.getStringList(prefSearchKey);
    // 4
    if (searches != null) {
      previousSearches = searches;
    } else {
      previousSearches = <String>[];
    }
  }
}
```

This method is also asynchronous. Here, you:

1. Use the `await` keyword to wait for an instance of `SharedPreferences`.

2. Check if a preference for your saved list already exists.

3. Get the list of previous searches.

4. If the list is not `null`, set the previous searches, otherwise initialize an empty list.

Finally, find `// TODO: Call getPreviousSearches` and substitute it with:

```
getPreviousSearches();
```

This loads any previous searches when the user restarts the app.

Adding the search functionality

To perform a search, you need to clear any of your variables and save the new search value. This method will not do an actual search just yet. Do this by replacing `// TODO: Add startSearch` with:

```
void startSearch(String value) {
  // 1
  setState(() {
    // 2
    currentSearchList.clear();
    currentCount = 0;
    currentEndPosition = pageCount;
    currentStartPosition = 0;
    hasMore = true;
    value = value.trim();

    // 3
    if (!previousSearches.contains(value)) {
      // 4
      previousSearches.add(value);
      // 5
      savePreviousSearches();
    }
  });
}
```

In this method, you:

1. Tell the system to redraw the widgets by calling `setState()`.

2. Clear the current search list and reset the count, start and end positions.

3. Check to make sure the search text hasn't already been added to the previous search list.

4. Add the search item to the previous search list.

5. Save the new list of previous searches.

Adding a search button

Next, you'll add a search button that saves terms each time the user performs a search.

In _buildSearchCard(), replace the const Icon(Icons.search), with the following:

```
IconButton(
  icon: const Icon(Icons.search),
  // 1
  onPressed: () {
    // 2
    startSearch(searchTextController.text);
    // 3
    final currentFocus = FocusScope.of(context);
    if (!currentFocus.hasPrimaryFocus) {
      currentFocus.unfocus();
    }
  },
),
```

This replaces the icon with an IconButton that the user can tap to perform a search.

1. Add onPressed to handle the tap event.

2. Use the current search text to start a search.

3. Hide the keyboard by using the FocusScope class.

Next, replace everything in between // *** Start Replace and // *** End Replace with:

```
Expanded(
  child: Row(
    children: <Widget>[
      Expanded(
        // 3
        child: TextField(
          decoration: const InputDecoration(
            border: InputBorder.none, hintText: 'Search'),
          autofocus: false,
```

```
      // 4
      textInputAction: TextInputAction.done,
      // 5
      onSubmitted: (value) {
        if (!previousSearches.contains(value)) {
          previousSearches.add(value);
          savePreviousSearches();
        }
      },
      controller: searchTextController,
    )),
    // 6
    PopupMenuButton<String>(
      icon: const Icon(
        Icons.arrow_drop_down,
        color: lightGrey,
      ),
      // 7
      onSelected: (String value) {
        searchTextController.text = value;
        startSearch(searchTextController.text);
      },
      itemBuilder: (BuildContext context) {
        // 8
        return previousSearches
            .map<CustomDropdownMenuItem<String>>((String
value) {
          return CustomDropdownMenuItem<String>(
            text: value,
            value: value,
            callback: () {
              setState(() {
                // 9
                previousSearches.remove(value);
                Navigator.pop(context);
              });
            },
          );
        }).toList();
      },
    ),
  ],
),
),
```

In this code, you:

3. Add a `TextField` to enter your search queries.

4. Set the keyboard action to `TextInputAction.done`. This closes the keyboard when the user presses the **Done** button.

5. Save the search when the user finishes entering text.

6. Create a `PopupMenuButton` to show previous searches.

7. When the user selects an item from previous searches, start a new search.

8. Build a list of custom drop-down menus (see **widgets/custom_dropdown.dart**) to display previous searches.

9. If the **X** icon is pressed, remove the search from the previous searches and close the pop-up menu.

To show the list of previous text searches, you used a text field with a drop-down menu. That is a row with a `TextField` and a `Customdrop-downMenuItem`. The menu item shows the search term and an icon on the right. It will look something like:

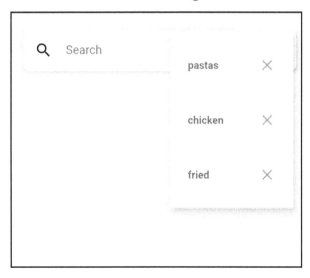

Clicking the **X** will delete the corresponding entry from the list.

Test the app

It's time to test the app. Because you added a new dependency, quit the running instance and run it again (Note that you do not always need to restart when adding dependencies). You'll see something like this:

The PopupMenuButton displays a menu when tapped and calls the method onSelected() when the user selects a menu item.

Enter a food item like **pastas** and make sure that, when you hit the search button, the app adds your search entry to the drop-down list.

Don't worry about the progress circle running — that happens when there's no data. Your app should look like this when you tap the drop-down arrow:

Now, stop the app by tapping the red stop button.

Run the app again and tap the drop-down button. The pastas entry is there. It's time to celebrate :]

The next step is to use the same approach to save the selected tab.

Saving the selected tab

In this section, you'll use shared_preferences to save the current UI tab that the user has navigated to.

Open **main_screen.dart** and add the following import:

```
import 'package:shared_preferences/shared_preferences.dart';
```

Next, replace `// TODO: Add index` key with:

```
static const String prefSelectedIndexKey = 'selectedIndex';
```

That is the constant you will use for the selected index preference key.

Next, add this new method:

```
void saveCurrentIndex() async {
  // 1
  final prefs = await SharedPreferences.getInstance();
  // 2
  prefs.setInt(prefSelectedIndexKey, _selectedIndex);
}
```

Here, you:

1. Use the `await` keyword to wait for an instance of the shared preference plugin.

2. Save the selected index as an integer.

Now, add this method:

```
void getCurrentIndex() async {
  // 1
  final prefs = await SharedPreferences.getInstance();
  // 2
  if (prefs.containsKey(prefSelectedIndexKey)) {
    // 3
    setState(() {
      final index = prefs.getInt(prefSelectedIndexKey);
      if (index != null) {
        _selectedIndex = index;
      }
    });
  }
}
```

With this code, you:

1. Use the `await` keyword to wait for an instance of the shared preference plugin.

2. Check if a preference for your current index already exists.

3. Get the current index and update the state accordingly.

Now, replace `// TODO: Call getCurrentIndex` with:

```
getCurrentIndex();
```

That will retrieve the currently-selected index when the page is loaded.

Finally, you need to call `saveCurrentIndex()` when the user taps a tab.

To do this, substitute `// TODO: Call saveCurrentIndex` with:

```
saveCurrentIndex();
```

This saves the current index every time the user selects a different tab.

Now, hot reload the app and select either the second or the third tab.

Quit the app and run it again to make sure the app uses the saved index when it starts.

At this point, your app should show a list of previously-searched items and also take you to the last selected tab when you start the app again. Here's a sample:

Congratulations! You've saved the state for both the current tab and any previous searches the user made.

Key points

- There are multiple ways to save data in an app: to files, in shared preferences and to a SQLite database.

- Shared preferences are best used to store simple, key-value pairs of primitive types like strings, numbers and Booleans.

- An example of when to use shared preferences is to save the tab a user is viewing, so the next time the user starts the app, they're brought to the same tab.

- The `async`/`await` keyword pair let you run asynchronous code off the main UI thread and then wait for the response. An example is getting an instance of `SharedPreferences`.

- The shared_preferences plugin should not be used to hold sensitive data. Instead, consider using the **flutter_secure_storage** plugin.

Where to go from here?

In this chapter, you learned how to persist simple data types in your app using the shared_preferences plugin.

If you want to learn more about Android **SharedPreferences**, go to https://developer.android.com/reference/kotlin/android/content/SharedPreferences?hl=en.

For iOS, check **UserDefaults**:
https://developer.apple.com/documentation/foundation/userdefaults.

In the next chapter, you'll continue building the same app and learn how to serialize JSON in preparation for getting data from the internet. See you there!

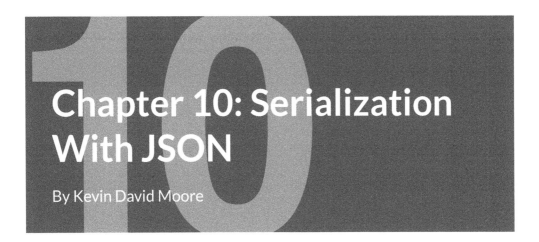

Chapter 10: Serialization With JSON

By Kevin David Moore

In this chapter, you'll learn how to serialize JSON data into model classes. A model class represents data for a particular object. An example is a recipe model class, which usually has a title, an ingredient list and steps to cook it.

You'll continue with the previous project, which is the starter project for this chapter, and you'll add a class that models a recipe and its properties. Then you'll integrate that class into the existing project.

By the end of the chapter, you'll know:

- How to serialize JSON into model classes.

- How to use Dart tools to automate the generation of model classes from JSON.

What is JSON?

JSON, which stands for **JavaScript Object Notation**, is an open-standard format used on the web and in mobile clients. It's the most widely used format for Representational State Transfer (REST)-based APIs that servers provide (https://w.wiki/7iv). If you talk to a server that has a REST API, it will most likely return data in a JSON format. An example of a JSON response looks something like this:

```
{
  "recipe": {
    "uri": "http://www.edamam.com/ontologies/
edamam.owl#recipe_b79327d05b8e5b838ad6cfd9576b30b6",
    "label": "Chicken Vesuvio"
  }
}
```

That is an example recipe response that contains two fields inside a recipe object.

While it's possible to treat the JSON as just a long string and try to parse out the data, it's much easier to use a package that already knows how to do that. Flutter has a built-in package for decoding JSON, but in this chapter, you'll use the **json_serializable** and **json_annotation** packages to help make the process easier.

Flutter's built-in **dart:convert** package contains methods like `json.decode` and `json.encode`, which converts a JSON string to a `Map<String, dynamic>` and back. While this is a step ahead of manually parsing JSON, you'd still have to write extra code that takes that map and puts the values into a new class.

The json_serializable package comes in handy because it can generate model classes for you according to the annotations you provide via json_annotation. Before taking a look at automated serialization, you'll see in the next section what manual serialization entails.

Writing the code yourself

So how do you go about writing code to serialize JSON yourself? Typical model classes have `toJson()` and `fromJson()` methods.

In the next section you learn how to use automated serialization. For now, you don't need to type this into your project, but need to understand the methods to convert the JSON above to a model class.

First, you'd create a `Recipe` model class:

```
class Recipe {
  final String uri;
  final String label;

  Recipe({this.uri, this.label});
}
```

Then you'd add a `toJson()` factory method and a `fromJson()` method:

```
factory Recipe.fromJson(Map<String, dynamic> json) {
  return Recipe(json['uri'] as String, json['label'] as String);
}

Map<String, dynamic> toJson() {
  return <String, dynamic>{ 'uri': uri, 'label': label}
}
```

In `fromJson()`, you grab data from the JSON map variable named `json` and convert it to arguments you pass to the `Recipe` constructor. In `toJson()`, you construct a map using the JSON field names.

While it doesn't take much effort to do that by hand for two fields, what if you had multiple model classes, each with, say, five fields, or more? What if you renamed one of the fields? Would you remember to rename all of the occurrences of that field?

The more model classes you have, the more complicated it becomes to maintain the code behind them. Fear not, that's where automated code generation comes to the rescue.

Automating JSON serialization

You'll use two packages in this chapter: json_annotation and json_serializable from Google.

You use the first to add annotations to model classes so that json_serializable can generate helper classes to convert JSON from a string to a model and back.

To do that, you mark a class with the `@JsonSerializable()` annotation so the builder package can generate code for you. Each field in the class should either have the same name as the field in the JSON string or use the `@JsonKey()` annotation to give it a different name.

Most builder packages work by importing what's called a **.part** file. That will be a file that is generated for you. All you need to do is create a few factory methods which will call the generated code.

Adding the necessary dependencies

Continue with your current project or open the **starter** project in the **projects** folder. Add the following package to **pubspec.yaml** in the Flutter dependencies section underneath and aligned with shared_preferences:

```
json_annotation: ^4.1.0
```

In the dev_dependencies section, after the flutter_test section, add:

```
build_runner: ^2.1.1
json_serializable: ^4.1.4
```

Make sure these are all indented correctly. The result should look like this:

```
dependencies:
  flutter:
    sdk: flutter

  cupertino_icons: ^1.0.3
  cached_network_image: ^3.1.0
  flutter_slidable: ^0.6.0
  flutter_svg: ^0.22.0
  shared_preferences: ^2.0.7
  json_annotation: ^4.1.0

dev_dependencies:
  flutter_test:
    sdk: flutter

  build_runner: ^2.1.1
  json_serializable: ^4.1.4
```

build_runner is a package that all code generators require in order to build **.part** file classes.

Finally, press the **Pub get** button you should see at the top of the file. You're now ready to generate model classes.

Generating classes from JSON

The JSON that you're trying to serialize looks something like:

```
{
  "q": "pasta",
  "from": 0,
  "to": 10,
  "more": true,
  "count": 33060,
  "hits": [
    {
      "recipe": {
        "uri": "http://www.edamam.com/ontologies/
edamam.owl#recipe_09b4dbdf0c7244c462a4d2622d88958e",
        "label": "Pasta Frittata Recipe",
        "image": "https://www.edamam.com/web-img/
5a5/5a5220b7a65c911a1480502ed0532b5c.jpg",
        "source": "Food Republic",
        "url": "http://www.foodrepublic.com/2012/01/21/pasta-
frittata-recipe",
      }
    ]
  }
}
```

The q field is the query. In this instance, you're querying about pasta. from is the starting index and to is the ending one. more is a boolean that tells you whether there are more items to retrieve, while count is the total number of items you could receive. The hits array is the actual list of recipes.

In this chapter, you'll use the label and image fields of the recipe item. Your next step is to generate the classes that model that data.

Creating model classes

Start by creating a new directory named **network** in the **lib** folder. Inside this folder, create a new file named **recipe_model.dart**. Then add the needed imports:

```
import 'package:json_annotation/json_annotation.dart';

part 'recipe_model.g.dart';
```

The json_annotation library lets you mark classes as serializable. The file **recipe_model.g.dart** doesn't exist yet; you'll generate it in a later step.

Next, add a class named `APIRecipeQuery` with a `@JsonSerializable()` annotation:

```
@JsonSerializable()
class APIRecipeQuery {
  // TODO: Add APIRecipeQuery.fromJson
}

// TODO: Add @JsonSerializable() class APIHits
// TODO: Add @JsonSerializable() class APIRecipe
// TODO: Add @JsonSerializable() class APIIngredients
```

That marks the `APIRecipeQuery` class as serializable so the **json_serializable** package can generate the **.g.dart** file.

Command-Click on `JsonSerializable` and you'll see its definition:

```
/// If a field is annotated with `JsonKey` with a non-`null`
value for
/// `includeIfNull`, that value takes precedent.
final bool? includeIfNull;

/// Creates a new [JsonSerializable] instance.
const JsonSerializable({
  @Deprecated('Has no effect') bool? nullable,
  this.anyMap,
  this.checked,
  this.createFactory,
  this.createToJson,
  this.disallowUnrecognizedKeys,
  this.explicitToJson,
  this.fieldRename,
  this.ignoreUnannotated,
  this.includeIfNull,
  this.genericArgumentFactories,
});
```

For example, you can make the class `nullable` and add extra checks for validating JSON properly.

Converting to and from JSON

Now, you need to add JSON conversion methods within the `APIRecipeQuery` class. Return to **recipe_model.dart** and replace `// TODO: Add APIRecipeQuery.fromJson` with:

```
factory APIRecipeQuery.fromJson(Map<String, dynamic> json) =>
  _$APIRecipeQueryFromJson(json);
```

```
Map<String, dynamic> toJson() => _$APIRecipeQueryToJson(this);
```

Note that the methods on the right of the arrow operator don't exist yet, so ignore any red squiggles. You'll create them later by running the **build_runner** command.

Note also that the first call is a `factory` method. That's because you need a class-level method when you're creating the instance, while you use the other method on an object that already exists.

Now, add the following fields right after the conversion methods:

```
@JsonKey(name: 'q')
String query;
int from;
int to;
bool more;
int count;
List<APIHits> hits;
```

The `@JsonKey` annotation states that you represent the `query` field in JSON with the string q. The rest of the fields look in JSON just like their names here. You'll define `APIHits` in a couple of steps.

Next, add this constructor, again ignoring the red squiggles:

```
APIRecipeQuery({
    required this.query,
    required this.from,
    required this.to,
    required this.more,
    required this.count,
    required this.hits,
});
```

The `required` annotation says that these fields are mandatory when creating a new instance.

Then, find `TODO: Add @JsonSerializable() class APIHits` and replace it with a new class named `APIHits`:

```
// 1
@JsonSerializable()
class APIHits {
  // 2
  APIRecipe recipe;

  // 3
  APIHits({
```

```
    required this.recipe,
  });

  // 4
  factory APIHits.fromJson(Map<String, dynamic> json) =>
    _$APIHitsFromJson(json);
  Map<String, dynamic> toJson() => _$APIHitsToJson(this);
}
```

Here's what this code does:

1. Marks the class serializable.

2. Defines a field of class `APIRecipe`, which you'll create soon.

3. Defines a constructor that accepts a `recipe` parameter.

4. Adds the methods for JSON serialization.

Add the `APIRecipe` class definition by replacing `// TODO: Add @JsonSerializable() class APIRecipe` with:

```
@JsonSerializable()
class APIRecipe {
  // 1
  String label;
  String image;
  String url;
  // 2
  List<APIIngredients> ingredients;
  double calories;
  double totalWeight;
  double totalTime;

  APIRecipe({
    required this.label,
    required this.image,
    required this.url,
    required this.ingredients,
    required this.calories,
    required this.totalWeight,
    required this.totalTime,
  });

  // 3
  factory APIRecipe.fromJson(Map<String, dynamic> json) =>
    _$APIRecipeFromJson(json);
  Map<String, dynamic> toJson() => _$APIRecipeToJson(this);
}

// TODO: Add global Helper Functions
```

Here you:

1. Define the fields for a recipe. `label` is the text shown and `image` is the URL of the image to show.

2. State that each recipe has a list of ingredients.

3. Create the factory methods for serializing JSON.

Now replace the `TODO: Add global Helper Functions` with:

```
// 4
String getCalories(double? calories) {
  if (calories == null) {
    return '0 KCAL';
  }
  return calories.floor().toString() + ' KCAL';
}


// 5
String getWeight(double? weight) {
  if (weight == null) {
    return '0g';
  }
  return weight.floor().toString() + 'g';
}
```

4. Add a helper method to turn a calorie into a string.

5. Add another helper method to turn the weight into a string.

Finally, replace `// TODO: Add @JsonSerializable() class APIIngredients` with:

```
@JsonSerializable()
class APIIngredients {
  // 1
  @JsonKey(name: 'text')
  String name;
  double weight;

  APIIngredients({
    required this.name,
    required this.weight,
  });

  // 2
  factory APIIngredients.fromJson(Map<String, dynamic> json) =>
      _$APIIngredientsFromJson(json);
  Map<String, dynamic> toJson() => _$APIIngredientsToJson(this);
}
```

Here you:

1. State that the `name` field of this class maps to the JSON field named `text`.

2. Create the methods to serialize JSON.

For your next step, you'll create the **.part** file.

Generating the .part file

Open the terminal in Android Studio by clicking on the `Terminal` panel in the lower left, or by selecting **View ▸ Tool Windows ▸ Terminal**, and type:

```
flutter pub run build_runner build
```

The expected output will look something like this:

```
[INFO] Generating build script...
...
[INFO] Creating build script snapshot......
...
[INFO] Running build...
...
[INFO] Succeeded after ...
```

> **Note**: If you have problems running the command, make sure that you've installed Flutter on your computer and you have a path set up to point to it.

This command creates **recipe_model.g.dart** in the **network** folder. If you don't see the file, right-click on the network folder and choose **Reload from disk**.

> **Note**: If you still don't see it, restart Android Studio so it recognizes the presence of the new generated file when it starts up.

If you want the program to run every time you make a change to your file, you can use the `watch` command, like this:

```
flutter pub run build_runner watch
```

The command will continue to run and watch for changes to files. To stop the process you can press Ctrl-C. Now, open **recipe_model.g.dart**. Here is the first generated method:

```
// 1
APIRecipeQuery _$APIRecipeQueryFromJson(Map<String, dynamic>
json) =>
    APIRecipeQuery(
        // 2
        query: json['q'] as String,
        // 3
        from: json['from'] as int,
        to: json['to'] as int,
        more: json['more'] as bool,
        count: json['count'] as int,
        // 4
        hits: (json['hits'] as List<dynamic>)
            .map((e) => APIHits.fromJson(e as Map<String,
dynamic>))
            .toList(),
    );
```

Notice that it takes a map of `String` to `dynamic`, which is typical of JSON data in Flutter. The key is the string and the value will be either a primitive, a list or another map. The method:

1. Returns a new `APIRecipeQuery` class.

2. Maps the q key to a `query` field.

3. Maps the `from` integer to the `from` field, and maps the other fields.

4. Maps each element of the `hits` list to an instance of the `APIHits` class.

You could have written this code yourself, but it can get a bit tedious and is error-prone. Having a tool generate the code for you saves a lot of time and effort. Look through the rest of the file to see how the generated code converts the JSON data to all the other model classes.

Hot restart the app to make sure it still compiles and works as before. You won't see any changes in the UI, but the code is now set up to parse recipe data.

Testing the generated JSON code

Now that you can parse model objects from JSON, you'll read one of the JSON files included in the starter project and show one card to make sure you can use the generated code.

Open **ui/recipes/recipe_list.dart** and add the following imports at the top:

```
import 'dart:convert';
import '../../network/recipe_model.dart';
import 'package:flutter/services.dart';
import '../recipe_card.dart';
import 'recipe_details.dart';
```

In `_RecipeListState`, replace `// TODO: Add _currentRecipes1` with:

```
APIRecipeQuery? _currentRecipes1 = null;
```

Next, replace `// TODO: Add loadRecipes` with:

```
Future loadRecipes() async {
  // 1
  final jsonString = await rootBundle.loadString('assets/
recipes1.json');
  setState(() {
    // 2
    _currentRecipes1 =
APIRecipeQuery.fromJson(jsonDecode(jsonString));
  });
}
```

This method:

1. Loads **recipes1.json** from the **assets** directory. `rootBundle` is the top-level property that holds references to all the items in the asset folder. This loads the file as a string.

2. Uses the built-in `jsonDecode()` method to convert the string to a map, then uses `fromJson()`, which was generated for you, to make an instance of an `APIRecipeQuery`.

Now, replace `// TODO: Call loadRecipes()` with:

```
loadRecipes();
```

At the bottom, replace `// TODO: Add _buildRecipeCard` with:

```
Widget _buildRecipeCard(
  BuildContext topLevelContext, List<APIHits> hits, int index) {
  // 1
  final recipe = hits[index].recipe;
  return GestureDetector(
    onTap: () {
      Navigator.push(topLevelContext, MaterialPageRoute(
        builder: (context) {
          return const RecipeDetails();
        },
      ));
    },
    // 2
    child: recipeStringCard(recipe.image, recipe.label),
  );
}
```

This method:

1. Finds the recipe at the given index.

2. Calls `recipeStringCard()`, which shows a nice card below the search field.

Now, locate `// TODO: Replace` method and substitute the existing `_buildRecipeLoader()` with the following:

```
Widget _buildRecipeLoader(BuildContext context) {
  // 1
  if (_currentRecipes1 == null || _currentRecipes1?.hits ==
null) {
    return Container();
  }
  // Show a loading indicator while waiting for the recipes
  return Center(
    // 2
    child: _buildRecipeCard(context, _currentRecipes1!.hits, 0),
  );
}
```

This code now:

1. Checks to see if the list of recipes is `null`.

2. If not, calls `_buildRecipeCard()` using the first item in the list.

Perform a hot restart (not hot reload) and the app will show a **Chicken Vesuvio** sample card:

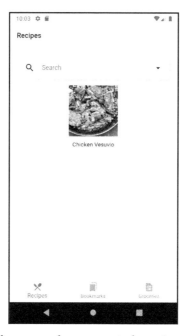

Now that the data model classes work as expected, you're ready to load recipes from the web. Fasten your seat belt. :]

Key points

- JSON is an open-standard format used on the web and in mobile clients, especially with REST APIs.

- In mobile apps, JSON code is usually parsed into the model objects that your app will work with.

- You can write JSON parsing code yourself, but it's usually easier to let a JSON package generate the parsing code for you.

- **json_annotation** and **json_serializable** are packages that will let you generate the parsing code.

Where to go from here?

In this chapter, you've learned how to create models that you can parse from JSON and then use when you fetch JSON data from the network. If you want to learn more about json_serializable, go to https://pub.dev/packages/json_serializable.

In the next chapter, you build on what you've done so far and learn about getting data from the internet.

Chapter 11: Networking in Flutter

By Kevin David Moore

Loading data from the network to show it in a UI is a very common task for apps. In the previous chapter, you learned how to serialize JSON data. Now, you'll continue the project to learn about retrieving JSON data from the network.

> **Note**: You can also start fresh by opening this chapter's **starter** project. If you choose to do this, remember to click the **Get dependencies** button or execute `flutter pub get` from Terminal.

By the end of the chapter, you'll know how to:

- Sign up for a recipe API service.

- Trigger a search for recipes by name.

- Convert data returned by the API to model classes.

With no further ado, it's time to get started!

Signing up with the recipe API

For your remote content, you'll use the Edamam Recipe API. Open this link in your browser: https://developer.edamam.com/.

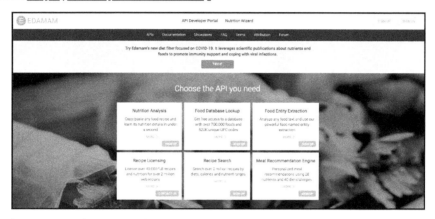

Click the **SIGN UP** button at the top-right and choose the **Recipe Search API** option.

The page will display multiple subscription choices. Choose the free option by clicking the **START NOW** button in the **Developer** column:

On the **Sign Up Info** pop-up window, enter your information and click **SIGN UP**. You'll receive an email confirmation shortly.

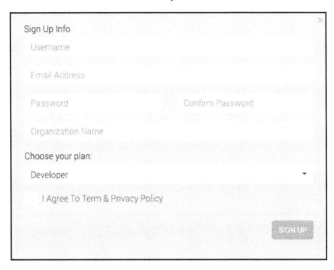

Once you've received the email and verified your account, return to the site and sign in. On the menu bar, click the **Get an API key now!** button:

Next, click the **Create a new application** button.

On the **Select service** page, click the **Recipe Search API** link.

A **New Application** page will come up. Enter **raywenderlich.com Recipes** for the app's name and **An app to display raywenderlich.com recipes** as the description — or use any values you prefer. When you're done, press the **Create Application** button.

Once the site generates the API key, you'll see a screen with your **Application ID** and **Application Key**.

You'll need your API Key and ID later, so save them somewhere handy or keep the browser tab open. Now, check the API documentation, which provides important information about the API including paths, parameters and returned data.

Accessing the API documentation

At the top of the window, right-click the **API Developer Portal** link and select **Open Link in New Tab**.

In the new tab, click the **Documentation** menu and choose **Recipe Search API**.

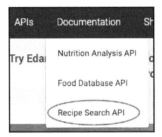

This page has a wealth of information about the API you're going to use. At the top, you'll see the **Path** and a list of the parameters available to use for the GET request you'll make.

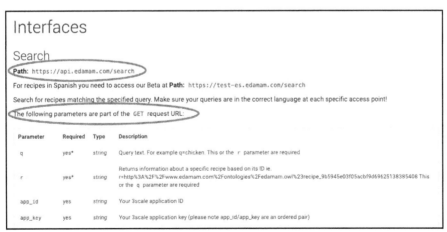

There's much more API information on this page than you'll need for your app, so you might want to bookmark it for the future.

Using your API key

For your next step, you'll need to use your newly created API key.

> **Note**: The free developer version of the API is rate-limited. If you use the API a lot, you'll probably receive some JSON responses with errors and emails warning you about the limit.

If you closed your browser, sign in again. Click the **Dashboard** button, then choose **Applications** from the menu bar. You'll see something like this:

Click the **View** button to see your ID and key(s):

Keep this page open so you can copy the values into your code. Your first step is to import a handy package to perform HTTP requests.

Preparing the Pubspec file

Open either your project or the chapter's **starter** project. To use the **http** package for this app, you need to add it to **pubspec.yaml**, so open that file and add the following after the **json_annotation** package:

```
http: ^0.13.3
```

Click the **Pub get** button to install the package, or run `flutter pub get` from the **Terminal** tab.

Using the HTTP package

The **HTTP** package contains only a few files and methods that you'll use in this chapter. The REST protocol has methods like:

- **GET**: Retrieves data.

- **POST**: Saves new data.

- **PUT**: Updates data.

- **DELETE**: Deletes data.

You'll use GET, specifically the function `get()` in the **HTTP** package, to retrieve recipe data from the API. This function uses the API's **URL** and a list of optional headers to retrieve data from the API service. In this case, you'll send all the information via query parameters, and you don't need to send headers.

Connecting to the recipe service

To fetch data from the recipe API, you'll create a Dart class to manage the connection. This Dart class file will contain your API Key, ID and URL.

In the Project sidebar, right-click **lib/network**, create a new Dart file and name it **recipe_service.dart**. After the file opens, import the **HTTP** package:

```
import 'package:http/http.dart';
```

Now, add the constants that you'll use when calling the APIs:

```
const String apiKey = '<Your Key>';
const String apiId = '<your ID>';
const String apiUrl = 'https://api.edamam.com/search';
```

Copy the API ID and key from your Edamam account and replace the existing `apiKey` and `apiId` assigned strings with your values. Do not copy the ending spaces and dash shown below:

The `apiUrl` constant holds the **URL** for the Edamam search API, from the recipe API documentation.

Still in **recipe_service.dart** add the following class and function to get the data from the API:

```
class RecipeService {
  // 1
  Future getData(String url) async {
    // 2
    print('Calling url: $url');
    // 3
    final response = await get(Uri.parse(url));
    // 4
    if (response.statusCode == 200) {
      // 5
      return response.body;
    } else {
      // 6
      print(response.statusCode);
    }
  }
  // TODO: Add getRecipes
}
```

Here's a breakdown of what's going on:

1. `getData` returns a `Future` (with an upper case "F") because an API's returned data type is determined in the future (lower case "f"). `async` signifies this method is an asynchronous operation.

2. For debugging purposes, you print out the passed-in URL.

3. response doesn't have a value until await completes. Response and get() are from the **HTTP** package. get fetches data from the provided url.

4. A statusCode of 200 means the request was successful.

5. You return the results embedded in response.body.

6. Otherwise, you have an error — print the statusCode to the console.

Now, replace // TODO: Add getRecipes with:

```
// 1
Future<dynamic> getRecipes(String query, int from, int to) async
{
  // 2
  final recipeData = await getData(
      '$apiUrl?
app_id=$apiId&app_key=$apiKey&q=$query&from=$from&to=$to');
  // 3
  return recipeData;
}
```

In this code, you:

1. Create a new method, getRecipes(), with the parameters query, from and to. These let you get specific pages from the complete query. from starts at 0 and to is calculated by adding the from index to your page size. You use type Future<dynamic> for this method because you don't know which data type it will return or when it will finish. async signals that this method runs asynchronously.

2. Use final to create a non-changing variable. You use await to tell the app to wait until getData returns its result. Look closely at getData() and note that you're creating the API URL with the variables passed in (plus the IDs previously created in the Edamam dashboard).

3. return the data retrieved from the API.

> **Note:** This method doesn't handle errors. You'll learn how to address those in Chapter 12, "Using the Chopper library".

Now that you've written the service, it's time to update the UI code to use it.

Building the user interface

Every good collection of recipes starts with a recipe card, so you'll build that first.

Creating the recipe card

The file **ui/recipe_card.dart** contains a few methods for creating a card for your recipes. Open it now and add the following import:

```
import '../network/recipe_model.dart';
```

Now, find`// TODO: Replace with new class` and replace it and the line beneath it:

```
Widget recipeCard(APIRecipe recipe) {
```

This creates a card using `APIRecipe`, but you'll notice some red squiggles indicating that there are errors. To correct these, replace`// TODO: Replace with image from recipe` and the line beneath it with:

```
imageUrl: recipe.image,
```

You're now using an image from the recipe.

To use the label returned with the recipe, locate`// TODO: Replace with label from recipe` and replace it and the line below with:

```
recipe.label,
```

Now, to use `getCalories()` created in the previous chapter, find `// TODO: Replace Padding section with getCalories()` and replace it and the whole `Padding()` widget below it with:

```
Padding(
  padding: const EdgeInsets.only(left: 8.0),
  child: Text(
    getCalories(recipe.calories),
    style: const TextStyle(
      fontWeight: FontWeight.normal,
      fontSize: 11,
    ),
  ),
),
```

Finally, open **ui/recipes/recipe_list.dart** and at the bottom replace `// TODO: Replace with recipeCard` and the line below it with:

```
child: recipeCard(recipe),
```

No more red squiggles, and now your stomach is growling. It's time to see some recipes :]

Adding a recipe list

Your next step is to create a way for your users to find which recipe they want to try: a recipe list.

Still in **recipe_list.dart**, after the last import, add:

```
import '../../network/recipe_service.dart';
```

At `// TODO: Replace with new API class`, replace it and the `List currentSearchList = [];` line beneath it with:

```
List<APIHits> currentSearchList = [];
```

You're getting close to running the app. Hang in there! It's time to use the recipe service.

Retrieving recipe data

Still in **recipe_list.dart**, you need to create a method to get the data from `RecipeService`. You'll pass in a query along with the starting and ending positions and the API will return the decoded JSON results.

Find `// TODO: Add getRecipeData()` here and replace it with this new method:

```
// 1
Future<APIRecipeQuery> getRecipeData(String query, int from, int
to) async {
    // 2
    final recipeJson = await RecipeService().getRecipes(query,
from, to);
    // 3
    final recipeMap = json.decode(recipeJson);
    // 4
    return APIRecipeQuery.fromJson(recipeMap);
}
```

Here's what this does:

1. The method is asynchronous and returns a `Future`. It takes a `query` and the start and the end positions of the recipe data, which `from` and `to` represent, respectively.

2. You define `recipeJson`, which stores the results from `RecipeService().getRecipes()` after it finishes. It uses the `from` and `to` fields from step 1.

3. The variable `recipeMap` uses Dart's `json.decode()` to decode the string into a map of type `Map<String, dynamic>`.

4. You use the JSON parsing method you created in the previous chapter to create an `APIRecipeQuery` model.

Now that you've created a way to get the data, it's time to put it to use. After `_buildRecipeLoader()`, find and replace `// TODO: Add _buildRecipeList()` with the following:

```
// 1
Widget _buildRecipeList(BuildContext recipeListContext,
List<APIHits> hits) {
  // 2
  final size = MediaQuery.of(context).size;
  const itemHeight = 310;
  final itemWidth = size.width / 2;
  // 3
  return Flexible(
    // 4
    child: GridView.builder(
      // 5
      controller: _scrollController,
      // 6
      gridDelegate: SliverGridDelegateWithFixedCrossAxisCount(
        crossAxisCount: 2,
        childAspectRatio: (itemWidth / itemHeight),
      ),
      // 7
      itemCount: hits.length,
      // 8
      itemBuilder: (BuildContext context, int index) {
        return _buildRecipeCard(recipeListContext, hits, index);
      },
    ),
  );
}
```

Here's what's going on:

1. This method returns a widget and takes `recipeListContext` and a list of recipe `hits`.

2. You use `MediaQuery` to get the device's screen size. You then set a fixed item height and create two columns of cards whose width is half the device's width.

3. You return a widget that's flexible in width and height.

4. `GridView` is similar to `ListView`, but it allows for some interesting combinations of rows and columns. In this case, you use `GridView.builder()` because you know the number of items and you'll use an `itemBuilder`.

5. You use `_scrollController`, created in `initState()`, to detect when scrolling gets to about 70% from the bottom.

6. The `SliverGridDelegateWithFixedCrossAxisCount` delegate has two columns and sets the aspect ratio.

7. The length of your grid items depends on the number of items in the `hits` list.

8. `itemBuilder` now uses `_buildRecipeCard()` to return a card for each recipe. `_buildRecipeCard()` retrieves the recipe from the hits list by using `hits[index].recipe`.

Great, now it's time for a little housekeeping.

Removing the sample code

In the previous chapter, you added code to **recipe_list.dart** to show a single card. Now that you're showing a list of cards, you need to clean up some of the existing code to use the new API.

At the top of `_RecipeListState`, remove this variable declaration:

```
APIRecipeQuery? _currentRecipes1 = null;
```

Find `// TODO: Remove call to loadRecipes()` and remove it and the next line that calls to `loadRecipes()`.

Now, find `// TODO: Delete loadRecipes()` and remove it and `loadRecipes()`.

Locate `// TODO: Replace this _buildRecipeLoader` definition and replace the existing `_buildRecipeLoader()` with the code below. Ignore any warning squiggles in the code for now:

```
Widget _buildRecipeLoader(BuildContext context) {
  // 1
  if (searchTextController.text.length < 3) {
    return Container();
  }
  // 2
  return FutureBuilder<APIRecipeQuery>(
    // 3
    future: getRecipeData(searchTextController.text.trim(),
        currentStartPosition, currentEndPosition),
    // 4
    builder: (context, snapshot) {
      // 5
      if (snapshot.connectionState == ConnectionState.done) {
        // 6
        if (snapshot.hasError) {
          return Center(
            child: Text(snapshot.error.toString(),
                textAlign: TextAlign.center, textScaleFactor:
1.3),
          );
        }

        // 7
        loading = false;
        final query = snapshot.data;
        inErrorState = false;
        if (query != null) {
          currentCount = query.count;
          hasMore = query.more;
          currentSearchList.addAll(query.hits);
          // 8
          if (query.to < currentEndPosition) {
            currentEndPosition = query.to;
          }
        }
        // 9
        return _buildRecipeList(context, currentSearchList);
      }
      // TODO: Handle not done connection
    },
  );
}
```

Here's what's going on:

1. You check there are at least three characters in the search term. You can change this value, but you probably won't get good results with only one or two characters.

2. `FutureBuilder` determines the current state of the `Future` that `APIRecipeQuery` returns. It then builds a widget that displays asynchronous data while it's loading.

3. You assign the `Future` that `getRecipeData` returns to `future`.

4. `builder` is required; it returns a widget.

5. You check the `connectionState`. If the state is **done**, you can update the UI with the results or an error.

6. If there's an error, return a simple `Text` element that displays the error message.

7. If there's no error, process the query results and add `query.hits` to `currentSearchList`.

8. If you aren't at the end of the data, set `currentEndPosition` to the current location.

9. Return `_buildRecipeList()` using `currentSearchList`.

For your next step, you'll handle the case where `snapshot.connectionState` isn't complete.

Replace `// TODO: Handle not done connection` with the following:

```
// 10
else {
  // 11
  if (currentCount == 0) {
    // Show a loading indicator while waiting for the recipes
    return const Center(child: CircularProgressIndicator());
  } else {
    // 12
    return _buildRecipeList(context, currentSearchList);
  }
}
```

Walking through this, step-by-step:

10. You check that `snapshot.connectionState` isn't done.

11. If the current count is 0, show a progress indicator.

12. Otherwise, just show the current list.

> **Note**: If you need a refresher on scrolling, check out Chapter 5, "Scrollable Widgets".

Great, it's time to try out the app!

Perform a hot reload, if needed. Type **Chicken** in the text field and press the **Search** icon. While the app pulls data from the API, you'll see the circular progress bar:

After the app receives the data, you'll see a grid of images with different types of chicken recipes.

Well done! You've updated your app to receive real data from the internet. Try different search queries and go show your friends what you've created. :]

> **Note**: If you make too many queries, you could get an error from the Edamam site. That's because the free account limits the number of calls you can make.

Key points

- The **HTTP** package is a simple-to-use set of methods for retrieving data from the internet.

- The built-in `json.decode` transforms JSON strings into a map of objects that you can use in your code.

- `FutureBuilder` is a widget that retrieves information from a `Future`.

- `GridView` is useful for displaying columns of data.

Where to go from here?

You've learned how to retrieve data from the internet and parse it into data models. If you want to learn more about the **HTTP** package and get the latest version, go to https://pub.dev/packages/http.

In the next chapter, you'll learn about the **Chopper** package, which will make handling data from the internet even easier. Till then!

Chapter 12: Using the Chopper Library

By Kevin David Moore

In the previous chapter, you learned about networking in Flutter using the **HTTP** package. Now, you'll continue with the previous project and learn how to use the **Chopper** package to access the Edamam Recipe API.

> **Note**: You can also start fresh by opening this chapter's **starter** project. If you choose to do this, remember to click the **Pub Get** button or execute `flutter pub get` from Terminal. You'll also need your API Key and ID.

By the end of the chapter, you'll know:

- How to set up Chopper and use it to fetch data from a server API.

- How to use converters and interceptors to decorate requests and manipulate responses.

- How to log requests.

Why Chopper?

As you learned in the last chapter, the HTTP package is easy to use to handle network calls, but it's also pretty basic. Chopper does a lot more. For example:

- It generates code to simplify the development of networking code.

- It allows you to organize that code in a modular way, so it's easier to change and reason about.

> **Note**: If you come from the Android side of mobile development, you're probably familiar with the **Retrofit** library, which is similar. If you have an iOS background, **AlamoFire** is a very similar library.

Preparing to use Chopper

To use Chopper, you need to add the package to **pubspec.yaml**. To log network calls, you also need the **logging** package.

Open **pubspec.yaml** and replace the **http** package line with:

```
chopper: ^4.0.1
logging: ^1.0.1
```

You also need **chopper_generator**, which is a package that generates the boilerplate code for you in the form of a **part** file. In the **dev_dependencies** section, after **json_serializable**, add this:

```
chopper_generator: ^4.0.1
```

Next, either click **Pub get** or run `flutter pub get` in Terminal to get the new packages.

Now that the new packages are ready to be used... fasten your seat belt! :]

Handling recipe results

In this scenario, it's a good practice to create a generic response class that will hold either a successful response or an error. While these classes aren't required, they make it easier to deal with the responses that the server returns.

Right-click on **lib/network** and create a new Dart file named **model_response.dart**. Add the following classes to it:

```
// 1
abstract class Result<T> {
}

// 2
class Success<T> extends Result<T> {
  final T value;

  Success(this.value);
}

// 3
class Error<T> extends Result<T> {
  final Exception exception;

  Error(this.exception);
}
```

Here, you've:

1. Created an `abstract class`. It's a simple blueprint for a result with a generic type `T`.

2. Created the `Success` class to extend `Result` and hold a value when the response is successful. This could hold JSON data, for example.

3. Created the `Error` class to extend `Result` and hold an exception. This will model errors that occur during an HTTP call, like using the wrong credentials or trying to fetch data without authorization.

> **Note**: To refresh your knowledge of abstract classes in Dart, check out our **Dart Apprentice** book
>
> https://www.raywenderlich.com/books/dart-apprentice/.

You'll use these classes to model the data fetched via HTTP using Chopper.

Preparing the recipe service

Open **recipe_service.dart**. You need to have your API Key and ID for this next step.

Delete all the code in the file and add the following, making sure to re-enter your API Key and ID:

```
// 1
import 'package:chopper/chopper.dart';
import 'recipe_model.dart';
import 'model_response.dart';
import 'model_converter.dart';

// 2
const String apiKey = '<Your Key Here>';
const String apiId = '<Your Id here>';
// 3
const String apiUrl = 'https://api.edamam.com';

// TODO: Add @ChopperApi() here
```

1. This adds the Chopper package and your models.

2. Here is where you re-enter your API Key and ID.

3. The `/search` was removed from the URL so that you can call other APIs besides `/search`.

It's now time to set up Chopper!

Setting up the Chopper client

Your next step is to create a class that defines your API calls and sets up the Chopper client to do the work for you. Still in **recipe_service.dart**, replace `// TODO: Add @ChopperApi() here` with:

```
// 1
@ChopperApi()
// 2
abstract class RecipeService extends ChopperService {
  // 3
  @Get(path: 'search')
  // 4
  Future<Response<Result<APIRecipeQuery>>> queryRecipes(
    // 5
      @Query('q') String query, @Query('from') int from,
  @Query('to') int to);
  // TODO: Add create()
```

```
}
// TODO: Add _addQuery()
```

There's quite a lot to understand here. To break it down:

1. @ChopperApi() tells the Chopper generator to build a **part** file. This generated file will have the same name as this file, but with **.chopper** added to it. In this case, it will be **recipe_service.chopper.dart**. Such a file will hold the boilerplate code.

2. RecipeService is an abstract class because you only need to define the method signatures. The generator script will take these definitions and generate all the code needed.

3. @Get is an annotation that tells the generator this is a **GET** request with a path named search, which you previously removed from the apiUrl. There are other HTTP methods you can use, such as @Post, @Put and @Delete, but you won't use them in this chapter.

4. You define a function that returns a Future of a Response using the previously created APIRecipeQuery. The abstract Result that you created above will hold either a value or an error.

5. queryRecipes() uses the Chopper @Query annotation to accept a query string and from and to integers. This method doesn't have a body. The generator script will create the body of this function with all the parameters.

Notice that, so far, you have defined a generic interface to make network calls. There's no actual code that performs tasks like adding the API key to the request or transforming the response into data objects. This is a job for converters and interceptors!

Converting request and response

To use the returned API data, you need a converter to transform requests and responses. To attach a converter to a Chopper client, you need an interceptor. You can think of an interceptor as a function that runs every time you send a request or receive a response — a sort of hook to which you can attach functionalities, like converting or decorating data, before passing such data along.

Right-click on **lib/network**, create a new file named **model_converter.dart** and add the following:

```
import 'dart:convert';
import 'package:chopper/chopper.dart';
import 'model_response.dart';
import 'recipe_model.dart';
```

This adds the built-in Dart **convert** package, which transforms data to and from JSON, plus the Chopper package and your model files.

Next, create ModelConverter by adding:

```
// 1
class ModelConverter implements Converter {
  // 2
  @override
  Request convertRequest(Request request) {
    // 3
    final req = applyHeader(
      request,
      contentTypeKey,
      jsonHeaders,
      override: false,
    );

    // 4
    return encodeJson(req);
  }

  Request encodeJson(Request request) {}

  Response decodeJson<BodyType, InnerType>(Response response) {}

  @override
  Response<BodyType> convertResponse<BodyType,
InnerType>(Response response) {}
}
```

Here's what you're doing with this code:

1. Use ModelConverter to implement the Chopper Converter abstract class.

2. Override convertRequest(), which takes in a request and returns a new request.

3. Add a header to the request that says you have a request type of **application/ json** using jsonHeaders. These constants are part of Chopper.

4. Call encodeJson() to convert the request to a JSON-encoded one, as required by the server API.

The remaining code consists of placeholders, which you'll include in the next section.

Encoding and decoding JSON

To make it easy to expand your app in the future, you'll separate encoding and decoding. This gives you flexibility if you need to use them separately later.

Whenever you make network calls, you want to ensure that you **encode** the request before you send it and **decode** the response string into your model classes, which you'll use to display data in the UI.

Encoding JSON

To encode the request in JSON format, replace the existing encodeJson() with:

```
Request encodeJson(Request request) {
  // 1
  final contentType = request.headers[contentTypeKey];
  // 2
  if (contentType != null && contentType.contains(jsonHeaders))
  {
    // 3
    return request.copyWith(body: json.encode(request.body));
  }
  return request;
}
```

In this code, you:

1. Extract the content type from the request headers.

2. Confirm contentType is of type application/json.

3. Make a copy of the request with a JSON-encoded body.

Essentially, this method takes a Request instance and returns a encoded copy of it, ready to be sent to the server. What about decoding? Glad you asked. :]

Decoding JSON

Now, it's time to add the functionality to decode JSON. A server response is usually a string, so you'll have to parse the JSON string and transform it into the `APIRecipeQuery` model class.

Replace `decodeJson()` with:

```
Response<BodyType> decodeJson<BodyType, InnerType>(Response
response) {
  final contentType = response.headers[contentTypeKey];
  var body = response.body;
  // 1
  if (contentType != null && contentType.contains(jsonHeaders))
{
    body = utf8.decode(response.bodyBytes);
  }
  try {
    // 2
    final mapData = json.decode(body);
    // 3
    if (mapData['status'] != null) {
      return response.copyWith<BodyType>(
          body: Error(Exception(mapData['status'])) as
BodyType);
    }
    // 4
    final recipeQuery = APIRecipeQuery.fromJson(mapData);
    // 5
    return response.copyWith<BodyType>(
        body: Success(recipeQuery) as BodyType);
  } catch (e) {
    // 6
    chopperLogger.warning(e);
    return response.copyWith<BodyType>(
        body: Error(e as Exception) as BodyType);
  }
}
```

There's a lot to think about here. To break it down, you:

1. Check that you're dealing with JSON and decode the `response` into a string named body.

2. Use JSON decoding to convert that string into a map representation.

3. When there's an error, the server returns a field named `status`. Here, you check to see if the map contains such a field. If so, you return a response that embeds an instance of `Error`.

4. Use `APIRecipeQuery.fromJson()` to convert the map into the model class.

5. Return a successful response that wraps `recipeQuery`.

6. If you get any other kind of error, wrap the response with a generic instance of `Error`.

You still have to overwrite one more method: `convertResponse()`. This method changes the given response to the one you want.

Replace the existing `convertResponse()` with:

```
@override
Response<BodyType> convertResponse<BodyType, InnerType>(Response
response) {
  // 1
  return decodeJson<BodyType, InnerType>(response);
}
```

1. This simply calls `decodeJson`, which you defined earlier.

Now it's time to use the converter in the appropriate spots and to add some interceptors.

Using interceptors

As mentioned earlier, interceptors can intercept either the request, the response or both. In a request interceptor, you can add headers or handle authentication. In a response interceptor, you can manipulate a response and transform it into another type, as you'll see shortly. You'll start with decorating the request.

Automatically including your ID and key

To request any recipes, the API needs your `app_id` and `app_key`. Instead of adding these fields manually to each query, you can use an interceptor to add them to each call.

Open **recipe_service.dart** and replace `// TODO: Add _addQuery()` with:

```
Request _addQuery(Request req) {
  // 1
  final params = Map<String, dynamic>.from(req.parameters);
  // 2
  params['app_id'] = apiId;
  params['app_key'] = apiKey;
```

```
    // 3
    return req.copyWith(parameters: params);
}
```

This is a request interceptor that adds the API key and ID to the query parameters. Here's what the code does:

1. Creates a Map, which contains key-value pairs from the existing Request parameters.

2. Adds the app_id and the app_key parameters to the map.

3. Returns a new copy of the Request with the parameters contained in the map.

The benefit of this method is that, once you hook it up, all your calls will use it. While you only have one call for now, if you add more, they'll include those keys automatically. And if you want to add a new parameter to every call you'll change only this method. Are you starting to see the advantages of Chopper? :]
You have interceptors to decorate requests and you have a converter to transform responses into model classes. Next, you'll put them to use!

Wiring up interceptors & converters

It's time to create an instance of the service that will fetch recipes.
Still in **recipe_service.dart**, locate // TODO: Add create() and replace it with the following code. Don't worry about the red squiggles; they're warning you that the boilerplate code is missing, because you haven't generated it yet.

```
static RecipeService create() {
  // 1
  final client = ChopperClient(
    // 2
    baseUrl: apiUrl,
    // 3
    interceptors: [_addQuery, HttpLoggingInterceptor()],
    // 4
    converter: ModelConverter(),
    // 5
    errorConverter: const JsonConverter(),
    // 6
    services: [
      _$RecipeService(),
    ],
  );
  // 7
  return _$RecipeService(client);
}
```

In this code, you:

1. Create a `ChopperClient` instance.

2. Pass in a base URL using the `apiUrl` constant.

3. Pass in two interceptors. `_addQuery()` adds your key and ID to the query. `HttpLoggingInterceptor` is part of Chopper and logs all calls. It's handy while you're developing to see traffic between the app and the server.

4. Set the `converter` as an instance of `ModelConverter`.

5. Use the built-in `JsonConverter` to decode any errors.

6. Define the services created when you run the generator script.

7. Return an instance of the generated service.

It's all set, you are ready to generate the boilerplate code!

Generating the Chopper file

Your next step is to generate **recipe_service.chopper.dart**, which works with the `part` keyword. Remember from Chapter 10, "Serialization With JSON", `part` will include the specified file and make it part of one big file.

Import the file that you'll generate. Still in **recipe_service.dart**, add this after the `import` statements at the top:

```
part 'recipe_service.chopper.dart';
```

Ignore the red squiggles. They'll disappear after you've generated the file.

> **Note**: It might seem weird to import a file before it's been created but the generator script will fail if it doesn't know what file to create.

Now, open **Terminal** in Android Studio. By default, it will be in your project folder. Execute:

```
flutter pub run build_runner build --delete-conflicting-outputs
```

> **Note**: Using `--delete-conflicting-outputs` will delete all generated files before generating new ones.

While it's executing, you'll see something like this:

```
Terminal:  Local   +
↑ starter git:(master) ↑ flutter pub run build_runner build --delete-conflicting-outputs
[INFO] Generating build script...
[INFO] Generating build script completed, took 354ms

[WARNING] Deleted previous snapshot due to missing asset graph.
[INFO] Creating build script snapshot......
[INFO] Creating build script snapshot... completed, took 11.8s

[INFO] Initializing inputs
[INFO] Building new asset graph...
[INFO] Building new asset graph completed, took 622ms

[INFO] Checking for unexpected pre-existing outputs....
[INFO] Deleting 1 declared outputs which already existed on disk.
[INFO] Checking for unexpected pre-existing outputs. completed, took 3ms

[INFO] Running build...
[INFO] Generating SDK summary...
[INFO] 3.8s elapsed, 0/12 actions completed.
[INFO] Generating SDK summary completed, took 3.8s

[INFO] 5.0s elapsed, 0/12 actions completed.
[INFO] 6.0s elapsed, 2/12 actions completed.
[INFO] 7.1s elapsed, 2/12 actions completed.
[INFO] 8.1s elapsed, 2/12 actions completed.
[INFO] 10.5s elapsed, 2/12 actions completed.
[INFO] 11.5s elapsed, 2/12 actions completed.
[INFO] 16.3s elapsed, 4/12 actions completed.
[INFO] 17.3s elapsed, 7/12 actions completed.
[INFO] Running build completed, took 17.8s

[INFO] Caching finalized dependency graph...
[INFO] Caching finalized dependency graph completed, took 41ms

[INFO] Succeeded after 17.9s with 3 outputs (39 actions)

↑ starter git:(master) ↑ ▯
```

Once it finishes, you'll see the new **recipe_service.chopper.dart** in **lib/network**. You may need to refresh the **network** folder before it appears.

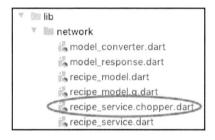

> **Note**: In case you don't see the file or Android Studio doesn't detect its presence, restart Android Studio.

Open it and check it out. The first thing you'll see is a comment stating not to modify the file by hand.

Looking farther down, you'll see a class called _$RecipeService. Below that, you'll notice that queryRecipes() has been overridden to build the parameters and the request. It uses the client to send the request.

It may not seem like much, but as you add different calls with different paths and parameters, you'll start to appreciate the help of a code generator like the one included in Chopper. :]

Now that you've changed RecipeService to use Chopper, it's time to put on the finishing touches: Set up logging and use the new method to fetch data.

Logging requests & responses

Open **main.dart** and add the following import:

```
import 'package:logging/logging.dart';
```

This is from the **logging** package you added to **pubspec.yaml** earlier.

Locate // TODO: Add _setupLogging() and replace it with:

```
void _setupLogging() {
  Logger.root.level = Level.ALL;
  Logger.root.onRecord.listen((rec) {
    print('${rec.level.name}: ${rec.time}: ${rec.message}');
  });
}
```

This initializes the **logging** package and allows Chopper to log requests and responses. Set the level to Level.ALL so that you see every log statement.

> **Note**: You can try changing ALL to WARNING, SEVERE or one of the other levels to see what happens.

Now, replace `// TODO: Call _setupLogging()` with:

```
_setupLogging();
```

Logging is all set now. It's time to use the new functionalities based on Chopper :]

Using the Chopper client

Open **ui/recipes/recipe_list.dart**. You'll see some errors due to the changes you've made.

If you see the following `import` delete it, as it's already imported in other classes:

```
import 'dart:convert';
```

Now, add the following imports:

```
import 'package:chopper/chopper.dart';
import '../../network/model_response.dart';
```

Find `// TODO: Delete getRecipeData()` and delete it and `getRecipeData()`.

In `_buildRecipeLoader()`, replace the line below `// TODO: change with new response` from:

```
return FutureBuilder<APIRecipeQuery>(
```

to:

```
return FutureBuilder<Response<Result<APIRecipeQuery>>>(
```

This uses the new response type that wraps the result of an API call.

Now, replace the `future` below `// TODO: change with new RecipeService` with:

```
future: RecipeService.create().queryRecipes(
    searchTextController.text.trim(),
    currentStartPosition,
    currentEndPosition),
```

The `future` now creates a new instance of `RecipeService` and calls its method, `queryRecipes()`, to perform the query.

Finally, replace the line below `// TODO: change with new snapshot` from:

```
final query = snapshot.data;
```

to:

```
// 1
final result = snapshot.data?.body;
// 2
if (result is Error) {
  // Hit an error
  inErrorState = true;
  return _buildRecipeList(context, currentSearchList);
}
// 3
final query = (result as Success).value;
```

Here's what you did in the code above:

1. `snapshot.data` is now a `Response` and not a string anymore. The body field is either the `Success` or `Error` that you defined above. Extract the value of body into `result`.

2. If `result` is an error, return the current list of recipes.

3. Since `result` passed the error check, cast it as `Success` and extract its value into `query`.

Stop the app, run it again and choose the search value **chicken** from the drop-down button. Verify that you see the recipes displayed in the UI.

Now, look in the **Run** window of Android Studio, where you'll see lots of `flutter:` `INFO` messages related to your network calls. This is a great way to see how your requests and responses look and to figure out what's causing any problems.

You made it! You can now use Chopper to make calls to the server API and retrieve recipes.

Key points

- The **Chopper** package provides easy ways to retrieve data from the internet.

- You can add headers to each network request.

- Interceptors can intercept both requests and responses and change those values.

- Converters can modify requests and responses.

- It's easy to set up global logging.

Where to go from here?

If you want to learn more about the Chopper package, go to
https://pub.dev/packages/chopper.
For more info on the **Logging** library, visit https://pub.dev/packages/logging.

In the next chapter, you'll learn about the important topic of state management. Until then!

Chapter 13: State Management

By Kevin David Moore

The main job of a UI is to represent **state**. Imagine, for example, you're loading a list of recipes from the network. While the recipes are loading, you show a spinning widget. When the data loads, you swap the spinner with the list of loaded recipes. In this case, you move from a **loading** to a **loaded** state. Handling such state changes manually, without following a specific pattern, quickly leads to code that's difficult to understand, update and maintain. One solution is to adopt a pattern that programmatically establishes how to track changes and how to broadcast details about states to the rest of your app. This is called **state management**.

To learn about state management and see how it works for yourself, you'll continue working with the previous project.

> **Note**: You can also start fresh by opening this chapter's **starter** project. If you choose to do this, remember to click the **Get dependencies** button or execute `flutter pub get` from Terminal. You'll also need to add your API Key and ID to **lib/network/recipe_service.dart**.

By the end of the chapter, you'll know:

- Why you need state management.

- How to implement state management using **Provider**.

- How to save the current list of bookmarks and ingredients.

- How to create a repository.

- How to create a mock service.

- Different ways to manage state.

Architecture

When you write apps and the amount of code gets larger and larger over time, you learn to appreciate the importance of separating code into manageable pieces. When files contain more than one class or classes combine multiple functionalities, it's harder to fix bugs and add new features.

One way to handle this is to follow **Clean Architecture** principles by organizing your project so it's easy to change and understand. You do this by separating your code into separate directories and classes, with each class handling just one task. You also use interfaces to define contracts that different classes can implement, allowing you to easily swap in different classes or reuse classes in other apps.

You should design your app with some or all of the components below:

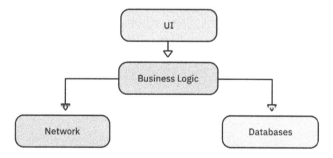

Notice that the UI is separate from the business logic. It's easy to start an app and put your database and business logic into your UI code — but what happens when you need to change the behavior of your app and that behavior is spread throughout your UI code? That makes it difficult to change and causes duplicate code that you might forget to update.

Communicating between these layers is important as well. How does one layer talk to the other? The easy way is to just create those classes when you need them. But this results in multiple instances of the same class, which causes problems coordinating calls.

For example, what if two classes each have their own database handler class and make conflicting calls to the database? Both Android and iOS use **Dependency Injection** or **DI** to create instances in one place and inject them into other classes that need them. This chapter will cover the Provider package, which does something similar.

Ultimately, the business logic layer should be in charge of deciding how to react to the user's actions and how to delegate tasks like retrieving and saving data to other classes.

Why you need state management

First, what do the terms **state** and **state management** mean? State is when a widget is active and stores its data in memory. The Flutter framework handles some state, but as mentioned earlier, Flutter is declarative. That means it rebuilds a UI `StatefulWidget` from memory when the state or data changes or when another part of your app uses it.

State management is, as the name implies, how you manage the state of your widgets and app.

Two state types to consider are **ephemeral state**, also known as **UI state** and **app state**:

- Use **Ephemeral state** when no other component in the widget tree needs to access a widget's data. Examples include whether a `TabBarView` tab is selected or `FloatingActionButton` is pressed.

- Use **App state** when other parts of your app need to access a widget's state data. One example is an image that changes over time, like an icon for the current weather. Another example is information that the user selects on one screen and which should then display on another screen, like when the user adds an item to a shopping cart.

Next, you'll learn more about the different types of state and how they apply to your recipe app.

Widget state

In Chapter 4, "Understanding Widgets", you saw the difference between stateless and stateful widgets. A **stateless widget** is drawn with the same state it had when it was created. A **stateful widget** preserves its state and uses it to (re)draw itself in the future.

Your current **Recipes** screen has a card with the list of previous searches and a `GridView` with a list of recipes:

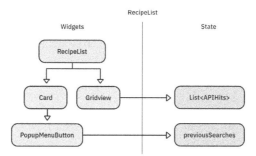

The left side shows some of the `RecipeList` widgets, while the right side shows the state objects that store the information each widget uses. An element tree stores both the widgets themselves and the states of all the stateful widgets in `RecipeList`:

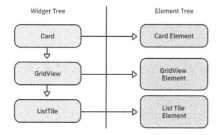

If the state of a widget updates, the state object also updates and the widget is redrawn with that updated state.

This kind of management handles state only for a specific widget. But what if you want to manage state for your whole app or share state between widgets and screens? You do this using **application state**.

Application state

In Flutter, a stateful widget can hold state, which its children can access, and pass data to another screen in its constructor. However, that complicates your code and you have to remember to pass data objects down the tree. Wouldn't it be great if child widgets could easily access their parent data without having to pass in that data?

There are several different ways to achieve that, both with built-in widgets and with third-party packages. You'll look at built-in widgets first.

Managing state in your app

Your app needs to save three things: the list to show in the **Recipes** screen, the user's bookmarks and the ingredients. In this chapter, you'll use state management to save this information so other screens can use it.

At this point, you'll only save this data in memory so when the user restarts the app, those selections won't be available. Chapter 15, "Saving Data With SQLite", will show how to save that data locally to a database for more permanent persistence.

These methods are still relevant for sharing data between screens. Here's a general idea of how your classes will look:

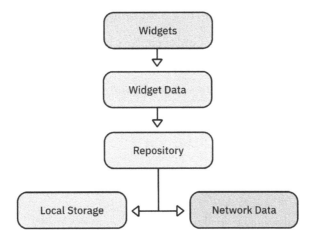

Stateful widgets

StatefulWidget is one of the most basic ways of saving state. The RecipeList widget, for example, saves several fields for later usage, including the current search list and the start and end positions of search results for pagination.

When you create a stateful widget, you call createState(), which stores the state internally in Flutter to reuse when the parent needs to rebuild the widget tree. When the widget is rebuilt, Flutter reuses the existing state.

You use initstate() for one-time work, like initializing text controllers. Then you use setState() to change state, triggering a rebuild of the widget with the new state.

For example, in Chapter 9, "Shared Preferences", you used setState() to set the selected tab. This tells the system to rebuild the UI to select a page. StatefulWidget is great for maintaining internal state, but not for state outside of the widget.

One way to achieve an architecture that allows sharing state between widgets is to adopt **InheritedWidget**.

InheritedWidget

InheritedWidget is a built-in class that allows its child widgets to access its data. It's the basis for a lot of other state management widgets. If you create a class that extends InheritedWidget and give it some data, any child widget can access that data by calling context.dependOnInheritedWidgetOfExactType<class>().

Wow, that's quite a mouthful! As shown below, <class> represents the name of the class extending InheritedWidget.

```
class RecipeWidget extends InheritedWidget {
  final Recipe recipe;
  RecipeWidget(Key? key, required this.recipe, required Widget
child}) :
        super(key: key, child: child);

  @override
  bool updateShouldNotify(RecipeWidget oldWidget) => recipe !=
oldWidget.recipe;

  static RecipeWidget of(BuildContext context) =>
context.dependOnInheritedWidgetOfExactType<RecipeWidget>()!;
}
```

You can then extract data from that widget. Since that's such a long method name to call, the convention is to create an of() method.

> **Note**: updateShouldNotify() compares two recipes, which requires Recipe to implement equals. Otherwise, you need to compare each field.

Then a child widget, like the text field that displays the recipe title, can just use:

```
RecipeWidget recipeWidget = RecipeWidget.of(context);
print(recipeWidget.recipe.label);
```

An advantage of using InheritedWidget is it's a built-in widget so you don't need to worry about using external packages.

A disadvantage of using InheritedWidget is that the value of a recipe can't change unless you rebuild the whole widget tree because InheritedWidget is immutable. So, if you want to change the displayed recipe title, you'll have to rebuild the whole RecipeWidget.

For a while, **scoped_model** (https://pub.dev/packages/scoped_model) was an interesting solution. It comes from the Fuchsia codebase and builds on top of InheritedWidget to separate UI and data, making the process easier than just using InheritedWidget.

However, since its version 1.0.0 release in November 2018, Google started recommending Provider as a better solution that provides similar functionalities to scoped_model and more. You'll use Provider to implement state management in your app.

Provider

Remi Rousselet designed Provider to wrap around InheritedWidget, simplifying it. Google had already created their own package to handle state management, but realized Provider was better. They now recommend using it, instead.

Google even includes details about it in their state management docs: https://bit.ly/3AhE6xb.

In essence, Provider is a set of classes that simplifies building a state management solution on top of InheritedWidget.

Classes used by Provider

Provider has several commonly used classes that you'll learn about in more detail:
ChangeNotifierProvider, Consumer, FutureProvider, MultiProvider and
StreamProvider.

One of the key classes, built in the Flutter SDK, is ChangeNotifier.

ChangeNotifier

ChangeNotifier is a class that adds and removes listeners, then notifies those
listeners of any changes. You usually extend the class for models so you can send
notifications when your model changes. When something in the model changes, you
call notifyListeners() and whoever is listening can use the newly changed model
to redraw a piece of UI, for example.

ChangeNotifierProvider

ChangeNotifierProvider is a widget that wraps a class, implementing
ChangeNotifier and uses the child widget for display. When changes are broadcast,
the widget rebuilds its tree. The syntax looks like this:

```
ChangeNotifierProvider(
  create: (context) => MyModel(),
  child: <widget>,
);
```

Provider offers a central point to manage state, so that you don't need to manually
update different widgets via setState() every time that state changes.

But what happens if you create a model in that widget each time? That creates a new
one! Any work that model did is lost the next time. By using create, Provider saves
that model instead of re-creating it each time.

Consumer

Consumer is a widget that listens for changes in a class that implements
ChangeNotifier, then rebuilds the widgets below itself when it finds any. When
building your widget tree, try to put a Consumer as deep as possible in the UI
hierarchy, so updates don't recreate the whole widget tree.

```
Consumer<MyModel>(
  builder: (context, model, child) {
    return Text('Hello ${model.value}');
  }
```

```
  );
```

If you only need access to the model and don't need notifications when the data changes, use `Provider.of`, like this:

```
  Provider.of<MyModel>(context, listen: false).<method name>
```

`listen: false` indicates you don't want notifications for any updates. This parameter is required to use `Provider.of()` inside `initState()`.

FutureProvider

`FutureProvider` works like other providers and uses the required `create` parameter that returns a `Future`.

```
  FutureProvider(
    initialData: null,
    create: (context) => createFuture(),
    child: <widget>,
  );

  Future<MyModel> createFuture() async {
    return Future.value(MyModel());
  }
```

A `Future` is handy when a value is not readily available but will be in the future. Examples include calls that request data from the internet or asynchronously read data from a database.

MultiProvider

What if you need more than one provider? You could nest them, but it'd get messy, making them hard to read and maintain.

```
  Provider<MyModel>(
    create: (_) => Something(),
    child: Provider<MyDatabase>(
      create: (_) => SomethingMore()
      child: <widget>
    ),
  );
```

Instead, use `MultiProvider` to create a list of providers and a single `child`:

```
  MultiProvider(
    providers: [
      Provider<MyModel>(create: (_) => Something()),
```

```
    Provider<MyDatabase>(create: (_) => SomethingMore()),
  ],
  child: <widget>
);
```

StreamProvider

You'll learn about **streams** in detail in the next chapter. For now, you just need to know that Provider also has a provider that's specifically for streams and works the same way as `FutureProvider`. Stream providers are handy when data comes in via streams and values change over time like, for example, when you're monitoring the connectivity of a device.

It's time to use Provider to manage state in **Recipe Finder**. The next step is to add it to the project.

Using Provider

Open **pubspec.yaml** and add the following packages after `logging`:

```
provider: ^6.0.0
equatable: ^2.0.3
```

Provider contains all the classes mentioned above. **Equatable** helps with equality checks by providing `equals()` and `toString()` as well as `hashcode`. This allows you to check models for equality in maps and it's necessary for providers.

Run **Pub Get** to install the new packages.

UI Models

In earlier chapters, you created models for the **Recipe** API. Here, you'll create simple models to share data between screens.

In **lib**, create a new directory named **data** and within it create a new file named **repository.dart**. Leave that file empty for now.

In **data**, create a new directory named **models**. Within it create a new file named **ingredient.dart** and add the following class:

```
import 'package:equatable/equatable.dart';
```

```
// 1
class Ingredient extends Equatable {
  // 2
  int? id;
  int? recipeId;
  final String? name;
  final double? weight;

  // 3
  Ingredient({this.id, this.recipeId, this.name, this.weight});

  // 4
  @override
  List<Object?> get props => [recipeId, name, weight];
}
```

Here's what's happening in this code:

1. The `Ingredient` class extends `Equatable`, to provide support for equality checks.

2. Add the properties an ingredient needs. You don't declare `recipeId` or `id` as `final` so you can change those values later.

3. Declare a constructor with all the fields.

4. When equality checks are performed, `Equatable` uses the `props` value. Here, you provide the fields you want to use to check for equality.

The next step is to create a class to model a recipe.

Creating the recipe class

In **models**, create **recipe.dart** then add the following code:

```
import 'package:equatable/equatable.dart';
import 'ingredient.dart';

class Recipe extends Equatable {
  // 1
  int? id;
  final String? label;
  final String? image;
  final String? url;
  // 2
  List<Ingredient>? ingredients;
  final double? calories;
  final double? totalWeight;
  final double? totalTime;
```

```
  // 3
  Recipe(
      {this.id,
      this.label,
      this.image,
      this.url,
      this.calories,
      this.totalWeight,
      this.totalTime});

  // 4
  @override
  List<Object?> get props =>
      [label, image, url, calories, totalWeight, totalTime];
}
```

The code includes:

1. Recipe properties for the recipe text: label, image and url. id is not final so you can update it.

2. A list of ingredients that the recipe contains along with its calories, weight and time to cook.

3. A constructor with all fields except ingredients, which you'll add later.

4. Equatable properties, which you'll use for comparison.

Instead of importing the same files multiple times, you'll use a single Dart file that exports all the files you need. Essentially, you'll group multiple imports into a single one.

Remember barrel files introduced in Chapter 5, "Scrollable Widgets"? Well, it's time to create another one. In the **models** folder, create **models.dart** and add the following:

```
export 'recipe.dart';
export 'ingredient.dart';
```

Now, you can just import **models.dart** instead of having to import both **recipe.dart** and **ingredient.dart** every time you need them.

With the models in place, it's now time to implement the conversion from data received via the network to model objects.

Convert data into models to display

Open **lib/network/recipe_model.dart** and import your new **models.dart** file:

```
import '../data/models/models.dart';
```

You need a new method to convert a network ingredient model to a display ingredient model.

Locate `// TODO: Add convertIngredients()` here and replace it with the following:

```
List<Ingredient> convertIngredients(List<APIIngredients>
apiIngredients) {
  // 1
  final ingredients = <Ingredient>[];
  // 2
  apiIngredients.forEach((ingredient) {
    ingredients
        .add(Ingredient(name: ingredient.name, weight:
ingredient.weight));
  });
  return ingredients;
}
```

In this code, you:

1. Create a new list of ingredients to return.

2. Convert each `APIIngredients` into an instance of `Ingredient` and add it to the list.

You're now ready to create a repository to handle the creation, fetching and deletion of recipes.

Creating a repository

Next, you'll create a repository interface that will provide methods to add and delete recipes and ingredients.

Open **data/repository.dart** and add the following:

```
import 'models/models.dart';

abstract class Repository {
```

```
  // TODO: Add find methods

  // TODO: Add insert methods

  // TODO: Add delete methods

  // TODO: Add initializing and closing methods
}
```

Remember that Dart doesn't have the keyword interface; instead, it uses abstract class. That means you need to add the methods that you want all repositories to implement. You'll do that next.

Finding recipes and ingredients

Replace // TODO: Add find methods with the following to help find recipes and ingredients:

```
// 1
List<Recipe> findAllRecipes();

// 2
Recipe findRecipeById(int id);

// 3
List<Ingredient> findAllIngredients();

// 4
List<Ingredient> findRecipeIngredients(int recipeId);
```

In this code, you define interfaces to:

1. Return all recipes in the repository.

2. Find a specific recipe by its ID.

3. Return all ingredients.

4. Find all the ingredients for the given recipe ID.

Adding recipes and ingredients

Next, replace // TODO: Add insert methods to insert a new recipe and any ingredients.

```
// 5
int insertRecipe(Recipe recipe);
```

```
// 6
List<int> insertIngredients(List<Ingredient> ingredients);
```

Here, you declare methods to:

5. Insert a new recipe.

6. Add all the given ingredients.

Deleting unwanted recipes and ingredients

Then, replace `// TODO: Add delete methods` to include delete methods:

```
// 7
void deleteRecipe(Recipe recipe);

// 8
void deleteIngredient(Ingredient ingredient);

// 9
void deleteIngredients(List<Ingredient> ingredients);

// 10
void deleteRecipeIngredients(int recipeId);
```

In this code, you add methods to:

7. Delete the given recipe.

8. Delete the given ingredient.

9. Delete all the given ingredients.

10. Delete all the ingredients for the given recipe ID.

Initializing and closing the repository

Now, you'll add two final methods. Replace `// TODO: Add initializing and closing` methods with:

```
// 11
Future init();
// 12
void close();
```

In this final bit of code, you:

11. Allow the repository to initialize. Databases might need to do some startup work.

12. Close the repository.

Now that you've defined the interface, you need to create a concrete implementation that stores these items in memory.

Creating a memory repository

The memory repository is where you store the ingredients in memory. This is a temporary solution, as they are lost each time you restart the app.

In **data**, create a new file named **memory_repository.dart** and add these imports:

```
import 'dart:core';
import 'package:flutter/foundation.dart';
// 1
import 'repository.dart';
// 2
import 'models/models.dart';
```

To break this code down:

1. **repository.dart** contains the interface definition.

2. **models.dart** exports the Recipe and Ingredient class definitions.

Defining the memory repository

Now, define MemoryRepository by adding the following:

> **Note**: MemoryRepository will have red squiggles until you finish adding all the required methods.

```
// 3
class MemoryRepository extends Repository with ChangeNotifier {
  // 4
  final List<Recipe> _currentRecipes = <Recipe>[];
  // 5
  final List<Ingredient> _currentIngredients = <Ingredient>[];
```

```
  // TODO: Add find methods

  // TODO: Add insert methods

  // TODO: Add delete methods

  // 6
  @override
  Future init() {
    return Future.value(null);
  }

  @override
  void close() {}
}
```

Here's what's going on in this code:

3. `MemoryRepository` extends `Repository` and uses Flutter's `ChangeNotifier` to enable listeners and notify those listeners of any changes.

4. You initialize your current list of recipes.

5. Then you initialize your current list of ingredients.

6. Since this is a memory repository, you don't need to do anything to initialize and close but you need to implement these methods.

Since this class just saves into memory, you store the recipes and ingredients using lists.

Now, you're ready to add the methods you need to find, insert and delete recipe data.

Finding stored recipes and ingredients

Replace `// TODO: Add find methods` with these:

```
  @override
  List<Recipe> findAllRecipes() {
    // 7
    return _currentRecipes;
  }

  @override
  Recipe findRecipeById(int id) {
    // 8
    return _currentRecipes.firstWhere((recipe) => recipe.id ==
id);
  }
```

```
@override
List<Ingredient> findAllIngredients() {
  // 9
  return _currentIngredients;
}

@override
List<Ingredient> findRecipeIngredients(int recipeId) {
  // 10
  final recipe =
      _currentRecipes.firstWhere((recipe) => recipe.id ==
recipeId);
  // 11
  final recipeIngredients = _currentIngredients
      .where((ingredient) => ingredient.recipeId == recipe.id)
      .toList();
  return recipeIngredients;
}
```

This code:

7. Returns your current RecipeList.

8. Uses firstWhere to find a recipe with the given ID.

9. Returns your current ingredient list.

10. Finds a recipe with the given ID.

11. Uses where to find all the ingredients with the given recipe ID.

These methods help find any recipe or set of ingredients you need to display on the screen.

Adding recipes and ingredient lists

Replace // TODO: Add insert methods with these, which let you add recipes and lists of ingredients:

```
@override
int insertRecipe(Recipe recipe) {
  // 12
  _currentRecipes.add(recipe);
  // 13
  if (recipe.ingredients != null) {
    insertIngredients(recipe.ingredients!);
  }
  // 14
  notifyListeners();
```

```
  // 15
  return 0;
}

@override
List<int> insertIngredients(List<Ingredient> ingredients) {
  // 16
  if (ingredients.length != 0) {
    // 17
    _currentIngredients.addAll(ingredients);
    // 18
    notifyListeners();
  }
  // 19
  return <int>[];
}
```

In this code, you:

12. Add the recipe to your list.

13. Call the method to add all the recipe's ingredients.

14. Notify all listeners of the changes.

15. Return the ID of the new recipe. Since you don't need it, it'll always return 0.

16. Check to make sure there are some ingredients.

17. Add all the ingredients to your list.

18. Notify all listeners of the changes.

19. Return the list of IDs added. An empty list for now.

Deleting recipes and ingredients

Replace // TODO: Add delete methods with these, to delete a recipe or ingredient:

```
@override
void deleteRecipe(Recipe recipe) {
  // 20
  _currentRecipes.remove(recipe);
  // 21
  if (recipe.id != null) {
    deleteRecipeIngredients(recipe.id!);
  }
  // 22
  notifyListeners();
}
```

```
@override
void deleteIngredient(Ingredient ingredient) {
  // 23
  _currentIngredients.remove(ingredient);
}

@override
void deleteIngredients(List<Ingredient> ingredients) {
  // 24
  _currentIngredients
      .removeWhere((ingredient) =>
ingredients.contains(ingredient));
  notifyListeners();
}

@override
void deleteRecipeIngredients(int recipeId) {
  // 25
  _currentIngredients
     .removeWhere((ingredient) => ingredient.recipeId ==
recipeId);
  notifyListeners();
}
```

Here, you:

20. Remove the recipe from your list.

21. Delete all the ingredients for this recipe.

22. Notify all listeners that the data has changed.

23. Remove the ingredients from your list.

24. Remove all ingredients that are in the passed-in list.

25. Go through all ingredients and look for ingredients that have the given recipe ID, then remove them.

You now have a complete `MemoryRepository` class that can find, add and delete recipes and ingredients. You'll use this repository throughout the app.

Using the repository via Provider

It's time to use your newly created repository and Provider. Open **main.dart** and add these imports:

```
import 'package:provider/provider.dart';
import 'data/memory_repository.dart';
```

Now, replace the build() method inside **MyApp**, including the @override, with:

```
@override
Widget build(BuildContext context) {
  // 1
  return ChangeNotifierProvider<MemoryRepository>(
    // 2
    lazy: false,
    // 3
    create: (_) => MemoryRepository(),
    // 4
    child: MaterialApp(
      title: 'Recipes',
      debugShowCheckedModeBanner: false,
      theme: ThemeData(
        brightness: Brightness.light,
        primaryColor: Colors.white,
        primarySwatch: Colors.blue,
        visualDensity: VisualDensity.adaptivePlatformDensity,
      ),
      home: const MainScreen(),
    ),
  );
}
```

In this code, you:

1. Use the ChangeNotifierProvider that has the type MemoryRepository.

2. Set lazy to false, which creates the repository right away instead of waiting until you need it. This is useful when the repository has to do some background work to start up.

3. Create your repository.

4. Return MaterialApp as the child widget.

> **Note:** If your code doesn't automatically format when you save your changes, remember that you can always reformat it by going to the **Code** menu and choosing **Reformat Code**.

The code for the model is all in place. It's now time to use it in the UI.

Using the repository for recipes

You'll implement code to add a recipe to the **Bookmarks** screen and ingredients to the **Groceries** screen. Open **ui/recipes/recipe_details.dart** and add the following imports:

```
import 'package:provider/provider.dart';
import '../../network/recipe_model.dart';
import '../../data/models/models.dart';
import '../../data/memory_repository.dart';
```

This includes the Provider package, the models and the repository. To show a recipe's details, you need to pass in the recipe you want to show.

Replace `// TODO: Replace with new constructor` and the line below it with:

```
final Recipe recipe;
const RecipeDetails({Key? key, required this.recipe}) :
super(key: key);
```

Displaying the recipes' details

You need to show the recipe's image, label and calories on the **Details** page. The repository already stores all of your currently bookmarked recipes.

Still in **ui/recipes/recipe_details.dart**, add this as the first line of the `build()` method:

```
final repository = Provider.of<MemoryRepository>(context);
```

This uses Provider to retrieve the repository created in **main.dart**. You'll use it to add the bookmark.

> **Note**: If your **recipe_details.dart** file does not have the `// TODO` comments, take a look at the starter project for the next few steps.

Find `// TODO: Replace imageUrl` and replace it and the hard-coded `imageUrl` with:

```
imageUrl: recipe.image ?? '',
```

Locate `// TODO: Replace hardcoded Chicken Vesuvio`, and make note of where `const` is used. Now, replace `// TODO: Replace hardcoded Chicken Vesuvio` and the whole `Padding` widget beneath it with the following - notice that it's not a `const` anymore:

```
Padding(
  padding: const EdgeInsets.only(left: 16.0),
  child: Text(
    recipe.label ?? '',
    style: const TextStyle(
        fontSize: 22, fontWeight: FontWeight.bold),
  ),
),
```

You're now using the `recipe.label`, which can change. This is why the `const` usage changed. The widgets that don't change have `const`.

Replace `// TODO: Replace hardcoded calories` and the lines below with:

```
Padding(
  padding: const EdgeInsets.only(left: 16.0),
  child: Chip(
    label: Text(getCalories(recipe.calories)),
  ),
),
```

(Notice the change of `const`). `getCalories()` is from **recipe_model.dart**.

Next, you'll enable the user to tap the **Bookmark** button to add the recipe to the list of bookmarks.

Bookmarking recipes

The first step is to insert the recipe into the repository.

Continuing to work in **ui/recipes/recipe_details.dart**, replace `// TODO: Add insertRecipe here`, and not the line beneath, with:

```
repository.insertRecipe(recipe);
```

This adds the recipe to your repository. To receive that recipe, you need to update **recipe_list.dart** to send the recipe to the details page.

Open **ui/recipes/recipe_list.dart** and add the models import:

```
import '../../data/models/models.dart';
```

Then go to _buildRecipeCard() and change return const RecipeDetails(); to:

```
final detailRecipe = Recipe(
    label: recipe.label,
    image: recipe.image,
    url: recipe.url,
    calories: recipe.calories,
    totalTime: recipe.totalTime,
    totalWeight: recipe.totalWeight);

detailRecipe.ingredients =
convertIngredients(recipe.ingredients);
return RecipeDetails(recipe: detailRecipe);
```

This creates a new Recipe from the network recipe using the convertIngredients method to convert each ingredient.

Now, hot reload the app. Enter **chicken** in the search box and tap the magnifying glass to perform the search. You'll see something like this:

Select a recipe to go to the details page:

Click the **Bookmark** button and the details page will disappear. Now, select the **Bookmarks** tab. At this point, you'll see a blank screen — you haven't implemented it yet. You'll add that functionality next.

Implementing the Bookmarks screen

Open **ui/myrecipes/my_recipes_list.dart** and add the following imports:

```
import 'package:provider/provider.dart';
import '../../data/models/recipe.dart';
import '../../data/memory_repository.dart';
```

This includes Provider to retrieve the repository as well as the `Recipe` class.

On the **Bookmarks** page, the user can delete a bookmarked recipe by swiping left or right and selecting the delete icon. To implement this, find and replace `// TODO: Add deleteRecipe() here` with:

```
void deleteRecipe(MemoryRepository repository, Recipe recipe)
async {
  if (recipe.id != null) {
    // 1
    repository.deleteRecipeIngredients(recipe.id!);
    // 2
    repository.deleteRecipe(recipe);
    // 3
    setState(() {});
  } else {
    print('Recipe id is null');
  }
}
```

In this code, you use:

1. The repository to delete any recipe ingredients.

2. The repository to delete the recipe.

3. `setState()` to redraw the view.

Still in `_MyRecipesListState`, replace the line below `// TODO: Update recipes declaration` with:

```
List<Recipe> recipes = [];
```

At `// TODO: Remove initState()`, remove the whole definition of `initState()` because you'll fill the list from the repository.

Replace `// TODO: Add Consumer` with the following:

```
return Consumer<MemoryRepository>(builder: (context, repository,
child) {
  recipes = repository.findAllRecipes();
```

This creates a `Consumer` of a MemoryRepository, which receives the repository. Remember that `Consumer` is a widget that can receive a class from a parent `Provider`.

The method `findAllRecipes()` will return either all the current recipes or an empty list.

At `// TODO: Add recipe definition`, add:

```
final recipe = recipes[index];
```

`itemBuilder` receives the current index so that we can retrieve the recipe at that index.

Now, replace all the hard-coded values:

At `// TODO: Replace imageUrl hardcoding`, replace `imageUrl` with:

```
imageUrl: recipe.image ?? '',
```

At `// TODO: Replace title hardcoding`, replace `title` with:

```
title: Text(recipe.label ?? ''),
```

At `// TODO: Update first onTap`, replace the `onTap(){})` declaration with, ignoring the red squiggles these will go away in two more steps:

```
onTap: () => deleteRecipe(
    repository,
    recipe)),
```

This calls `deleteRecipe()`, which you defined above.

At `// TODO: Update second onTap`, replace the other `onTap(){})` with, again ignore the red squiggles:

```
onTap: () => deleteRecipe(
      repository,
    recipe)),
```

Finally, to get rid of those annoying red squiggles, replace `// TODO: Add final brace and parenthesis` with:

```
    },
  );
```

Hot reload the app and make sure the recipe you bookmarked earlier shows up now. You'll see:

You're almost done, but the **Groceries** view is currently blank. Your next step is to add the functionality to show the ingredients of a bookmarked recipe.

Implementing the Groceries screen

Open **ui/shopping/shopping_list.dart** and add the following:

```
import 'package:provider/provider.dart';
import '../../data/memory_repository.dart';
```

Here you import Provider and the repository.

Remove the line below // TODO: Remove ingredients declaration.

Replace // TODO: Add Consumer widget with:

```
return Consumer<MemoryRepository>(builder: (context, repository,
  child) {
    final ingredients = repository.findAllIngredients();
```

This adds a Consumer widget to display the current ingredients.

Replace the line below `// TODO: Update title to include name` with:

```
title: Text(ingredients[index].name ?? ''),
```

This will display the ingredient's `name` property.

At `// TODO: Add closing brace and parenthesis`, add:

```
    },
  );
```

This closes the `Consumer` widget.

Hot reload and make sure you still have one bookmark saved.

Now, go to the **Groceries** tab to see the ingredients of the recipe you bookmarked. You'll see something like this:

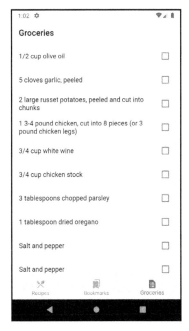

Congratulations, you made it! You now have an app where state changes can be monitored and notified across different screens, thanks to the infrastructure of Provider.

But there's one more thing to think about: Hitting the real web server with a request every time you want to try a code change isn't a good idea. It's time-consuming and doesn't give you control over the returned data. Your next step is to build a mock service that returns specific responses that imitate the real API.

Using a mock service

You'll add an alternate way to retrieve data. This is handy because:

- The Edamam site limits the number of queries you can make for the developer account.

- It's good practice to have a service that returns a mocked version of the data, especially for testing.

In **assets**, there are two recipe JSON files. You'll create a mock service provider that randomly returns one of those files.

If you get errors when you retrieve data from a production server, you can just swap out the current repository with the mock service.

Start by creating a new directory under **lib** named **mock_service**. Next, create **mock_service.dart** in that new directory.

Add the imports:

```
import 'dart:convert';
import 'dart:math';
import 'package:http/http.dart' as http;

// 1
import 'package:chopper/chopper.dart';
// 2
import 'package:flutter/services.dart' show rootBundle;
import '../network/model_response.dart';
import '../network/recipe_model.dart';
```

Here's what you're doing:

1. You import Chopper to create instances of `Response`.

2. `show` means that you want a specific class or classes to be visible in your app. In this case, you want `rootBundle` to be visible for loading JSON files.

> **Note**: You can hide classes by using `hide`.

Now, add `MockService`:

```
class MockService {
  // 1
  late APIRecipeQuery _currentRecipes1;
  late APIRecipeQuery _currentRecipes2;
  // 2
  Random nextRecipe = Random();

  // TODO: Add create and load methods

  // TODO: Add query method

}
```

Here's what this code does:

1. Use `_currentRecipes1` and `_currentRecipes2` to store the results loaded from the two JSON files.

2. `nextRecipe` is an instance of `Random` that creates a number between 0 and 1.

Next, you'll load recipes from the JSON files.

Implementing methods to create and load recipes

Now, replace `// TODO: Add create and load methods` with:

```
// 3
void create() {
  loadRecipes();
}

void loadRecipes() async {
  // 4
  var jsonString = await rootBundle.loadString('assets/
recipes1.json');
  // 5
  _currentRecipes1 =
APIRecipeQuery.fromJson(jsonDecode(jsonString));
  jsonString = await rootBundle.loadString('assets/
recipes2.json');
  _currentRecipes2 =
APIRecipeQuery.fromJson(jsonDecode(jsonString));
}
```

To break down this code:

3. The `create()` method, which **Provider** will call, just calls `loadRecipes()`.

4. `rootBundle` loads the JSON file as a string.

5. `jsonDecode()` creates a map that `APIRecipeQuery` will use to get a list of recipes.

Next, replace `// TODO: Add query method` with the following:

```
Future<Response<Result<APIRecipeQuery>>> queryRecipes(
  String query, int from, int to) {
    // 6
    switch(nextRecipe.nextInt(2)) {
      case 0:
        // 7
        return Future.value(Response(http.Response('Dummy', 200,
request: null),
            Success<APIRecipeQuery>(_currentRecipes1)));
      case 1:
        return Future.value(Response(http.Response('Dummy', 200,
request: null),
            Success<APIRecipeQuery>(_currentRecipes2)));
      default:
        return Future.value(Response(http.Response('Dummy', 200,
request: null),
            Success<APIRecipeQuery>(_currentRecipes1)));
    }
  }
```

Here, you:

6. Use your random field to pick a random integer, either 0 or 1.

7. Wrap your `APIRecipeQuery` result in `Success`, `Response` and `Future`.

You'll notice that this looks like the method from `RecipeService`. That's because the mock service should look the same.

That's all for mocking. Now you'll use it in the app, instead of the real service.

Using the mock service

Open up **main.dart** and add the `MockService` interface:

```
import 'mock_service/mock_service.dart';
```

Currently, build() is using ChangeNotifierProvider. Now, you need to use multiple providers so it can also use MockService. MultiProvider will accomplish this.

Replace the whole build() method with this:

```
@override
Widget build(BuildContext context) {
  return MultiProvider(
    // 1
    providers: [
      // 2
      ChangeNotifierProvider<MemoryRepository>(
        lazy: false,
        create: (_) => MemoryRepository(),
      ),
      // 3
      Provider(
        // 4
        create: (_) => MockService()..create(),
        lazy: false,
      ),
    ],
    // 5
    child: MaterialApp(
      title: 'Recipes',
      debugShowCheckedModeBanner: false,
      theme: ThemeData(
        brightness: Brightness.light,
        primaryColor: Colors.white,
        primarySwatch: Colors.blue,
        visualDensity: VisualDensity.adaptivePlatformDensity,
      ),
      home: const MainScreen(),
    ),
  );
}
```

Here's what's going on in the code above:

1. MultiProvider uses the providers property to define multiple providers.

2. The first provider is your existing ChangeNotifierProvider.

3. You add a new provider, which will use the new mock service.

4. Create the MockService and call create() to load the JSON files (notice the .. cascade operator).

5. The only child is a MaterialApp, like before.

Now, you're ready to load and display mocked recipes.

Loading mocked recipes

Open **ui/recipes/recipe_list.dart** and add the `MockService` and `Provider` imports:

```
import '../../mock_service/mock_service.dart';
import 'package:provider/provider.dart';
```

In `_buildRecipeLoader()`, change the `RecipeService.create()` to:

```
Provider.of<MockService>(context)
```

It should now look like this:

```
future: Provider.of<MockService>(context).queryRecipes(
    searchTextController.text.trim(),
    currentStartPosition,
    currentEndPosition),
```

Stop and restart the app and search for any term in the **Recipes** tab. Notice how, no matter what you type, you only get chicken or pasta recipes. That's because `MockService` only provides those two results. In the future, it will be easier to test specific changes or add more mocked data.

Congratulations, you now have a service that works even if you don't have an account or your network isn't working. You can even use `MockService` for testing. The advantage is that you know what results you'll get because data is stored in static JSON files.

Amazing work! There was a lot in this chapter to learn, but it's important work. State management is a key concept for Flutter development.

Is Provider the only option for state management? No. Brace yourself for a quick tour of alternative libraries.

Other state management libraries

There are other packages that help with state management and provide even more flexibility when managing state in your app. While Provider features classes for widgets lower in the widget tree, other packages provide more generic state management solutions for the whole app, often enabling a unidirectional data flow architecture.

Such libraries include **Redux**, **BLoC**, **MobX** and **Riverpod**. Here's a quick overview of each.

Redux

If you come from web or React development, you might be familiar with Redux, which uses concepts such as actions, reducers, views and store. The flow looks like this:

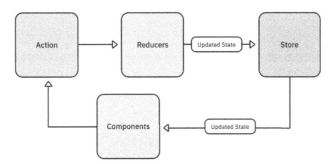

Actions, like clicks on the UI or events from network operations, are sent to reducers, which turn them into a state. That state is saved in a store, which notifies listeners, like views and components, about changes.

The nice thing about the Redux architecture is that a view can simply send actions and wait for updates from the store.

To use Redux in Flutter, you need two packages: **redux** and **flutter_redux**.

For React developers migrating to Flutter, an advantage of Redux is that it's already familiar. If you are not familiar with it, it might take a bit to learn it.

BLoC

BLoC stands for **B**usiness **Lo**gic **C**omponent. It's designed to separate UI code from the data layer and business logic, helping you create reusable code that's easy to test. Think of it as a stream of events: some widgets submit events and other widgets respond to them. BLoC sits in the middle and directs the conversation, leveraging the power of streams.

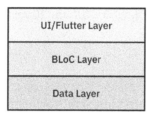

It's quite popular in the Flutter Community and very well documented.

MobX

MobX comes to Dart from the web world. It uses the following concepts:

- **Observables**: Hold the state.

- **Actions**: Mutate the state.

- **Reactions**: React to the change in observables.

MobX comes with annotations that help you write your code and make it simpler.

One advantage is that MobX allows you to wrap any data in an observable. It's relatively easy to learn and requires smaller generated code files than BLoC does.

Riverpod

Provider's author, Remi Rousselet, wrote Riverpod to address some of Provider's weaknesses. In fact, Riverpod is an anagram of Provider! Rousselet wanted to solve the following problems:

1. Remove the dependency on Flutter to make it usable with pure Dart code.

2. Be compile safe. Have the compiler catch errors that occur with Provider.

3. Have more features.

4. Be more flexible.

Riverpod is pretty new and it looks like a promising state management package to use in the future.

Key points

- State management is key to Flutter development.
- **Provider** is a great package that helps with state management.
- Other packages for handling application state include **Redux**, **Bloc**, **MobX** and **Riverpod**.
- Repositories are a pattern for providing data.
- By providing an `Interface` for the repository, you can switch between different repositories. For example, you can switch between real and mocked repositories.
- Mock services are a way to provide dummy data.

Where to go from here?

If you want to learn more about:

1. State management, go to
   https://flutter.dev/docs/development/data-and-backend/state-mgmt/intro.
2. For Flutter **Redux** go to https://pub.dev/packages/flutter_redux.
3. For **Bloc**, go to https://bloclibrary.dev/#/.
4. For **MobX**, go to https://github.com/mobxjs/mobx.dart.
5. For **Riverpod**, go to https://riverpod.dev/.
6. For Clean Architecture, go to
   https://pusher.com/tutorials/clean-architecture-introduction.

In the next chapter you'll learn all about streams, to handle data that can be sent and received continuously. See you there!

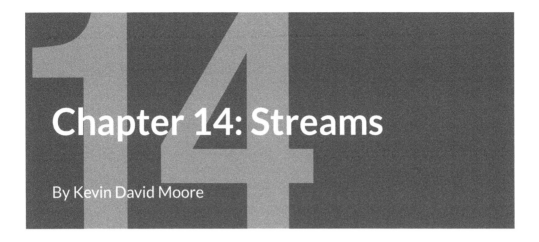

Chapter 14: Streams

By Kevin David Moore

Imagine yourself sitting by a creek, having a wonderful time. While watching the water flow, you see a piece of wood or a leaf floating down the stream and you decide to take it out of the water. You could even have someone upstream purposely float things down the creek for you to grab.

You can imagine Dart streams in a similar way: as data flowing down a creek, waiting for someone to grab it. That's what a stream does in Dart — it sends data events for a listener to grab.

With Dart streams, you can send one data event at a time while other parts of your app listen for those events. Such events can be collections, maps or any other type of data you've created.

Streams can send errors in addition to data; you can also stop the stream, if you need to.

In this chapter, you'll update your recipe project to use streams in two different locations. You'll use one for bookmarks, to let the user mark favorite recipes and automatically update the UI to display them. You'll use the second to update your ingredient and grocery lists.

But before you jump into the code, you'll learn more about how streams work.

Types of streams

Streams are part of Dart, and Flutter inherits them. There are two types of streams in Flutter: single subscription streams and broadcast streams.

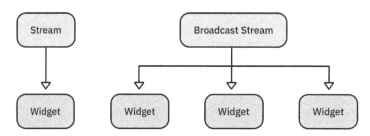

Single subscription streams are the default. They work well when you're only using a particular stream on one screen.

A single subscription stream can only be listened to once. It doesn't start generating events until it has a listener and it stops sending events when the listener stops listening, even if the source of events could still provide more data.

Single subscription streams are useful to download a file or for any single-use operation. For example, a widget can subscribe to a stream to receive updates about a value, like the progress of a download, and update its UI accordingly.

If you need multiple parts of your app to access the same stream, use a broadcast stream, instead.

A **broadcast stream** allows any number of listeners. It fires when its events are ready, whether there are listeners or not.

To create a broadcast stream, you simply call `asBroadcastStream()` on an existing single subscription stream.

```
final broadcastStream = singleStream.asBroadcastStream();
```

You can differentiate a broadcast stream from a single subscription stream by inspecting its Boolean property `isBroadcast`.

In Flutter, there are some key classes built on top of `Stream` that simplify programming with streams.

The following diagram shows the main classes used with streams:

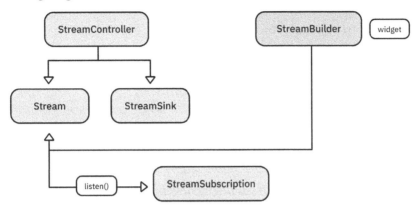

Next, you'll take a deeper look at each one.

StreamController and sink

When you create a stream, you usually use StreamController, which holds both the stream and StreamSink.

Sink

A sink is a destination for data. When you want to add data to a stream, you will add it to the sink. Since the StreamController owns the sink, it listens for data on the sink and sends the data to it's stream listeners.

Here's an example that uses StreamController:

```
final _recipeStreamController =
StreamController<List<Recipe>>();
final _stream = _recipeStreamController.stream;
```

To add data to a stream, you add it to its sink:

```
_recipeStreamController.sink.add(_recipesList);
```

This uses the sink field of the controller to "place" a list of recipes on the stream. That data will be sent to any current listeners.

When you're done with the stream, make sure you close it, like this:

```
_recipeStreamController.close();
```

StreamSubscription

Using listen() on a stream returns a StreamSubscription. You can use this subscription class to cancel the stream when you're done, like this:

```
StreamSubscription s = stream.listen((value) {
    print('Value from controller: $value');
});
...
...
// You are done with the subscription
subscription.cancel();
```

Sometimes, it's helpful to have an automated mechanism to avoid managing subscriptions manually. That's where StreamBuilder comes in.

StreamBuilder

StreamBuilder is handy when you want to use a stream. It takes two parameters: a stream and a builder. As you receive data from the stream, the builder takes care of building or updating the UI.

Here's an example:

```
final repository = Provider.of<Repository>(context, listen:
false);
  return StreamBuilder<List<Recipe>>(
    stream: repository.recipesStream(),
    builder: (context, AsyncSnapshot<List<Recipe>> snapshot) {
      // extract recipes from snapshot and build the view
    }
  )
...
```

StreamBuilder is handy because you don't need to use a subscription directly and it unsubscribes from the stream automatically when the widget is destroyed.

Now that you understand how streams work, you'll convert your existing project to use them.

Adding streams to Recipe Finder

You're now ready to start working on your recipe project. If you're following along with your app from the previous chapters, open it and keep using it with this chapter. If not, just locate the **projects** folder for this chapter and open **starter** in Android Studio.

> **Note**: If you use the starter app, don't forget to add your apiKey and apiId in **network/recipe_service.dart**.

To convert your project to use streams, you need to change the memory repository class to add two new methods that return one stream for recipes and another for ingredients. Instead of just returning a list of static recipes, you'll use streams to modify that list and refresh the UI to display the change.

This is what the flow of the app looks like:

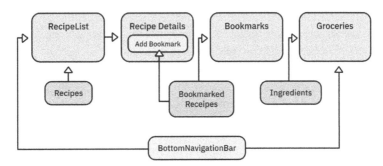

Here, you can see that the **RecipeList** screen has a list of recipes. Bookmarking a recipe adds it to the bookmarked recipe list and updates both the bookmark and the groceries screens.

You'll start by converting your repository code to return Streams and Futures.

Adding futures and streams to the repository

Open **data/repository.dart** and change all of the return types to return a `Future`. For example, change the existing `findAllRecipes()` to:

```
Future<List<Recipe>> findAllRecipes();
```

Do this for all the methods except `init()` and `close()`.

Your final class should look like:

```
Future<List<Recipe>> findAllRecipes();

Future<Recipe> findRecipeById(int id);

Future<List<Ingredient>> findAllIngredients();

Future<List<Ingredient>> findRecipeIngredients(int recipeId);

Future<int> insertRecipe(Recipe recipe);

Future<List<int>> insertIngredients(List<Ingredient>
ingredients);

Future<void> deleteRecipe(Recipe recipe);

Future<void> deleteIngredient(Ingredient ingredient);

Future<void> deleteIngredients(List<Ingredient> ingredients);

Future<void> deleteRecipeIngredients(int recipeId);

Future init();

void close();
```

These updates allow you to have methods that work asynchronously to process data from a database or the network.

Next, add two new `Stream`s after `findAllRecipes()`:

```
// 1
Stream<List<Recipe>> watchAllRecipes();
// 2
Stream<List<Ingredient>> watchAllIngredients();
```

Here's what this code does:

1. `watchAllRecipes()` watches for any changes to the list of recipes. For example, if the user did a new search, it updates the list of recipes and notifies listeners accordingly.

2. `watchAllIngredients()` listens for changes in the list of ingredients displayed on the **Groceries** screen.

You've now changed the interface, so you need to update the memory repository.

Cleaning up the repository code

Before updating the code to use streams and futures, there are some minor housekeeping updates.

Open **data/memory_respository.dart**, import the the Dart **async** library:

```
import 'dart:async';
```

Now **remove**:

```
import 'package:flutter/foundation.dart';
```

Then, update the `MemoryRepository` class definition to remove `ChangeNotifier`, so it looks like:

```
class MemoryRepository extends Repository {
```

Next, add a few new fields after the existing two `List` declarations, ignoring all the red squiggles:

```
//1
Stream<List<Recipe>>? _recipeStream;
Stream<List<Ingredient>>? _ingredientStream;
// 2
final StreamController _recipeStreamController =
    StreamController<List<Recipe>>();
final StreamController _ingredientStreamController =
    StreamController<List<Ingredient>>();
```

Here's what's going on:

1. `_recipeStream` and `ingredientStream` are private fields for the streams. These will be captured the first time a stream is requested, which prevents new streams from being created for each call.

2. Creates `StreamControllers` for recipes and ingredients.

And now, add these new methods before `findAllRecipes()`:

```
// 3
@override
Stream<List<Recipe>> watchAllRecipes() {
  if (_recipeStream == null) {
    _recipeStream = _recipeStreamController.stream as
Stream<List<Recipe>>;
  }
  return _recipeStream!;
}

// 4
@override
Stream<List<Ingredient>> watchAllIngredients() {
  if (_ingredientStream == null) {
    _ingredientStream =
      _ingredientStreamController.stream as
Stream<List<Ingredient>>;
  }
  return _ingredientStream!;
}
```

These streams will:

3. Check to see if you already have the stream. If not, call the stream method, which creates a new stream, then return it.

4. Do the same for ingredients.

Updating the existing repository

`MemoryRepository` is full of red squiggles. That's because the methods all use the old signatures, and everything's now based on `Futures`.

Still in **data/memory_repository.dart**, replace the existing `findAllRecipes()` with this:

```
@override
// 1
```

```
Future<List<Recipe>> findAllRecipes() {
  // 2
  return Future.value(_currentRecipes);
}
```

These updates:

1. Change the method to return a `Future`.

2. Wrap the return value with a `Future.value()`.

There are a few more updates you need to make before moving on to the next section.

First, in `init()` remove the `null` from the `return` statement so it looks like this:

```
@override
Future init() {
  return Future.value();
}
```

Then update `close()` so it closes the streams.

```
@override
void close() {
  _recipeStreamController.close();
  _ingredientStreamController.close();
}
```

In the next section, you'll update the remaining methods to return futures and add data to the stream using `StreamController`.

Sending recipes over the stream

As you learned earlier, `StreamController`'s `sink` property adds data to streams. Since this happens in the future, you need to change the return type to `Future` and then update the methods to add data to the stream.

To start, change `insertRecipe()` to:

```
@override
// 1
Future<int> insertRecipe(Recipe recipe) {
  _currentRecipes.add(recipe);
  // 2
  _recipeStreamController.sink.add(_currentRecipes);
```

```
    if (recipe.ingredients != null) {
      insertIngredients(recipe.ingredients!);
    }
    // 3
    // 4
    return Future.value(0);
  }
```

Here's what you have updated:

1. Update the method's return type to be `Future`.

2. Add `_currentRecipes` to the recipe sink.

3. Removed `notifyListeners();`.

4. Return a `Future` value. You'll learn how to return the ID of the new item in a later chapter.

This replaces the previous list with the new list and notifies any stream listeners that the data has changed.

You might wonder why you call `add` with the same list instead of adding a single ingredient or recipe. The reason is that the stream expects a list, not a single value. By doing it this way, you replace the previous list with the updated one.

Now that you know how to convert the first method, it's time to convert the rest of the methods as an exercise. Don't worry, you can do it! :]

Exercise

Convert the remaining methods, just like you just did with `insertRecipe()`. You'll need to do the following:

1. Update `MemoryRepository` methods to return a `Future` that matches the new `Repository` interface methods.

2. For all methods that change a watched item, add a call to add the item to the sink.

3. Remove all the calls to `notifyListeners()`. Hint: not all methods have this statement.

4. Wrap the return values in `Futures`.

For a method that returns a `Future<void>`, what do you think the return will look like? Hint: there's a `return` statement.

```
return Future.value();
```

If you get stuck, check out **memory_repository.dart** in the **challenge** project in this chapter's folder — but give it your best shot first!

After you complete the exercise, `MemoryRepository` shouldn't have any more red squiggles — but you still have a few more tweaks to make before you can run your new, stream-powered app.

Switching between services

In the previous chapter, you created a MockService to provide local data that never changes, but you also have access to RecipeService. It's still a bit tedious to switch between the two, so you'll take care of that before integrating streams.

An easy way to do that is with an interface — or, as it's known in Dart, an abstract class. Remember that an interface or abstract class is just a contract that implementing classes will provide the given methods.

Once you create your interface, it will look like this:

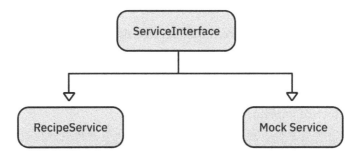

To start creating the interface, go to the **network** folder, create a new Dart file named **service_interface.dart** and add the following imports:

```
import 'package:chopper/chopper.dart';
import 'model_response.dart';
import 'recipe_model.dart';
```

Next, add a new class:

```
abstract class ServiceInterface {
  Future<Response<Result<APIRecipeQuery>>> queryRecipes(
      String query, int from, int to);
}
```

This defines a class with one method named queryRecipes. It has the same parameters and return values as RecipeService and MockService. By having each service implement this interface, you can change the providers to provide this interface instead of a specific class.

Implementing the new service interface

Open **network/recipe_service.dart** and add the **service_interface** import:

```
import 'service_interface.dart';
```

Now, have RecipeService implement ServiceInterface:

```
abstract class RecipeService extends ChopperService
    implements ServiceInterface {
```

Then, add @override right above:

```
@Get(path: 'search')
```

Next, do the same in **mock_service/mock_service.dart**. Add the **service_interface** import:

```
import '../network/service_interface.dart';
```

Now, have the service implement this interface:

```
class MockService implements ServiceInterface {
```

and add the @override above queryRecipes(). With this done, you can now change the provider in **main.dart**.

Changing the provider

You'll now adopt the new service interface instead of the specific services you used in the current code.

Open **main.dart** and add these imports:

```
import 'data/repository.dart';
import 'network/recipe_service.dart';
import 'network/service_interface.dart';
```

Then, remove the existing import of **mock_service.dart**.

Find `// TODO: Update ChangeNotifierProvider` replace it and `ChangeNotifierProvider` with this:

```
Provider<Repository>(
  lazy: false,
  create: (_) => MemoryRepository(),
),
```

When you provide a `Repository`, you can change the type of repository you create. Here, you're using `MemoryRepository`, but you could also use something else, as you'll do in the next chapter.

Now, just below the last change, replace the `Provider` with:

```
Provider<ServiceInterface>(
  create: (_) => RecipeService.create(),
  lazy: false,
),
```

Here, you use `RecipeService`, but if you start having problems with API rate-limiting, you can switch to `MockService`.

Next, open **ui/recipes/recipe_details.dart** and replace the **memory_repository** import with the `Repository` import:

```
import '../../data/repository.dart';
```

Now, replace the line below `// TODO: change to new repository` with:

```
final repository = Provider.of<Repository>(context);
```

Now, you can finally replace the specific service with your interface. Open **ui/recipes/recipe_list.dart**, replace the existing import of **mock_service.dart** with the following import:

```
import '../../network/service_interface.dart';
```

Next, in `_buildRecipeLoader()`, replace the line below `// TODO: replace with new interface` with:

```
future: Provider.of<ServiceInterface>(context).queryRecipes(
```

You're now ready to integrate the new code based on streams. Fasten your seat belt! :]

Adding streams to Bookmarks

The **Bookmarks** page uses `Consumer`, but you want to change it to a stream so it can react when a user bookmarks a recipe. To do this, you need to replace the reference to `MemoryRepository` with `Repository` and use a `StreamBuilder` widget.

Start by opening **ui/myrecipes/my_recipe_list.dart** and changing the memory_repository import to:

```
import '../../data/repository.dart';
```

Inside `_buildRecipeList()`, replace the `return Consumer` and the line below it with the following:

```
// 1
final repository = Provider.of<Repository>(context, listen:
false);
// 2
return StreamBuilder<List<Recipe>>(
  // 3
  stream: repository.watchAllRecipes(),
  // 4
  builder: (context, AsyncSnapshot<List<Recipe>> snapshot) {
    // 5
    if (snapshot.connectionState == ConnectionState.active) {
      // 6
      final recipes = snapshot.data ?? [];
```

Don't worry about the red squiggles for now. This code:

1. Uses `Provider` to get your `Repository`.

2. Uses `StreamBuilder`, which uses a `List<Recipe>` stream type.

3. Uses the new `watchAllRecipes()` to return a stream of recipes for the builder to use.

4. Uses the builder callback to receive your snapshot.

5. Checks the state of the connection. When the state is **active**, you have data.

Now, at the end of `_buildRecipeList()`, find `// TODO: Add else here` and replace it with:

```
} else {
  return Container();
}
```

This returns a container if the snapshot isn't ready.

Next, in `deleteRecipe()`, change `MemoryRepository` to `Repository` so it looks like this:

```
void deleteRecipe(Repository repository, Recipe recipe) async {
```

> **Note**: You can always use Android Studio's **Reformat Code** command from the **Code** menu to clean up your formatting.

All these changes ensure that the class depends on the new, generic `Repository`.

At this point, you've achieved one of your two goals: you've changed the **Recipes** screen to use streams. Next, you'll do the same for the **Groceries** tab.

Adding streams to Groceries

Start by opening **ui/shopping/shopping_list.dart** and replacing the
memory_repository.dart import with:

```
import '../../data/repository.dart';
import '../../data/models/ingredient.dart';
```

Just as you did in the last section, find the `build()` method and change the `return`
`Consumer` line and the line below it to the following:

```
final repository = Provider.of<Repository>(context);
return StreamBuilder(
  stream: repository.watchAllIngredients(),
  builder: (context, snapshot) {
    if (snapshot.connectionState == ConnectionState.active) {
      final ingredients = snapshot.data as List<Ingredient>?;
      if (ingredients == null) {
        return Container();
      }
```

Once again, ignore the red squiggles. This is just like the code from Recipe Details,
except it uses `watchAllIngredients()`.

Next, at the end of `ListView.builder` replace `// TODO: Add else here` with:

```
} else {
  return Container();
}
```

As before, this just returns a container if the snapshot isn't ready.

No more red squiggles. Yay! :]

Stop and restart your app and make sure it works as before. Your main screen will look like this after a search:

Click a recipe. The **Details** page will look like this:

Next, click the **Bookmark** button to return to the **Recipes** screen, then go to the **Bookmarks** page to see the recipe you just added:

Finally, go to the **Groceries** tab and make sure the recipe ingredients are all showing.

Congratulations! You're now using streams to control the flow of data. If any of the screens change, the other screens will know about that change and will update the screen.

You're also using the `Repository` interface so you can go back and forth between a memory class and a different type in the future.

Key points

- Streams are a way to asynchronously send data to other parts of your app.
- You usually create streams by using `StreamController`.
- Use `StreamBuilder` to add a stream to your UI.
- Abstract classes, or interfaces, are a great way to abstract functionality.

Where to go from here?

In this chapter, you learned how to use streams. If you want to learn more about the topic, visit the Dart documentation at https://dart.dev/tutorials/language/streams.

In the next chapter, you'll learn about databases and how to persist your data locally.

Chapter 15: Saving Data With SQLite

By Kevin David Moore

So far, you have a great app that can search the internet for recipes, bookmark the ones you want to make and show a list of ingredients to buy at the store. But what happens if you close the app, go to the store and try to look up your ingredients? They're gone! As you might have guessed, having an in-memory repository means that the data doesn't persist after your app closes.

One of the best ways to persist data is with a database. Both Android and iOS provide access to the **SQLite** database system. This allows you to insert, read, update and remove structured data that are persisted on disk.

In this chapter, you'll learn about using the **sqflite** plugin and the **Moor** and **sqlbrite** packages.

By the end of the chapter, you'll know:

- How to create SQLite-based databases.

- How to insert, fetch and remove recipes or ingredients.

- How to use the sqflite plugin.

- How to use the sqlbrite library and receive updates via streams.

- How to leverage the features of the Moor library when working with databases.

Databases

Databases have been around for a long time, but being able to put a full-blown database on a phone is pretty amazing.

What *is* a database? Think of it like a file cabinet that contains folders with sheets of paper in them. A database has tables (file folders) that store data (sheets of paper).

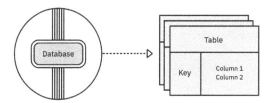

Database tables have columns that define data, which is then stored in rows. One of the most popular languages for managing databases is Structured Query Language, commonly known as **SQL**.

You use SQL commands to get the data in and out of the database. In this chapter, you'll learn about SQL commands that create SQL statements that:

1. Manage a database.

2. Manage data in the database's tables.

Using SQL

The SQLite database system on Android and iOS is an embedded engine that runs in the same process as the app. SQLite is lightweight, taking up less than 500 Kb on most systems.

When SQLite creates a database, it stores it in one file inside an app. These files are cross-platform, meaning you can pull a file off a phone and read it on a regular computer.

Unlike a database server, SQLite needs no server configuration or server process.

While SQLite is small and runs fast, it still requires some knowledge of the SQL language and how to create databases, tables and execute SQL commands.

Writing queries

One of the most important parts of SQL is writing a query. To make a query, use the `SELECT` command followed by any columns you want the database to return, then the table name. For example:

```
// 1
SELECT name, address FROM Customers;
// 2
SELECT * FROM Customers;
// 3
SELECT name, address FROM Customers WHERE name LIKE 'A%';
```

Here's what's happening in the code above:

1. Returns the name and address columns from the `CUSTOMERS` table.

2. Using `*`, returns all columns from the specified table.

3. Uses `WHERE` to filter the returned data. In this case, it only returns data where `NAME` starts with `A`.

Adding data

You can add data using the `INSERT` statement:

```
INSERT INTO Customers (NAME, ADDRESS) VALUES (value1, value2);
```

While you don't have to list all the columns, if you want to add all the values, the values must be in the order you used to define the columns. It's a best practice to list the column names whenever you insert data. That makes it easier to update your values list if, say, you add a column in the middle.

Deleting data

To delete data, use the `DELETE` statement:

```
DELETE FROM Customers WHERE id = '1';
```

If you don't use the `WHERE` clause, you'll delete all the data from the table. Here, you delete the customer whose `id` equals 1. You can use broader conditions of course. For example, you might delete all the customers with a given city.

Updating data

You use UPDATE to update your data. You won't need this command for this app, but for reference, the syntax is:

```
UPDATE customers
SET
  phone = '555-12345',
WHERE id = '1';
```

This updates the phone number of the customer whose id equals 1.

To store recipes and ingredients in a database, you'll start by adding two new libraries to your app: **sqflite** and **sqlbrite**.

sqflite

The sqflite plugin provides SQLite database access on iOS, Android and macOS. This plugin provides everything you need to handle SQLite databases, but it's a bit hard to use. Later, you'll use the Moor package, which makes things easier. First, however, it's important to learn how to use the underlying plugin.

> **Note**: sqflite is a plugin and not a package because it requires platform-specific code.

With sqflite, you need to manually create all the database's tables and put SQL statements together by hand.

To start, you need to create the database and then create the table(s). This means you need to understand SQL's CREATE TABLE. Here's how it looks:

```
CREATE TABLE mytable (
  id INTEGER PRIMARY KEY,
  namo TEXT,
  value INTEGER,
  NUM REAL
);
```

This creates a table named `mytable` with the following columns:

- **id**: Defined as an integer, it's also the primary key.

- **name**: A string.

- **value**: An integer.

- **num**: Of type `REAL`, this is stored as an 8-byte floating-point value.

A primary key is very important because it makes each row unique. This way, you can easily find or delete entries by using the `id` column.

Once you have a reference to the database, you can insert, delete, update or query its table(s). When you query the database, you'll get a `List<Map<String, dynamic>>` back. You then need to take each item in the `List` and use a function to convert the `Map` into a class. This is similar to how you convert JSON into classes.

sqlbrite

The sqlbrite library is a reactive stream wrapper around sqflite. It allows you to set up streams so you can receive events when there's a change in your database. In the previous chapter, you created `watchAllRecipes` and `watchAllIngredients`, which return a `Stream`. To create these streams from a database, sqlbrite uses `watch` methods.

Adding a database to the project

If you're following along with your app, open it and keep using it with this chapter. If not, locate the **projects** folder for this chapter and open the **starter** folder.

> **Note**: If you use the starter app, don't forget to add your **apiKey** and **apiId** in **network/recipe_service.dart**.

Your app manages two types of data: recipes and ingredients, which you'll model according to this diagram:

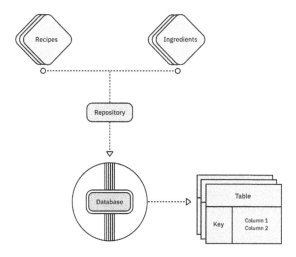

In this chapter, you'll implement two different solutions: one with sqflite and one with Moor. This will give you the experience to decide which one you prefer. You'll then swap the memory repository for the new database repository.

Adding sqflite

To use the sqflite plugin, open **pubspec.yaml** and add the following packages after the **equatable** package:

```
sqflite: ^2.0.0+4
path_provider: ^2.0.2
synchronized: ^3.0.0
sqlbrite: ^2.1.0
```

These packages provide the following:

1. **sqflite**: Provides SQLite database access.

2. **path_provider**: Simplifies dealing with common file system locations.

3. **synchronized**: Helps implement lock mechanisms to prevent concurrent access, when needed.

4. **sqlbrite**: Reactive wrapper around sqflite that receives changes happening in the database via streams.

Run **Pub Get**. Now, you're ready to create your first database.

Setting up the database

In the **data** folder, create a new folder named **sqlite**. Inside that folder, create a new file called **database_helper.dart**. This class will handle all the SQLite database operations.

Start by adding all the imports you'll need:

```
import 'package:path/path.dart';
import 'package:sqflite/sqflite.dart';
import 'package:path_provider/path_provider.dart';
import 'package:sqlbrite/sqlbrite.dart';
import 'package:synchronized/synchronized.dart';
import '../models/models.dart';
```

This provides access to all your packages.

Now, define the class:

```
class DatabaseHelper {
}
```

Next, define some fields and constants:

```
// 1
static const _databaseName = 'MyRecipes.db';
static const _databaseVersion = 1;

// 2
static const recipeTable = 'Recipe';
static const ingredientTable = 'Ingredient';
static const recipeId = 'recipeId';
static const ingredientId = 'ingredientId';

// 3
static late BriteDatabase _streamDatabase;

// make this a singleton class
// 4
DatabaseHelper._privateConstructor();
static final DatabaseHelper instance =
DatabaseHelper._privateConstructor();
// 5
static var lock = Lock();

// only have a single app-wide reference to the database
// 6
static Database? _database;

// TODO: Add create database code here
```

Here's what's happening in the code:

1. Constants for the database name and version.

2. Define the names of the tables.

3. Your sqlbrite database instance. `late` indicates the variable is non-nullable and that it will be initialized after it's been declared.

4. Make the constructor private and provide a public static `instance`.

5. Define `lock`, which you'll use to prevent concurrent access.

6. Private sqflite database instance.

You need to create the database once, then you can access it through your `instance`. This prevents other classes from creating multiple instances of the helper and initializing the database more than once.

Creating tables

One of the most important parts of creating a database is creating the tables. Your app will have two tables: `recipeTable` and `ingredientTable`.

While it isn't required, it's a good practice for tables to have a `PRIMARY KEY`, which is a unique ID for each record or row of data. You can automatically create this ID when a new record is created.

The `TEXT` SQL type represents all the strings, while the `INTEGER` SQL type represents the integers.

Locate `// TODO: Add create database code here` and replace it with the following to create two databases:

```
// SQL code to create the database table
// 1
Future _onCreate(Database db, int version) async {
  // 2
  await db.execute('''
      CREATE TABLE $recipeTable (
        $recipeId INTEGER PRIMARY KEY,
        label TEXT,
        image TEXT,
        url TEXT,
        calories REAL,
        totalWeight REAL,
        totalTime REAL
      )
```

```
        ''');
  // 3
  await db.execute('''
      CREATE TABLE $ingredientTable (
        $ingredientId INTEGER PRIMARY KEY,
        $recipeId INTEGER,
        name TEXT,
        weight REAL
      )
      ''');
}

// TODO: Add code to open database
```

In the code above, you:

1. Pass an sqflite database db into the method. It will create the tables.

2. Create `recipeTable` with the same columns as the model using `CREATE TABLE`.

3. Create `ingredientTable`.

> **Note**: You use REAL for double values.

For this example, your app's tables only have a few columns. You can use additional statements to add more tables and/or columns, if you need to.

Now that you've created the tables, you'll learn how to access them.

Opening the database

Before you can use the database, you have to open it. `_initDatabase()` uses sqflite's `openDatabase()`. That method requires a path where it should create the database, the current database version and a "create" method name.

Replace the line that reads `// TODO: Add code to open database` with the following:

```
// this opens the database (and creates it if it doesn't exist)
// 1
Future<Database> _initDatabase() async {
  // 2
  final documentsDirectory = await
getApplicationDocumentsDirectory();

  // 3
```

```
  final path = join(documentsDirectory.path, _databaseName);

  // 4
  // TODO: Remember to turn off debugging before deploying app
to store(s).
  Sqflite.setDebugModeOn(true);

  // 5
  return openDatabase(path,
      version: _databaseVersion, onCreate: _onCreate);
}

// TODO: Add initialize getter here
```

In the code above, you:

1. Declare that the method returns a Future, as the operation is asynchronous.

2. Get the app document's directory name, where you'll store the database.

3. Create a path to the database by appending the database name to the directory path.

4. Turn on debugging. Remember to turn this off when you're ready to deploy your app to the store(s).

5. Use sqflite's openDatabase() to create and store the database file in the path.

Next, since _database is private, you need to create a getter that will initialize the database. Replace // TODO: Add initialize getter here with this:

```
// 1
Future<Database> get database async {
  // 2
  if (_database != null) return _database!;
  // Use this object to prevent concurrent access to data
  // 3
  await lock.synchronized(() async {
    // lazily instantiate the db the first time it is accessed
    // 4
    if (_database == null) {
      // 5
      _database = await _initDatabase();
      // 6
      _streamDatabase = BriteDatabase(_database!);
    }
  });
  return _database!;
}
```

```
// TODO: Add getter for streamDatabase
```

Using the methods you created earlier, this method will open and create the database, if it hasn't been created before. Specifically:

1. Other methods and classes can use this getter to access (get) the database.

2. If `_database` is not `null`, it's already been created, so you return the existing one.

3. Use `lock` to ensure that only one process can be in this section of code at a time.

4. Check to make sure the database is null.

5. Call the `_initDatabase()`, which you defined above.

6. Create a `BriteDatabase` instance, wrapping the database.

> **Note**: When you run the app a second time, it won't call `_onCreate()` because the database already exists.

Now that you have a getter for the database, create a getter for the stream database by replacing `// TODO: Add getter for streamDatabase` with:

```
// 1
Future<BriteDatabase> get streamDatabase async {
  // 2
  await database;
  return _streamDatabase;
}

// TODO: Add parseRecipes here
```

Here, you:

1. Define an asynchronous getter method.

2. Await the result — because it also creates `_streamDatabase`.

You'll use the stream database for the stream methods in your repository, as well as to insert and delete data.

The infrastructure is now in place, but the database speaks SQL and your app deals with either JSON or Dart classes. It's time to add some helper methods to convert SQL data to JSON and vice versa.

Converting data to classes

To convert the stored map of data from the database to classes, you'll need to add `fromJson()` and `toJson()` to the model classes.

> **Note**: If you need more information on JSON, see Chapter 10, "Serialization With JSON".

Open **data/models/recipe.dart**. Add the following at the bottom, before the closing }:

```
// Create a Recipe from JSON data
factory Recipe.fromJson(Map<String, dynamic> json) => Recipe(
    id: json['recipeId'],
    label: json['label'],
    image: json['image'],
    url: json['url'],
    calories: json['calories'],
    totalWeight: json['totalWeight'],
    totalTime: json['totalTime'],
);

// Convert our Recipe to JSON to make it easier when you store
// it in the database
Map<String, dynamic> toJson() => {
    'recipeId': id,
    'label': label,
    'image': image,
    'url': url,
    'calories': calories,
    'totalWeight': totalWeight,
    'totalTime': totalTime,
};
```

These two methods convert a Map<String, dynamic> to a Recipe and vice versa.

Open **data/models/ingredient.dart**. Add these two methods at the bottom, before the closing }:

```
// Create a Ingredient from JSON data
factory Ingredient.fromJson(Map<String, dynamic> json) =>
Ingredient(
    id: json['ingredientId'],
    recipeId: json['recipeId'],
    name: json['name'],
    weight: json['weight'],
);
```

```
// Convert our Ingredient to JSON to make it easier when you
// store it in the database
Map<String, dynamic> toJson() => {
  'ingredientId': id,
  'recipeId': recipeId,
  'name': name,
  'weight': weight,
};
```

Similar to Recipe's methods, these let you convert an Ingredient to a Map and vice versa.

Now, return to **database_helper.dart** and replace // TODO: Add parseRecipes here with the following:

```
List<Recipe> parseRecipes(List<Map<String, dynamic>> recipeList)
{
  final recipes = <Recipe>[];
  // 1
  recipeList.forEach((recipeMap) {
    // 2
    final recipe = Recipe.fromJson(recipeMap);
    // 3
    recipes.add(recipe);
  });
  // 4
  return recipes;
}

List<Ingredient> parseIngredients(List<Map<String, dynamic>>
ingredientList) {
  final ingredients = <Ingredient>[];
  ingredientList.forEach((ingredientMap) {
    // 5
    final ingredient = Ingredient.fromJson(ingredientMap);
    ingredients.add(ingredient);
  });
  return ingredients;
}

// TODO: Add findAppRecipes here
```

In the code above, you:

1. Iterate over a list of recipes in JSON format.

2. Convert each recipe into a Recipe instance.

3. Add the recipe to the recipe list.

4. Return the list of `recipes`.

5. Convert each ingredient in JSON format into a list of `Ingredients`.

With the conversion code in place, it's now time to integrate it into the existing repository.

Implementing repository-like functions

Your next step is to create functions that return the information that the repository expects. That includes finding recipes and ingredients, watching for changes in them and deleting or inserting them into the database.

Start with the first three methods of the repository pattern: `findAllRecipes()`, `watchAllRecipes()` and `watchAllIngredients()`. This is the pattern you'll use:

- Get the database.

- Perform the query and return the parsed results.

Locate `// TODO: Add findAppRecipes` here and replace it with the following:

```
Future<List<Recipe>> findAllRecipes() async {
  // 1
  final db = await instance.streamDatabase;
  // 2
  final recipeList = await db.query(recipeTable);
  // 3
  final recipes = parseRecipes(recipeList);
  return recipes;
}

// TODO: Add watchAllRecipes() here
```

In this code, you:

1. Get your database `instance`.

2. Use the database `query()` to get all the recipes. `query()` has other parameters, but you don't need them here.

3. Use `parseRecipes()` to get a list of recipes.

Now, you need to handle the two `watch` methods, which are a bit different. You'll use `yield*` with a query to create a stream and `async*` on the method name.

Replace // TODO: Add watchAllRecipes() here with:

```
Stream<List<Recipe>> watchAllRecipes() async* {
  final db = await instance.streamDatabase;
  // 1
  yield* db
    // 2
    .createQuery(recipeTable)
    // 3
    .mapToList((row) => Recipe.fromJson(row));
}

// TODO: Add watchAllIngredients() here
```

Here's what's happening:

1. yield* creates a Stream using the query.

2. Create a query using recipeTable.

3. For each row, convert the row to a list of recipes.

Now, for the ingredients, you need a similar method.

Replace // TODO: Add watchAllIngredients() here with:

```
Stream<List<Ingredient>> watchAllIngredients() async* {
  final db = await instance.streamDatabase;
  yield* db
      .createQuery(ingredientTable)
      .mapToList((row) => Ingredient.fromJson(row));
}

// TODO: Add findRecipeByID() here
```

Here you watch for results of a query to the ingredients table, which is delivered via a stream. Notice the async* and the yield* keywords used to signal a stream.

Now that you've ensured that the repository will get the data it expects, your next step is to let the user find the recipes they need.

Finding recipes

After the user has added recipes, they'll want a quick way to find the one they have in mind for dinner. That's what you'll work on next.

While you could use rawQuery(), which uses raw SQL commands, it's easier to pull data from a database if you use query(), instead. query() lets you pass the columns you want to be returned and even include a where filter. You can also group, order or add limits with an offset.

To find a specific recipe, you need to query using the unique recipe ID. To enable this, replace // TODO: Add findRecipeByID() here with this code:

```
Future<Recipe> findRecipeById(int id) async {
  final db = await instance.streamDatabase;
  final recipeList = await db.query(recipeTable, where: 'id =
$id');
  final recipes = parseRecipes(recipeList);
  return recipes.first;
}

// TODO: Put findAllIngredients() here
```

This is similar to findAllRecipes(); the only difference is that you pass the id to where. The query method returns a list, even when there is one item on the list.

Next, replace // TODO: Put findAllIngredients() here with findAllIngredients():

```
Future<List<Ingredient>> findAllIngredients() async {
  final db = await instance.streamDatabase;
  final ingredientList = await db.query(ingredientTable);
  final ingredients = parseIngredients(ingredientList);
  return ingredients;
}

// TODO: findRecipeIngredients() goes here
```

Here, you use ingredientTable and pass the results to parseIngredients().

To find all the ingredients for a specific recipe, you need to use the where clause when searching for ingredients with a specific recipe ID. Replace // TODO: findRecipeIngredients() goes here with:

```
Future<List<Ingredient>> findRecipeIngredients(int recipeId)
async {
  final db = await instance.streamDatabase;
```

```
  final ingredientList =
      await db.query(ingredientTable, where: 'recipeId =
$recipeId');
  final ingredients = parseIngredients(ingredientList);
  return ingredients;
}

// TODO: Insert methods go here
```

Here you query the ingredients table by recipe ID, parse the results and return the list of ingredients.

Inserting data into tables

The user will want to add the delicious recipes they find to the app. To let them do this, you need a way to insert data into tables.

BriteDatabase provides insert(). This method takes a table name and the JSON to do the insertion. As long as the models have a toJson() and a fromJson(), you can easily write methods to insert an entry into a table.

Locate and replace // TODO: Insert methods go here with the following methods:

```
// 1
Future<int> insert(String table, Map<String, dynamic> row) async
{
  final db = await instance.streamDatabase;
  // 2
  return db.insert(table, row);
}

Future<int> insertRecipe(Recipe recipe) {
  // 3
  return insert(recipeTable, recipe.toJson());
}

Future<int> insertIngredient(Ingredient ingredient) {
  // 4
  return insert(ingredientTable, ingredient.toJson());
}

// TODO: Delete methods go here
```

Here's what's going on in this code:

1. Take the table name and the JSON map.

2. Use Sqlbrite's insert().

3. Return values from insert() using the recipe's table and JSON data.

4. Return values from insert() using the ingredient's table and JSON data.

But what if the user doesn't like the recipe they added? They need a way to remove data as well. That's the next step.

Deleting data

Deleting data is just as easy as inserting it; you just need the table name and a row ID. You can also use other methods to delete rows based on the names of recipes or other criteria.

Replace // TODO: Delete methods go here with the following:

```
// 1
Future<int> _delete(String table, String columnId, int id) async
{
  final db = await instance.streamDatabase;
  // 2
  return db.delete(table, where: '$columnId = ?',whereArgs:
[id]);
}

Future<int> deleteRecipe(Recipe recipe) async {
  // 3
  if (recipe.id != null) {
    return _delete(recipeTable, recipeId, recipe.id!);
  } else {
    return Future.value(-1);
  }
}

Future<int> deleteIngredient(Ingredient ingredient) async {
  if (ingredient.id != null) {
    return _delete(ingredientTable, ingredientId,
ingredient.id!);
  } else {
    return Future.value(-1);
  }
}

Future<void> deleteIngredients(List<Ingredient> ingredients) {
    // 4
  ingredients.forEach((ingredient) {
    if (ingredient.id != null) {
      _delete(ingredientTable, ingredientId, ingredient.id!);
    }
  });
  return Future.value();
```

```
  }

  Future<int> deleteRecipeIngredients(int id) async {
    final db = await instance.streamDatabase;
    // 5
    return db
        .delete(ingredientTable, where: '$recipeId = ?',
    whereArgs: [id]);
  }

  // TODO: Add close() here
```

Here's what this does:

1. Create a private function, _delete, which will delete data from the table with the provided column and row id.

2. Delete a row where columnId equals the passed-in id.

3. Call _delete(), which deletes a recipe with the passed ID.

4. For each ingredient, delete that entry from the ingredients table.

5. Delete all ingredients that have the given recipeId.

_delete() and deleteRecipeIngredients() use the where and whereArgs parameters. If you use whereArgs, you need to use a ? for each item in the list of arguments. Notice the last method. It uses whereArgs: [id]. This is an array of parameters. For every question mark, you need an entry in the array.

You could also delete a recipe based on the label string, but this causes problems if you have multiple entries with the same label.

You're nearly done with the setup! You just need a way to open and close the database.

Initializing and closing

SQLite databases need to be opened and closed. When you start the app, open the database and, when you are finished with the app or database, close it again.

Using providers is a nice way to open and close the database. Your helper class doesn't need its own init, but it does have the database getter that needs time to open up the database. When it finishes processing, you need to close the getter.

Replace `// TODO: Add close()` here with your last method:

```
void close() {
  _streamDatabase.close();
}
```

Closing `_streamDatabase` will close the regular sqflite database, as well as any subscriptions. The extra curly brace closes the declaration of `DatabaseHelper`, in case your IDE didn't add it already automatically.

Now on to integrate the new code with the existing repository-based code.

Adding an SQLite repository

Just like your `MemoryRepository`, you need a repository class for your database. You'll create `SqliteRepository` to fulfill this need.

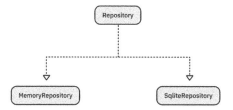

This class will implement the `Repository` interface.

In the **sqlite** folder, create a new file called **sqlite_repository.dart** and add the following, ignoring the red squiggles:

```
import 'dart:async';
// 1
import '../repository.dart';
import 'database_helper.dart';
import '../models/models.dart';

// 2
class SqliteRepository extends Repository {
  // 3
  final dbHelper = DatabaseHelper.instance;

  // TODO: Add methods to use dbHelper here
}
```

Here's what these imports do:

1. Include helper class, models and repository interface.

2. Create a new class named `SqliteRepository` that extends `Repository`.

3. Add a `dbHelper` field, which is just a single instance of `DatabaseHelper`.

Replace `// TODO: Add methods to use dbHelper here` with the following methods that use `dbHelper`:

```
@override
Future<List<Recipe>> findAllRecipes() {
  return dbHelper.findAllRecipes();
}

@override
Stream<List<Recipe>> watchAllRecipes() {
  return dbHelper.watchAllRecipes();
}

@override
Stream<List<Ingredient>> watchAllIngredients() {
  return dbHelper.watchAllIngredients();
}

@override
Future<Recipe> findRecipeById(int id) {
  return dbHelper.findRecipeById(id);
}

@override
Future<List<Ingredient>> findAllIngredients() {
  return dbHelper.findAllIngredients();
}

@override
Future<List<Ingredient>> findRecipeIngredients(int id) {
  return dbHelper.findRecipeIngredients(id);
}

// TODO: Add recipe insert here
```

These methods just call the helper class, but the insert methods do a bit more. To set the `recipeId` for each ingredient, you first have to insert the recipe into the database and get the returned recipe ID from the insert call. You can then set this ID on each ingredient. Those ingredients are then ready to be added to the database.

Setting the recipe's ID

If the ingredient's `recipeId` isn't set, the database won't know which ingredient belongs to which recipe.

Replace `// TODO: Add recipe insert here` with the following method:

```
@override
Future<int> insertRecipe(Recipe recipe) {
  // 1
  return Future(() async {
    // 2
    final id = await dbHelper.insertRecipe(recipe);
    // 3
    recipe.id = id;
    if (recipe.ingredients != null) {
      recipe.ingredients!.forEach((ingredient) {
        // 4
        ingredient.recipeId = id;
      });
      // 5
      insertIngredients(recipe.ingredients!);
    }
    // 6
    return id;
  });
}

// TODO: Insert ingredients
```

Here's what's happening:

1. Return an asynchronous `Future`.

2. Use your helper to insert the recipe and save the `id`.

3. Set your recipe class's id to this `id`.

4. Set each ingredient's `recipeId` field to this `id`.

5. Insert all the ingredients.

6. Return the new `id`.

Before you can insert the ingredient, you need to update all the ingredients' `recipeIds` to the new ID of the inserted recipe.

Inserting the ingredients

Next, you'll insert the ingredients.

Replace `// TODO: Insert ingredients` with:

```
@override
Future<List<int>> insertIngredients(List<Ingredient>
ingredients) {
  return Future(() async {
    if (ingredients.length != 0) {
      // 1
      final ingredientIds = <int>[];
      // 2
      await Future.forEach(ingredients, (Ingredient ingredient)
async {
        // 3
        final futureId = await
dbHelper.insertIngredient(ingredient);
        ingredient.id = futureId;
        // 4
        ingredientIds.add(futureId);
      });
      // 5
      return Future.value(ingredientIds);
    } else {
      return Future.value(<int>[]);
    }
  });
}

// TODO: Delete methods go here
```

Here's what's going on:

1. Create a list of new ingredient IDs.

2. Since you need to use `await` with `insertIngredient`, you need to wrap everything in an asynchronous `Future`. This is a bit tricky, but it allows you to wait for each ID. It returns a `Future` so the whole method can still run asynchronously.

3. Get the new ingredient's ID.

4. Add the ID to your return list.

5. Return the list of new IDs.

Deleting recipes

Now that you have the delete methods in the helper class, you need to implement them in the repository. Most of these just call the helper's methods.

Locate and replace `// TODO: Delete methods go here` with:

```
@override
Future<void> deleteRecipe(Recipe recipe) {
  // 1
  dbHelper.deleteRecipe(recipe);
  // 2
  if (recipe.id != null) {
    deleteRecipeIngredients(recipe.id!);
  }
  return Future.value();
}

@override
Future<void> deleteIngredient(Ingredient ingredient) {
  dbHelper.deleteIngredient(ingredient);
  // 3
  return Future.value();
}

@override
Future<void> deleteIngredients(List<Ingredient> ingredients) {
  // 4
  dbHelper.deleteIngredients(ingredients);
  return Future.value();
}

@override
Future<void> deleteRecipeIngredients(int recipeId) {
  // 5
  dbHelper.deleteRecipeIngredients(recipeId);
  return Future.value();
}

// TODO: initialize and close methods go here
```

Here's what these methods do:

1. Call the helper's `deleteRecipe()`.

2. Delete all of this recipe's ingredients.

3. Delete ingredients and ignore the number of deleted rows.

4. Delete all ingredients in the list passed in.

5. Delete all ingredients with the given recipe ID.

These methods just call the helper class and return an empty `Future`.

Initializing and closing

Remember that databases need to be opened and closed. To do this, your repository just needs to call `dbHelper`'s methods.

Replace `// TODO: initialize and close methods go here` with:

```
@override
Future init() async {
  // 1
  await dbHelper.database;
  return Future.value();
}

@override
void close() {
  // 2
  dbHelper.close();
}
```

In this code, you:

1. Await for the database to initialize.

2. Call the helper's `close()` method.

Running the app

After all that work, it's time to see your changes. For your last change before you run, open **main.dart**.

First, import the new repository:

```
import 'data/sqlite/sqlite_repository.dart';
```

Second, initialize the repository in main() and pass that repository to the widget by replacing the line that reads runApp(const MyApp()); with the following:

```
final repository = SqliteRepository();
await repository.init();

runApp(MyApp(repository: repository));
```

These lines use await to wait for the repository to initialize, then run the app.

At the top of MyApp, add a new repository field by replacing const MyApp({Key? key}) : super(key: key); with:

```
final Repository repository;
const MyApp({Key? key, required this.repository}) : super(key:
key);
```

Scroll down and find a line that reads create: (_) => MemoryRepository(),. Replace it with:

```
// 1
create: (_) => repository,
// 2
dispose: (_, Repository repository) => repository.close(),
```

Here's what this code does:

1. create passes in repository (the repository was created earlier).

2. dispose calls close() to close the database.

Stop and restart the app and search for **pastas**. You'll see something like:

Click the first entry. You'll see a details page, similar to this:

Clicking the **Bookmark** button will bring you back to the **Recipes** tab. Now, select the **Bookmarks** tab, and check that it displays the recipe you just bookmarked.

Now, tap the **Groceries** tab and you'll see the grocery list with the ingredients for your bookmarked recipe:

Stop the app by clicking the red **Stop** button in Android Studio and build and run again.

You'll now see the same bookmarks and groceries as before. Phew! That was a lot of work, but you did it. Pretty amazing!

All the recipes that you bookmarked are saved in the database and will be available each time you run the app.

Congratulations, you achieved the first milestone! Is there something to improve? Is there a simpler and more maintainable way to achieve the same result? Yes, there is. In the next section, you'll see how to use Moor.

Using Moor

As you saw, that was a lot of work. Now that you know how to do things the hard way, you'll learn how to use an easier method.

Moor is a package that's intentionally similar to the **Room** library on Android. In fact, Moor is just **Room** spelled backward.

Unlike sqflite, you don't need to write SQL code and the setup is a lot easier. You'll write specific Dart classes and Moor will take care of the necessary translations to and from SQL code.

You need one file for dealing with the database and one for the repository. To start, add Moor to **pubspec.yaml**, after `sqlbrite`:

```
moor_flutter: ^4.0.0
```

Next, add the Moor generator, which will write code for you, in the dev_dependencies section after `chopper_generator`:

```
moor_generator: ^4.4.1
```

Finally, run any of the following:

- `flutter pub get` from Terminal

- **Pub get** from the IDE window

- **Tools ▸ Flutter ▸ Flutter Pub Get**

Database classes

For your next step, you need to create a set of classes that will describe and create the database, tables and Data Access Objects (DAOs).

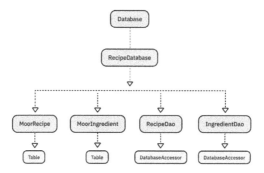

`Table` and `DatabaseAccessor` are from Moor. You'll create the other classes.

> **Note**: A DAO is a class that is in charge of accessing data from the database. It's used to separate your business logic code (e.g., the one that fetches the ingredients of a recipe) from the details of the persistence layer (SQLite in this case). A DAO can be a class, an interface or an abstract class. In this chapter, you'll implement DAOs using classes.

Create a new folder inside **data** called **moor**. Inside **moor**, create a file called **moor_db.dart** and add the following imports:

```
import 'package:moor_flutter/moor_flutter.dart';
import '../models/models.dart';
```

This will add Moor and your models.

Now, add a `part` statement:

```
part 'moor_db.g.dart';

// TODO: Add MoorRecipe table definition here

// TODO: Add MoorIngredient table definition here

// TODO: Add @UseMoor() and RecipeDatabase() here

// TODO: Add RecipeDao here
```

```
// TODO: Add IngredientDao

// TODO: Add moorRecipeToRecipe here

// TODO: Add MoorRecipeData here

// TODO: Add moorIngredientToIngredient and
MoorIngredientCompanion here
```

Remember, this is a way to combine one file into another to form a whole file. The Moor generator will create this file for you later, when you run the `build_runner` command. Until then, it'll display a red squiggle.

Creating tables

To create a table in Moor, you need to create a class that extends `Table`. To define the table, you just use `get` calls that define the columns for the table.

Still in **moor_db.dart**, replace `// TODO: Add MoorRecipe table definition here` with the following:

```
// 1
class MoorRecipe extends Table {
  // 2
  IntColumn get id => integer().autoIncrement()();

  // 3
  TextColumn get label => text()();

  TextColumn get image => text()();

  TextColumn get url => text()();

  RealColumn get calories => real()();

  RealColumn get totalWeight => real()();

  RealColumn get totalTime => real()();
}
```

Here's what you do in this code:

1. Create a class named `MoorRecipe` that extends `Table`.

2. You want a column named `id` that is an integer. `autoIncrement()` automatically creates the IDs for you.

3. Create a label column made up of text.

This definition is a bit unusual. You first define the column type with type classes that handle different types:

- **IntColumn**: Integers.

- **BoolColumn**: Booleans.

- **TextColumn**: Text.

- **DateTimeColumn**: Dates.

- **RealColumn**: Doubles.

- **BlobColumn**: Arbitrary blobs of data.

It also uses a "double" method call, where each call returns a builder. For example, to create IntColumn, you need to make a final call with the extra () to create it.

Defining the Ingredient table

Now, find and replace `// TODO: Add MoorIngredient table definition here` with:

```
class MoorIngredient extends Table {
  IntColumn get id => integer().autoIncrement()();

  IntColumn get recipeId => integer()();

  TextColumn get name => text()();

  RealColumn get weight => real()();
}
```

This is similar to the sqflite `recipe` table.

Now, for the fun part: creating the database class.

Creating the database class

Moor uses annotations. The first one you need is `@UseMoor`. This specifies the tables and Data Access Objects (DAO) to use.

Still in **moor_db.dart**, add this class with the annotation by replacing `// TODO: Add @UseMoor and RecipeDatabase()` here with:

```
// 1
@UseMoor(tables: [MoorRecipe, MoorIngredient], daos: [RecipeDao,
IngredientDao])
```

```
// 2
class RecipeDatabase extends _$RecipeDatabase {
  RecipeDatabase()
    // 3
      : super(FlutterQueryExecutor.inDatabaseFolder(
            path: 'recipes.sqlite', logStatements: true));

  // 4
  @override
  int get schemaVersion => 1;
}
```

Here's what the code above does:

1. Describe the tables — which you defined above — and DAOs this database will use. You'll create the DAOs next.

2. Extend _$RecipeDatabase, which the Moor generator will create. This doesn't exist yet, but the part command at the top will include it.

3. When creating the class, call the super class's constructor. This uses the built-in Moor query executor and passes the pathname of the file. It also sets logging to true.

4. Set the database or schema version to 1.

Now, if you compare this class to what you did for sqflite, you'll notice that it's much simpler and doesn't involve any SQL statements. Starting to notice the advantages of using Moor? :]

There is still a bit more to do. You need to create DAOs, which are classes that are specific to a table and allow you to call methods to access that table. They're similar to the methods in DatabaseHelper and have the same names.

Creating the DAO classes

Your first step is to create the RecipeDao class. You'll see more red squiggles, just ignore them for now. With **moor_db.dart** still open, replace // TODO: Add RecipeDao here with the following:

```
// 1
@UseDao(tables: [MoorRecipe])
// 2
class RecipeDao extends DatabaseAccessor<RecipeDatabase> with
_$RecipeDaoMixin {
  // 3
  final RecipeDatabase db;
```

```
  RecipeDao(this.db) : super(db);

  // 4
  Future<List<MoorRecipeData>> findAllRecipes() =>
select(moorRecipe).get();

  // 5
  Stream<List<Recipe>> watchAllRecipes() {
    // TODO: Add watchAllRecipes code here
  }

  // 6
  Future<List<MoorRecipeData>> findRecipeById(int id) =>
      (select(moorRecipe)..where((tbl) =>
tbl.id.equals(id))).get();

  // 7
  Future<int> insertRecipe(Insertable<MoorRecipeData> recipe) =>
      into(moorRecipe).insert(recipe);

  // 8
  Future deleteRecipe(int id) => Future.value(
      (delete(moorRecipe)..where((tbl) =>
tbl.id.equals(id))).go());
}
```

Here's what's going on:

1. @UseDao specifies the following class is a DAO class for the MoorRecipe table.

2. Create the DAO class that extends the Moor DatabaseAccessor with the mixin, _$RecipeDaoMixin.

3. Create a field to hold an instance of your database.

4. Use a simple select query to find all recipes.

5. Define watchAllRecipes(), but skip the implementation for now.

6. Define a more complex query that uses where to fetch recipes by ID.

7. Use into() and insert() to add a new recipe.

8. Use delete() and where() to delete a specific recipe.

In some ways, Moor is a bit more complex than sqflite, but it also doesn't require as much setup. Most of these calls are one-liners and quite easy to read.

Inserting data is pretty simple. Just specify the table and pass in the class. Notice that you're not passing the model recipe, you're passing `Insertable`, which is an interface that Moor requires. When you generate the `part` file, you'll see a new class, `MoorRecipeData`, which implements this interface.

Deleting requires the table and a `where`. This function just returns `true` for those rows you want to delete. Instead of `get()`, you use `go()`.

Now, replace `// TODO: Add IngredientDao` with the following. Again ignoring the red squiggles. They'll go away when all the new classes are in place.

```
// 1
@UseDao(tables: [MoorIngredient])
// 2
class IngredientDao extends DatabaseAccessor<RecipeDatabase>
    with _$IngredientDaoMixin {
  final RecipeDatabase db;

  IngredientDao(this.db) : super(db);

  Future<List<MoorIngredientData>> findAllIngredients() =>
      select(moorIngredient).get();

  // 3
  Stream<List<MoorIngredientData>> watchAllIngredients() =>
      select(moorIngredient).watch();

  // 4
  Future<List<MoorIngredientData>> findRecipeIngredients(int id)
=>
      (select(moorIngredient)..where((tbl) =>
tbl.recipeId.equals(id))).get();

  // 5
  Future<int> insertIngredient(Insertable<MoorIngredientData>
ingredient) =>
      into(moorIngredient).insert(ingredient);

  // 6
  Future deleteIngredient(int id) =>
      Future.value((delete(moorIngredient)..where((tbl) =>
          tbl.id.equals(id))).go());
}
```

Here's what's going on:

1. Similar to `RecipeDao`, you define the table to use.

2. Extend `DatabaseAccessor` with `_$IngredientDaoMixin`.

3. Call `watch()` to create a stream.

4. Use `where()` to select all ingredients that match the recipe ID.

5. Use `into()` and `insert()` to add a new ingredient.

6. Use `delete()` plus `where()` to delete a specific ingredient.

Now it's time to generate the part file.

Generating the part file

Now, you need to create the Moor part file. In Terminal, run:

```
flutter pub run build_runner build --delete-conflicting-outputs
```

This generates **moor_db.g.dart**.

> **Note**: `--delete-conflicting-outputs` deletes previously generated files, then rebuilds them.

After the file has been generated, open **moor_db.g.dart** and take a look. It's a very large file. It generated several classes, saving you a lot of work!

Now that you've defined these tables, you need to create methods that convert your database classes to your regular model classes and back.

> **Note**: Restart Android Studio if doesn't detect the presence of the newly generated **moor_db.g.dart** file.

Converting your Moor recipes

At the end of **moor_db.dart**, replace `// TODO: Add moorRecipeToRecipe here` with:

```
// Conversion Methods
Recipe moorRecipeToRecipe(MoorRecipeData recipe) {
  return Recipe(
      id: recipe.id,
      label: recipe.label,
      image: recipe.image,
      url: recipe.url,
      calories: recipe.calories,
      totalWeight: recipe.totalWeight,
      totalTime: recipe.totalTime
  );
}
```

This converts a Moor recipe to a model recipe.

The next method converts `Recipe` to a class that you can insert into a Moor database. Replace `// TODO: Add MoorRecipeData here` with this:

```
Insertable<MoorRecipeData> recipeToInsertableMoorRecipe(Recipe
recipe) {
  return MoorRecipeCompanion.insert(
      label: recipe.label ?? '',
      image: recipe.image ?? '',
      url: recipe.url ?? '',
      calories: recipe.calories ?? 0,
      totalWeight: recipe.totalWeight ?? 0,
      totalTime: recipe.totalTime ?? 0
  );
}
```

`Insertable` is an interface for objects that can be inserted into the database or updated. Use the generated `MoorRecipeCompanion.insert()` to create that class.

Creating classes for Ingredients

Next, you'll do the same for the ingredients models. Replace `// TODO: Add moorIngredientToIngredient and MoorIngredientCompanion here` with the following:

```
Ingredient moorIngredientToIngredient(MoorIngredientData
ingredient) {
  return Ingredient(
      id: ingredient.id,
      recipeId: ingredient.recipeId,
```

```
        name: ingredient.name,
        weight: ingredient.weight);
  }

  MoorIngredientCompanion ingredientToInsertableMoorIngredient(
      Ingredient ingredient) {
    return MoorIngredientCompanion.insert(
        recipeId: ingredient.recipeId ?? 0,
        name: ingredient.name ?? '',
        weight: ingredient.weight ?? 0);
  }
```

These methods convert a Moor ingredient into an instance of `Ingredient` and vice versa.

Updating watchAllRecipes()

Now that you've written the conversion methods, you can update `watchAllRecipes()`.

You'll notice most of the red squiggles in **data/moor/moor_db.dart** are now gone. There's one left.

> **Note**: Run `flutter clean` and `flutter pub get` in case your IDE is not up to date with the newly generated files.

Locate `// TODO: Add watchAllRecipes code here` and replace it with:

```
// 1
return select(moorRecipe)
    // 2
    .watch()
    // 3
    .map((rows) {
      final recipes = <Recipe>[];
      // 4
      rows.forEach((row) {
        // 5
        final recipe = moorRecipeToRecipe(row);
        // 6
        if (!recipes.contains(recipe)) {
          recipe.ingredients = <Ingredient>[];
          recipes.add(recipe);
        }
      },);
      return recipes;
    },);
```

Here's the step-by-step:

1. Use `select` to start a query.

2. Create a stream.

3. Map each list of rows.

4. For each row, execute the code below.

5. Convert the recipe row to a regular recipe.

6. If your list doesn't already contain the recipe, create an empty ingredient list and add it to your recipes list.

In addition to creating a stream with `watch()`, you map the results into a model recipe and add an empty ingredient list. You then return the list of recipes.

No more red squiggles. :]

Creating the Moor repository

Now that you have the Moor database code written, you need to write a repository to handle it. You'll create a class named `MoorRepository` that implements `Repository`:

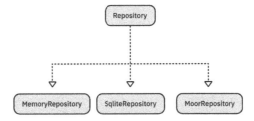

In the **moor** directory, create a new file named **moor_repository.dart**. Add the following imports:

```
import 'dart:async';
import '../models/models.dart';

import '../repository.dart';
import 'moor_db.dart';
```

This imports your models, the repository interface and your just-created **moor_db.dart**.

Next, create MoorRepository and some fields:

```
class MoorRepository extends Repository {
  // 1
  late RecipeDatabase recipeDatabase;
  // 2
  late RecipeDao _recipeDao;
  // 3
  late IngredientDao _ingredientDao;
  // 3
  Stream<List<Ingredient>>? ingredientStream;
  // 4
  Stream<List<Recipe>>? recipeStream;

  // TODO: Add findAllRecipes()
  // TODO: Add watchAllRecipes()
  // TODO: Add watchAllIngredients()
  // TODO: Add findRecipeById()
  // TODO: Add findAllIngredients()
  // TODO: Add findRecipeIngredients()
  // TODO: Add insertRecipe()
  // TODO: Add insertIngredients()
  // TODO: Add Delete methods

  @override
  Future init() async {
    // 6
    recipeDatabase = RecipeDatabase();
    // 7
    _recipeDao = recipeDatabase.recipeDao;
    _ingredientDao = recipeDatabase.ingredientDao;
  }

  @override
  void close() {
    // 8
    recipeDatabase.close();
  }
}
```

Here's what's happening in the code above:

1. Stores an instance of the Moor RecipeDatabase.

2. Creates a private RecipeDao to handle recipes.

3. Creates a private IngredientDao that handles ingredients.

4. Creates a stream that watches ingredients.

5. Creates a stream that watches recipes.

6. Creates your database.

7. Gets instances of your DAOs.

8. Closes the database.

Implementing the repository

As you did in past chapters, you'll now add all the missing methods following the
TODO: indications.Replace // TODO: Add findAllRecipes() with:

```
@override
Future<List<Recipe>> findAllRecipes() {
  // 1
  return _recipeDao
      .findAllRecipes()
  // 2
      .then<List<Recipe>>((List<MoorRecipeData> moorRecipes) {
    final recipes = <Recipe>[];
    // 3
    moorRecipes.forEach((moorRecipe) async {
      // 4
      final recipe = moorRecipeToRecipe(moorRecipe);
      // 5
      if (recipe.id != null) {
        recipe.ingredients = await
findRecipeIngredients(recipe.id!);
      }
      recipes.add(recipe);
    },);
    return recipes;
  },);
}
```

The code above does the following:

1. Uses RecipeDao to find all recipes.

2. Takes the list of MoorRecipeData items, executing then after findAllRecipes()
    finishes.

3. For each recipe:

4. Converts the Moor recipe to a model recipe.

5. Calls the method to get all recipe ingredients, which you'll define later.

The next step is simple. Find `// TODO: Add watchAllRecipes()` and substitute it with:

```
@override
Stream<List<Recipe>> watchAllRecipes() {
  if (recipeStream == null) {
    recipeStream = _recipeDao.watchAllRecipes();
  }
  return recipeStream!;
}
```

This just calls the same method name on the recipe DAO class, then saves an instance so you don't create multiple streams.

Next, replace `// TODO: Add watchAllIngredients()` with:

```
@override
Stream<List<Ingredient>> watchAllIngredients() {
  if (ingredientStream == null) {
    // 1
    final stream = _ingredientDao.watchAllIngredients();
    // 2
    ingredientStream = stream.map((moorIngredients) {
      final ingredients = <Ingredient>[];
      // 3
      moorIngredients.forEach((moorIngredient) {

ingredients.add(moorIngredientToIngredient(moorIngredient));
      },);
      return ingredients;
    },);
  }
  return ingredientStream!;
}
```

This:

1. Gets a stream of ingredients.

2. Maps each stream list to a stream of model ingredients

3. Converts each ingredient in the list to a model ingredient.

Finding recipes

The find methods are a bit easier, but they still need to convert each database class to a model class.

Replace `// TODO: Add findRecipeById()` with:

```
@override
Future<Recipe> findRecipeById(int id) {
  return _recipeDao
      .findRecipeById(id)
      .then((listOfRecipes) =>
  moorRecipeToRecipe(listOfRecipes.first));
}
```

Since `findRecipeById()` returns a list, just take the first one and convert it.

Look for `// TODO: Add findAllIngredients()` and replace it with:

```
@override
Future<List<Ingredient>> findAllIngredients() {
  return
  _ingredientDao.findAllIngredients().then<List<Ingredient>>(
      (List<MoorIngredientData> moorIngredients) {
        final ingredients = <Ingredient>[];
        moorIngredients.forEach(
          (ingredient) {

  ingredients.add(moorIngredientToIngredient(ingredient));
        },
      );
      return ingredients;
    },
  );
}
```

This method is almost like `watchAllIngredients()`, except that it doesn't use a stream.

Finding all the ingredients for a recipe is similar. Replace `// TODO: Add findRecipeIngredients()` with:

```
@override
Future<List<Ingredient>> findRecipeIngredients(int recipeId) {
  return _ingredientDao.findRecipeIngredients(recipeId).then(
      (listOfIngredients) {
        final ingredients = <Ingredient>[];
        listOfIngredients.forEach(
          (ingredient) {
```

```
        ingredients.add(moorIngredientToIngredient(ingredient));
          },
        );
        return ingredients;
      },
    );
}
```

This method finds all the ingredients associated with a single recipe.Now it's time to look at inserting recipes.

Inserting recipes

To insert a recipe, first you insert the recipe itself and then insert all its ingredients. Replace // TODO: Add insertRecipe() with:

```
@override
Future<int> insertRecipe(Recipe recipe) {
  return Future(() async {
    // 1
    final id =
        await
_recipeDao.insertRecipe(recipeToInsertableMoorRecipe(recipe));
    if (recipe.ingredients != null) {
      // 2
      recipe.ingredients!.forEach((ingredient) {
        ingredient.recipeId = id;
      },);
      // 3
      insertIngredients(recipe.ingredients!);
    }
    return id;
  },);
}
```

Here you:

1. Use the recipe DAO to insert a converted model recipe.

2. Set the recipe ID for each ingredient.

3. Insert all the ingredients. You'll define these next.

Now, it's finally time to add methods to insert ingredients. Replace // TODO: Add insertIngredients() with:

```
@override
Future<List<int>> insertIngredients(List<Ingredient>
```

```
ingredients) {
  return Future(() {
    // 1
    if (ingredients.length == 0) {
      return <int>[];
    }
    final resultIds = <int>[];
    ingredients.forEach((ingredient) {
      // 2
      final moorIngredient =
ingredientToInsertableMoorIngredient(ingredient);
      // 3
      _ingredientDao
          .insertIngredient(moorIngredient)
          .then((int id) => resultIds.add(id));
    },);
    return resultIds;
  },);
}
```

This code:

1. Checks to make sure you have at least one ingredient.

2. Converts the ingredient.

3. Inserts the ingredient into the database and adds a new ID to the list.

Now it's time to add code to delete recipes and ingredients.

Deleting

Deleting is much easier. You just need to call the DAO methods. Replace `// TODO: Add Delete methods` with:

```
@override
Future<void> deleteRecipe(Recipe recipe) {
  if (recipe.id != null) {
    _recipeDao.deleteRecipe(recipe.id!);
  }
  return Future.value();
}

@override
Future<void> deleteIngredient(Ingredient ingredient) {
  if (ingredient.id != null) {
    return _ingredientDao.deleteIngredient(ingredient.id!);
  } else {
    return Future.value();
  }
}
```

```
  }

  @override
  Future<void> deleteIngredients(List<Ingredient> ingredients) {
    ingredients.forEach((ingredient) {
      if (ingredient.id != null) {
        _ingredientDao.deleteIngredient(ingredient.id!);
      }
    });
    return Future.value();
  }

  @override
  Future<void> deleteRecipeIngredients(int recipeId) async {
    // 1
    final ingredients = await findRecipeIngredients(recipeId);
    // 2
    return deleteIngredients(ingredients);
  }
```

The last method is the only one that's different. In the code above, you:

1. Find all ingredients for the given recipe ID.

2. Delete the list of ingredients.

Phew! The hard work is over.

Replacing the repository

Now, you just have to replace your SQL repository with your shiny new Moor repository.

Open **main.dart**. Add the import:

```
import 'data/moor/moor_repository.dart';
```

Delete the two import statements: import 'data/memory_repository.dart'; and import 'data/sqlite/sqlite_repository.dart';.

Replace this:

```
final repository = SqliteRepository();
```

with the following:

```
final repository = MoorRepository();
```

Running the app

Stop the running app, build and run. Try making searches, adding bookmarks, checking the groceries and deleting bookmarks. It will work just the same as with `SqliteRepository`. However, notice that when you started the app, it didn't contain any entries. Do you know why?

Answer: The app now uses a different database file.

Congratulations! Now, your app is using all the power provided by **Moor** to store data in a local database!

Cleaning up (Optional)

In the next chapter you will not need the sqflite plugin now that you're using Moor. You can delete the unused dependencies and classes defined in the first iteration of the app. Note that this is optional.To do so, delete the folder **lib/data/sqlite** and all its files. Then open **pubspec.yml** and remove the following libraries:

```
sqflite: ^2.0.0+4
path_provider: ^2.0.2
synchronized: ^3.0.0
```

Run **Pub get** then hot restart the app and verify that it works as before.

Key points

- Databases persist data locally to the device.

- Data stored in databases are available after the app restarts.

- The **sqflite** plugin requires some SQL knowledge to set up the database.

- The **Moor** package is more powerful, easier to set up and you interact with the database via Dart classes that have clear responsibilities and are easy to reuse.

Where to go from here?

To learn about:

- **Databases and SQLite**, go to https://flutter.dev/docs/cookbook/persistence/sqlite.

- **sqflite**, go to https://pub.dev/packages/sqflite.

- **Moor**, go to https://pub.dev/packages/moor_flutter.

- **sqlbrite** go to https://pub.dev/packages/sqlbrite.

- **The database that started it all**, go to https://www.sqlite.org/index.html.

In the next section, you'll learn all about deploying your apps.

Section V: Deployment

Building an app for you own devices is great; sharing your app with the world is even better!

In this section you'll go over the steps and process needed to release your apps to the iOS App Store and Google Play Store. You'll also see how to use platform-specific assets in your apps.

Chapter 16: Platform Specific App Assets

By Michael Katz

So far, you've built Flutter apps for the Flutter toolkit using the Dart language and the various Flutter idioms. You then built and deployed those apps to iOS and Android devices without having to do anything special. It's almost magical.

However, sometimes you'll need to add platform-specific code to cater to the needs of the particular store or operating system.

For example, you might need to change how you specify the app icon, the launch assets and the splash screen to suit each platform.

In this chapter, you'll go through the process of setting up some important parts of your app to look great regardless of which platform your users choose. You'll continue using the **Recipe Finder** app from the previous section.

> **Note:** You can also start fresh by opening this chapter's **starter** project. If you choose to do this, remember to click the **Get dependencies** button or execute `flutter pub get` from Terminal. You'll also need to add your API Key and ID in **lib/network/recipe_service.dart**.

You'll want to use native development tools when working with platform-specific assets, so you'll need to install Xcode 12 to complete this chapter. Once that's done, begin by opening the chapter's starter project.

Setting the app icon

The app icon is one of the most important pieces of any app's branding. It's what shows up on the store page and the home screen as well as in notifications and settings. It's the avatar for the app, so it must look just right.

To do this, you need to use constraints. Android and iOS not only use different constraints, but they also specify them differently, which means you need to tweak your icon for each platform.

By default, when you create a new Flutter project with the `flutter` tool, it sets the Flutter **F logo** as the project's icon:

Not only is this not branded to your recipe app, but the app stores aren't likely to approve it. Your first task will be to update to a custom image that looks great on each platform.

Optimizing the app icon for Android

With the project open in Android Studio, open **android/app/src/main/AndroidManifest.xml**. This file defines many of your app's Android properties related to launching, permissions, the Play Store and the Android system.

One of the properties under `application` defines the launcher screen icon:

```
android:icon="@mipmap/ic_launcher"
```

The `@mipmap` part means that it resolves to a **mipmap-{resolution}** folder to load a graphic of the correct device's screen scale. **ic_launcher** is the filename of the icon.

Under **main/res**, you'll find the various **mpimap-** subfolders.

In Finder, open **assets/icons/android** from the chapter materials. Copy the **res** folder from Finder and replace **android/app/src/main/res** in Android Studio.

If you receive a pop-up confirming you want to copy the folders to the specified directories, click **Refactor** or **OK**, depending on your Android Studio version.

Expand the **android/app/src/main/res** folder and verify you've pasted the **res** folder in the correct place. It should be at the same level as the **java** and **kotlin** folders, not inside the existing **res** folder.

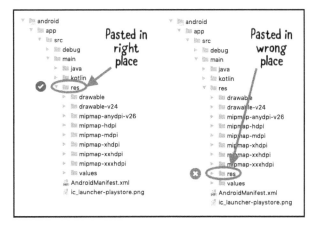

Hot reload doesn't update the launcher icon (hot restart doesn't, either). For these changes to take effect, you need to stop the app and run it again.

On the home screen, you'll now see the new launcher icon. Run the app on an Android device or emulator to see the following:

Great, you've just swapped the default assets for some cool custom ones. If you need to adjust the icon fill size, or if you're working on your own app later and want to import Android images, you'll need to import and resize the artwork. That's next!

Personalizing the app icon for Android

When you work with your own custom artwork, there are a few more steps you need to take, beyond just copying and pasting from a folder. You need to work in the Android portion of your app and not within the Flutter project.

Open the Android folder directly from the Android Studio menu, choose **File ▸ Open** and navigate to your project's **android** folder. Finally, click **Open**.

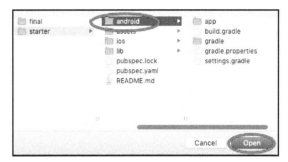

Wait until the Gradle sync is complete. The time it takes your project to finish might vary.

Navigate to the **app** folder, right-click on **res** and choose **New ▸ Image Asset**.

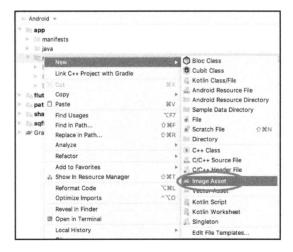

The **Configure Image Asset** pop-up window will display. Click the folder icon to open the custom image.

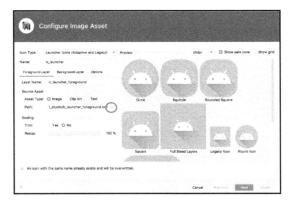

Locate your master artwork image. In this case, you'll find it in the **assets**/. Select the **IconArtwork_1024x1024.png** image and click on **Open**.

The loaded image will appear like this.

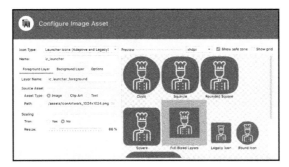

If the cook figure is outside the **safe zone**, use the **Resize** slider to adjust the size. Make sure the cook figure is inside the circle, which is the safe zone, as shown below. When done click **Next**.

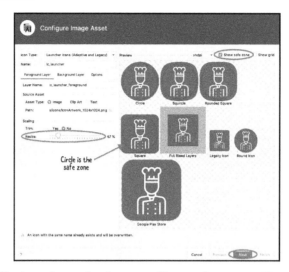

The next screen displays the path where you'll save the assets. Keep in mind this is for the Android project, not your Flutter project, so the folder layers look different from what you've worked with so far.

Leave the defaults and click **Finish**.

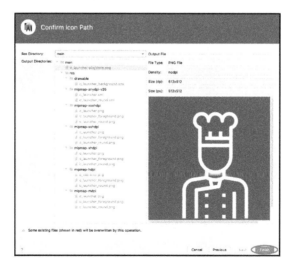

Close this Android project and go back to your Flutter project.

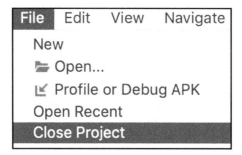

You've now seen how to resize custom artwork for your Android app. What's great is that after you finish these updates, your Flutter app updates automatically!

As before, for these changes to take effect, you need to stop the app and run it again. You'll see the same launcher icon. Run the app on an Android device or emulator to see the following:

Recipe Fi...

Next, you'll work on the iOS app icon.

Optimizing the app icon for iOS

When you create a Flutter project that supports iOS, Flutter generates an **ios** subfolder in the project at the same level as the **android** folder. This contains the libraries and support files to run on iOS. In that folder is an Xcode workspace, **Runner.xcworkspace**.

> **Note:** iOS developers, Flutter apps use **Runner.xcworkspace** instead of the traditional **Runner.xcodeproj**.

In Finder, open **starter/ios** from the chapter materials and double-click **Runner.xcworkspace**. If you have Xcode open, you can also navigate to the folder and open it.

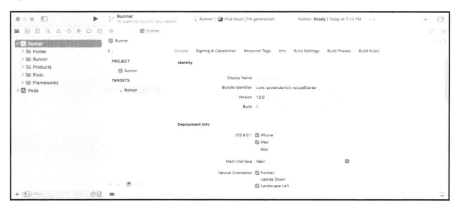

Flutter uses a workspace to build the app because, under the hood, it uses **Cocoapods** to manage iOS-specific dependencies required to build and deploy iOS apps. The workspace contains the main runner project and the Cocoapods project as well as all the supporting files to build and deploy an iOS app.

This project contains a lot of boilerplate and helpers to run the app within the iOS app context. Don't worry about building the app from the project. Continue to use Android Studio or the command line to build and deploy to a simulator.

Viewing the app icon

To see the app icon, open **Runner ▸ Runner ▸ Assets.xcassets**. This is an **asset catalog**, a way of organizing assets in an Xcode project in a configuration-aware way.

Inside, you'll see **AppIcon** and **LaunchImage**.

Click **AppIcon** to see all the devices and resolutions supported by the default Flutter icon.

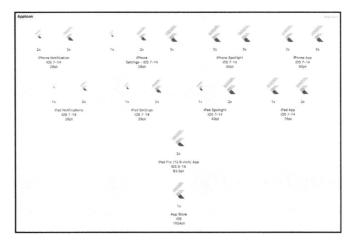

In Finder, open **assets/icons/ios** from the chapter materials. Drag each of the images inside into the asset catalog, grabbing the right one for each size. You can tell which is which by the name.

Don't worry if you grab the wrong one: A yellow warning triangle will appear next to any image that isn't the right size.

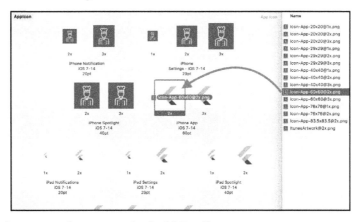

Save these changes and return to Android Studio.

Perform a full stop and run again on an iOS simulator to see the new icon on the Home Screen.

Setting the app's name

Now that you have a shiny new icon on the device launch screens, you'll notice that the app's name isn't formatted nicely, which detracts from the experience.

Setting the launcher name is an easy fix, but you also have to do it for each platform.

Return to **AndroidManifest.xml**. Find the `android:label` property of the `application` node and change the text to:

Build and run the app again. By choosing a shorter label, the name will fit on more Android launchers.

You can do the same on iOS as well. Go back to Xcode and open **Runner ▸ Runner ▸ Info.plist**. This file is similar to **AndroidManifest.xml** in that it contains information about your app for the OS to use.

Under **Information Property List**, change the **Bundle name** to Recipe 🔍 as well.

Back in Android Studio, build and run the app for iOS.

There, that looks better!

Adding a launch screen

The next finishing touch you'll put on your app is a launch screen. It takes a few moments for the Dart VM to spin up when users launch the app, so you'll add polish by giving them something to look at other than a white screen. Once again, you need to set this up separately for iOS and Android.

Setting a launch image in iOS

On iOS, setting a launch image is straightforward.

In Xcode, open **ios/Runner.xcworkspace** again, select **Assets.xcassets**, and this time select **LaunchImage**.

You'll see three boxes to represent the image at **1x**, **2x** and **3x** resolution. Because you've only defined one version of the image, you need to tell iOS to scale it for the other high-resolution screens.

To do that, select one of the boxes. Then in the **Attributes inspector** select from the **Scales** drop-down: **Single Scale**.

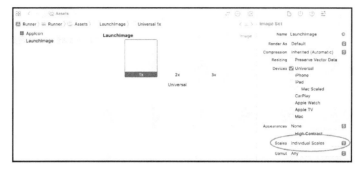

This setting lets the system know there's just one version of the image. This is preferred for images like photographs, which have a native resolution.

Find **splash.png** under **assets/launch image** from the chapter materials, then drag it onto the **All** square for the launch image.

The user will see this image from the time when the app launches until the main screen is ready. Since the image has text in it, you'd normally supply high-resolution images as well, but in this case, you'll modify it later.

Build and run on iOS from Android Studio again.

On some simulators it's a little squished and on others it doesn't even show up, but you'll fix that now.

Showing a more sophisticated launch UI

A good image can go a long way toward making your app look sophisticated. However, the one you just used is problematic because the built-in text is hard to get right across a wide variety of device sizes and resolutions. This adds a layer of complexity to the translation.

Right now, UIImageView in **LaunchScreen.storyboard** uses the launch image you added to the asset catalog earlier. The app loads this storyboard when it launches and displays it until it finishes loading. In Xcode, open the storyboard from **Runner ▸ Runner ▸ LaunchScreen.storyboard**.

Adding constraints

Your first step is to make the image fill the screen without distorting its contents. That will make it look good on all device sizes.

Expand **View Controller Scene** ▸ **View Controller** ▸ **View** and select **LaunchImage**.

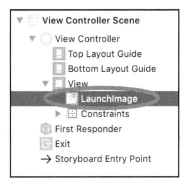

Then, click the **Add New Constraints** button at the bottom.

Set all four constraints to **0** and make sure **Constrain to margins** isn't selected. Then, click **Add 4 Constraints** to set the constraints. This forces the image to fill its superview.

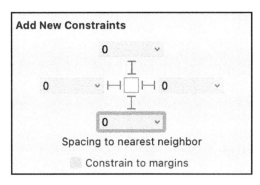

Next, in the **Attributes inspector**, change the **Content Mode** to **Aspect Fill**. This will resize the image to fill the image view, but keep the aspect ratio intact, truncating it as necessary.

Replacing the title with a label

It's not ideal to have text attached to the image, so you'll replace it with a label that has its own constraints, instead. To do that, you'll need a new image.

Returning to **Runner ▸ Runner ▸ Assets.xcassets** open **LaunchImage** in the asset catalog. In the same assets folder as the original splash image, you'll also find **alloo.jpg**. Drag this to the catalog to replace the existing image.

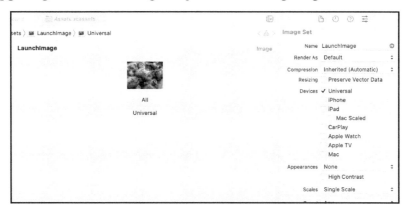

Back in **LaunchScreen.storyboard**, drag a **Label** from the **Library** onto the view. If it's not already visible, you can access the Library from **View ▸ Show Library**.

Add constraints to the label, as you did for the image, but this time, add these three constraints:

- **Top** to **140**.
- **Leading** and **Trailing** space to **0**.
- Leave the **bottom** constraint unset.

Then, in the **Attribute inspector**, set the following values:

- **Text** to **Recipe Finder**.
- **Color** to **White Color**.
- **Font** to **System**, **Style** to **Heavy** and **Size** to **100**.
- **Alignment** to **Center**.
- **Lines** to **2**.
- **Line Break** to **Word Wrap**.
- **Shadow** to **Dark Grey Color** and **Shadow Offset** to a **Height** of **2** and a **Width** of **2**.

Hold your breath for one last finishing step in the name of aesthetics. With the label still selected, move to the **Size inspector**. Double-click the **Vertical** constraint to open the constraint in the editor. Change the **Second Item** from **Top.Layout Guide.Bottom** to **Superview.Top**.

This changes the anchor for the label's top from the layout guide, which changes during launch, to the top of the screen. This ensures consistent placement of the label.

Phew… that was a lot of settings, but the result really makes a *statement*. When you're done, the storyboard will look like this:

In Android Studio, if your app is still running perform a full stop. Build and run again to see the new launch screen.

Now, the image is no longer squished, the text is readable and your launch screen looks great.

Setting a launch image in Android

Setting a launch image is less user-friendly on Android. In Android Studio, navigate in the Project browser to **android/app/src/main/res/drawable/** and open **launch_background.xml**.

This file is a **layer-list drawable**, which describes a drawable user interface that displays on app launch. Since this is a drawable, it doesn't have all the options that an iOS storyboard does, so you can't add separate text or an advanced layout. On the plus side, rendering is fast and efficient.

In the file, add the following code inside the `layer-list` node, after the first `item`:

```
<item>
  <bitmap
    android:gravity="fill"
    android:src="@drawable/splash" />
</item>
```

This loads the image **splash** from the **drawable** folder and stretches it to fill the window.

Next, copy **splash.png** from the chapter assets folder to **android/app/src/main/res/drawable**.

Build and run and the splash image will show until the UI is ready.

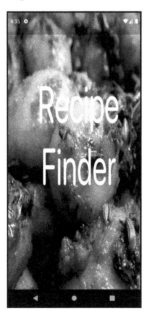

Using Android's two-phase launch

The app goes through two phases when it launches. The first is **app launch**, which occurs between when the user taps the launcher icon and when the app code starts to execute. The second is between that point and when Flutter renders the first frame of the main activity. For each of these phases, you can supply different drawable assets for the launch screens.

In **AndroidManifest.xml**, you define the first phase for the main activity with the property:

```
android:theme="@style/LaunchTheme"
```

This corresponds to a style named **LaunchTheme**, defined in **android/app/src/ main/res/values/styles.xml**. It sets the background to the drawable you already looked at.

The second phase, from Flutter launch to the first screen, is defined by a `meta-data` node, which you'll find under a comment explaining just that:

```
<meta-data
  android:name="io.flutter.embedding.android.SplashScreenDrawable"
    android:resource="@drawable/launch_background"
    />
```

This means you can redefine them separately.

Change `android:resource` to `@drawable/loading_background`; this lets you use a different drawable than before.

Next, duplicate **launch_background.xml** and name it **loading_background.xml**.

Open the newly created **loading_background.xml**. Change the `android:src` of the **bitmap** to `@drawable/loading`. This will now load an image named **loading** instead.

Finally, copy and paste **assets/launch image/loading.png** from the materials folder to **drawable**, alongside the other Android resources.

This file is a static image of the general first UI. Showing this to the user before loading the real UI but make the load time seem faster.

Build and run. Now, you'll see you've replaced the first launch screen with the placeholder image before the app starts.

You did it! You've updated your app's icons and launch screens in both Android and iOS.

Key points

- Flutter generates **app projects** for iOS and Android, which you can edit to brand your app.

- These projects contain resources and code related to **launching the app** and preparing to start the Flutter main view.

- You need to set assets related to app launch **separately** for each platform.

Where to go from here?

You may have seen other apps with more dynamic or animated splash screens. These are generally created as a whole-screen stateful widget that displays for a predetermined time between the Flutter VM load and launching your main screen widget.

Dynamic splash screens give your app launch a little more flair, but you should still include an image-based launch screen to show before the splash loads. The **splashscreen** package is a good place to start if you want to implement one in your app: https://pub.dev/packages/splashscreen.

Chapter 17: Build & Release an Android App

By Michael Katz

So you've finished building your app and you're ready to let the world try it out. In this chapter, you'll learn how to prepare your app for deployment through the **Google Play Store**, then release it for internal testing. In the next chapter, you'll do the same for Apple's **App Store**.

The steps you'll follow to launch your app are straightforward:

1. Create a signed release build.

2. Prepare the Play Store for upload.

3. Upload the build.

4. Notify testers that the build is ready.

To complete this chapter, you'll need a Google Play developer account and a physical Android device.

Set up for release

Before you can upload a build for distribution, you need to build it with a release configuration. When you create a new Flutter project, you automatically create a debug build configuration. This is helpful while in development, but it's not suitable for store submission for several reasons:

- **App bloat**: A debug build is extra large because of the symbols and overhead needed for hot reload/restart and for source debugging.

- **Resource keys**: It's typical to point your debug app at a sandbox environment for services and analytics so you don't pollute production data or violate user privacy.

- **Unsigned**: Debug builds aren't signed yet. To upload to the store, you need to sign the app to verify you are the one who built it.

- **Google says so**: The Play Store won't allow you to upload a debuggable app.

The app's configuration spreads across several files. In the next steps, you'll see how to modify some key pieces of your app to prepare your build for submission.

If you're following along with your app from the previous chapters, open it and keep using it with this chapter. If not, just locate the **projects** folder for this chapter, open the **starter** project in Android Studio and remember to get dependencies.

> **Note**: If you use the starter app, don't forget to add your `apiKey` and `apiId` in **network/recipe_service.dart**.

Preparing the manifest

Debug builds get broad permissions, but apps released through reputable stores need to declare which aspects of the user's hardware or systems they need to access. The **Android Manifest** file is where you declare permissions.

Open **android/app/src/main/AndroidManifest.xml**. This file describes the app to the Android OS.

Add the following permission beneath the closing `</application>` tag. Look for the comment that reads `<!-- add permissions here -->` and add the following code beneath it:

```
<uses-permission android:name="android.permission.INTERNET" />
```

With this line, you tell Android that your app needs access to the internet to run. The Flutter template manifest does not include any permissions.

> **Note**: If your next app requires additional permissions, such as access to the camera or location information, add them here.

Updating build.gradle

build.gradle is where you describe different build configurations. You'll change it next. When you set up the app, you used the default debug configuration. Now, you'll add a release configuration to produce a bundle you can upload to the Play Store.

Open **android/app/build.gradle**.

Under `android {`, you'll see a definition for `defaultConfig`. This describes the app ID, versioning information and SDK version.

When assigning `applicationId`, you usually use your name or your company's name.

```
applicationId "com.raywenderlich.recipe_finder"
```

This book uses **com.raywenderlich.recipe_finder**, which means you need to use a different name when you submit to the stores. To avoid errors because the app already exists in the Play Store, use something unique to you or your business name when you upload your app. Be sure to use lowercase letters and don't use spaces or special characters.

Change `applicationId` to something unique. For example you could add letters to the end of the text inside the quotes. Be creative :]

Change **targetSdkVersion** to **29**, if it isn't 29 or higher already:

```
targetSdkVersion 29
```

While `minSdkVersion` is the earliest version of Android OS that supports the app, `targetSdkVersion` is the version you designed the app for. Setting this kicks in compatibility modes on earlier OS versions and triggers different checks on the Play Store.

Your next step is to create a signing key to make your app secure enough to be in the Play Store.

Creating a signing key

Before you can distribute the app, you need to sign it. This ensures that all future versions come from the same developer.

To sign the app, you first need to make a signing key by creating a **keystore**, which is a secure repository of certificates and private keys.

During the next step, you'll see a prompt to enter a password. There are some key things to know:

- Use any six-character password you like, but **be sure to remember it**. You'll need it whenever you access the keystore, which you need to do every time you upload a new version of the app.

- In addition to a password, you need to provide information about yourself and your organization. This is part of the certificate, so don't enter anything you don't want someone else to see.

- Once you've entered and confirmed that information, the tool will create the .jks file and save it in the directory that ran the command.

Open a terminal window and navigate to the root project directory.

> **Note**: If you started this chapter with the starter project, then the root project directory is the starter folder.

Run the following command:

```
keytool -genkey -v -keystore recipes.jks -keyalg RSA -keysize
2048 -validity 10000 -alias recipes
```

keytool is a Java command run from **Terminal** that generates a keystore. You save it in the file, **recipes.jks**.

The keystore contains one key with the specified -alias recipes. You'll use this key later to sign the bundle that you'll upload to the Play Store.

> **Note**: It's important to keep the keystore secure and out of any public repositories. Adding it to **.gitignore** will help protect your file. If someone gets access to the key, they can cause all sorts of mayhem, such as pretending to be you when distributing malicious apps.

Accessing the signing key

Now that you've created a key, you need to supply the build system with the information necessary to access it. To do that, you'll create a separate file to store the password information.

> **Note**: It's important to keep this file a secret and not to check it into a public repository, just like the keystore file. If a malicious actor has this file and your keystore, they can easily impersonate you.

In the **android** folder, create a new file: **key.properties**.

Set its contents to:

```
storePassword={YOUR PASSWORD}
keyPassword={YOUR PASSWORD}
keyAlias=recipes
storeFile=../../recipes.jks
```

storePassword and keyPassword should be the same password you supplied the keytool command, without any punctuation.

keyAlias is the same as the –alias listed at the end of the keytool command.

storeFile is the path of the keystore you created. It's relative to **android/app**, so be sure to change the path, if necessary.

You need these values to unlock the key in the keystore and sign the app. In the next step, you'll read from the file during the build process.

Referencing the signing key

You now have a key and its password, but signing doesn't happen automatically. During the build, you need to open the keystore and sign the app bundle. To do this, you need to modify the build... and when you think about modifying the build process, you should think about **build.gradle**.

Open **android/app/build.gradle**.

Before the `android {` section, locate `// Add keystore properties here` and add the following:

```
def keystoreProperties = new Properties()
def keystorePropertiesFile = rootProject.file('key.properties')
if (keystorePropertiesFile.exists()) {
    keystoreProperties.load(new
FileInputStream(keystorePropertiesFile))
}
```

Here, you define a new `Properties` that reads **key.properties** and loads the content into `keystoreProperties`. At the top of the file, you'll see something similar that loads the Flutter properties from **local.properties**.

Next, at the top of the `android` section, make sure `compileSdkVersion` matches `targetSdkVersion`, which you set above. It should be **29**. If `compileSdkVersion` isn't 29 or higher, update it.

```
compileSdkVersion 29
```

Also, inside the `android` section, locate `// add signing release config here` just after the `defaultConfig` block and add:

```
signingConfigs {
    release {
        keyAlias keystoreProperties['keyAlias']
        keyPassword keystoreProperties['keyPassword']
        storeFile keystoreProperties['storeFile'] ?
file(keystoreProperties['storeFile']) : null
        storePassword keystoreProperties['storePassword']
    }
}
```

This defines a signing configuration, then directly maps the values loaded from the properties file to the `release` configuration.

Finally, replace the existing `buildTypes` block with:

```
buildTypes {
    release {
        signingConfig signingConfigs.release
    }
}
```

This defines the release `signingConfig`, which is a specific Android build construct, created using the previously declared `release` signing configuration. You'll use this when you create a release build.

Now, you've created a release configuration and set it up. The next step is to build the app for release.

Build an app bundle

With **build.gradle** in place, you can leave the final steps to create a signed Android App Bundle up to the Flutter build system. The bundle will contain everything you need to upload your app to the Play store.

Open a terminal window, navigate to the project directory and run:

```
flutter build appbundle
```

This will build an **Android App Bundle** (**AAB**) for the project. It may take several minutes to complete. When it's done, the command output will tell you where to find the .aab file.

> **Note**: If you receive an error message stating the keystore file was not found, make sure the path you have in **key.properties** for the `storeFile=` line has the correct path to the generated **recipes.jks**.

The bundle is just a .zip file containing the compiled code, assets and metadata. You'll send this to Google in the next section.

AAB versus APK

If you've been working with Android for a while, you might be expecting to create an **APK** file. When you do a debug build from Android studio, you get an APK file.

You can distribute an Android app as an APK or an AAB. App bundles are preferred by the Play Store, but you can use APKs to distribute in other stores or for sideloading to a device.

> **Note**: Sideloading means installing an app on an Android device without using the official Google Play store. After configuring your device to allow running apps from unknown sources, you can install apps that are typically distributed as APK files.

If you want to create an APK release, use the following command:

```
flutter build apk --split-per-abi
```

This creates release build APKs. The `--split-per-abi` flag makes separate APKs for each supported target, such as x86, arm64 and so on. This reduces the file size for the output. A "fat" APK, which contains support for all targets, could be substantial in size. To make a fat APK rather than a split APK, just omit that flag.

Uploading to the Google Play Store

Your next step to getting your app out in the wide world is to upload it to the Google Play Store. You'll need a Google Play Developer account to do that.

Open https://play.google.com/console/. If you see a prompt to sign up, follow the onscreen instructions to create a developer account. There is a nominal fee to join the Google Developer Program. If you don't want to sign up, you can continue to distribute APK files via sideloading.

This book won't cover the specific steps for creating an account, as those instructions change faster than this book. Just follow along with Google's guidance until you are at the **Google Play Console**.

Creating a new app

Once you're in the Play Console, the next step is to create an app. This gives you a place to upload your build. The big **Create app** button will do the trick — click it to get started. The location of the button depends on whether this is your first app.

Next, you'll see prompts for some basic information about the app. You'll also need to agree to the Developer Program Policies.

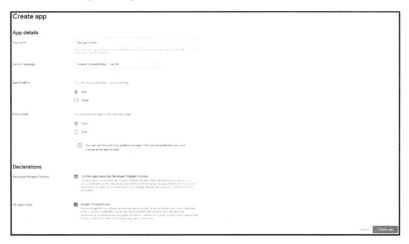

If you're satisfied with accepting the declarations, click **Create app** once again.

Note that creating an app just creates a record in the Play Store. This lets you deal with pre-release activities, uploading builds and filling out store information. It doesn't publish anything to the store or make anything public yet. You have a lot more information to add before you can publish the app.

Providing assets and a description

Your next step before publishing is to upload app assets, such as icons and screenshots, and provide a description for the app. You'll do this in the **Main store listing** tab.

On the left, expand **Store presence** under the **Grow** section and select **Main store listing**.

Here, you'll enter the customer-facing information about your app, which is required for release. The page has two sections: **App Details** and **Graphics**.

In the **App Details** section, enter a **Short description** and a **Full description**.

For example, a short description for this app might be:

```
This is an app to find recipes on the web.
```

Here's an example for the full description:

```
With Recipe Finder, the world's premier recipe search app,
you'll find all sorts of interesting things to cook. Bookmark
your favorite ones to put together a shopping list.
```

The **Graphics** section lets you upload special art and screenshots. You'll find sample versions of these in **assets\store graphics** at the top of this chapter's materials.

For the **App icon**, upload **app_icon.png**. This is a large, 512×512px version of the launcher icon.

The **Feature graphic** is the image you use to promote your app in the Play Store. Upload **feature_graphic.png** for this asset. It's a 1024×500px stylized image that promotes the app branding.

Next, you need to add the screenshots. The store asks for phone, 7-inch tablet and 10-inch tablet image sizes. Fortunately, you don't have to upload screenshots for every possible screen size, just a representative.

For the **Phone screenshots**, upload **phone1.png**, **phone2.png** and **phone3.png**. These all come from screenshots taken on the simulator.

Even though Recipe Finder isn't designed for a tablet, it will run on one. It's good practice to include screenshots for these cases, as well.

For **7-inch tablet screenshots** upload **7in.png**.

For **10-inch tablet screenshots** upload **10in.png**.

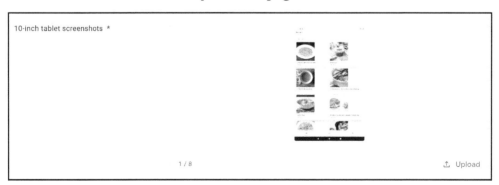

For this chapter, you won't upload a **Video** because that requires setting up a YouTube account. However, a video that shows off your app's features is a good idea for your production apps.

Click **Save** to save the images and details you've entered so far.

Now, you've defined enough of a presence to make an impression.

Entering the rest of the information

However, you still haven't added enough information for the Play Store to allow you to distribute your app. Because you can promote an uploaded build for sale in the store, the Play Console wants you to fill out a lot of information first.

Click the **Dashboard** button, which is the top item in the left navigation bar in the console, and find the **Set up your app** section. This shows a checklist of all the items you need to fill out before you can distribute your app.

The steps you performed earlier completed the **Set up your store listing** goal, so it's already checked.

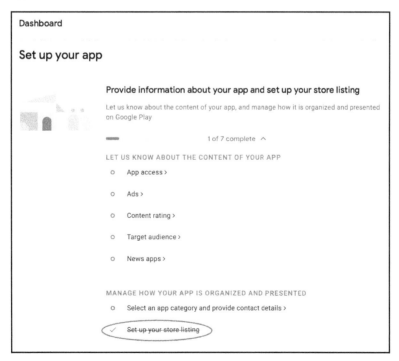

Click each of those items to fill out the required information. If you get lost in the process, go back to the Dashboard and find the **Set up your app** section again.

Because this is a simple recipe app without a lot of controversial content — other than what counts as a "sandwich" — the answers are straightforward. You also have time before your app goes live in the Play Store to modify any of your choices.

The following are sample settings to get you started.

Be sure to click **Save** after updating each page, then navigate back to the Dashboard to choose the next step.

App access

For **App access**, select that all functionality is available since there are no restrictions.

Ads

For **Ads**, indicate that the app doesn't contain ads.

Content rating

To receive a content rating, you'll have to answer a questionnaire. Click **Start questionnaire**.

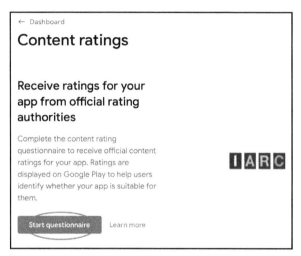

The questionnaire has several steps. The first is specifying the **Category**. Enter your email address, select the **Reference, News, or Educational** category and click **Next**.

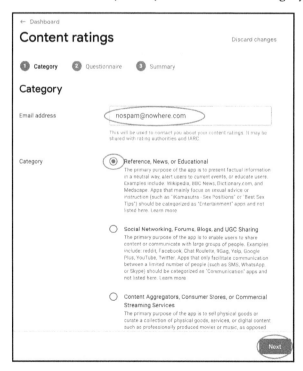

You need to answer several questions regarding your app's content. Be sure to read each before making your selection. Your app just contains recipes without any functionality to even buy the ingredients, so you can select **No** for all the content questions. When you're finished, click **Save**.

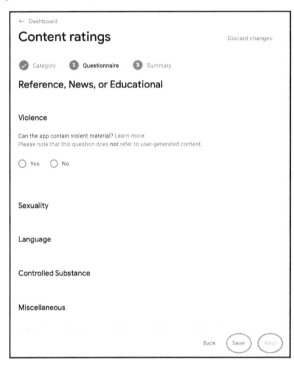

After you've saved your choices, click **Next** and review the **Summary** page.

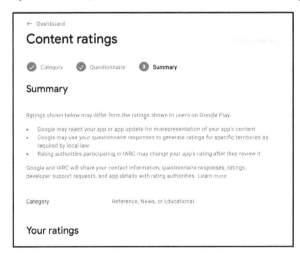

If everything looks good, click **Submit**. You'll then see the **Content ratings** page.

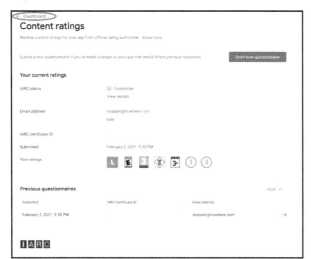

Click the **Back arrow** at the top to return to the Dashboard and continue with **Target audience and content**.

Target audience and content

This app is not for children, so simply select 18 and up. That way, there's no problem if a user looks up a saucy dish, like a bolognese.

The next question asks about your **Store presence**. Choose your preferred option and click **Next**.

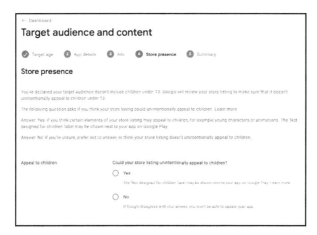

The screen will show you a summary. Note the differences between choosing **Yes** and **No**.

Click the **Back arrow** again to go back to the Dashboard and get ready to set details for the **News** section.

News

This is not a news app.

App category

Return to the Dashboard and click **Select an app category and provide contact details**.

For the app category, select **Books & Reference** because this is a reference app. For the contact details, you need some real business contact info to publish to the store. For testing, however, it's OK to fill out nonsense.

Click **Save** at the bottom right.

App pricing and merchant info

If your Google Play Store account is new and you haven't set up your financial information yet, you need to let Google know where to send money. In this case, though, it's not a big deal because this is a free app.

To change the price, find the search field at the top of the Dashboard page. Enter **pricing** and click **App Pricing**.

In this case, you'll publish a free app, which is the default value.

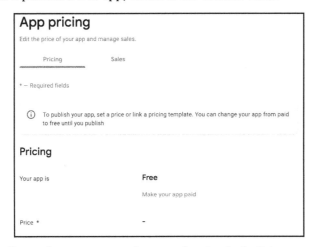

Now, you're finally ready to set up a release and upload a build.

Uploading a build

The next step in your app's journey is to upload a build for testing. The Play Store provides different levels of testing:

- **Internal testing**: Intended for testing within your organization or with a small group of friends or customers, it's limited to 100 people. You'll generally use this for releases during the development cycle.

- **Closed testing**: Allows you to send builds to an invite-only list. Use this for alpha or beta releases, experiments and gathering feedback from a wider set of customers or reviewers.

- **Open testing**: A public test that anyone can join. Use this to gather feedback on a polished release.

In any of these tracks, the steps to upload a build are similar. This chapter focuses on internal testing.

Go to the **Release** section in the left menu. Expand **Testing ▸ Internal testing** and click **Create new release**.

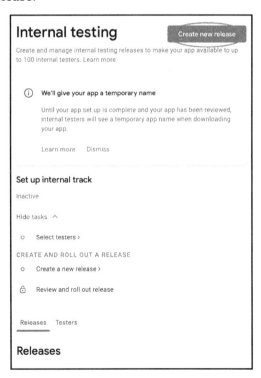

If prompted, read the Terms and Conditions. If you don't object to them, accept them.

To use an Android App Bundle, which Google prefers, you must allow Google Play to create your app signing. For more information, click **Learn more**. When you're done, click **Continue**.

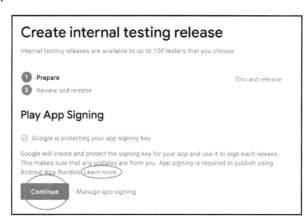

When you ran `flutter build`, it placed **app-release.aab** in your current project's folder hierarchy. The location isn't part of your Flutter project and it isn't visible in your IDE.

By default, the directory is: **build/app/outputs/bundle/release/**. Open Finder or Windows Explorer and navigate to this release folder.

Drag the app bundle file to the box for dropping or uploading a file, in the middle of the **Releases** page.

After the upload has completed, all that's left to do is create a **Release name** and **Release notes**.

The release name defaults to the version number, but you can rename it to something that will be helpful if you need to refer to the version later. For example, **First Testing Release**.

Use the release notes to notify the users about what's changed or if you want them to look for particular issues. You can provide this message in multiple languages.

For example:

```
<en-US>
This release is just to demonstrate uploading and sending out a
build.
</en-US>
```

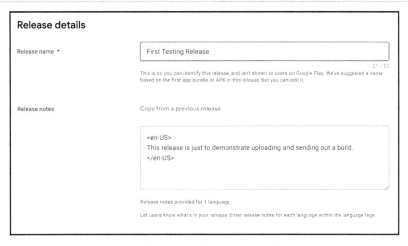

When you're done, click **Save**. This saves the release information.

To distribute it, next click **Review release**.

Distribution

On the next screen, if there are any **errors** listed under **Errors, warnings and messages**, you'll have to resolve them before you can proceed. It's OK to roll out with warnings, such as a lack of debug symbols.

Once you've resolved all the issues, click **Start rollout to Internal testing**.

You'll get one more confirmation dialog. Click **Rollout**.

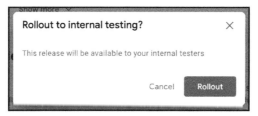

When the release says **Available to internal testers**, your app is ready for testing. Congratulations!

> **Note**: It will take some time before the app becomes available, from minutes to possibly a few days. Stay patient.

Click the **Testers tab**, then **Create email list** to create a new list of testers.

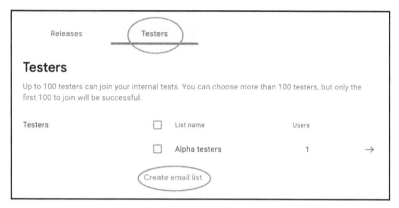

Give the list a name and add the Google account email that you use for the Play Store on your phone.

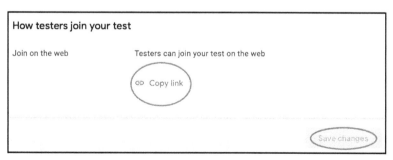

There are a few ways to get the app on your phone. The easiest is to use the web link, which you can find under **How testers join your test**.

Click **Copy link** and send it to yourself on an Android device. Be sure to click **Save changes**.

Installing the app

Using the web browser on your Android device, navigate to that link and you'll see the invitation to join the test.

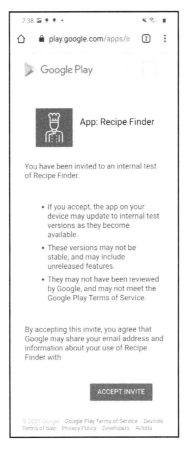

Tapping **ACCEPT INVITE** will give you a link to the Play Store to download the app. Once you're in the Play Store, just tap **Install**.

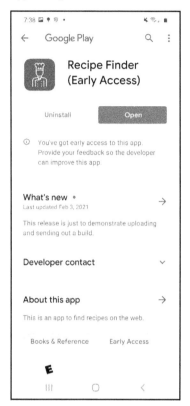

After the app loads, you're ready to go.

Congratulations, you just built a Flutter app on your local machine, uploaded it to Google Play and downloaded it to your device! Take a bow, this is a real accomplishment.

Key points

- Release builds need a signed release configuration.

- To upload to the Google Play Store, you'll need to list all necessary permissions.

- To test an app, go to the Google Play Console, create the app with store metadata, create a release, upload the build and invite testers.

Where to go from here?

For the most part, you don't need the Flutter tools to prepare the app bundle for release. It's all Android-specific work. To learn more about how Android Studio can help prepare and sign release builds and how to use the Google Play Console, check out our Android Apprentice book:
https://www.raywenderlich.com/books/android-apprentice.
This covers the Google Play Console more in-depth.

In particular, once you've done enough internal testing of your app, you can **promote** the release for **closed testing**. This means that your app goes through App Review and is available in the Play Store, but it's unlisted. This lets you share it with even more testers.

After that, you can promote that release for **open testing**, which is a public beta that anyone can join, or send it out as an official **production** release.

In the next chapter you'll release **Recipe Finder** on Apple's App Store. Get ready!

Chapter 18: Build & Release an iOS App

By Michael Katz

In this chapter, you'll learn how to use Xcode and TestFlight to distribute your Flutter app's iOS version.

Unlike with Android, apps can't be sideloaded onto iOS devices. To distribute your app to users and testers, you have to go through App Store Connect, Apple's developer portal for the App Store. TestFlight allows you to send apps to testers and gather feedback from both your internal team and the outside world.

For this chapter, you'll need to use a Mac with Xcode installed. You'll also need a valid Apple Developer Program account to access the App Store.

If you're following along with your app, open it and keep using it with this chapter. If not, locate the **projects** folder for this chapter and open the **starter** folder.

> **Note**: If you use the starter app, don't forget to add your **apiKey** and **apiId** in **network/recipe_service.dart**. Also, run `flutter pub get` from the IDE's terminal.

Run your app on an iOS simulator to set up the necessary files in the **iOS** folder.

Creating the signing

It's time to leave Android Studio (or VS Code) and move over to Xcode. Open the workspace file **ios/Runner.xcworkspace**. This workspace includes the main app projects and the CocoaPods dependencies you need to build the app.

In the Project navigator, check if there's a folder arrow next to **Pods**. If not, close the Xcode project, return to Android Studio and run your app on an iOS simulator. This will pull all the required files. When you're done, re-open **ios/Runner.xcworkspace**.

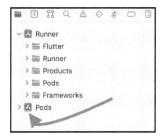

Select **Runner** in the Project navigator to open the project editor. Select the **Runner** target and open the **General** tab.

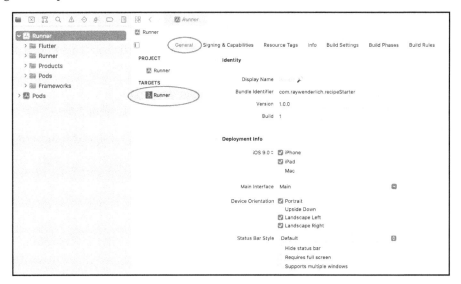

For app submission, it's important to check the **Bundle Identifier**. This has to be unique for your app. If you want to follow along with this tutorial to test out the process — that is, *not submit* — you still have to change the existing value. Try using a random unique string if you are out of ideas.

Creating an Apple Developer Program account

If you already have a valid Apple Developer Program account, move on to the next section: **Creating an app identifier**.

If you want to enroll in the Apple Developer Program, open https://developer.apple.com/account and sign in with your Apple ID. If you see a page prompting you to join the Apple Developer Program, you need to click the link and follow the instructions to enroll.

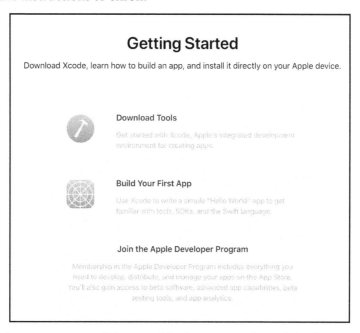

The instructions are ever-evolving, so this chapter won't explain them. Just follow the prompts, enter all your personal or business information and pay the fee. Once registered, you'll be able to access the Apple Developer Portal and the App Store.

Creating an app identifier

In the developer portal, you'll tell Apple about your app.

From https://developer.apple.com/account, click **Certificates, IDs & Profiles** from the **Program Resources**.

From there, choose **Identifiers** to get to the identifiers list. This list contains all the app identifiers associated with your developer account. It will include all the IDs you create manually or through Xcode.

Click the + button to create a new identifier.

You'll see a long list of identifiers supported by the portal. For this task, select **App IDs** and click **Continue**.

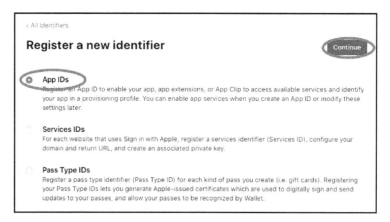

You'll get a chance to choose between an **App** and an **App Clip**.

> **Note**: App Clips are lightweight versions of your app that users can download quickly and start using. Later, they can download the full app. At the time of writing, these are only experimentally supported with Flutter and are out of the scope of this book.
>
> See https://flutter.dev/docs/development/platform-integration/ios-app-clip for more details.

Choose **App** and click **Continue**.

Next, you have the opportunity to set an explicit App ID.

Copy the Bundle Identifier you previously chose for your app from Xcode and paste it in the **Bundle ID** field. Remember, this has to be unique so don't use **com.raywenderlich.recipefinder**.

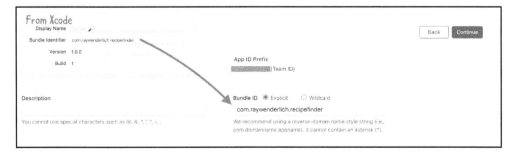

Next, set the description. This is for your use only. It helps you find the app you want from a long list in the console as you make more apps.

There's also a long list of **Capabilities**, which are special entitlements that let your app access parts of the operating system, hardware or Apple's Cloud services. The app for this chapter doesn't require any special capabilities, so you don't need to worry about setting up any of these.

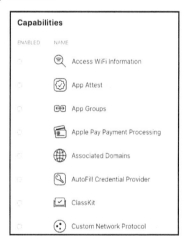

Click **Continue**, then **Register**. After a moment for processing, you'll see the app ID listed in the **Identifiers** list.

Now that Apple knows the identifier, you need to update Xcode. You'll bounce back and forth between the web and Xcode a few times.

Setting the team

From the project editor, click the **Signing & Capabilities** tab. This will allow you to select a team. Select your developer team in the drop-down. If you aren't signed in through Xcode, choose **Add an Account...** to sign in.

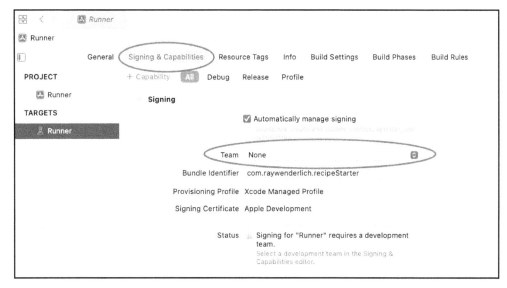

Once you've set the team and fixed any errors, Xcode will create the signing certificates.

> **Note**: Instead of letting Xcode manage your app profile, you can deal with those issues manually. You usually do this if you're working in a continuous integration environment. Manual signing is outside the scope of this book, but it's covered in *iOS App Distribution & Best Practices*: https://bit.ly/3iBgy0x.

Setting up the App Store

When you submit an Android app, you first have to have a Google Play developer account and then set up the app in the Play Store. For iOS (and macOS) apps, you need to follow the same procedure for Apple.

The first step is to set up a spot for the app in **App Store Connect**. This is Apple's administrative console for developers in the App Store.

Navigate to the App Store Connect website: https://appstoreconnect.apple.com/

> **Note**: You'll need a valid Apple Developer Program account to access App Store Connect. If you log in and see an **Enroll** button, then you still have to sign up. Use the instructions above to create an account.

Creating a new app

Before you can upload and distribute a build, you first have to create a record for the app by adding some basic information.

From the main App Store Connect login menu, select **My Apps**. This is where you'll create your app's store listing.

To create a new app record, click the + button and select **New App**.

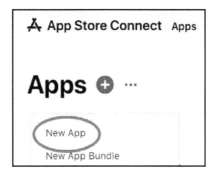

Note: You may have to accept the App Store terms and conditions or enter business or legal info. This might happen now or at any point in the process. The site will let you know when you need to agree and will not let you proceed otherwise. Any time you see that request, resolve the issue and come back.

You'll see a window where you can fill in some basic app information:

Fill in the following information:

1. Select the **iOS** platform.

2. **Name** is important here because your customers will see it. As with the Android app, you'll need to use something unique. **Recipe Finder** is already taken, and you'll get an error message if you pick a name that someone has already used.

3. **Primary Language** is the default language for the app — in this case, US English.

4. For **Bundle ID**, select the identifier you used in the developer portal from the drop-down. If it doesn't show up here, go back to the Identifiers list and make sure you created an app ID.

5. **SKU** is a unique identifier used for financial reports. Pick one that you'll recognize when counting the money. :]

6. **User Access** controls access to your team's App Store Connect users. This is important if you have a large team and don't want to show the app to everyone in your organization.

When you're done, your responses should look like this:

New App

Platforms ?
☑ iOS   macOS   tvOS

Name ?

Recipe Finder

Primary Language ?

English (U.S.)

Bundle ID ?

Recipe Finder - com.raywenderlich.recipefinder

SKU ?

FlutterApprentice1

User Access   ?

Limited Access   ◉ Full Access

Cancel   Create

Click **Create** and you'll see a new screen showing your app's App Store Connect entry.

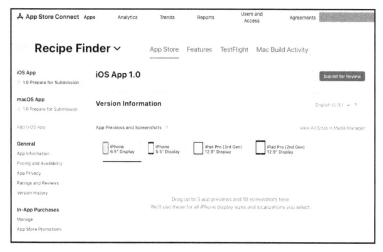

Voilà! Your app is now ready for you to upload.

Uploading to the App Store

On Android, you made an **appbundle** to distribute to the Play Store. iOS has a parallel concept. You'll need to build an archive to upload to the App Store. You can do this from either Xcode or the command line. For this chapter, you'll use Xcode.

In Xcode, just above the section where you entered the Bundle Identifier, you'll see the tiny app icon with a device.

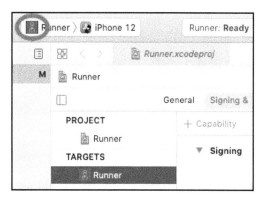

To the right of the tiny app icon, click the device name and set the device to **Any iOS Device** as the build destination. This is important because you can make deployable builds only for actual devices, not the simulator.

When you upload your app to the App Store, you upload an app **archive**. To create an archive from the menu, go to **Product ▸ Archive**.

Archive builds the app for distribution and packages it for uploading to the App Store. You'll see a progress bar across the top of your Xcode window.

> Archiving Runner: sqlite | Building 153 of 235 tasks

When it completes, the **Organizer** window will pop up and display the archive.

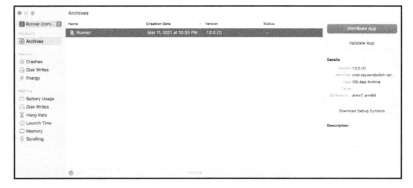

The archive file contains the app binary along with metadata and symbols. The App Store will process this file and get the version that users will finally download on their devices.

Uploading the build

From the organizer window, click **Distribute App**.

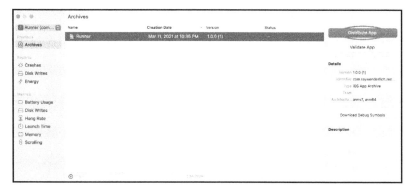

You'll see a list of distribution methods. Choose **App Store Connect** and click **Next**. The other options are for custom distributions typically used in enterprise contexts.

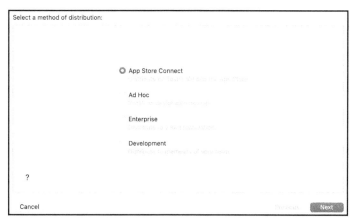

In the next dialog, choose **Upload** to send the build directly to Apple. The **Export** option creates an artifact that you can upload later, through other means. Click **Next**.

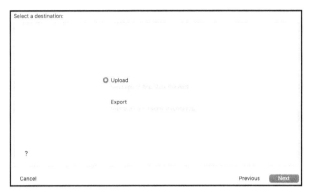

The next form covers distribution options. You have the option to strip the Swift symbols, which reduces app size. The other option is to upload the debug symbols, which makes it possible to symbolicate crash reports that come in from users. Click **Next**.

> **Note**: The Xcode project generated by Flutter is not bitcode-enabled by default. To configure it for bitcode see https://git.io/JVWH5.

The next form is about app signing. It's easier to let Xcode manage your signing, but if you have a CI system doing your builds and uploading to the App Store, you'll have more control with manual signing. For now, click **Automatically manage signing** then click **Next**.

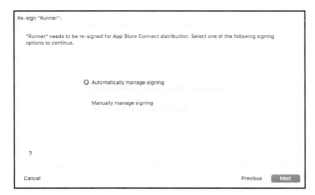

If you have an **Apple Distribution certificate**, skip to the next step. If you don't know what an Apple Distribution certificate is, then you're in the right place.

You need a certificate to upload to App Store Connect. Xcode can generate one for you. If your account doesn't have a certificate yet, you'll see the following screen. Select **Generate an Apple Distribution certificate** and click **Next**.

While the certificate generates, you'll see a screen with a spinning wheel. It can flash by or take a little while to generate. When it's done, you'll see the following screen. Be sure to read it.

You'll notice that it warns you that the private key is stored locally and cannot be recovered if lost. Apple recommends saving the certificate and key in a safe place.

Click **Export Signing Certificate**, add a password and save it somewhere you can remember. After you've exported the certificate, click **Next**.

Xcode will then sign the app and prepare it for upload.

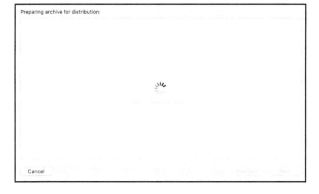

After Xcode creates the archive, the final form will show you the app contents and metadata. This includes any frameworks — such as Flutter — and other dependencies, as well as all the signing and entitlement information. Click **Upload** to send it to the App Store.

Now, it's important that you've already set up the record in the App Store so there's a place for this information to go. If there are no issues with App Store Connect, like having to accept agreements, then you're done working in Xcode. Otherwise, resolve any errors and try again. Click **Done** when prompted.

In a few minutes, the app will show up under the iOS builds in App Store Connect. Go to https://appstoreconnect.apple.com/apps, click your app and go to the **TestFlight** tab. Select **Builds ▸ iOS** on the left to see the list of uploaded builds. You'll see yours is **Processing**.

After some time, the status will update to **Ready to Submit**.

Alternately, you might see an error like **Missing Compliance**:

If there's an error, follow the instructions at the link to fix it. If this is the first time you uploaded the build, you'll likely get a compliance issue. Follow your local legal advice on how to answer those questions.

Once your app is ready to submit, you can continue with the TestFlight process.

Sharing builds through TestFlight

Now, you're ready to test your build. There are two options for test builds: **Internal Testing** and **External Testing**.

Internal testing is for sharing within your own team or company for quality assurance or feedback. Typically, this includes other developers, quality engineers, product managers, designers and marketing specialists. Your mileage may vary.

External testing is for a limited group of testers. These can include people within your organization as well as beta test customers, friends, journalists and anyone you want to try your app before you release it.

Internal testing

You can begin internal testing as soon as the app finishes processing. To add testers from the **TestFlight** tab of the App store console, just select **App Store Connect Users** under the **Internal Testing** header.

Click + next to **Testers**.

You'll get a list of users to add as testers. Internal testing is only open to users who have accounts in your App Store Connect. At a minimum, you'll be listed as available. To add more people to your account, you'll have to go through the **Users and Access** link from the top navigation bar.

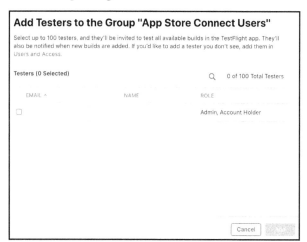

Once you add a tester, they'll appear in the **Testers** list.

That tester will have to accept the email invite before they can install a build.

The invite will provide instructions or a button to launch TestFlight. From there, the user will receive a prompt to install the app.

And that's all it takes for the user to get your app on their device. From then on, the App Store will automatically notify your testers when a new build is available.

From the same **Testers** list in App Store Connect, you can monitor the app's usage for crashes or feedback submitted through the TestFlight tool.

External testing

Internal testing is limited to a few people who are in your store account. Obviously, you don't want to give store access to testers who aren't part of your organization.

To get started with external testing, you first have to make a group. The App Store lets you separate testers into groups, so you don't have to release every build to every tester. For example, you might want a test team to get every build, but update customer beta builds only once a week.

Click the + next to **External Testing** in the left navigation bar to create a new group.

You'll see a window for you to enter the **Group Name**. Enter a name and click **Create**.

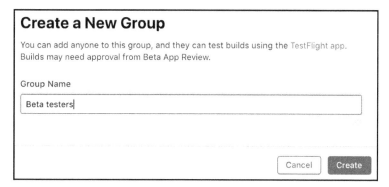

After you create the group, you'll see it listed in the sidebar.

You can now add testers to your group. One difference from internal testing is that you can invite testers right from this panel. You can also create a web link to share, letting testers invite themselves to the group.

Before you can create a link or add users, you need to add a build. Click + next to **Builds**.

Apple reviews apps before it releases them to beta testers. The next window allows you to choose which build you wish to submit to Apple for Beta App Review.

Select the build that you want Beta App Review to test. Click **Next** to go to the next screen.

Next, enter contact information. This lets your readers supply user feedback and lets Beta App Review ask any questions they have. If your app has a login, you have to create an account that app review can use to log in and check out the app. Fortunately, **Recipe Finder** has no login. :]

Enter the information and click **Next** to continue.

Your last step is to enter a little message that will be included with the build notification. This an opportunity to ask people to check out certain things or to notify them about changes.

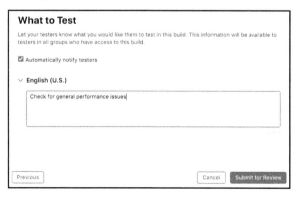

Enter a message and click **Submit for Review**.

This sends your build to Apple for a quick version of an app review. Within a short time — anywhere from a few minutes to a few days — the app will be ready to test, assuming there aren't any issues.

Congratulations, now you can distribute the app for testing.

To submit your app to the App Store for download or purchase, you need to add all the information required under the **App Store** tab, such as screenshots, marketing copy, privacy policy and age rating.

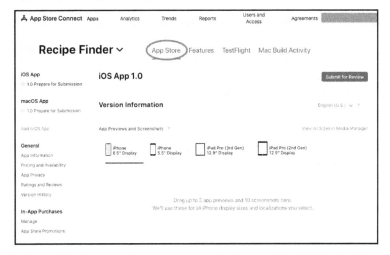

Once that information is complete, you can submit your TestFlight build to the full app review. After testing, you can submit your app for release.

And there you have it: simple Flutter app distribution on iOS.

Key points

- You have to configure the Apple Developer Portal and App Store Connect before you can upload a build.

- Use Xcode to archive the project to easily upload your app to the App Store.

- Use TestFlight for internal and external testing of iOS apps.

Where to go from here?

If you want to take this to the next level and learn more about app signing or distributing and selling to customers in the App Store,
then iOS App Distribution & Best Practices
https://www.raywenderlich.com/books/ios-app-distribution-best-practices is for you.

Apple's documentation is also helpful if you have questions about terms not covered here: https://apple.co/3FmLlrq.

Section VI: Working With Firebase Cloud Firestore

In this section you will learn how to create and use a Firebase Cloud Firestore. You will learn how to use it to add and retrieve data. Then you will learn about authentication and how to secure your data.

Chapter 19: Firebase Cloud Firestore

By Vincenzo Guzzi & Kevin David Moore

When you want to store information for hundreds of people, you can't store it on one person's phone. It has to be in a storage cloud. You could hire a team of developers to design and implement a backend system that connects to a database via a set of APIs. This could take months of development time. Wouldn't it be great if you could just connect to an existing system?

This is where **Firebase Cloud Firestore** comes in. You no longer need to write complicated apps that use thousands of lines of async tasks and threaded processes to simulate reactiveness. With Cloud Firestore, you'll be up and running in no time.

In this chapter, you will create an instant messaging app called **RayChat**. While creating RayChat, you'll learn:

- About Cloud Firestore and when to use it.

- The steps required to set up a Firebase project with the Cloud Firestore.

- How to connect to, query and populate the Cloud Firestore.

- How to use the Cloud Firestore to build your own instant messaging app.

Getting started

First, open the starter project from this chapter's project materials and run `flutter pub get`.

Next, build and run your project on an Android device. Don't worry, you'll run on iOS later.

You'll see the RayChat home page:

Right now, your app doesn't do much. You'll need to add your own Cloud Firestore to send and receive messages.

What is a Cloud Firestore?

Google gives you the option for two real-time NoSQL document databases within the Firebase suite of tools: Realtime Database and Firebase Cloud Firestore. But what's the difference?

Firestore is Google's newest offering. Google created Firestore to better cope with large-scale software with deeply layered data. You can query data and receive it separately, creating a truly elastic environment that copes well as your data set grows.

Realtime Database, though still a document-driven NoSQL database, returns data in JSON format. When you query a tree of JSON data, it includes all of its child nodes. To keep your transactions light and nimble, you have to keep your data hierarchy as flat as possible.

Both of these solutions are great, so it's important to know when to use them. Here are some key metrics for each database:

Realtime Database

- Has a free plan, but charges per transaction and to a lesser extent for storage used, past the limit.

- It's easy to scale.

- Can handle complex, deeply layered data sets and relations.

- Available for mobile and web.

Firebase Cloud Firestore

- Also has a free plan, but charges for storage used, not for queries made, past the limit.

- Extremely low latency.

- Easy to store simple data using JSON.

- Available for mobile only.

You will be using Cloud Firestore.

> **Note**: Check out the full list of comparisons on Google's product page
>
> https://cloud.google.com/products/databases.
>
> And have a look at our Cloud Firestore tutorial
>
> https://www.raywenderlich.com/7426050-firebase-chapter-for-flutter-getting-started#toc-anchor-005 if you're looking to explore the Firestore solution.

Setting up a Google project and Database

Before you can use any of Google's cloud services, you have to set up a project on the Firebase Console; then you can create your Cloud Firestore and manage it directly from the console. You'll use the free tier.

First, go to https://console.firebase.google.com. Then, click **Create a project**:

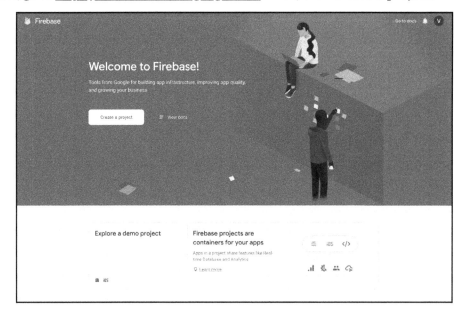

Name your project **RayChat** and click **Continue**:

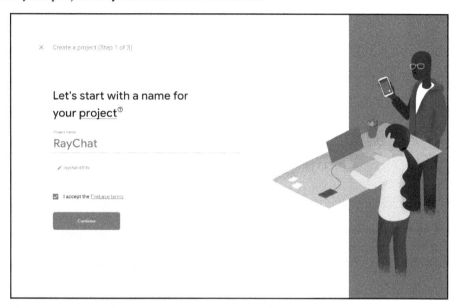

Disable Google Analytics since you don't need it for this chapter.

Finally, click **Create project** at the bottom of the page:

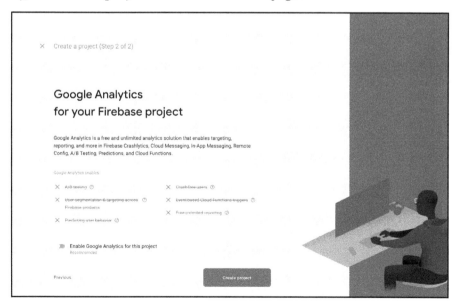

Give Google a minute to load and then your project will be ready.

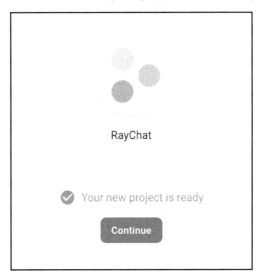

Click **Continue**.

To create your Cloud Firestore, go back to your Firebase home page and select **See all Build features**:

Scroll down and click **Cloud Firestore**:

Then select **Create Database**.

Select **Start in test mode**. This ensures you can read and write data easily while developing your app.

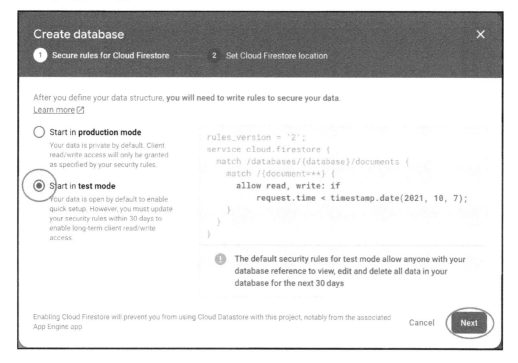

Select your region for your **Cloud Firestore location** and then click **Enable**:

You'll see a step displayed while your database is being created:

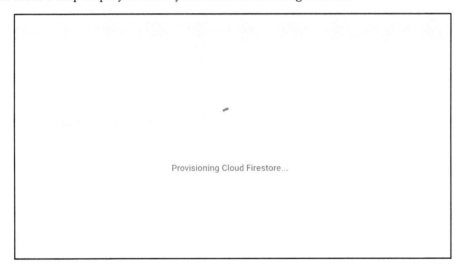

After your database has been created, you'll be redirected to your database console. You can come back to this page later to see your app data in real time:

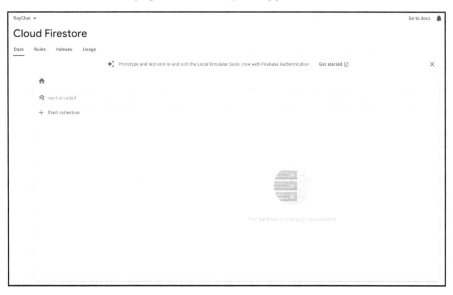

Next, you'll connect your Flutter app with your new Google project.

Creating Google Services files

Google uses a config file that contains all of the API keys for your Firebase project. You'll need to create a config file for your Android and iOS apps individually. You'll start with Android.

Setting up Android

If you only see icons in the left margin, click on the arrow at the bottom of the list to expand the menu.

Click on the **Project Overview** button and make sure you have **RayChat** selected as your active project. Then click the **Android symbol**:

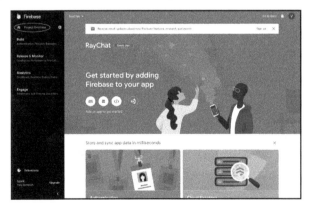

This takes you to a helper page for creating your Android config file. The Android package name is typically your app name in reverse-DNS format. Add **com.raywenderlich.RayChat** in the **package name** field and **RayChat** in the **App nickname** field. Then click **Register app**:

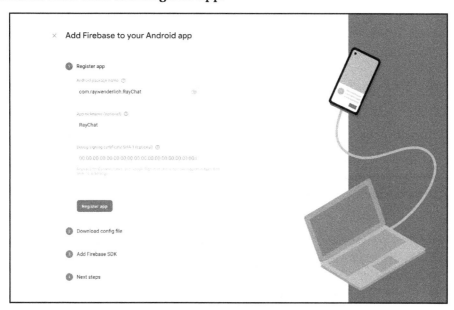

Wait a few seconds for the file to generate. Then click **Download google-services.json** (if prompted remember to allow the download:

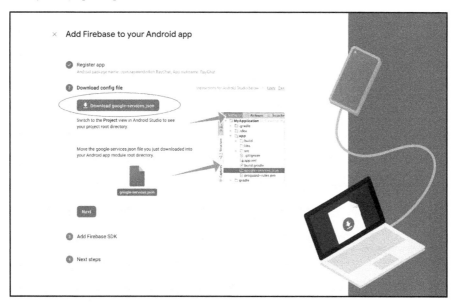

Click **Next**. You can read the directions but don't follow them.

Click **Next** again and then **Continue to console**.

Now, move **google-services.json** from the download location to your project's **android/app** folder.

> **Note:** Don't follow the Firebase console steps under **Add Firebase SDK** as they assume you're developing an Android native app. Flutter does things a little differently.

Returning to Android Studio, in your project, open **android/build.gradle**. Then add the following dependency at the end of the list in the `dependencies` section of `buildscript`:

```
classpath 'com.google.gms:google-services:4.3.10'
```

```
buildscript {
    ext.kotlin_ver
    repositories {
        google()
        jcenter()
    }

    dependencies {
        classpath
        classpath
    }
```

Now open **android/app/build.gradle** and add the Google services plugin after the other `apply plugin` and `apply from` entries:

```
apply plugin: 'com.google.gms.google-services'
```

Don't worry about the Gradle errors. Run the app again to make sure it still runs. You should see the same screen you saw before:

Now that Android is set up and works, you'll work on iOS.

Setting up iOS

You'll need Xcode to set up your iOS project. If you're not using a Mac, feel free to skip this section.

Head back to your Firebase Console home page and click **Add app**. Then select **iOS**:

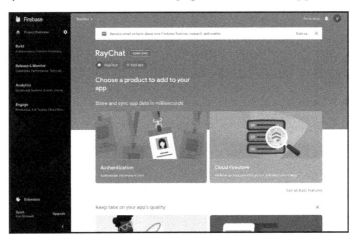

This brings you to the config file generation page for iOS. Like before, add **com.raywenderlich.RayChat** as your iOS Bundle ID and **RayChat** as your app nickname. Click **Register app**:

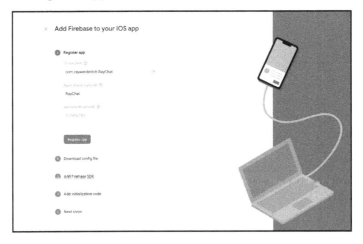

As before, once your app is registered, download **GoogleService-info.plist**.

Note: Don't follow the Firebase console steps for the **Add Firebase SDK** section as they are not suited to Flutter.

Click on **Next** until you get to the end of the steps and then click **Continue to console**.

Move the **GoogleService-info.plist** file to the **ios/Runner** folder.

Next, open **ios/Runner.xcworkspace** in **Xcode**.

In Xcode's Project navigator, expand the top-level **Runner**. Then right-click **Runner** beneath it and select **Add Files to "Runner"…**:

Then select **Google-Services-Info.plist** from the **Runner** folder. Make sure you have **Copy items if needed** checked. Then click **Add**:

And you're done! Close Xcode. Now you can communicate with your Google project in both your iOS and Android apps produced by Flutter.

Run the app in the iOS simulator to make sure it works.

Time to start writing some code.

Adding Flutter dependencies

FlutterFire is the set of Flutter Firebase packages. You will use them to save and retrieve data. Go back to Android Studio and add the following dependencies in your **pubspec.yaml**. Add them underneath the `intl` dependency:

```
firebase_core: ^1.6.0
cloud_firestore: ^2.5.3
```

Press the **Pub get** button.

Before creating the model class, it's time to talk about collections.

Understanding Collections

Firestore stores data in collections, which are similar to tables in a traditional database. They have a name and a list of **Documents**.

These documents usually have a unique generated key (also known as document ID) in the database, and they store data in key/value pairs.

These fields can have several different types:

- String

- Number

- Boolean

- Map

- Array

- Null

- Timestamp

- Geopoint

- Reference to another document

You can use Firestore's console to manually enter data and see the data appear almost immediately in your app. If you enter data in your app, you'll see it appear on the web and other apps almost immediately.

Now that you know about collections, it's time to create the models for your app.

Modeling data

Add a new directory inside **lib** called **data**. You'll use this folder to store your data models and data access objects.

Adding a data model

Create a new file in the **data** directory called **message.dart**. Then add a new class with three fields, text, date and email:

```
import 'package:cloud_firestore/cloud_firestore.dart';

class Message {
  final String text;
  final DateTime date;
  final String? email;

  DocumentReference? reference;

  Message({
    required this.text,
    required this.date,
    this.email,
    this.reference
  });
  // TODO: Add JSON converters
}
```

You also need a way to transform your Message model from JSON since that's how it's stored in your Cloud Firestore. Replace // TODO: Add JSON converters with:

```
factory Message.fromJson(Map<dynamic, dynamic> json) => Message(
    text: json['text'] as String,
    date: DateTime.parse(json['date'] as String),
    email: json['email'] as String?);

Map<String, dynamic> toJson() => <String, dynamic>{
      'date': date.toString(),
      'text': text,
      'email': email,
    };
// TODO: Add fromSnapshot
```

The first definition will help you transform the JSON you receive from the Cloud Firestore, into a Message. The second will do the opposite — transform the Message into JSON, for saving.

Replace `// TODO: Add fromSnapshot` with:

```
factory Message.fromSnapshot(DocumentSnapshot snapshot) {
  final message = Message.fromJson(snapshot.data() as
Map<String, dynamic>);
  message.reference = snapshot.reference;
  return message;
}
```

This takes a Firestore snapshot and converts it to a message.

Adding a data access object (DAO)

Create a new file in **data** called **message_dao.dart**. This is your DAO for your messages.

Add the following:

```
import 'package:cloud_firestore/cloud_firestore.dart';
import 'message.dart';

class MessageDao {
  // 1
  final CollectionReference collection =
    FirebaseFirestore.instance.collection('messages');
  // TODO: Add saveMessage
}
```

This code:

1. Gets an instance of `FirebaseFirestore` and then gets the root of the messages collection by calling `collection()`.

Now, you need `MessageDao` to perform two functions: saving and retrieving.

Replace `// TODO: Add saveMessage` with:

```
void saveMessage(Message message) {
    collection.add(message.toJson());
}
// TODO: Add getMessageStream
```

This function takes a `Message` as a parameter and uses your `CollectionReference` to save the JSON message to your Cloud Firestore:

1. `toJson()` converts the message to a JSON string.

2. `add()` Adds the string to the collection. This updates the database immediately.

For the retrieval method, you only need to expose a `Stream<QuerySnapshot>` which interacts directly with your `DatabaseReference`.

Replace `// TODO: Add getMessageStream` with:

```
Stream<QuerySnapshot> getMessageStream() {
  return collection.snapshots();
}
```

This returns a stream of data at the root level. Now you have your message DAO. As the name states, the data access object helps you access whatever data you have stored at the given Cloud Firestore reference. It will also let you store new data, as you send messages. Now all you have to do is build your UI.

Provider

As you saw in Chapter 13, "State Management", **Provider** is a great package for providing classes to its children. Open **pubspec.yaml** and add the `provider` package:

```
provider: ^6.0.0
```

Run `flutter pub get`.

Open up **main.dart** and add the imports:

```
import 'package:firebase_core/firebase_core.dart';
import 'package:provider/provider.dart';
import '../data/message_dao.dart';
```

Replace `// TODO: Add Firebase Initialization` with:

```
await Firebase.initializeApp();
```

This will initialize a new Firebase instance.

In the build method, replace `// TODO: Add MultiProvider` and the `return` keyword on the next line with:

```
return MultiProvider(
  providers: [
    // TODO: Add ChangeNotifierProvider<UserDao> here
    Provider<MessageDao>(
      lazy: false,
```

```
      create: (_) => MessageDao(),
    ),
  ],
  child:
```

Next replace `// TODO: Add closing parenthesis` with:

```
),
```

You've now created an instance of `MessageDao` once so that other screens can use it.

Creating new messages

Open **ui/message_list.dart** and add `Message` and `MessageDao` as imports at the top of the file:

```
import 'package:provider/provider.dart';
import '../data/message.dart';
import '../data/message_dao.dart';
```

Next, get the `MessageDao` inside `build` at the top by replacing `// TODO: Add MessageDao` with:

```
final messageDao = Provider.of<MessageDao>(context, listen:
false);
```

Now replace `// TODO: Add Message DAO 1` and the line beneath it with:

```
_sendMessage(messageDao);
```

Do the same thing with `// TODO: Add Message DAO 2` and the line beneath it.

Replace `// TODO: Replace _sendMessage` and the line beneath it with your send message code:

```
void _sendMessage(MessageDao messageDao) {
  if (_canSendMessage()) {
    final message = Message(
      text: _messageController.text,
      date: DateTime.now(),
      // TODO: add email
    );
    messageDao.saveMessage(message);
    _messageController.clear();
    setState(() {});
```

```
    }
  }
```

This code creates a new Message with the _messageController text populated by a TextField in your widget tree. It then uses your MessageDao to save that message to your Cloud Firestore.

Stop the app and run for iOS. You'll see the same screen as you did before:

Note: Compilation at this point might take some time, even many minutes. See this issue to know more and find some workaround:

https://github.com/FirebaseExtended/flutterfire/issues/2751

Try typing in your first message and click the → button.

Now, go back to your Firebase Console and open your project's Cloud Firestore. You'll see your message as an entry:

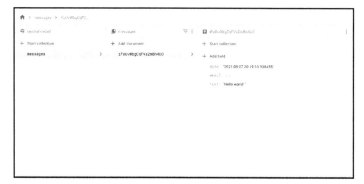

Note that all of the random letters will be different for each person. Great job. You now have implemented a remote database and added an entry with very little code.

Try adding a few more messages. You can even watch your Cloud Firestore as you enter each message to see them appear in real time.

Now it's time to display those messages in **RayChat**.

Reactively displaying messages

Since `MessageDao` has a `getMessageStream()` method that returns a stream, you will use a `StreamBuilder` to display messages.

Add the following imports at the top of **message_list.dart**:

```
import 'package:cloud_firestore/cloud_firestore.dart';
import 'message_widget.dart';
```

Then replace `// TODO: Add _buildListItem` with:

```
Widget _buildListItem(BuildContext context, DocumentSnapshot
snapshot) {
  // 1
  final message = Message.fromSnapshot(snapshot);
  // 2
  return MessageWidget(
    message.text,
    message.date,
    message.email
  );
}
```

1. Create a new message from the given snapshot.

2. Pass the message info to the MessageWidget.

Then replace `// TODO: Add _buildList` with:

```
Widget _buildList(BuildContext context, List<DocumentSnapshot>?
snapshot) {
  // 1
  return ListView(
    controller: _scrollController,
    physics: const BouncingScrollPhysics(),
    padding: const EdgeInsets.only(top: 20.0),
    // 2
    children: snapshot!.map((data) => _buildListItem(context,
data)).toList(),
  );
}
```

Here you:

1. Return a `ListView` with our `_scrollController` and some physics.

2. Map each snapshot item and send it to `_buildListItem()`.

Then replace `// TODO: Replace _getMessageList` and the `_getMessageList()`
method below it with this code:

```
Widget _getMessageList(MessageDao messageDao) {
  return Expanded(
    // 1
    child: StreamBuilder<QuerySnapshot>(
      // 2
      stream: messageDao.getMessageStream(),
      // 3
      builder: (context, snapshot) {
        // 4
        if (!snapshot.hasData)
          return const Center(child: LinearProgressIndicator());

        // 5
        return _buildList(context, snapshot.data!.docs);
      },
    ),
  );
}
```

Here you:

1. Create a `StreamBuilder` widget.

2. Use your `messageDao` to get a stream of messages.

3. Use a builder that contains your snapshot.

4. If you don't have any data yet, use a `LinearProgressIndicator`.

5. Call `_buildList()` with your snapshot data.

Now replace `// TODO: Add Message DAO to _getMessageList` and the line below it with:

```
_getMessageList(messageDao),
```

Trigger a hot reload, and you'll see your messages in a list:

Enter a new message, and you'll see it appear before your eyes:

Magic!

Try loading your app on two different devices or simulators and watch as you communicate in real time.

Now you have an app that can write and display messages, but you can only have one set of messages. What if you wanted each person to have their own set of messages? For that to happen, each user needs to have their own identity in the system. This is done with user authorization and authentication.

Authentication

Firebase provides user authorization and authentication with the `FirebaseAuth` class, which allows you to:

- Create a new user.

- Sign in a user.

- Sign out a user.

- Get data from that user.

Setting up Firebase Authentication

Return to the Firebase console. Click on the **Authentication** card and if prompted with **Get started** click on it, too:

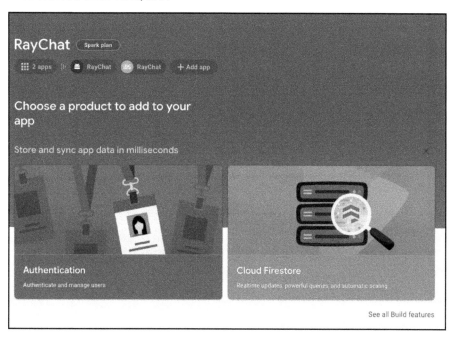

Next Click the **Set up sign-in** method button:

You are going to choose the first entry, **Email/Password**:

Click the **Enable** switch and click **Save**:

Next, click on **Firestore Database** on the left panel:

Delete any messages you have so that you can start over.

Click on the three vertical dots to the right of the **messages** title to delete. Select
Delete collection:

You will get a warning dialog. You must confirm the deletion by following the
instructions. You'll see here that you need to type the collection ID. Enter `messages`
and click **Delete** to delete all data:

Rules

Firebase database security consists of rules, which limit who can read and/or write to specific paths. The rules consist of a JSON string in the **Rules** tab.

On the Firebase console, go to the **Cloud Firestore** section and select the second tab: **Rules**:

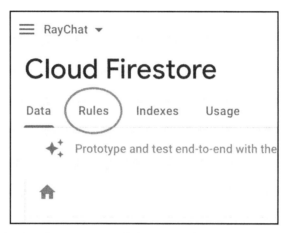

When you set up the database, you used the test ruleset. Now you need to lock down the database so that only those who have logged into your chat app can read and write messages. Replace the current rules with:

```
rules_version = '2';
service cloud.firestore {
  match /databases/{database}/documents {
    match /{document=**} {
      allow read, write: if request.auth != null;
    }
  }
}
```

It will look like this:

`auth` is a special variable and contains the current user information. By checking to make sure that it is not `null`, you ensure a user is logged in.

When you are ready, press the **Publish** button to save the changes.

Now that the database is ready, you'll change the app.

Firebase Authentication

To use authentication with Firebase, you will need the Firebase Authentication package. Add the following to the **pubspec.yaml**:

```
firebase_auth: ^3.1.1
```

Then, press **Pub get** to update the dependencies.

User authentication

Just as you created a DAO for messages, you will create a DAO for users. In the **data** folder, create a new file named **user_dao.dart** and add the following imports:

```
import 'package:firebase_auth/firebase_auth.dart';
import 'package:flutter/foundation.dart';
```

Next, create the `UserDao` class:

```
class UserDao extends ChangeNotifier {
  final auth = FirebaseAuth.instance;
  // TODO: Add helper methods
}
```

This class extends `ChangeNotifier` so that we can notify any listeners whenever a user has logged in or logged out. The `auth` variable is used to hold on to an instance of `FirebaseAuth`.

Replace `// TODO: Add helper methods` with:

```
// 1
bool isLoggedIn() {
  return auth.currentUser != null;
}

// 2
String? userId() {
  return auth.currentUser?.uid;
}

//3
String? email() {
  return auth.currentUser?.email;
}
// TODO: Add signup
```

In this code you:

1. Return `true` if the user is logged in. If the current user is `null`, they are logged out.

2. Return the id of the current user, which could be `null`.

3. Return the email of the current user.

Signing up

The first task a user will need to perform is to create an account. Replace `// TODO: Add signup` with:

```
// 1
void signup(String email, String password) async {
  try {
    // 2
    await auth.createUserWithEmailAndPassword(
      email: email,
```

```
    password: password,
  );
  // 3
  notifyListeners();
} on FirebaseAuthException catch (e) {
  // 4
  if (e.code == 'weak-password') {
    print('The password provided is too weak.');
  } else if (e.code == 'email-already-in-use') {
    print('The account already exists for that email.');
  }
} catch (e) {
  // 5
  print(e);
}
}
// TODO: Add login
```

Here you:

1. Pass in the email and password the user entered. For a real app, you will need to make sure those strings meet your requirements.

2. Call the Firebase method to create a new account.

3. Notify all listeners so they can then check when a user is logged in.

4. Handle some common errors.

5. Catch any other type of exception.

Logging in

Once a user has created an account, they can log back in. Replace `// TODO: Add login` with:

```
// 1
void login(String email, String password) async {
  try {
    // 2
    await auth.signInWithEmailAndPassword(
        email: email,
        password: password,
    );
    // 3
    notifyListeners();
  } on FirebaseAuthException catch (e) {
    if (e.code == 'weak-password') {
      print('The password provided is too weak.');
    } else if (e.code == 'email-already-in-use') {
```

```
      print('The account already exists for that email.');
    }
  } catch (e) {
    print(e);
  }
}
// TODO: Add logout
```

Here, you:

1. Pass in the email and password the user entered.

2. Call the Firebase method to log in to their account.

3. Notify all listeners.

Logging out

The final feature is **logout**. Replace `// TODO: Add logout` with:

```
void logout() async {
  await auth.signOut();
  notifyListeners();
}
```

Now that all the logic is in place, you'll build the UI to log in.

Login screen

To get into the system, a user needs to log in. To do that, they need to create an account. You will be creating a dual-use login screen that will allow a user to either log in or sign up for a new account.

To keep things simple you'll skip error handling. Just remember to implement it before you ship the app to the store :]

In the **ui** folder, create a new file called **login.dart**. Add the following imports:

```
import 'package:flutter/material.dart';
import 'package:flutter/services.dart';
import 'package:flutter/widgets.dart';
import 'package:provider/provider.dart';
import '../data/user_dao.dart';
```

Next, add the `Login` class as follows, ignoring the red squiggles for now:

```
class Login extends StatefulWidget {
  const Login({Key? key}) : super(key: key);

  @override
  _LoginState createState() => _LoginState();
}

class _LoginState extends State<Login> {
  // 1
  final _emailController = TextEditingController();
  // 2
  final _passwordController = TextEditingController();
  // 3
  final GlobalKey<FormState> _formKey = GlobalKey<FormState>();

  @override
  void dispose() {
    // 4
    _emailController.dispose();
    _passwordController.dispose();
    super.dispose();
  }
// TODO: Add build
```

Here, you:

1. Create a text controller for the email field.

2. Create a text controller for the password field.

3. Create a key needed for a form.

4. Dispose of the editing controllers.

Now, you'll add the UI. Still ignoring the red squiggles, replace `// TODO: Add build` with:

```
@override
Widget build(BuildContext context) {
  // 1
  final userDao = Provider.of<UserDao>(context, listen: false);
  return Scaffold(
    // 2
    appBar: AppBar(
      title: const Text('RayChat'),
    ),
    body: Padding(
      padding: const EdgeInsets.all(32.0),
      // 3
```

```
    child: Form(
      key: _formKey,
      // TODO: Add Column & Email
```

In this code, you:

1. Use Provider to get an instance of the `UserDao`.

2. Create an `AppBar` with the name of your app.

3. Create the `Form` with the global key.

Next, you'll create a column with four rows. The first row will have the email address field, the second a password field, the third a login button and the fourth will have a signup button.

Replace `// TODO: Add Column & Email` with:

```
    child: Column(
      children: [
        Row(
          children: [
            const SizedBox(height: 80),
            Expanded(
              // 1
              child: TextFormField(
              decoration: const InputDecoration(
                  border: UnderlineInputBorder(),
                  hintText: 'Email Address',),
              autofocus: false,
              // 2
              keyboardType: TextInputType.emailAddress,
              // 3
              textCapitalization: TextCapitalization.none,
              autocorrect: false,
              // 4
              controller: _emailController,
              // 5
              validator: (String? value) {
                if (value == null || value.isEmpty) {
                  return 'Email Required';
                }
                return null;
              },
              ),
            ),
          ],
        ),
        // TODO: Add Password
```

Here, you:

1. Create the field for the email address.

2. Use an email address keyboard type.

3. Turn off auto-correction and capitalization.

4. Set the editing controller.

5. Define a validator to check for empty strings. You can use regular expressions or any other type of validation if you like.

Next, add the password field. Replace `// TODO: Add Password` with:

```
Row(
  children: [
    const SizedBox(height: 20),
    Expanded(
        child: TextFormField(
      decoration: const InputDecoration(
          border: UnderlineInputBorder(), hintText: 'Password'),
      autofocus: false,
      obscureText: true,
      keyboardType: TextInputType.visiblePassword,
      textCapitalization: TextCapitalization.none,
      autocorrect: false,
      controller: _passwordController,
      validator: (String? value) {
        if (value == null || value.isEmpty) {
          return 'Password Required';
        }
        return null;
      },
    ),
    ),
  ],
),
const Spacer(),
// TODO: Add Buttons
```

This is almost the same except for the password field. Now replace `// TODO: Add Buttons` with:

```
Row(
  children: [
    const SizedBox(height: 20),
    Expanded(
      child: ElevatedButton(
        onPressed: () {
          // 1
```

```
              userDao.login(
                _emailController.text, _passwordController.text);
            },
            child: const Text('Login'),
          ),
        )
      ],
    ),
    Row(
      children: [
        const SizedBox(height: 20),
        Expanded(
          child: ElevatedButton(
            onPressed: () {
              // 2
              userDao.signup(
                _emailController.text, _passwordController.text);
            },
            child: const Text('Sign Up'),
          ),
        ),
        const SizedBox(height: 60),
      ],
    ),
    // TODO: Add parentheses
```

Here, you:

1. Set the first button to call the `login()` method.

2. Set the second button to call the `signup()` method.

Now, replace `// TODO: Add parentheses` with:

```
            ],
          ),
        ),
      ),
    );
  }
}
```

Reformat the code to clean things up. You now have a screen that accepts an email address and password and can log in or sign up a user.

Open up **main.dart** and add the following imports:

```
import '../data/user_dao.dart';
import 'ui/login.dart';
```

Replace `// TODO: Add ChangeNotifierProvider<UserDao>` here with:

```
ChangeNotifierProvider<UserDao>(
  lazy: false,
  create: (_) => UserDao(),
),
```

This provides `UserDao` to other screens.

Now, replace `// TODO: Add Consumer<UserDao>` here and the line beneath it with:

```
// 1
home: Consumer<UserDao>(
  // 2
  builder: (context, userDao, child) {
    // 3
    if (userDao.isLoggedIn()) {
      return const MessageList();
    } else {
      return const Login();
    }
  },
),
```

Here's what's happening above:

1. You want a `Consumer` of a `UserDao`.

2. In the builder, you are passed in an instance of `UserDao`.

3. Check to see if the user is logged in. If so, show the `MessageList` otherwise show the login screen.

Stop and restart the app, and you should see the login screen:

Enter an email and a password (remember the password) and press **Sign up**.

Note: Use at least eight characters for the password.

The app will show the Messages screen. Check the Firebase **Authentication** panel on the **Users** tab. You should see the added email address:

It's time to add the user handling code.

Adding user handling code

First, return to **message_list.dart** and add this import:

```
import '../data/user_dao.dart';
```

Then replace `// TODO: Add Email String` with:

```
String? email;
```

To save the current email, replace `// TODO: Add UserDao` with:

```
final userDao = Provider.of<UserDao>(context, listen: false);
email = userDao.email();
```

This saves the current user's email so that we can pass it to the `Message` class.

Next in `_sendMessage`, replace `// TODO: add email` with:

```
email: email,
```

This adds the email as the last parameter.

Run the app again, add a few new messages and make sure you see the emails on the new messages (old messages will not have an email saved):

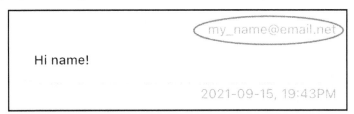

How will the user log out? Next, you'll add a logout button on the Messages screen.

Adding a logout button

Still in **message_list.dart**, replace `// TODO: Replace with actions` with:

```
actions: [
  IconButton(
    onPressed: () {
      userDao.logout();
    },
    icon: const Icon(Icons.logout),
  ),
],
```

This will add the logout icon to the top bar and call `logout()` on the instance of `UserDao`.

Trigger a hot reload, and you'll see the Messages screen. Then click the **Logout** button:

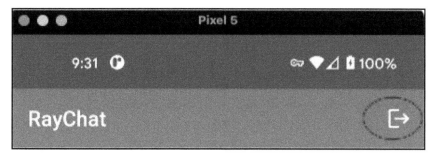

This will take you back to the login screen. Enter your email and password and click **Login**. And here you can see again the messages you have already sent. Magic!

You now have a fully working chat app that can be used by multiple people. Great job!

Key points

- **Cloud Firestore** is a good solution for low-latency database storage.

- **FlutterFire** provides an easy way to use Firebase packages.

- Firebase provides **authentication** and security through **Rules**.

- Creating data access object (**DAO**) files helps to put Firebase functionalities in one place.

- You can choose many different types of authentication, from email to other services.

Where to go from here?

There are plenty of other Cloud Firestore features, which can supercharge your app and give it enterprise-grade features. These include:

- **Offline capabilities**: Keep your data in sync even when offline, here: https://firebase.google.com/docs/firestore/manage-data/enable-offline.

- **Database Rules**: Make your database more secure, here: https://firebase.google.com/docs/database/security.

- **More sign-up methods**: Use similar features to Google and Apple sign-in.

Your _databaseReference has access to a method called onValue that returns a Stream<Event> directly.

Use this if you like to integrate with another state management library like **BLoC**, **Redux**, **MobX** or **Riverpod**; see Chapter 13, "State Management", for more details.

There are plenty of other great Firebase products you can integrate with. Check out the rest of the Firebase API, here: https://firebase.flutter.dev/docs/overview/#next-steps.

You can also read our article, "Firebase Tutorial for Flutter: Getting Started", here: https://www.raywenderlich.com/7426050.

Conclusion

Congratulations! You've completed your introduction to building apps with Flutter. The skills you've honed throughout these chapters will set you up for developing production apps with this exciting toolkit.

If you want to further your understanding of Flutter development with Dart after working through *Flutter Apprentice*, we suggest you read the *Dart Apprentice*, available here https://www.raywenderlich.com/books/dart-apprentice/.

If you have any questions or comments as you work through this book, please stop by our forums at https://forums.raywenderlich.com/c/books/flutter-apprentice/ and look for the particular forum category for this book.

Thank you again for purchasing this book. Your continued support is what makes the books, tutorials, videos and other things we do at https://raywenderlich.com possible. We truly appreciate it!

– The *Flutter Apprentice* team

Appendices

In this section, you'll find the solutions to the challenges presented in the book chapters.

Appendix A: Chapter 5 Solution 1

By Vincent Ngo

First, you need to make `ExploreScreen` a `StatefulWidget` because you need to preserve the state of the scroll controller.

Next, add a `ScrollController` property in `_ExploreScreenState`:

```
late ScrollController _controller;
```

Then, add a function called `scrollListener()`, which is the function callback that will listen to the scroll offsets.

```
void _scrollListener() {
  // 1
  if (_controller.offset >= _controller.position.maxScrollExtent
&&
      !_controller.position.outOfRange) {
    print('i am at the bottom!');
  }
  // 2
  if (_controller.offset <= _controller.position.minScrollExtent
&&
      !_controller.position.outOfRange) {
    print('i am at the top!');
  }
}
```

Here's how the code works:

1. Check the scroll offset to see if the position is greater than or equal to the `maxScrollExtent`. If so, the user has scrolled to the very bottom.

2. Check if the scroll offset is less than or equal to `minScrollExtent`. If so, the user has scrolled to the very top.

Within _ExploreScreenState, override initState(), as shown below:

```
@override
void initState() {
  // 1
  _controller = ScrollController();
  // 2
  _controller.addListener(_scrollListener);
  super.initState();
}
```

Here's how the code works:

1. You initialize the scroll controller.

2. You add a listener to the controller. Every time the user scrolls,
    scrollListener() will get called.

Within the ExploreScreen's parent ListView, all you have to do is set the scroll
controller, as shown below:

```
return ListView(
        controller: _controller,
        ...
```

That will tell the scroll controller to listen to this particular list view's scroll events.

Finally, add a function called dispose().

```
@override
void dispose() {
  _controller.removeListener(_scrollListener);
  super.dispose();
}
```

The framework calls dispose() when you permanently remove the object and its
state from the tree. It's important to remember to handle any memory cleanup, such
as unsubscribing from streams and disposing of animations or controllers. In this
case, you're removing the scroll listener.

Hot restart, scroll to the botton and top, and see the printed statements in the **Run**
console:

```
Performing hot restart...
Syncing files to device iPhone 8...
Restarted application in 1,086ms.
flutter: i am at the bottom!
flutter: i am at the top!
```

```
flutter: i am at the bottom!
flutter: i am at the top!
```

Here are some examples of when you might need a scroll controller:

- Detect if you're at a certain offset.

- Control the scroll movement by animating to a specific index.

- Check to see if the scroll view has started, stopped or ended.

Appendix B: Chapter 5 Solution 2

By Vincent Ngo

In **recipes_grid_view.dart**, replace the gridDelegate parameter with the following:

```
const SliverGridDelegateWithMaxCrossAxisExtent(
  maxCrossAxisExtent: 500.0),
```

Recall that the GridView is set to scroll in the vertical direction. That means the cross axis is horizontal. According to Flutter's documentation, maxCrossAxisExtent sets the maximum extent of tiles in the cross axis. So making maxCrossAxisExtent greater than the device's width would allow for only one column!

CPSIA information can be obtained
at www.ICGtesting.com
Printed in the USA
LVHW111930040122
707835LV00005B/279